Christian hymns

Christian hymns

First published 1977
Standard binding ISBN 0 900898 30 5
De Luxe binding ISBN 0 900898 31 3

This new edition 2004
ISBN 1 85049 207 7

Published by the Evangelical Movement of Wales
Bryntirion, Bridgend, South Wales CF31 4DX;
and the Christian Hymns Committee,
33 Hyde Way, Welwyn Garden City, Herts AL7 3UQ.

Printed in Great Britain by Bath Press, Bath.

PREFACE

More than twenty-five years ago, when the first edition of Christian Hymns was published, the editors hardly anticipated that all these years later they would be involved in a revision of that volume. It has been the remarkably wide acceptance of that book, not only in the UK but in many other countries of the English-speaking world, that has led to this present publication.

As with the original book, we have sought the co-operation of a good number of churches from widely representative backgrounds. This has assisted us in discovering those hymns that have not been greatly used, and also in identifying the sort of compositions that are being sung with acceptance in many of our churches. The result has been the addition of well over 200 new items and the omission of about 190 little-used hymns from the first edition.

The last quarter of a century has seen many changes in worship style and practices, not least in the sung praise of God. Consequently we have included quite a number of more modern compositions, as well as rediscovering a few hymns from former generations that have either lingered in undeserved obscurity, or whose non-inclusion in the earlier edition created perhaps justifiable disappointment amongst many.

It has not been an easy task, not least because historically music has been such a powerful medium amongst the people of God. The hymns that poured from the pen of Charles Wesley had a powerful effect upon the Methodists. They learned their theology and had it confirmed to them very largely through the biblical truth often expressed in memorable poetic forms in his hymns.

A veritable torrent of material continues to pour forth, both from pens and keyboards, no doubt assisted, if not occasioned, by the technological revolution that has transformed the contemporary musical scene. Inevitably, a substantial amount that has come has already gone; of the rest, time will tell how much is ephemeral and what is of lasting value. It is the lot of editors to attempt some assessment of available material, and this we have tried to do – with how much success others must judge.

PREFACE

As with the first edition, and following the principle which determined C. H. Spurgeon's selection of hymns, we have resolutely refused to adopt a sectarian agenda and have considered each hymn on its biblical, spiritual and poetic merit, irrespective of the background of the author.

A new section of 'Songs and Choruses' has been included for those who like to make use of these items, and the number of Psalm versions and hymns based on Psalms has been considerably increased. As in the first edition, these are distributed throughout the book according to their appropriate classification. A separate index of these is provided to facilitate their selection.

With regard to tunes, we have aimed at a policy of flexibility that will accommodate the preferences of a wide variety of congregations. Such flexibility has been achieved in a number of cases by printing more than one tune to a hymn, and in others by providing cross-references to other suitable tunes found elsewhere in the book. Often a perceptive accompanist will be able to adapt to a particular spiritual mood by varying the tune to be chosen for a hymn.

We recognize that many tunes are 'wedded' to certain words and that it would be needlessly offensive to ride roughshod over such established usage. But sometimes a new or alternative tune can add freshness and new vigour to a hymn whose very familiarity has brought with it a tiredness that limits its usefulness. It isalso true that within the wider context of evangelicalism there are a number of 'families', each of which connects certain tunes with particular words. A measure of cross-fertilization can be helpful and we have endeavoured to achieve this.

Many readers will immediately notice one of the major differences between this book and its predecessor, namely that we have attempted a measure of modernization of the linguistic forms in which the hymns are expressed. This will be seen in the general adoption of 'You' in place of 'Thou', with the accompanying changes in verbal inflections. This has only been done if such substitutions have not played havoc with the author's original rhyming scheme, nor involved our attempting to replace poetry with our doggerel, even if the latter rhymes and scans. It has not been followed in a slavish manner, and in several hymns that justifiably could be regarded as 'classics' we have retained the older forms. We understand the arguments put forward on both sides of this contentious divide, and some might judge us to have adopted something of a mediating position. Apart from such modernizations, an asterisk (*) has been used where we are aware that the printed text differs significantly from that of the author's original version.

The section of hymns and songs for children has been considerably reduced. In part this is a reflection of the changes that have come about in this area and which have resulted in many churches ceasing to use such hymns. Children can be helped to learn and sing some of the great hymns of the church, many of which express exalted truth in quite simple language.

The committee which compiled this selection has been greatly assisted from the musical side by Philip Watson (who was involved in the original publication) together with Brian Freer and Peter Moss. We are much in debt to them for their advice and expertise, although final responsibility for the selection of tunes rests with the editors. Once again we are greatly indebted to the Revd J W West, now of Westbury, for his work in compiling the Index of Biblical References and Allusions. We would wish also to express our deep gratitude for the invaluable help given us on the technical and administrative side by Mrs Pat Goodrich, Mr Peter Goodrich, Mr James Gosling, Mrs Joyce Walkey-Morais, Mrs Jackie Friston and Mrs Jeannette Watson. Their contribution has been invaluable.

We send forth this revised edition of Christian Hymns with the earnest prayer that the Lord will condescend to bless it, and with the hope that an even wider range of His people will find it of help as they engage in the greatest activity open to us on earth – the worship of the true and living God.

Paul E. G. Cook, Graham Harrison,
David Clark, Robert Strivens
Editorial Committee

PREFACE TO THE ORIGINAL EDITION

Many churches have long felt the need for the publication of a new hymn-book. Such a book should be firmly representative of all that is best in the great evangelical tradition to which we belong. It should be large enough to provide ample choice of hymns suitable for the public worship and for the more informal gatherings of the church. Its scope should be sufficiently broad to enable Christians in different denominations and churches to use it with satisfaction and profit. Musically it should ensure the retention of those tunes whose merits have been proved, while at the same time introducing new or alternative tunes that will adorn the hymns they are designed to accompany. In an attempt to meet these needs *Christian Hymns* has been produced.

It has been compiled with certain clearly held convictions uppermost in the minds of the Editors. Any collection of hymns for use in the public worship of the church, if it is to be successful, must be wide-ranging both in the subject matter of the hymns themselves and in the moods that they express and evoke. But the basis of a hymn-book that is to be spiritually healthy will be a solid core of hymns that are robustly objective in their statement of God's glories and in the ascription of His praise. Such hymns will set Him forth in the majesty and sovereignty of His Being, the magnificence of His attributes, the greatness of His works, the unfettered freedom of His grace. Hymns that do this will say to the congregation: 'Behold your God!' In addition, they will provide the congregation with a fit and worthy vehicle by means of which they can ascribe to that God the glory due to His Name. Our hymnody, as is the case with our theology, must begin with God, proceed in dependence upon Him, and redound to His glory.

To this extent our experience of God must take a secondary place and certainly must not become the determining factor in the shaping of our hymns and hymn-books. God is there before our experience. And He is there sometimes despite our experience — or the lack of it. Indeed, the realization, and perhaps even the singing, of such truths about Him may well become the channel by which His Spirit draws near to bless us richly in our souls.

However, psalms and hymns serve a deeper function than simply to state in true but objective fashion the glory of our God. If the old Puritan was right who advocated the preaching of a 'felt Christ', surely our singing should share this characteristic. The God of the Bible is One who is graciously pleased to come down and to manifest His presence to His children. By His Spirit He sheds His love abroad in their hearts and causes them to rejoice with joy unspeakable and full of glory. It would be strange indeed if such facts had left no mark upon the hymnody of the church.

To say this is not to say that our hymns should become self-centred, introspective and preoccupied with 'the diseases and distempers of the soul' (to quote Richard Baxter's phrase). There are such hymns and there are such hymn-books. Suffice it for the Editors to express the hope that this compilation will not add to their number.

But now that many of our churches have moved out of the sentimentality that largely characterized the life and hymns of an earlier generation, the need remains for the recovery of the great wealth of sound, warm, powerful hymns that are our heritage.

Users of this hymn-book will observe that many hymns by Isaac Watts and Charles Wesley have been included. As Louis F. Benson points out in his standard work, *The English Hymn*, many of Wesley's compositions have been confined largely to the Wesleyan denominations and have thus been virtually unknown to the wider Christian public. In the case of Watts it must be said that despite the efforts of many successors, few of them have managed to attain so consistently high a standard. In both instances, therefore, we feel justified in including a larger number of hymns by these supreme masters of the art of hymn-writing than might usually be found in present-day compilations. There is surely no virtue in singing hymns merely because they are old, but it must be admitted that the general quality of hymn-writing in the present century has not been of a high order. It is therefore still necessary for the church to turn back to these hymns which at their best have something of a timeless quality about them.

There is likewise the need for the rediscovery and restoration to use of a considerable number of hymns from times of revival and evangelical awakening — particularly those from the eighteenth century. If it is not strictly true to say, as does the preface to one well-known hymn-book, that 'Methodism was born in song', we can say with no fear of contradiction that when Methodists were born again they began to sing. The result of this is the rich store of hymns deriving more or less directly from the Methodist Revival in England and Wales two centuries ago. From this treasure-house it has been our privilege to draw extensively, for many of the greatest hymns of the church come from this period.

Similarly, we have felt it to be our duty to include a good proportion of hymns that express the desire of the church for, and the longing of the soul after, God. Regretfully, we do not live at such a time of revival. But hopefully we continue to call upon our heavenly Father whose delight it is to hear and to answer the cries of His children. Nothing would give the Editors greater pleasure than for them to be forced to issue a revised edition of this hymn-book containing a much higher proportion of new compositions born out of a contemporary pouring forth of the Holy Spirit. Meanwhile we trust that in this hymn-book churches will find hymns that will express to their God their longings after Him.

Towards the close of the hymn-book we have included a section containing hymns for children. In connection with this it may be of help to readers to recall some of the words written by John Wesley in 1790 in the Preface to his brother Charles' *Hymns for Children and Others of Riper Years*:

> There are two ways of writing or speaking to children: the one is, to let ourselves down to them: the other to lift them up to us. Dr. Watts has wrote in the former way, and has succeeded admirably well, speaking to children as children, and leaving them as he found them. The following hymns are written on the other plan: they contain strong and manly sense, yet expressed in such plain and easy language, as even children may understand. But when they do understand them, they will be children no longer, only in years and stature.

Both types of hymn find their place in this hymn-book.

Hymns are written to be sung, not read. In fact a Christian sometimes is able to sing what he is not so able to say. Considerable importance, therefore, resides in the choice of tunes for a hymn-book such as this. The Editors have little time for those musicians who insist on giving congregations what they deem to be good for them, whether or not the congregations share their musical opinions. Consequently in the main we have followed the practice of setting well-known hymns to well-loved tunes. In many cases it would have been an impertinence to have attempted to sever such unions. However, there is a case to be argued for the introduction of a fresh element that can be the means of imparting new life and vigour to a familiar old hymn. Such can often be the effect of a new or different, but well-chosen, tune. We have not hesitated to make such suggestions where we have thought they would be helpful. Usually these are found either in the form of an alternative tune set beside the more familiar one, or else given in a cross-reference to another page in the hymn-book.

PREFACE TO THE ORIGINAL EDITION

What we believe will prove to be one of the features of this hymn-book much appreciated by churches in England and other countries beyond Wales is the large number of Welsh hymn-tunes that it contains. Several of them appear, we believe, for the first time in an English-language hymn-book. Their moods, harmonies and unique qualities should greatly enrich the musical repertoire of many congregations. In this connection we would mention also the inclusion of a number of translations of Welsh hymns. Several of these have been translated specially for *Christian Hymns*. Usually these carry with them the tunes with which their originals are commonly associated.

Generally speaking, a congregation that is able to sing its hymns in four-part harmony will find — other things being equal — that its worship is richer and more satisfying than if it is able to sing only the melody of the hymns. To this end we have sought to ensure that the harmonies of the tunes lend themselves to this type of singing. Without in any sense diminishing the emphasis that should be upon the words that are being sung, and paying due regard to the danger that congregational singing can become an end in itself, we would suggest that congregations using this hymn-book endeavour to familiarize themselves with these harmonies, that their praise may the more glorify God.

In this connection John Wesley's 'Rules for Methodist singers' are still instructive:

1. Learn the tunes.
2. Sing them as printed.
3. Sing all. If it is a cross to you, take it up and you will find it a blessing.
4. Sing lustily and with a good courage.
5. Sing modestly. Do not bawl.
6. Sing in time. Do not run before or stay behind.
7. Above all, sing spiritually. Have an eye to God in every word you sing. Aim at pleasing Him more than yourself or any other creature. In order to do this, attend strictly to the sense of what you sing, and see that your heart is not carried away with the sound, but offered to God continually.

It will be evident that we do not share the convictions of some fellow Christians who, prohibiting the use of what they call 'uninspired compositions', limit themselves to singing metrical psalms in the public worship of God. There are, we believe, sound biblical reasons for the view that we hold on this point in common with the great majority of Christians in the world. Not least is the fact that the progressive nature of biblical revelation imposes a necessary historical limitation upon the Psalmist. Despite the Messianic import of some of the psalms, the book as a whole by virtue of the position it occupies in the history of redemption cannot give full expression to the glories of the New Testament revelation. Moreover, there are indications within the pages of Scripture itself of the propriety of believers expressing their praise of God in words that are not necessarily of immediate divine inspiration. In a word, when the Psalmist said 'Sing unto the Lord a new song', we find it difficult to believe that what he really meant was 'Only sing unto the Lord an old psalm.'

Nevertheless, it would be nothing less than tragic if a book that is largely composed of post-biblical hymns were to ignore the wealth of praise, devotion and profound spiritual experience that is expressed so finely in the Psalms. Accordingly we have sought to include a number of metrical psalms. In addition to these there are several hymns which are either paraphrases of, or are closely based upon, particular psalms. To facilitate and encourage the use of all these we have listed them in a separate index under the number of the psalm from which they originate.

A word of explanation may be called for regarding the principles which have permitted us to include the work of some authors who may be noted for their heterodoxy in at least some aspects of their theology. At this point we are happy to follow the practice of C. H. Spurgeon who in his Preface to *Our Own Hymn-Book* wrote:

> Whatever may be thought of our taste we have used it without prejudice; and a good hymn has not been rejected because of the character of its author, or the heresies of the church in whose hymnal it first occurred; so long as the language and the spirit commended the hymn to our heart we included it, and believe that we have enriched our collection thereby.

In all cases resort has been made to the original text of the hymns. Only when infelicitous expressions, antiquity of language or doctrinal aberration have occurred have we felt at all justified in making alterations. John Wesley (who evidently suffered much at the hands of eighteenth-century piratical publishers) is on record as requesting those who reprinted, and in the process amended, his and his brother's hymns 'to add the true reading in the margin, or at the bottom of the page'. He writes, '...I desire they would not attempt to mend them; for they really are not able'. He is a bold man who flies in the face of such a warning. But anyone who has compared John Wesley's altered (and much improved) version of Isaac Watts' paraphrase of Psalm 100 with the original will agree that there is sometimes a case to be made out for regarding Wesley's advice as a general principle rather than as an absolute rule. Thus, for example:

PREFACE TO THE ORIGINAL EDITION

Before Jehovah's aweful throne,
Ye nations, bow with sacred joy:
Know that the Lord is God alone,
He can create and He destroy.

is infinitely to be preferred to what Isaac Watts wrote:

Sing to the Lord with joyful voice,
Let every land His name adore;
The British Isles shall send the noise
Across the ocean to the shore.

It has the additional virtue of rescuing a magnificent hymn from the obscurity into which it would have sunk. If the alteration of the occasional word or phrase where Charles Wesley's Arminianism becomes belligerent has made some of his otherwise superb hymns singable by a wider Christian public, we feel that the risk of his brother's censure ('... we may no longer be accountable either for the nonsense or for the doggerel of other men') will prove easier to bear.

Some hymns which are more appropriate to private than to congregational use have been included, although not under a separate section. Opinions may vary as to exactly which should be included in such a section, and we have thought it preferable to leave such decisions to the discretion of the user of the hymn-book. Although they may rarely, if ever, be sung by a congregation, we have included such classics as Wesley's 'Come, O Thou Traveller Unknown' (full version) and Newton's 'I asked the Lord that I might grow'.

For a hymn-book to be adequate for use in the church's praise and worship of God demands of it several distinguishing features. It must maintain that scriptural balance between the objective and the experimental. It must be wide-ranging in its statement of the truths of the Christian faith, omitting none of which it should sing, nor yet giving undue prominence to any. It must be comprehensive in its expression of the needs, longings and aspirations, the joys and sorrows, the comforts that the church in general and individual Christians in particular experience in this present world. It must plumb the depths and soar to the heights. And all the while it must do these things in language and style that befit the themes with which it deals. Its music must not hinder or distract the worshipper, but rather assist him in the exercise of his worship. We may be permitted the hope that in some small measure *Christian Hymns* will go at least some way towards the realization of these objectives, and that a wide range of Evangelical churches of all denominations will find it of service to them in their worship of God.

Its compilation has been a work extending over several years, during which time we have received help and encouragement from many friends. In particular we would wish to express our appreciation of the help given to us in the earlier stages of our work by Mr S. M. Houghton, M.A. His knowledge of hymns and their writers is encyclopaedic, his care in verifying texts is meticulous, and his standards of literary taste and doctrinal accuracy are rightly demanding. Mr Philip B. Watson, B.A., A.R.C.M., Director of Musical Studies at Queen's High School, Newport, and Mr John Manton, M.A., of Loughborough University, have been largely responsible for the work on the musical side of this hymn-book. We are deeply indebted to them for their labours. Final responsibility for both texts and music, however, lies with the Editors. We are grateful also to Mr Andrew J. Hayden and Mr R. F. Newton (both members of 'The Hymn Society of Great Britain and Ireland') who very kindly checked the dates of hymn-writers and composers in the light of their extensive researches into this subject. Other friends too numerous to mention by name have helped in many ways. We express our gratitude to them all, not least to those whose suggestions, opinions and even compositions have, after consideration, been rejected.

This book was born out of the conviction that the time had come for the publication of a hymn-book that could minister to the needs of Evangelical churches as a whole. Accordingly, we have sought to transcend narrow party emphases and to direct the attention of the people of God to the rich store of hymnology that is available for their use. In desiring to produce a collection of hymns that could thus be used by Evangelical churches from different denominational backgrounds, the Editors were faced with a particular difficulty over the question of baptismal hymns. It would be futile to think that the differences over the doctrine of baptism could be bridged, far less solved, by a hymn-book! But we hope that our method of treatment will commend itself to Christians who conscientiously differ from one another in their judgment over this issue, and that accordingly they will afford it a sympathetic reception. Paedo-Baptists of necessity hold to the practice of baptizing believers in certain circumstances at least. And in the increasingly 'missionary' situation confronting Christians today, as a result of which they face a nation more overtly pagan than for centuries, it follows that many of the people converted will be from a non-church background. Hymns that are relevant to a service of the baptism of believers will be needed increasingly therefore by churches that formerly might have had occasion to use such but rarely. These churches may well find also that some of the hymns in the section entitled 'Marriage, home and family' will be acceptable to them for their services of infant baptism. The Editors, whose convictions in this matter lead them to administer baptism only to professing believers and not to infants, in no way feel that their principles or heritage have been compromised by this attempt to serve the larger cause of unity among Evangelical churches.

We trust that *Christian Hymns* will indeed help to enrich the worship of churches in the English-speaking world, and we send it forth with the prayer that the Lord, of whose glories these hymns sing, will deign to bless and use it for the furtherance of His glory and for the blessing of His people.

Paul E. G. Cook
Graham Harrison

ADDRESSES OF MAIN COPYRIGHT HOLDERS

Copycare Ltd
P.O. Box 77,
Hailsham, BN27 3EF
music@copycare.com

Daybreak Music Ltd
P.O. Box 2848,
Eastbourne, BN20 7XP
info@daybreakmusic.co.uk

The Jubilate Group
4 Thorne Park Road, Chelston,
Torquay, TQ2 6RX
enquiries@jubilate.co.uk

Kingsway Communications Ltd
26-28 Lottbridge Drove,
Eastbourne, BN23 6NT
info@kingsway.co.uk

Make Way Music
P.O. Box 263,
Croydon, CR9 5AP
info@makewaymusic.com

Novello & Co Ltd
8/9 Frith Street,
London W1D 3JB
promotion@musicsales.com

Sovereign Music UK
P.O. Box 356,
Leighton Buzzard, LU7 3WP
Sovereignmusic@aol.com

CONTENTS

LIST OF METRICAL PSALMS AND HYMNS BASED ON PSALMS

Psalm	First line	Hymn
Psalm 1	Blessed is the man, the man who does not walk	668
Psalm 1	Blessed is the one who turns away	725
Psalm 1	Blest is he who loves God's precepts	670
Psalm 1	Happy the people who refuse	365
Psalm 3	Your promise, Lord, is perfect peace	811
Psalm 4:8 Psalm 5:8	Lead me, Lord, lead me in Thy righteousness	82
Psalm 4	Lord of my life, my hope, my joy	688
Psalm 6	Gently, gently, lay Your rod	837
Psalm 9	Our God almighty be adored	114
Psalm 9:7-11, 19-20	The Lord for ever reigns on high	36
Psalm 11	In God will I trust, though my counsellors say	110
Psalm 18	Whom should we love like Thee	510
Psalm 19	God's law is perfect, and converts	349
Psalm 19	The heavens declare Thy glory, Lord	359
Psalm 19:7-10	The law of the Lord is perfect	360
Psalm 22:23-26, 31	All you that fear Jehovah's name	124
Psalm 23	My Shepherd will supply my need	112
Psalm 23	The King of love my Shepherd is	693
Psalm 23	The Lord is my shepherd, no want shall I know	628
Psalm 23	The Lord's my Shepherd, I'll not want....*And I will trust...*	808
Psalm 23	The Lord's my Shepherd, I'll not want	787
Psalm 24:3-6	O Lord, who shall ascend	676
Psalm 24:7-10	Ye gates, lift up your heads on high	293
Psalm 27	God is my strong salvation	750
Psalm 27	Whom shall I fear on earth below	766
Psalm 30	I worship You, O Lord	844
Psalm 34:1-10	At all times I will bless the Lord	5
Psalm 34	Through all the changing scenes of life	119
Psalm 36	High in the heavens, eternal God	11
Psalm 36:7-9	How precious, O Lord	923

LIST OF METRICAL PSALMS

List of Metrical Psalms

THE WORSHIP OF GOD

Praise and thanksgiving

1

PSALM 100

All people that on earth do dwell,
sing to the Lord with cheerful voice;
Him serve with fear, His praise forth tell,
come now before Him and rejoice.

2 Know that the Lord is God indeed;
without our aid He did us make;
we are His flock, He doth us feed,
and for His sheep He doth us take.

3 O enter then His gates with praise,
approach with joy His courts unto;
praise Him and bless His Name always,
for it is seemly so to do.

4 For why? The Lord our God is good;
His mercy is for ever sure;
His truth at all times firmly stood,
and shall from age to age endure.

William Kethe, d. 1594

2

PSALM 100

Before Jehovah's awesome throne,
you nations, bow with sacred joy;
know that the Lord is God alone,
He can create, and He destroy.

2 His sovereign power, without our aid,
made us of clay, and formed us men;
and when like wandering sheep we strayed,
He brought us to His fold again.

3 We are His people, we His care,
our souls and all our mortal frame;
what lasting honours shall we rear,
Almighty Maker, to Your Name?

4 We'll crowd Your gates with thankful songs,
high as the heavens our voices raise;
and earth, with her ten thousand tongues,
shall fill Your courts with sounding praise.

5 Wide as the world is Your command,
vast as eternity Your love;
firm as a rock Your truth shall stand,
when rolling years shall cease to move.

Isaac Watts, 1674-1748;
altd. by John Wesley, 1703-91

3

Angel voices, ever singing
round Thy throne of light,
angel harps, for ever ringing,
rest not day nor night;
thousands only live to bless Thee,
and confess Thee
Lord of might.

2 Thou who art beyond the farthest
mortal eye can scan,
can it be that Thou regardest
songs of sinful man?
Can we know that Thou art near us
and wilt hear us?
Yes, we can.

3 In Thy house, great God, we offer
of Thine own to Thee,
and for Thine acceptance proffer,
all unworthily,
hearts, and minds, and hands, and voices
in our choicest
psalmody.

4 Honour, glory, might, and merit
Thine shall ever be,
Father, Son, and Holy Spirit,
blessèd Trinity.
Of the best that Thou hast given
earth and heaven
render Thee.

Francis Pott, 1832-1909

4

Christ is our corner-stone,
on Him alone we build;
with His true saints alone
the courts of heaven are filled;
on His great love
our hopes we place
of present grace
and joys above.

2 O then with hymns of praise
these hallowed courts shall ring;
our voices we will raise
the Three in One to sing;
and so proclaim
in joyful song,
both loud and long,
that glorious Name.

3 Here may we gain from heaven
the grace which we implore;
and may that grace, once given,
be with us evermore,
until that day
when all the blest
to endless rest
are called away.

Latin, 6th or 7th cent.;
tr. by John Chandler, 1806-76

5

Psalm 34:1-10

At all times I will bless the Lord;
I'll praise Him with my voice.
Because I glory in the Lord
let troubled souls rejoice.
Together let us praise the Lord;
exalt His name with me.
I sought the Lord; His answer came:
from fears He set me free.

2 They look to Him and shine with joy;
they are not put to shame.
This suffering man cried to the Lord;
from Him deliverance came.
The angel of the Lord surrounds
and guards continually
all those who fear and honour Him;
He sets His people free.

3 Come, taste and see – the Lord is good;
who trusts in Him is blessed.
O fear the Lord, you saints; with need
you will not be oppressed.
Young lions may grow weak and faint
and hunger for their food;
but those who wait upon the Lord
will not lack any good.

Sing Psalms, 2003

6

Psalm 117

Come all you nations everywhere,
the praises of the Lord declare;
and all you peoples, now proclaim
the honours of His holy Name.

2 For wondrous is His steadfast love,
poured out upon us from above;
His faithfulness is unsurpassed;
through endless ages shall it last.

3 So join together, everyone,
to praise the Father, Spirit, Son;
the Lord of Heaven and earth adore
for ever and for evermore.

Graham D S Deans, b. 1953

7

Based on Psalm 95

Come, let us praise the Lord,
with joy our God acclaim,
His greatness tell abroad,
and bless His saving Name.
Lift high your songs
before His throne
to whom alone
all praise belongs.

2 Our God of matchless worth,
our King beyond compare,
the deepest bounds of earth,
the hills, are in His care.
He all decrees,
who by His hand
prepared the land
and formed the seas.

3 In worship bow the knee,
our glorious God confess;
the great Creator, He,
the Lord our Righteousness.
He reigns unseen:
His flock He feeds
and gently leads
in pastures green.

4 Come, hear His voice today,
receive what love imparts;
His holy will obey
and harden not your hearts.
His ways are best;
and lead at last,
all troubles past,
to perfect rest.

Timothy Dudley-Smith, b. 1926

8

Eternal Light! Eternal Light!
how pure the soul must be,
when, placed within Thy searching sight,
it shrinks not, but with calm delight
can live and look on Thee.

2 The spirits that surround Thy throne
may bear the burning bliss;
but that is surely theirs alone,
since they have never, never known
a fallen world like this.

3 O how shall I, whose native sphere
is dark, whose mind is dim,
before the Ineffable appear,
and on my naked spirit bear
the uncreated beam?

4 There is a way for man to rise
to that sublime abode:
an offering and a sacrifice,
a Holy Spirit's energies,
an Advocate with God.

5 These, these prepare us for the sight
of holiness above;
the sons of ignorance and night
can dwell in the eternal Light,
through the eternal Love.

Thomas Binney, 1798-1874

9

Psalm 117

From all that dwell below the skies
let the Creator's praise arise:
let the Redeemer's Name be sung,
through every land, by every tongue.

2 Eternal are Your mercies, Lord;
eternal truth attends Your Word:
Your praise shall sound from shore to
shore,
till suns shall rise and set no more.

Isaac Watts, 1674-1748

10

Psalm 136

Give to our God immortal praise;
mercy and truth are all His ways;
wonders of grace to God belong,
repeat His mercies in your song.

2 Give to the Lord of lords renown,
the King of kings with glory crown:
His mercies ever shall endure,
when lords and kings are known no more.

3 He built the earth, He spread the sky,
and fixed the starry lights on high:
wonders of grace to God belong,
repeat His mercies in your song.

4 He fills the sun with morning light,
He bids the moon direct the night:
His mercies ever shall endure,
when suns and moons shall shine no more.

5 He sent His Son with power to save
from guilt and darkness and the grave:
wonders of grace to God belong,
repeat His mercies in your song.

6 Through this vain world He guides our feet,
and leads us to His heavenly seat:
His mercies ever shall endure,
when this vain world shall be no more.

Isaac Watts, 1674-1748

11

Psalm 36

High in the heavens, eternal God,
Your goodness in full glory shines;
Your truth shall break through every cloud
that veils and darkens Your designs.

2 For ever firm Your justice stands,
as mountains their foundations keep;
wise are the wonders of Your hands;
Your judgments are a mighty deep.

3 Your providence is kind and large,
both man and beast Your bounty share:
the whole creation is Your charge,
but saints are Your especial care.

4 My God, how excellent Your grace,
whence all our hope and comfort springs!
The sons of Adam in distress
fly to the shadow of Your wings.

5 From the provisions of Your house
we shall be fed with sweet repast;
there mercy like a river flows,
and brings salvation to our taste.

6 Life, like a fountain rich and free,
springs from the presence of the Lord;
and in Your light our souls shall see
the glories promised in Your Word.

Isaac Watts, 1674-1748

12

Holy, holy, holy Lord,
God of hosts, when heaven and earth
out of darkness, at Thy Word,
issued into glorious birth,
all Thy works before Thee stood,
and Thine eye beheld them good;
while they sang with sweet accord,
holy, holy, holy Lord!

2 Holy, holy, holy! Thee,
one Jehovah evermore,
Father, Son and Spirit, we,
dust and ashes, would adore:

lightly by the world esteemed,
from that world by Thee redeemed,
sing we here with glad accord,
holy, holy, holy Lord!

3 Holy, holy, holy! all
heaven's triumphant choirs shall sing,
when the ransomed nations fall
at the footstool of their King:
then shall saints and seraphim,
harps and voices, swell one hymn,
blending in sublime accord,
holy, holy, holy Lord!

James Montgomery, 1771-1854

13

How shall I sing that majesty
which angels do admire?
Let dust in dust and silence lie;
sing, sing, ye heavenly choir.
Thousands of thousands stand around
Thy throne, O God most high;
ten thousand times ten thousand sound
Thy praise; but who am I?

2 Thy brightness unto them appears,
whilst I Thy footsteps trace;
a sound of God comes to my ears,
but they behold Thy face.
They sing because Thou art their sun;
Lord, send a beam on me;
for where heaven is but once begun
there hallelujahs be.

3 Enlighten with faith's light my heart,
inflame it with love's fire;
then shall I sing and bear a part
with that celestial choir.
I shall, I fear, be dark and cold,
with all my fire and light;
yet when Thou dost accept their gold,
Lord, treasure up my mite.

4 How great a being, Lord, is Thine,
which doth all beings keep!
Thy knowledge is the only line
to sound so vast a deep.
Thou art a sea without a shore,
a sun without a sphere;
Thy time is now and evermore,
Thy place is everywhere.

John Mason, c. 1646-94

14

PSALM 146

I'll praise my Maker while I've breath,
and when my voice is lost in death,
praise shall employ my nobler powers;
my days of praise shall ne'er be past,
while life, and thought, and being last,
or immortality endures.

2 Happy the man whose hopes rely
on Israel's God! He made the sky,
and earth, and seas, with all their train:
His truth for ever stands secure;
He saves the oppressed, He feeds the poor,
and none shall find His promise vain.

3 The Lord gives eyesight to the blind;
the Lord supports the fainting mind;
He sends the labouring conscience peace;
He helps the stranger in distress,
the widow and the fatherless,
and grants the prisoner sweet release.

4 I'll praise Him while He lends me breath,
and when my voice is lost in death,
praise shall employ my nobler powers;
my days of praise shall ne'er be past,
while life, and thought, and being last,
or immortality endures.

Isaac Watts, 1674-1748

15

In Your great Name, O Lord, we come
to worship at Your feet!
O pour Your Holy Spirit down
on all that now shall meet!

2 Teach us to pray, and praise, and hear,
and understand Your Word;
to feel Your blissful presence near,
and trust our living Lord.

3 This house with grace and glory fill,
this congregation bless:
Your great salvation now reveal,
Your glorious righteousness.

Joseph Hoskins, 1745-88

16

Immortal, invisible, God only wise,
in light inaccessible hid from our eyes,
most blessèd, most glorious, the Ancient of Days,
almighty, victorious, Thy great Name we praise.

2 Unresting, unhasting, and silent as light,
nor wanting, nor wasting, Thou rulest in might;
Thy justice like mountains high soaring above,
Thy clouds which are fountains of goodness and love.

3 To all life Thou givest, to both great and small;
in all life Thou livest, the true life of all;
we blossom and flourish as leaves on the tree,
and wither and perish – but nought changeth Thee.

4 Great Father of glory, pure Father of light,
Thine angels adore Thee, all veiling their sight;
all praise we would render; O help us to see
'tis only the splendour of light hideth Thee.

5 Immortal, invisible, God only wise,
in light inaccessible hid from our eyes,
most blessèd, most glorious, the Ancient of Days,
almighty, victorious, Thy great Name we praise.

Walter Chalmers Smith, 1824-1908

17

PSALM 136

Let us with a gladsome mind
praise the Lord, for He is kind:
for His mercies shall endure,
ever faithful, ever sure.

2 He, with all-commanding might,
filled the new-made world with light:
for His mercies shall endure,
ever faithful, ever sure.

3 All things living does He feed,
His full hand supplies their need:
for His mercies shall endure,
ever faithful, ever sure.

4 He His chosen race did bless
in the wasteful wilderness:
for His mercies shall endure,
ever faithful, ever sure.

5 He has with a piteous eye
looked upon our misery:
for His mercies shall endure,
ever faithful, ever sure.

6 Let us then with gladsome mind
praise the Lord, for He is kind:
for His mercies shall endure,
ever faithful, ever sure.

*John Milton**, 1608-74

18

Lo! God is here! let us adore,
and own how awesome is this place!
Let all within us feel His power
and silent bow before His face;
who know His power, His grace who prove,
serve Him with fear, with reverence love.

2 Lo! God is here! Him day and night
the united choirs of angels sing;
to Him, enthroned above all height,
heaven's host their noblest praises bring;
disdain not, Lord, our meaner song,
who praise You with a stammering tongue.

3 Being of beings! may our praise
Your courts with grateful fragrance fill;
still may we stand before Your face,
still hear and do Your sovereign will;
to You may all our thoughts arise,
ceaseless, accepted sacrifice.

Gerhard Tersteegen, 1697-1769;
tr. by John Wesley, 1703-91

19

PSALM 145

Long as I live I'll bless Your Name,
my King, my God of love;
my work and joy shall be the same
in the bright world above.

2 Great is the Lord, His power unknown,
and let His praise be great:
I'll sing the honours of Your throne,
Your works of grace repeat.

3 Your grace shall dwell upon my tongue,
and while my lips rejoice,
the men that hear my sacred song
shall join their cheerful voice.

4 Fathers to sons shall teach Your Name,
and children learn Your ways;
ages to come Your truth proclaim,
and nations sound Your praise.

5 Your glorious deeds of ancient date
shall through the world be known;
Your arm of power, Your heavenly state,
with public splendour shown.

6 The world is managed by Your hands,
Your saints are ruled by love;
and Your eternal kingdom stands,
though rocks and hills remove.

Isaac Watts, 1674-1748

20

My God, how wonderful Thou art,
Thy majesty how bright!
How beautiful Thy mercy-seat,
in depths of burning light!

2 How dread are Thine eternal years,
O everlasting Lord,
by prostrate spirits day and night
incessantly adored!

3 How wonderful, how beautiful,
the sight of Thee must be,
Thine endless wisdom, boundless power,
and aweful purity!

4 O how I fear Thee, living God,
with deepest, tenderest fears,
and worship Thee with trembling hope
and penitential tears!

5 Yet I may love Thee, too, O Lord,
almighty as Thou art;
for Thou hast stooped to ask of me
the love of my poor heart.

6 No earthly father loves like Thee;
no mother, e'er so mild,
bears and forbears as Thou hast done
with me, Thy sinful child.

7 Father of Jesus, love's reward,
what rapture will it be
prostrate before Thy throne to lie,
and ever gaze on Thee!

Frederick William Faber, 1814-63

21

PSALM 103:1-7

O bless the Lord, my soul;
let all within me join,
and aid my tongue to bless His Name
whose favours are divine.

2 O bless the Lord, my soul,
nor let His mercies lie
forgotten in unthankfulness,
and without praises die.

3 'Tis He forgives your sins,
'tis He relieves your pain,
'tis He that heals your sicknesses,
and makes you young again.

4 He crowns your life with love,
when ransomed from the grave;
He that redeemed my soul from hell
has sovereign power to save.

5 He fills the poor with good,
He gives the sufferers rest;
the Lord has judgments for the proud,
and justice for the oppressed.

6 His wondrous works and ways
He made by Moses known;
but sent the world His truth and grace
by His belovèd Son.

Isaac Watts, 1674-1748

22

PSALM 95:1-6

O come, and let us to the Lord
in songs our voices raise;
with joyful noise let us the rock
of our salvation praise.

2 Let us before His presence come
with praise and thankful voice;
let us sing psalms to Him with grace,
and make a joyful noise.

3 For God, a great God and great king
above all gods He is;
depths of the earth are in His hand,
the strength of hills is His.

4 To Him the spacious sea belongs,
for He the same did make;
the dry land also from His hands
its form at first did take.

5 O come, and let us worship Him,
with meekness on Him call,
and on our knees before the Lord
our Maker let us fall.

SCOTTISH PSALTER*, 1650

23

O God beyond all praising,
we worship You today
and sing the love amazing
that songs cannot repay;
for we can only wonder
at every gift You send,
at blessings without number
and mercies without end.
We lift our hearts before You
and wait upon Your word,
we honour and adore You,
our great and mighty Lord.

2 Then hear, O gracious Saviour,
accept the love we bring,
that we who know Your favour
may serve You as our King;
and whether our tomorrows
be filled with good or ill,
we'll triumph through our sorrows
and rise to bless You still:
to marvel at Your beauty
and glory in Your ways,
and make a joyful duty
our sacrifice of praise.

Michael Perry, 1942-96

24

PSALM 96

O sing a new song,
O sing to the Lord;
O sing, all the earth:
His name be adored!
Tell forth His salvation
as day follows day;
among all the peoples
His wonders display.

2 For great is the Lord,
most worthily praised,
more awesome than gods
the heathen have raised;
the Lord made the heavens,
so great is His might,
and dwells amid majesty,
beauty and light.

3 Ascribe to the Lord,
all nations on earth,
due glory and strength,
due honour and worth;
let all the earth seek Him,
with offerings draw near,
in holiness worship
and bow down with fear.

4 Proclaim to all lands:
'The Lord reigns today!
This earth shall be freed
from change and decay:
His justice is coming' –
O heavens, rejoice,
and oceans re-echo
with thunderous voice!

5 Then forest and field
for gladness shall sing
to welcome the Lord,
their maker and king;
for by His true judgement
at last shall be weighed
all lands and all peoples,
the world that He made.

David G Preston, b. 1949

25

Based on PSALM 150

Sing praise to the Lord!
Praise Him in the height;
rejoice in His Word,
O angels of light:
O heavens, adore Him
by whom you were made,
and worship before Him,
in brightness arrayed.

2 Sing praise to the Lord!
Praise Him upon earth,
in tuneful accord,
O sons of new birth;
praise Him who has brought you
His grace from above,
praise Him who has taught you
to sing of His love.

3 Sing praise to the Lord!
Thanksgiving and song
to Him be outpoured
all ages along:
for love in creation,
for heaven restored,
for grace of salvation,
sing praise to the Lord!

Henry Williams Baker, 1821-77

26

O worship the Lord in the beauty of holiness;
bow down before Him, His glory proclaim;
with gold of obedience and incense of lowliness,
kneel and adore Him, the Lord is His name.

2 Low at His feet lay thy burden of carefulness;
high on His heart He will bear it for thee,
comfort thy sorrows, and answer thy prayerfulness,
guiding thy steps as may best for thee be.

3 Fear not to enter His courts in the slenderness
of the poor wealth thou wouldst reckon as thine;
truth in its beauty and love in its tenderness,
these are the offerings to lay on His shrine.

4 These, though we bring them in trembling and fearfulness,
He will accept for the name that is dear;
mornings of joy give for evenings of tearfulness,
trust for our trembling, and hope for our fear.

5 O worship the Lord in the beauty of holiness;
bow down before Him, His glory proclaim;
with gold of obedience and incense of lowliness,
kneel and adore Him, the Lord is His name.

John Samuel Bewley Monsell, 1811-75

27

Based on PSALM 65

Praise, Lord, for Thee in Zion waits;
prayer shall besiege Thy temple gates;
all flesh shall to Thy throne repair,
and find, through Christ, salvation there.

2 Our spirits faint, our sins prevail;
leave not our trembling hearts to fail:
O Thou that hearest prayer, descend,
and still be found the sinner's friend.

3 How blest Thy saints! how safely led!
how surely kept! how richly fed!
Saviour of all in earth and sea,
how happy they who rest in Thee!

4 Thy hand sets fast the mighty hills,
Thy voice the troubled ocean stills;
evening and morning hymn Thy praise,
and earth Thy bounty wide displays.

5 The year is with Thy goodness crowned;
Thy clouds drop wealth the world
around;
through Thee the deserts laugh and sing,
and nature smiles, and owns her King.

6 Lord, on our souls Thy Spirit pour;
the moral waste within restore;
O let Thy love our spring-tide be,
and make us all bear fruit to Thee.

Henry Francis Lyte, 1793-1847

28

**Praise to the Lord, the Almighty,
the King of creation;**
O my soul, praise Him, for He is thy
health and salvation;
all ye who hear,
brothers and sisters, draw near,
praise Him in glad adoration.

2 Praise to the Lord, who doth prosper
thy work and defend thee;
surely His goodness and mercy here
daily attend thee;
ponder anew
what the Almighty can do,
who with His love doth befriend thee.

3 Praise to the Lord, who, when tempests
their warfare are waging,
who, when the elements madly around
thee are raging,
biddeth them cease,
turneth their fury to peace,
whirlwinds and waters assuaging.

4 Praise to the Lord, who, when darkness
and sin are abounding,
who, when the godless do triumph, all
virtue confounding,
sheddeth His light,
chaseth the horrors of night,
saints with His mercy surrounding.

5 Praise to the Lord! O let all that is in me
adore Him!
All that hath life and breath, come now
with praises before Him!
Let the Amen
sound from His people again:
gladly for aye we adore Him.

Joachim Neander, 1650-80;
tr. by Catherine Winkworth, 1827-78, *and others*

29

Based on Psalm 103

**Praise, my soul, the King of
heaven,**
to His feet your tribute bring;
ransomed, healed, restored, forgiven,
who like you His praise should sing?
Praise Him! praise Him!
praise the everlasting King.

2 Praise Him for His grace and favour
to our fathers in distress;
praise Him, still the same for ever,
slow to chide and swift to bless:
Praise Him! praise Him!
glorious in His faithfulness.

3 Father-like, He tends and spares us,
well our feeble frame He knows;
in His hands He gently bears us,
rescues us from all our foes:
Praise Him! praise Him!
widely as His mercy flows.

4 Frail as summer's flower we flourish;
blows the wind, and it is gone;
but while mortals rise and perish
God endures unchanging on.
Praise Him! praise Him!
praise the high eternal One.

5 Angels, help us to adore Him;
you behold Him face to face;
sun and moon, bow down before Him,
dwellers all in time and space.
Praise Him! praise Him!
praise with us the God of grace.

Henry Francis Lyte, 1793-1847

30

Praise to Thee, Thou great Creator!
Praise be Thine from every tongue:
join, my soul, with every creature,
join the universal song.

2 Father! source of all compassion!
pure unbounded grace is Thine;
hail the God of our salvation!
Praise Him for His love divine.

3 For ten thousand blessings given,
for the hope of future joy,
sound His praise through earth and heaven,
sound Jehovah's praise on high.

4 Joyfully on earth adore Him,
till in heaven our song we raise;
there, enraptured, fall before Him,
lost in wonder, love and praise.

John Fawcett, 1740-1817

31

Based on PSALM 98

Sing to God new songs of worship –
all His deeds are marvellous;
He has brought salvation to us
with His hand and holy arm.
He has shown to all the nations
righteousness and saving power;
He recalled his truth and mercy
to His people Israel.

2 Sing to God new songs of worship –
earth has seen His victory;
let the lands of earth be joyful,
praising Him with thankfulness.
Sound upon the harps His praises,
play to Him with melody;
let the trumpets sound His triumph,
show your joy to God the King!

3 Sing to God new songs of worship –
let the sea now make a noise;
all on earth and in the waters
sound your praises to the Lord.
Let the hills rejoice together,
let the rivers clap their hands,
for with righteousness and justice
He will come to judge the earth.

Michael Baughen, b. 1930

32

Round the Lord in glory seated,
cherubim and seraphim
filled His temple, and repeated
each to each the alternate hymn:

Lord, Your glory fills the heaven,
earth is with Your fulness stored;
unto You be glory given,
holy, holy, holy Lord!

2 Heaven is still with glory ringing,
earth takes up the angels' cry,
holy, holy, holy singing,
Lord of hosts, the Lord most high:

3 With His seraphim before Him,
with His holy church below,
now unite we to adore Him,
let our joyful anthem flow:

*Richard Mant**, 1776-1848

33

Songs of praise the angels sang,
heaven with hallelujahs rang,
when creation was begun,
when God spoke and it was done.

2 Songs of praise awoke the morn,
when the Prince of peace was born;
songs of praise arose, when He
captive led captivity.

3 Heaven and earth must pass away,
songs of praise shall crown that day;
God will make new heavens, new earth,
songs of praise shall hail their birth.

4 And shall man alone be dumb,
till that glorious kingdom come?
No! the church delights to raise
psalms, and hymns, and songs of praise.

5 Saints below, with heart and voice,
still in songs of praise rejoice,
learning here, by faith and love,
songs of praise to sing above.

6 Borne upon their latest breath,
songs of praise shall conquer death;
then, amidst eternal joy,
songs of praise their powers employ.

James Montgomery, 1771-1854

34

Stand up, and bless the Lord,
ye people of His choice:
stand up, and bless the Lord your God
with heart and soul and voice.

2 Though high above all praise,
above all blessing high,
who would not fear His holy Name,
and praise and magnify?

3 O for the living flame
from His own altar brought,
to touch our lips, our minds inspire,
and wing to heaven our thought!

4 God is our strength and song,
and His salvation ours;
then be His love in Christ proclaimed
with all our ransomed powers.

5 Stand up, and bless the Lord,
the Lord your God adore;
stand up, and bless His glorious Name
henceforth for evermore.

James Montgomery, 1771-1854

35

LUKE 1:46-55

Tell out, my soul, the greatness of the Lord!
Unnumbered blessings, give my spirit voice;
tender to me the promise of His word;
in God my Saviour shall my heart rejoice.

2 Tell out, my soul, the greatness of His Name!
Make known His might, the deeds His arm has done;
His mercy sure, from age to age the same;
His holy Name, the Lord, the Mighty One.

3 Tell out, my soul, the greatness of His might!
Powers and dominions lay their glory by.
Proud hearts and stubborn wills are put to flight,
the hungry fed, the humble lifted high.

4 Tell out, my soul, the glories of His word!
Firm is His promise, and His mercy sure.
Tell out, my soul, the greatness of the Lord
to children's children and for evermore!

Timothy Dudley-Smith, b. 1926

36

PSALM 9:7-11,19-20

The LORD for ever reigns on high;
His throne for judgement stands.
He'll judge the world in righteousness,
with justice rule the lands.

2 The LORD will be a hiding place
for those who are oppressed,
and He will be a strong defence
for those who are distressed.

3 All those who know Your name, O LORD,
in You their trust will place,
for You do not abandon those
who seek Your gracious face.

4 Sing praises to the LORD who sits
in Zion on His throne;
among the nations of the world
proclaim what He has done.

5 Arise, LORD! let not man prevail;
judge nations from Your throne.
That they may know how frail they are,
with fear, LORD, strike them down.

SING PSALMS, 2003

37

PSALM 118

Unto the Lord come, raise together
glad songs of praise from earth below;
to Him whose mercy lasts for ever
true thankfulness now let us show:
when, in distress, my cry ascended,
He answered me and set me free;
I will not fear, by Him defended:
what can man do now unto me?

2 Better it is on Him relying
than confidence in man to place;
my enemies around defying,
undaunted in His Name I'll face:
my strength, my song and my salvation,
all has the Lord become to me!
Praise, then, with joyful acclamation,
His hand that brings the victory.

3 Thee will I praise – Thou hast protected
when Thou didst hear my helpless cry;
the stone by builders once rejected
now in its place is set on high.
Save, Lord, we plead, Thou great Defender,
send to us now prosperity;
with grateful hearts we then will render
our sacrifice of praise to Thee.

Graham Stuart Harrison, b. 1935

38

You holy angels bright,
who wait at God's right hand,
or through the realms of light
fly at your Lord's command,
assist our song,
or else the theme
too high does seem
for mortal tongue.

2 You blessèd souls at rest,
who ran this earthly race,
and now, from sin released,
behold your Saviour's face,
God's praises sound,
as in His sight
with sweet delight
you do abound.

3 You saints who toil below,
adore your heavenly King,
and, onward as you go,
some joyful anthem sing;
take what He gives,
and praise Him still
through good and ill,
who ever lives.

4 My soul, bear now your part,
triumph in God above,
and with a well-tuned heart
sing forth the songs of love.
Let all your days
till life shall end,
whate'er He send,
be filled with praise.

*Richard Baxter**, 1615-91;
v. 3 by John Hampden Gurney, 1802-62

39

PSALM 98

Unto God our Saviour
sing a joyful song;
wondrous are His doings,
for His arm is strong.
He has wrought salvation,
He has made it known,
and before the nations
is His justice shown.

2 Joyful, all ye people
sing before the Lord;
shout and sing His praises
now in glad accord;
with the harp and trumpet
joyful praises bring;
come, rejoice before Him,
God the Lord your King.

3 Waves of mighty ocean,
earth with fulness stored,
floods and fields and mountains,
sing before the Lord;
for He comes with justice,
evil to redress,
and to judge the nations
in His righteousness.

THE PSALTER, 1912

The Triune God

40

Begin, my soul, some heavenly theme;
awake, my voice, and sing
the mighty works, or mightier Name,
of our eternal King.

2 Tell of His wondrous faithfulness,
and sound His power abroad;
sing the sweet promise of His grace,
and the almighty God.

3 Proclaim salvation from the Lord,
for wretched, dying men:
His hand inscribed the sacred word
with an immortal pen.

4 Engraved as in eternal brass,
the mighty promise shines;
nor can the powers of darkness rase
those everlasting lines.

5 His every word of grace is strong
as that which built the skies;
the voice that rolls the stars along
speaks all the promises.

6 Now shall my fainting heart rejoice
to know my heaven secure;
I trust the all-creating voice,
and faith desires no more.

*Isaac Watts**, 1674-1748

41

Come, Thou almighty King,
help us Thy Name to sing,
help us to praise:
Father all-glorious,
o'er all victorious,
come and reign over us,
Ancient of Days!

2 Come, Thou incarnate Word,
gird on Thy mighty sword,
our prayers attend;
come, and Thy people bless,
and give Thy Word success;
Spirit of holiness,
on us descend!

3 Come, Holy Comforter,
Thy sacred witness bear
in this glad hour:
Thou, who almighty art,
now rule in every heart,
and never from us part,
Spirit of power!

4 To the great One in Three,
eternal praises be,
hence evermore:
His sovereign majesty
may we in glory see,
and to eternity
love and adore!

From Madan's Collection, 1760

42

Command Your blessing from above,
O God! on all assembled here;
behold us with a Father's love,
while we look up with filial fear.

2 Command Your blessing, Jesus, Lord!
May we Your true disciples be;
speak to each heart the mighty word,
say to the weakest, 'Follow Me!'

3 Command Your blessing in this hour,
Spirit of truth! and fill this place
with humbling and exalting power,
with quickening and confirming grace.

4 Almighty Maker, Saviour, Guide,
one true, eternal God confessed,
may nought in life or death divide
the saints in Your communion blest!

5 With You and Yours for ever bound,
may all, who here in prayer unite,
with harps and songs Your throne surround,
rest in Your love, and reign in light.

*James Montgomery**, 1771-1854

43

Father of heaven, whose love profound
a ransom for our souls has found,
before Your throne we sinners bend;
to us Your pardoning love extend.

2 Almighty Son, incarnate Word,
our Prophet, Priest, Redeemer, Lord,
before Your throne we sinners bend;
to us Your saving grace extend.

3 Eternal Spirit, by whose breath
the soul is raised from sin and death,
before Your throne we sinners bend;
to us Your quickening power extend.

4 Thrice holy: Father, Spirit, Son;
mysterious Godhead, Three in One,
before Your throne we sinners bend;
grace, pardon, life to us extend.

Edward Cooper, 1770-1833

44

Glory be to God the Father,
glory be to God the Son,
glory be to God the Spirit,
great Jehovah, Three in One:
glory, glory,
while eternal ages run!

2 Glory be to Him who loved us,
washed us from each spot and stain;
glory be to Him who bought us,
made us kings with Him to reign:
glory, glory,
to the Lamb that once was slain!

3 Glory to the King of angels,
glory to the church's King,
glory to the King of nations,
heaven and earth, your praises bring:
glory, glory,
to the King of glory bring!

4 'Glory, blessing, praise eternal!'
thus the choir of angels sings;
'Honour, riches, power, dominion!'
thus its praise creation brings.
Glory, glory,
glory to the King of kings!

Horatius Bonar, 1808-89

45

God is in His temple,
the almighty Father,
round His footstool let us gather;
Him with adoration
serve, the Lord most holy,
who has mercy on the lowly.
Let us raise
hymns of praise,
for His great salvation:
God is in His temple!

2 Christ comes to His temple:
we, His Word receiving,
are made happy in believing.
Lo! from sin delivered,
He has turned our sadness,
our deep gloom, to light and gladness.
Let us raise
hymns of praise,
for our bonds are severed:
Christ comes to His temple!

3 Come and claim Your temple,
gracious Holy Spirit!
In our hearts Your home inherit:
make in us Your dwelling,
Your high work fulfilling,
into ours Your will instilling;
till we raise
hymns of praise,
beyond mortal telling,
in the eternal temple.

William Tidd Matson, 1833-99

46

Heavenly Father, our Creator,
all You made declares Your praise;
source of life and light eternal,
endless love for endless days.
You have made us in Your image,
shaped and formed us from the clay;
marred by sin we bow before You,
now remake us, Lord, we pray.

2 Jesus Christ, God's Son, our Saviour,
seated at the Father's side;
You have come and shared our weakness,
for our sins You bled and died.
Now You reign in heavenly glory,
we on earth Your praises sing;
help us tell the wondrous story
of our risen, exalted King.

3 Holy Spirit, for our comfort,
poured on earth from heaven above;
gift of grace and hope of glory,
in our hearts form perfect love.
Daily make us more like Jesus,
grant that we, His church, be one,
one in truth and one in purpose,
that Your will on earth be done.

4 Father, Son and Holy Spirit,
we in Christ approach Your throne,
freed from fear of condemnation,
called to worship You alone.
Three in One, eternal Godhead,
let us know Your will today,
by Your grace, empower, enfold us,
lead us gladly to obey.

Andrew J Goddard, b. 1967

47

Holy, holy, holy, Lord God almighty!
early in the morning our song shall rise to Thee;
holy, holy, holy! merciful and mighty,
God in three Persons, blessèd Trinity!

2 Holy, holy, holy! all the saints adore Thee,
casting down their golden crowns around the glassy sea;
cherubim and seraphim falling down before Thee,
God from of old who evermore shall be!

3 Holy, holy, holy! though the darkness hide Thee,
though the eye of sinful man Thy glory may not see,
only Thou art holy, there is none beside Thee
perfect in power, in love, and purity.

4 Holy, holy, holy, Lord God almighty!
all Thy works shall praise Thy Name, in earth and sky and sea;
holy, holy, holy! merciful and mighty,
God in three Persons, blessèd Trinity!

Reginald Heber, 1783-1826

48

God of the covenant, triune Jehovah,
marvels of mercy adoring we see;
seeker of souls, in the counsels eternal
binding Thy lost ones for ever to Thee.

2 Not now by words bringing death to transgressors,
grace unto life the new covenant brings,
Jesus our surety, our Kinsman-Redeemer,
round us the robe of His righteousness flings.

3 Blessings on blessings through ages unending,
covenant fulness in glorious flood;
ours is a hope which no mortal can measure,
brought in by Jesus and sealed in His blood.

4 God of the covenant – changeless, eternal,
Father, Son, Spirit in blessing agree;
Thine be the glory, our weakness confessing,
triune Jehovah, we rest upon Thee.

Jessie F Webb, 1866-1964

49

God the Father, throned in splendour,
righteous, merciful and tender;
thankful songs Your people render –
sovereign Lord, we praise Your name!

2 God the Son, in glory seated,
Your redemptive act completed:
for Your mercy we entreated,
and You heard and loved and came.

3 God the Holy Spirit, filling
every contrite heart and willing;
grace and holiness instilling,
fruitful lives Your constant aim.

4 Father, Son and Holy Spirit,
source of riches we inherit:
glory, wisdom, truth and merit
we ascribe to Your great name!

Betty Stanley, b. 1921

50

Infinite God, to Thee we raise
our hearts in solemn songs of praise;
by all Thy works on earth adored,
we worship Thee, the common Lord;
the everlasting Father own,
and bow our souls before Thy throne.

2 Thee all the choir of angels sings,
the Lord of hosts, the King of kings;
cherubs proclaim Thy praise aloud,
and seraphs shout the triune God;
and, Holy, holy, holy! cry,
Thy glory fills both earth and sky!

3 God of the patriarchal race,
the ancient seers record Thy praise,
the goodly apostolic band
in highest joy and glory stand;
and all the saints and prophets join
to extol Thy majesty divine.

4 Head of the martyrs' noble host,
of Thee they justly make their boast;
the church, to earth's remotest bounds,
her heavenly Founder's praise resounds;
and strives, with those around the throne,
to hymn the mystic Three in One.

5 Father of endless majesty,
all might and love they render Thee;
Thy true and only Son adore,
the same in dignity and power;
and God the Holy Ghost declare,
the saints' eternal Comforter.

Ambrose, c. 339-97;
tr. by Charles Wesley, 1707-88

51

Now thank we all our God,
with hearts, and hands, and voices;
who wondrous things has done,
in whom His world rejoices;
who, from our mothers' arms,
has blessed us on our way
with countless gifts of love,
and still is ours today.

2 O may this bounteous God
through all our life be near us,
with ever-joyful hearts
and blessèd peace to cheer us,
and keep us in His grace,
and guide us when perplexed,
and free us from all ills
in this world and the next.

3 All praise and thanks to God
the Father now be given,
the Son, and Him who reigns
with Them in highest heaven:
the one eternal God,
whom earth and heaven adore;
for thus it was, is now,
and shall be evermore.

Martin Rinkart, 1586-1649;
tr. by Catherine Winkworth, 1827-78

52

The God of Abraham praise,
who reigns enthroned above,
ancient of everlasting days,
and God of love.
Jehovah! Great I AM!
By earth and heaven confessed;
I bow and bless the sacred Name,
for ever blessed.

2 The God of Abraham praise,
at whose supreme command
from earth I rise, and seek the joys
at His right hand.
I all on earth forsake –
its wisdom, fame, and power –
and Him my only portion make,
my shield and tower.

3 The God of Abraham praise,
whose all-sufficient grace
shall guide me all my happy days
in all my ways.
He is my faithful Friend,
He is my gracious God;
and He shall save me to the end
through Jesus' blood.

4 He by Himself has sworn,
I on His oath depend:
I shall, on eagles' wings upborne,
to heaven ascend;
I shall behold His face,
I shall His power adore,
and sing the wonders of His grace
for evermore.

5 There dwells the Lord our King,
the Lord our Righteousness,
triumphant o'er the world and sin,
the Prince of peace;
on Zion's sacred height
His kingdom He maintains,
and glorious with His saints in light
for ever reigns.

6 The whole triumphant host
give thanks to God on high.
Hail, Father, Son, and Holy Ghost!
they ever cry.
Hail, Abraham's God, and mine!
I join the heavenly lays;
all might and majesty are Thine,
and endless praise.

Thomas Olivers, 1725-99

53

To Him who chose us first,
before the world began;
to Him who bore the curse
to save rebellious man;
to Him who formed our hearts anew,
is endless praise and glory due.

2 The Father's love shall run
through our immortal songs;
we bring to God the Son
hosannas on our tongues;
our lips address the Spirit's Name,
with equal praise and zeal the same.

3 Let every saint above,
and angel round the throne,
for ever bless and love
the sacred Three in One;
thus heaven shall raise His honours
high,
when earth and time grow old and die.

Isaac Watts, 1674-1748

54

The Lord is King; lift up your voice,
O earth, and all you heavens rejoice!
From world to world the joy shall ring:
'The Lord omnipotent is King!'

2 The Lord is King! who then shall dare
resist His will, distrust His care,
or murmur at His wise decrees,
or doubt His royal promises?

3 The Lord is King! child of the dust,
the Judge of all the earth is just:
holy and true are all His ways;
let every creature speak His praise.

4 He reigns! you saints, exalt your strains:
your God is King, your Father reigns;
and He is at the Father's side,
the Man of love, the Crucified.

5 One Lord, one kingdom, all secures:
He reigns – and life and death are yours;
through earth and heaven one song
shall ring,
'The Lord omnipotent is King!'

Josiah Conder, 1789-1855

55

We give immortal praise
to God the Father's love,
for all our comforts here,
and better hopes above;
He sent His own eternal Son
to die for sins that man had done.

2 To God the Son belongs
immortal glory too,
who bought us with His blood
from everlasting woe;
and now He lives, and now He reigns,
and sees the fruit of all His pains.

3 To God the Spirit's Name
immortal worship give,
whose new-creating power
makes the dead sinner live;
His work completes the great design,
and fills the soul with joy divine.

4 Almighty God, to Thee
be endless honours done,
the undivided Three,
and the mysterious One:
where reason fails, with all her powers,
there faith prevails, and love adores.

Isaac Watts, 1674-1748

56

We praise Thee, O God,
for the Son of Thy love,
for Jesus, who died and
is now gone above.

Hallelujah! Thine the glory,
Hallelujah! we sing;
Hallelujah! Thine the glory,
our praise now we bring.

2 All glory and praise
to the Lamb that was slain,
who has borne all our sins
and has cleansed every stain.

3 We praise Thee, O God,
for Thy Spirit of light,
who has shown us our Saviour
and scattered our night.

4 All glory and praise
to the God of all grace,
who has bought us, and sought us,
and shown us His face.

5 Revive us again;
fill each heart with Thy love
may each soul be rekindled
with fire from above.

William P Mackay, 1839-85

57

We praise, we worship Thee, O God;
Thy sovereign power we sound abroad;
all nations bow before Thy throne,
and Thee the eternal Father own.

2 Loud hallelujahs to Thy Name
angels and seraphim proclaim;
the heavens and all the powers on high
with rapture constantly do cry:

3 'O holy, holy, holy Lord,
Thou God of hosts, by all adored,
earth and the heavens are full of Thee,
Thy light, Thy power, Thy majesty.'

4 Apostles join the glorious throng,
and swell the loud immortal song;
prophets enraptured hear the sound,
and spread the hallelujahs round.

5 Victorious martyrs join their praise
and shout the omnipotence of grace,
while all Thy church through all the earth
acknowledge and extol Thy worth.

6 Glory to Thee, O God most high!
Father, we praise Thy majesty:
the Son, the Spirit we adore;
one Godhead, blest for evermore.

Philip Gell's PSALMS AND HYMNS, 1815

58

What was it, O our God,
led You to give Your Son,
to yield Your well-beloved
for us by sin undone?
Unbounded love led You to give
Your well-loved Son that we might live.

2 What led the Son of God
to leave His throne on high,
to shed His precious blood,
to suffer and to die?
Unbounded love for sinners lost
led Him to suffer at such cost.

3 What moved You to impart
Your Spirit from above,
that He might fill our heart
with heavenly peace and love?
Unbounded love moved You to send
the Spirit as our guide and friend.

4 What love to You we owe,
our God, for all Your grace!
Our hearts may well o'erflow
in everlasting praise:
then let us raise our songs on high
such boundless love to magnify.

*Ann Gilbert**, 1782-1866

The Lord's Day

59

Come, let us join with one accord
in hymns around the throne:
this is the day our risen Lord
has made and called His own.

2 This is the day that God has blessed,
the brightest of the seven,
type of that everlasting rest
the saints enjoy in heaven.

3 Then let us in His name sing on,
and hasten to that day
when our Redeemer shall come down,
and shadows pass away.

4 Not one, but all our days below,
let us in hymns employ;
and in our Lord rejoicing, go
to His eternal joy.

Charles Wesley, 1707-88

60

Come, let us with our Lord arise,
our Lord, who made both earth and
skies;
who died to save the world He made,
and rose triumphant from the dead;
He rose, the Prince of life and peace,
and stamped the day for ever His.

2 This is the day the Lord has made,
that all may see His love displayed,
may feel His resurrection's power,
and rise again to fall no more,
in perfect righteousness renewed,
and filled with all the life of God.

3 Then let us render Him His own,
with solemn prayer approach the throne,
with meekness hear the gospel word,
with thanks His dying love record;
our joyful hearts and voices raise,
and fill His courts with songs of praise.

4 Honour and praise to Jesus pay
throughout His consecrated day;
be all in Jesu's praise employed,
nor leave a single moment void;
with utmost care the time improve,
and only breathe His praise and love.

Charles Wesley, 1707-88

61

Jesus, we look to Thee,
Thy promised presence claim;
Thou in the midst of us shalt be,
assembled in Thy Name.

2 Thy Name salvation is,
which here we come to prove;
Thy name is life, and health, and peace,
and everlasting love.

3 We meet, the grace to take
which Thou hast freely given;
we meet on earth for Thy dear sake,
that we may meet in heaven.

4 Present we know Thou art,
but O Thyself reveal!
now, Lord, let every bounding heart
the mighty comfort feel.

5 O may Thy quickening voice
the death of sin remove;
and bid our inmost souls rejoice
in hope of perfect love!

Charles Wesley, 1707-88

62

Now, gracious God, Thine arm reveal,
and make Thy glory known;
now let us all Thy presence feel,
and soften hearts of stone.

2 Help us to venture near Thy throne,
and plead a Saviour's name,
for all that we can call our own
is vanity and shame.

3 From all the guilt of former sin
may mercy set us free;
and let the week we now begin
begin and end with Thee.

4 Send down Thy Spirit from above,
that saints may love Thee more;
and sinners now may learn to love,
who never loved before.

John Newton, 1725-1807

63

O day of rest and gladness,
O day of joy and light,
O balm of care and sadness,
most beautiful, most bright!
On thee the high and lowly,
through ages joined in tune,
sing: Holy, holy, holy,
to the great God triune.

2 On thee, at the creation,
the light first had its birth;
on thee, for our salvation,
Christ rose from depths of earth;
on thee, our Lord victorious
the Spirit sent from heaven:
and thus on thee most glorious
a triple light was given.

3 Today on weary nations
the heavenly manna falls;
to holy convocations
the silver trumpet calls,
where gospel light is glowing
with pure and radiant beams,
and living water flowing
with soul-refreshing streams.

4 New graces ever gaining
from this our day of rest,
we reach the rest remaining
to spirits of the blest.
To Holy Ghost be praises,
to Father and to Son;
the church her voice upraises
to Thee, blest Three in One.

Christopher Wordsworth, 1807-85

64

Based on PSALM 92

Sweet is the work, my God, my King,
to praise Your Name, give thanks and sing;
to show Your love by morning light,
and talk of all Your truth at night.

2 Sweet is the day of sacred rest,
no mortal cares disturb my breast;
O may my heart in tune be found,
like David's harp of solemn sound!

3 My heart shall triumph in the Lord,
and bless His works and bless His Word;
Your works of grace, how bright they shine,
how deep Your counsels, how divine!

4 And I shall share a glorious part,
when grace has well refined my heart;
and fresh supplies of joy are shed,
like holy oil, to cheer my head.

5 Sin, my worst enemy before,
shall vex my eyes and ears no more;
my inward foes shall all be slain,
nor Satan break my peace again.

6 Then shall I see, and hear, and know
all I desired or wished below;
and every power find sweet employ
in that eternal world of joy.

Isaac Watts, 1674-1748

65

Based on Psalm 118:24-26

This is the day the Lord has made,
He calls the hours His own;
let heaven rejoice, let earth be glad,
and praise surround the throne.

2 Today He rose and left the dead,
and Satan's empire fell:
today the saints His triumph spread,
and all His wonders tell.

3 Hosanna to the anointed King,
to David's holy Son!
Help us, O Lord! descend and bring
salvation from Your throne.

4 Blest be the Lord, who comes to men
with messages of grace;
who comes in God His Father's name,
to save our sinful race.

5 Hosanna in the highest strains
the church on earth can raise;
the highest heavens in which He reigns
shall give Him nobler praise.

Isaac Watts, 1674-1748

66

Thou glorious Sun of righteousness,
on this day risen to set no more,
shine on us now, to heal and bless,
with brighter beams than e'er before.

2 Shine on Thy work of grace within,
on each celestial blossom there;
destroy each bitter root of sin,
and make Thy garden fresh and fair.

3 Shine on Thy pure, eternal Word,
its mysteries to our souls reveal;
and whether read, remembered, heard,
O let it quicken, strengthen, heal.

4 Shine on the temples of Thy grace,
in righteousness Thy priests be clad;
unveil the brightness of Thy face,
and make Thy chosen people glad.

5 Shine, till Thy glorious beams shall chase
the brooding cloud from every eye;
till every earthly dwelling-place
shall hail the Day-spring from on high.

6 Shine on, shine on, eternal Sun!
Pour richer floods of life and light,
till that bright sabbath be begun,
that glorious day which knows no
night.

Charlotte Elliott, 1789-1871

67

To Your temple I repair,
Lord I love to worship there,
when within the veil I meet
Christ before the mercy seat.

2 You, through Him, are reconciled,
I, through Him, became Your child;
Abba! Father! give me grace
in Your courts to seek Your face.

3 While Your glorious praise is sung,
touch my lips, unloose my tongue,
that my joyful soul may bless
Christ the Lord, my righteousness.

4 When Your people's prayers ascend,
God of love, to mine attend;
hear me, for Your Spirit pleads,
hear, for Jesus intercedes.

5 While I listen to Your law,
fill my soul with humble awe,
till Your gospel bring to me
life and immortality.

6 While Your ministers proclaim
peace and pardon in Your name,
through their voice, by faith may I
hear You speaking from on high.

7 From Your house, when I return,
may my heart within me burn,
and at evening let me say,
'I have walked with God today.'

James Montgomery, 1771-1854

Morning and evening

68

Awake, my soul, and with the sun
your daily stage of duty run;
shake off dull sloth, and joyful rise
to pay your morning sacrifice.

2 Your precious time mis-spent redeem,
each present day your last esteem;
improve your talent with due care;
for the great day yourself prepare.

3 Let all your converse be sincere;
your conscience as the noonday clear;
think how all-seeing God your ways
and all your secret thoughts surveys.

4 By influence of the light divine
let your own light in good works shine;
reflect all heaven's propitious ways
in ardent love and cheerful praise.

5 Wake, and lift up yourself, my heart,
and with the angels bear your part,
who all night long unwearied sing
high praise to the eternal King.

6 Praise God, from whom all blessings flow;
praise Him, all creatures here below;
praise Him above, you heavenly host;
praise Father, Son, and Holy Ghost.

Thomas Ken, 1637-1710

69

Begin the day with God:
He is the rising Sun,
His is the radiance of your dawn,
His the fresh day begun.

2 Sing a new song at morn;
join the glad woods and hills;
join the fresh winds and seas and plains;
join the bright flowers and rills.

3 Awake, cold lips, and sing;
arise, dull heart, and pray;
lift up, O man, your heart and eyes;
brush slothfulness away.

4 Cast every weight aside;
do battle with each sin;
fight with the faithless world without,
the faithless heart within.

5 Look up beyond these clouds,
for there your pathway lies;
mount up, away, and linger not,
your goal is yonder skies!

Horatius Bonar, 1808-89

70

PSALM 134

Come now with joyful hearts,
all you that serve the Lord,
and in His house, as day departs,
your praise to Him accord.

2 Lift up your hands on high
towards His holy place,
to bless and praise and magnify
the Lord of truth and grace.

3 For He who reigns above,
who heaven and earth did frame,
shall out of Zion send His love
to all who bless His name.

Graham D S Deans, b. 1953
Based on version by William Whittingham, 1534-79

71

O Jesus, Lord of heavenly grace,
the brightness of Your Father's face,
O fountain of eternal light,
whose beams disperse the shades of night;

2 Come, holy Sun of heavenly love,
shower down Your radiance from above,
and to our inmost hearts convey
the Holy Spirit's cloudless ray.

3 And we the Father's help will claim,
and sing the Father's glorious Name;
His powerful succour we implore,
that we may stand, to fall no more.

4 May He our actions deign to bless,
and loose the bonds of wickedness,
from sudden falls our feet defend,
and guide us safely to the end.

5 May faith, deep-rooted in the soul,
subdue our flesh, our minds control;
may guile depart, and discord cease,
and all within be joy and peace.

6 O hallowed be the approaching day;
let meekness be our morning ray,
and faithful love our noonday light,
and hope our sunset, calm and bright.

7 O Christ, with each returning morn
Your image to our hearts is borne;
O may we ever clearly view
our Saviour and our God in You.

Ambrose, c. 339-97;
tr. by John Chandler, 1806-76

72

Rise, my soul, adore your Maker:
angels praise;
join your lays,
with them be partaker.
Father, Lord of every spirit,
in Your light
lead me right,
through my Saviour's merit.

2 O my Jesus, God almighty,
pray for me,
till I see
You in Salem's city.
Holy Ghost, by Jesus given,
be my Guide,
lest my pride
shut me out of heaven.

3 You this night were my Protector:
with me stay
all the day,
ever my Director.
Holy, holy, holy Giver
of all good,
life and food,
reign, adored for ever!

John Cennick, 1718-55

73

When morning gilds the skies
my heart awaking cries,
'May Jesus Christ be praised!'
Alike at work and prayer
to Jesus I repair:
'May Jesus Christ be praised!'

2 To You, my God above,
I cry with glowing love,
'May Jesus Christ be praised!'
The fairest graces spring
in hearts that ever sing,
'May Jesus Christ be praised!'

3 Does sadness fill my mind?
A solace here I find,
'May Jesus Christ be praised!'
Or fades my earthly bliss?
My comfort still is this,
'May Jesus Christ be praised!'

4 When evil thoughts molest
with this I shield my breast,
'May Jesus Christ be praised!'
The powers of darkness fear
when this glad song they hear,
'May Jesus Christ be praised!'

5 Be this, while life is mine,
my canticle divine,
'May Jesus Christ be praised!'
Be this the eternal song
through all the ages long,
'May Jesus Christ be praised!'

German, 19th cent.;
tr. by Edward Caswall, 1814-78

74

At even, ere the sun was set,
the sick, O Lord, around Thee lay;
O in what various pains they met!
O with what joy they went away!

2 Once more 'tis eventide, and we
oppressed with various ills draw near;
what if Thy form we cannot see?
We know and feel that Thou art here.

3 O Saviour Christ, our woes dispel;
for some are sick, and some are sad,
and some have never loved Thee well,
and some have lost the love they had.

4 And some have found the world is vain,
yet from the world they break not free;
and some have friends who give them pain,
yet have not sought a friend in Thee.

5 And none, O Lord, have perfect rest,
for none are wholly free from sin;
and they who fain would serve Thee best
are conscious most of wrong within.

6 O Saviour Christ, Thou too art man;
Thou hast been troubled, tempted, tried;
Thy kind but searching glance can scan
the very wounds that shame would hide.

7 Thy touch has still its ancient power;
no word from Thee can fruitless fall;
hear in this solemn evening hour,
and in Thy mercy heal us all.

Henry Twells, 1823-1900

75

Ere I sleep, for every favour
this day showed
by my God,
I will bless my Saviour.

2 O my Lord, what shall I render
to Thy Name,
still the same,
merciful and tender?

3 Thou hast ordered all my goings
in Thy way,
heard me pray,
sanctified my doings.

4 Leave me not, but ever love me;
let Thy peace
be my bliss,
till Thou hence remove me.

5 Visit me with Thy salvation,
let Thy care
now be near
round my habitation.

6 Thou my rock, my guard, my tower,
safely keep,
while I sleep,
me, with all Thy power.

7 So, whene'er in death I slumber,
let me rise
with the wise,
counted in their number.

John Cennick, 1718-55

76

Glory to Thee, my God, this night,
for all the blessings of the light:
keep me, O keep me, King of kings,
beneath Thine own almighty wings.

2 Forgive me, Lord, for Thy dear Son,
the ill that I this day have done;
that with the world, myself, and Thee,
I, ere I sleep, at peace may be.

3 Teach me to live, that I may dread
the grave as little as my bed;
teach me to die, that so I may
rise glorious at the judgment day.

4 O may my soul on Thee repose,
and may sweet sleep mine eyelids close,
sleep that may me more vigorous make
to serve my God when I awake.

5 If in the night I sleepless lie,
my soul with heavenly thoughts supply;
let no ill dreams disturb my rest,
no powers of darkness me molest.

6 Praise God, from whom all blessings flow;
praise Him, all creatures here below;
praise Him above, ye heavenly host;
praise Father, Son, and Holy Ghost.

Thomas Ken, 1637-1710

77

Lord, keep us safe this night,
secure from all our fears;
may angels guard us while we sleep,
till morning light appears.

John Leland, 1754-1841

78

Saviour, again to Thy dear Name we raise
with one accord our parting hymn of praise;
we stand to bless Thee ere our worship cease,
then, humbly waiting, hear Thy word of peace.

2 Grant us Thy peace upon our homeward way;
with Thee began, with Thee shall end the day;
guard Thou the lips from sin, the hearts from shame,
that in this house have called upon Thy Name.

3 Grant us Thy peace, Lord, through the coming night,
turn Thou for us its darkness into light;
from harm and danger keep Thy children free,
for dark and light are both alike to Thee.

4 Grant us Thy peace throughout our earthly life,
our balm in sorrow, and our stay in strife;
then, when Thy voice shall bid our conflict cease,
call us, O Lord, to Thine eternal peace.

*John Ellerton**, 1826-93

79

The day Thou gavest, Lord, is ended,
the darkness falls at Thy behest;
to Thee our morning hymns ascended,
Thy praise shall sanctify our rest.

2 We thank Thee that Thy church unsleeping,
while earth rolls onward into light,
through all the world her watch is keeping,
and rests not now by day or night.

3 As o'er each continent and island
the dawn leads on another day,
the voice of prayer is never silent,
nor dies the strain of praise away.

4 The sun that bids us rest is waking
our brethren 'neath the western sky,
and hour by hour fresh lips are making
Thy wondrous doings heard on high.

5 So be it, Lord! Thy throne shall never,
like earth's proud empires, pass away;
Thy kingdom stands, and grows for ever,
till all Thy creatures own Thy sway.

John Ellerton, 1826-93

Close of worship

80

Come, dearest Lord, descend and dwell,
by faith and love, in every breast;
then shall we know, and taste, and feel
the joys that cannot be expressed.

2 Come, fill our hearts with inward strength,
make our enlargèd souls possess,
and learn the height and breadth and length
of Your immeasurable grace.

3 Now to the God whose power can do
more than our thoughts or wishes know,
be everlasting honours done
by all the church, through Christ His Son.

Isaac Watts, 1674-1748

81

May the grace of Christ our Saviour,
and the Father's boundless love,
with the Holy Spirit's favour,
rest upon us from above.

2 Thus may we abide in union
with each other and the Lord,
and possess, in sweet communion,
joys which earth cannot afford.
John Newton, 1725-1807

82

PSALMS 5:8; 4:8

Lead me, Lord, lead me in Thy righteousness,
make Thy way plain before my face.
Lead me, Lord, lead me in Thy righteousness,
make Thy way plain before my face.

2 For it is Thou Lord, Thou Lord only,
that makest me dwell in safety.
For it is Thou Lord, Thou Lord only,
that makest me dwell in safety.

83

Lord, dismiss us with Your blessing,
fill our hearts with joy and peace;
let us each, Your love possessing,
triumph in redeeming grace:
O refresh us!
travelling through this wilderness.

2 Thanks we give, and adoration,
for Your gospel's joyful sound;
may the fruits of Your salvation
in our hearts and lives abound;
may Your presence
with us evermore be found.

3 So, whene'er the signal's given
us from earth to call away,
borne on angels' wings to heaven,
glad the summons to obey,
may we ever
reign with Christ in endless day!
John Fawcett, 1740-1817

84

Now may He, who from the dead
brought the Shepherd of the sheep,
Jesus Christ, our King and Head,
all our souls in safety keep.

2 May He teach us to fulfil
what is pleasing in His sight,
perfect us in all His will,
and preserve us day and night.

3 To that dear Redeemer's praise,
who the covenant sealed with blood,
let our hearts and voices raise
loud thanksgivings to our God.
John Newton, 1725-1807

85

Once more before we part,
we bless the Saviour's name;
let every tongue and heart
join to extol the Lamb.

2 Jesus, the sinner's friend,
He whom our souls adore,
His praises have no end,
praise Him for evermore.

3 Lord, in Your grace we came,
Your blessing still impart;
we met in Jesus' name,
and in His name we part.

4 If here we meet no more,
may we in realms above,
with all the saints adore
redeeming grace and love.
Joseph Hart, 1712-68,
and Robert Hawker, 1753-1827

86

Based on JUDE 24,25

Now to Him whose power is able
to protect our stumbling feet,
and prepare our souls for glory
there with joy our King to meet;
so that we may stand before Him
faultless at His judgement seat.

2 To the only God our Saviour,
through our Lord Christ Jesus' name,
be dominion, power, glory,
majesty and matchless fame,
from before the world's foundation,
now and evermore the same!

Nick Needham, b. 1959

Doxologies

87

Praise God, from whom all blessings flow;
praise Him, all creatures here below;
praise Him above, ye heavenly host;
praise Father, Son, and Holy Ghost!

Thomas Ken, 1637-1710

88

To God the Father, God the Son,
and God the Spirit, Three in One,
be honour, praise and glory given,
by all on earth, and all in heaven.

Isaac Watts, 1674-1748

89

Give glory to God,
you children of men,
and publish abroad,
again and again,
the Son's glorious merit,
the Father's free grace,
the gift of the Spirit,
to Adam's lost race.

Joseph Hart, 1712-68

90

Now to Him who loved us, gave us
every pledge that love could give,
freely shed His blood to save us,
gave His life that we might live,
be the kingdom and dominion
and the glory evermore.

Samuel Miller Waring, 1792-1827

91

Based on PSALM 150

Hallelujah! Hallelujah!
earth and heaven, in sweet accord,
join to tell Jehovah's praises,
tell the glory of the Lord.

2 Hallelujah! Hallelujah!
magnify Jehovah's Name,
praise the living God, your maker;
all that breathe, His praise proclaim.

From the PSALTER HYMNAL, 1959

92

Praise the God of all creation,
praise the Father's boundless love;
praise the Lamb, our expiation,
Priest and King enthroned above.

2 Praise the Fountain of salvation,
Him by whom our spirits live;
undivided adoration
to the One Jehovah give.

Josiah Conder, 1789-1855

GOD THE FATHER

Creation

93

Based on Psalm 147

Fill your hearts with joy and gladness,
sing and praise your God and mine!
Great the Lord in love and wisdom,
might and majesty divine!
He who framed the starry heavens
knows and names them as they shine.

2 Praise the Lord, His people, praise Him!
wounded souls His comfort know;
those who fear Him find His mercies,
peace for pain and joy for woe;
humble hearts are high exalted,
human pride and power laid low.

3 Praise the Lord for times and seasons,
cloud and sunshine, wind and rain;
spring to melt the snows of winter
till the waters flow again;
grass upon the mountain pastures,
golden valleys thick with grain.

4 Fill your hearts with joy and gladness,
peace and plenty crown your days;
love His laws, declare His judgments,
walk in all His words and ways.
He the Lord and we His children:
praise the Lord, all people, praise!

Timothy Dudley-Smith, b. 1926

94

From mountain summit grand,
I view what God has planned,
and know that same dear hand
created me.
Cascading waterfall
thunders its mighty call,
the Lord who formed it all
created me.

And yet a cross upon a lonely hill
portrays a love and power greater still,
for on that bleak hillside,
my Lord and Saviour died;
His death can mean eternal life
to me.

Brian Deakin, b. 1935

95

I sing the almighty power of God,
that made the mountains rise,
that spread the flowing seas abroad,
and built the lofty skies.

2 I sing the wisdom that ordained
the sun to rule the day;
the moon shines full at His command,
and all the stars obey.

3 I sing the goodness of the Lord,
that filled the earth with food;
He formed the creatures with His word,
and then pronounced them good.

4 There's not a plant or flower below
but makes His glories known;
and clouds arise, and tempests blow,
by order from His throne.

5 Creatures, as numerous as they be,
are subject to His care;
there's not a place where we can flee
but God is present there.

6 In heaven He shines with beams of love,
with wrath in hell beneath:
'tis on His earth I stand or move,
and 'tis His air I breathe.

7 His hand is my perpetual guard,
He guides me with His eye;
why should I then forget the Lord,
who is for ever nigh?

Isaac Watts, 1674-1748

96

Lord of all being, throned afar,
Thy glory flames from sun and star;
centre and soul of every sphere,
yet to each loving heart how near.

2 Sun of our life, Thy quickening ray
sheds on our path the glow of day;
Star of our hope, Thy softened light
cheers the long watches of the night.

3 Our midnight is Thy smile withdrawn;
our noontide is Thy gracious dawn;
our rainbow arch, Thy mercy's sign;
all, save the clouds of sin, are Thine.

4 Lord of all life, below, above,
whose light is truth, whose warmth is love,
before Thy ever-blazing throne
we ask no lustre of our own.

5 Grant us Thy truth to make us free,
and kindling hearts that burn for Thee,
till all Thy living altars claim
one holy light, one heavenly flame.

Oliver Wendell Holmes, 1809-94

97

Based on PSALM 104

O worship the King,
all-glorious above;
O gratefully sing
His power and His love:
our Shield and Defender,
the Ancient of Days,
pavilioned in splendour
and girded with praise.

2 O tell of His might,
O sing of His grace,
whose robe is the light,
whose canopy space;
His chariots of wrath
the deep thunder-clouds form,
and dark is His path
on the wings of the storm.

3 The earth, with its store
of wonders untold,
Almighty, Your power
has founded of old,
established it fast
by a changeless decree,
and round it has cast,
like a mantle, the sea.

4 Your bountiful care
what tongue can recite?
It breathes in the air,
it shines in the light;
it streams from the hills,
it descends to the plain,
and sweetly distils
in the dew and the rain.

5 Frail children of dust,
and feeble as frail,
in You do we trust,
nor find You to fail;
Your mercies how tender,
how firm to the end,
our Maker, Defender,
Redeemer and Friend.

6 O measureless Might!
ineffable Love!
while angels delight
to hymn You above,
Your humbler creation,
though feeble their lays,
with true adoration
shall lisp to Your praise.

Robert Grant, 1779-1838

98 PSALM 148

Praise the Lord! O heavens adore Him;
praise Him, angels in the height;
sun and moon, rejoice before Him;
praise Him, all you stars and light.
Praise the Lord! for He has spoken;
worlds His mighty voice obeyed;
laws, that never shall be broken,
for their guidance He has made.

2 Praise the Lord! for He is glorious;
never shall His promise fail:
God has made His saints victorious;
sin and death shall not prevail.
Praise the God of our salvation!
hosts on high His power proclaim;
heaven and earth, and all creation,
praise and magnify His Name.

Anonymous:
FOUNDLING HOSPITAL PSALMS AND HYMNS,
1802-09 editions

99 PSALM 147

Praise ye the Lord; 'tis good to raise
our hearts and voices in His praise:
His nature and His works invite
to make His duty our delight.

2 He formed the stars, those heavenly flames,
He counts their numbers, calls their names;
His wisdom's vast, and knows no bound,
a deep where all our thoughts are drowned.

3 Sing to the Lord, exalt Him high,
who spreads His clouds along the sky;
there He prepares the fruitful rain,
nor lets the drops descend in vain.

4 He makes the grass the hills adorn,
and clothes the smiling fields with corn;
the beasts with food His hands supply,
and the young ravens when they cry.

5 What is the creature's skill or force,
the sprightly man, the warlike horse,
the nimble wit, the active limb?
All are too mean delights for Him.

6 But saints are lovely in His sight;
He views His children with delight;
He sees their hope, He knows their fear,
and looks, and loves His image there.

Isaac Watts, 1674-1748

Providence

100 PSALM 91

Call Jehovah your salvation,
rest beneath the Almighty's shade,
in His secret habitation
dwell, and never be dismayed:
there no tumult shall alarm you,
you shall dread no hidden snare:
guile nor violence can harm you,
in eternal safeguard there.

2 From the sword at noonday wasting,
from the fearsome pestilence,
in the depth of midnight blasting,
God shall be your sure defence.
He shall charge His angel legions
watch o'er all your paths to keep,
though you walk through hostile regions,
though in deserts wild you sleep.

3 Since, with pure and firm affection,
you on God have set your love,
with the wings of His protection
He will shield you from above.
You shall call on Him in trouble,
He will hearken, He will save,
here for grief reward you double,
crown with life beyond the grave.
James Montgomery, 1771-1854

101

Commit your every grief
and ways into His hands,
to His sure truth and tender care,
who heaven and earth commands.

2 Who points the clouds their course,
whom winds and seas obey,
He shall direct your wandering feet,
He shall prepare your way.

3 Then on the Lord rely,
who safely leads you on;
fix on His work your steadfast eye,
so shall your work be done.

4 No profit can you gain
from self-consuming care:
to Him commend your cause; His ear
attends the softest prayer.

5 He everywhere has sway,
and all things serve His might;
His every act pure blessing is,
His path unsullied light.

6 When He makes bare His arm,
who shall His work withstand?
When He His people's cause defends,
who, who shall stay His hand?

7 Put now your trust in God,
in duty's path go on;
walk in His strength with faith and hope,
so shall your work be done.
Paul Gerhardt, 1607-76;
*tr. by John Wesley**, 1703-91

102

PSALM 46

God is our refuge and our strength,
our ever-present aid,
and therefore, though the earth remove,
we will not be afraid;
though hills amidst the seas be cast,
though foaming waters roar,
yea, though the mighty billows shake
the mountains on the shore.

2 A river flows whose streams make glad
the city of our God,
the holy place wherein the Lord
Most High has His abode.
Since God is in the midst of her,
unmoved her walls shall stand,
for God will be her early help
when trouble is at hand.

3 The nations raged, the kingdoms moved,
but when His voice was heard,
the troubled earth was stilled to peace
before His mighty word.
The Lord of hosts is on our side,
our safety to secure;
the God of Jacob is for us
a refuge strong and sure.

4 O come, behold what wondrous works
Jehovah's hand has wrought;
come, see what desolations great
He on the earth has brought.
To utmost ends of all the earth
He causes wars to cease;
the weapons of the strong destroyed,
He makes abiding peace.

5 'Be still and know that I am God,
o'er all exalted high;
the subject nations of the earth
My Name shall magnify.'
The Lord of hosts is on our side,
our safety to secure;
the God of Jacob is for us
a refuge strong and sure.

THE PSALTER, 1912

103

PSALM 46

God is our strength and refuge,
our present help in trouble;
and we therefore will not fear,
though the earth should change!
Though mountains shake and tremble,
though swirling floods are raging,
God the Lord of hosts is with us
evermore!

2 There is a flowing river,
within God's holy city;
God is in the midst of her –
she shall not be moved!
God's help is swiftly given,
thrones vanish at His presence –
God the Lord of hosts is with us
evermore!

3 Come, see the works of our maker,
learn of His deeds all-powerful;
wars will cease across the world
when He shatters the spear!
Be still and know your Creator,
uplift Him in the nations –
God the Lord of hosts is with us
evermore!

Richard Bewes, b. 1934

104

PSALM 46

God is the refuge of His saints,
when storms of sharp distress invade;
ere we can offer our complaints,
behold Him present with His aid.

2 Let mountains from their seats be hurled
down to the deep, and buried there:
convulsions shake the solid world;
our faith shall never yield to fear.

3 Loud may the troubled ocean roar,
in sacred peace our souls abide;
while every nation, every shore,
trembles, and dreads the swelling tide.

4 There is a stream whose gentle flow
makes glad the city of our God,
life, love, and joy, still gliding through,
and watering our divine abode.

5 This sacred stream, Your holy Word,
thus all our raging fear controls;
sweet peace Your promises afford,
and give new strength to fainting souls.

6 Zion enjoys her Monarch's love,
secure against a threatening hour;
nor can her firm foundations move,
built on His truth, armed with His power.

Isaac Watts, 1674-1748

105

God moves in a mysterious way
His wonders to perform;
He plants His footsteps in the sea,
and rides upon the storm.

2 Deep in unfathomable mines
of never-failing skill
He treasures up His bright designs,
and works His sovereign will.

3 You fearful saints, fresh courage take;
the clouds you so much dread
are big with mercy, and shall break
in blessings on your head.

4 Judge not the Lord by feeble sense,
but trust Him for His grace;
behind a frowning providence
He hides a smiling face.

5 His purposes will ripen fast,
unfolding every hour;
the bud may have a bitter taste,
but sweet will be the flower.

6 Blind unbelief is sure to err,
and scan His work in vain;
God is His own interpreter,
and He will make it plain.

William Cowper, 1731-1800

106

'Great is Thy faithfulness', O God my Father,
there is no shadow of turning with Thee;
Thou changest not, Thy compassions they fail not;
as Thou hast been Thou forever wilt be.

'Great is Thy faithfulness! Great is Thy faithfulness!'
Morning by morning new mercies I see!
All I have needed Thy hand hath provided –
'Great is Thy faithfulness', Lord, unto me!

2 Summer and winter, and springtime and harvest,
sun, moon and stars in their courses above,
join with all nature in manifold witness
to Thy great faithfulness, mercy and love.

3 Pardon for sin and a peace that endureth,
Thy own dear presence to cheer and to guide,
strength for today and bright hope for tomorrow,
blessings all mine, with ten thousand beside!

Thomas O Chisholm, 1866-1960

107

Great providence of heaven –
what wonders shine
in its profound display
of God's design:
it guards the dust of earth,
commands the hosts above,
fulfils the mighty plan
of His great love.

2 The kingdoms of this world
lie in its hand;
see how they rise or fall
at its command!
Through sorrow and distress,
tempestuous storms that rage,
God's kingdom yet endures
from age to age.

3 Its darkness dense is but
a radiant light;
its oft-perplexing ways
are ordered right.

Soon all its winding paths
will end, and then the tale
of wonder shall be told
beyond the veil.

David Charles, 1762-1834;
tr. by Edmund Tudor Owen, b. 1935

108 ISAIAH 40:28-31

Have you not known, have you not heard,
that firm remains on high
the everlasting throne of Him
who formed the earth and sky?

2 Are you afraid His power shall fail
when comes your evil day?
And can an all-creating arm
grow weary or decay?

3 Supreme in wisdom as in power
the Rock of Ages stands;
though Him you cannot see, nor trace
the working of His hands.

4 He gives the conquest to the weak,
supports the fainting heart;
and courage in the evil hour
His heavenly aids impart.

5 Mere human power shall fast decay,
and youthful vigour cease;
but they who wait upon the Lord
in strength shall still increase.

6 The saints shall mount on eagles' wings,
and taste the promised bliss,
till their unwearied feet arrive
where perfect pleasure is.

Isaac Watts, 1674-1748;
as in SCOTTISH PARAPHRASES, 1781

109

How gentle God's commands,
how kind His precepts are!
Come, cast your burdens on the Lord,
and trust His constant care.

2 While providence supports,
let saints securely dwell;
that hand which bears all nature up
shall guide His children well.

3 Why should this anxious load
press down your weary mind?
Haste to your heavenly Father's throne,
and sweet refreshment find.

4 His goodness stands approved,
down to the present day;
I'll drop my burden at His feet,
and bear a song away.

Philip Doddridge, 1702-51

110 PSALM 11

In God will I trust, though my counsellors say,
O flee as a bird to your mountain away;
the wicked are strong and the righteous are weak,
foundations are shaken, yet God will I seek.

2 The Lord in His temple shall ever abide;
His throne is eternal whatever betide.
The children of men He beholds from on high,
the wicked to punish, the righteous to try.

3 The Lord is most righteous, the Lord loves the right,
the evil He hates and will surely requite;
the wicked His anger will drive from their place,
the upright in rapture shall gaze on His face.

THE PSALTER, 1912

111

My God, I thank Thee, who hast made
the earth so bright,
so full of splendour and of joy,
beauty and light;
so many glorious things are here,
noble and right.

2 I thank Thee, too, that Thou hast made
joy to abound,
so many gentle thoughts and deeds
circling us round,
that in the darkest spot of earth
some love is found.

3 I thank Thee more, that all our joy
is touched with pain,
that shadows fall on brightest hours,
that thorns remain;
so that earth's bliss may be our guide,
and not our chain.

4 For Thou, who knowest, Lord, how soon
our weak heart clings,
hast given us joys, tender and true,
yet all with wings,
so that we see, gleaming on high,
diviner things.

5 I thank Thee, Lord, that Thou hast kept
the best in store:
we have enough, but not too much
to long for more –
a yearning for a deeper peace
not known before.

6 I thank Thee, Lord, that here our souls,
though amply blest,
can never find, although they seek,
a perfect rest,
nor ever shall, until they lean
on Jesus' breast.

Adelaide Anne Procter, 1825-64

112

Psalm 23

My Shepherd will supply my need,
Jehovah is His name;
in pastures fresh He makes me feed
beside the living stream.
He brings my wandering spirit back
when I forsake His ways;
and leads me for His mercy's sake
in paths of truth and grace.

2 When I walk through the shades of death,
Your presence is my stay;
a word of Your supporting breath
drives all my fears away.
Your hand in sight of all my foes
does still my table spread;
my cup with blessings overflows,
Your oil anoints my head.

3 The sure provisions of my God
attend me all my days:
O may Your house be my abode,
and all my work be praise!
There would I find a settled rest,
while others go and come;
no more a stranger or a guest,
but like a child at home.

Isaac Watts, 1674-1748

113

O Father, You are sovereign
in all the worlds You made;
Your mighty Word was spoken
and light and life obeyed.
Your voice commands the seasons
and bounds the ocean shore,
sets stars within their courses
and stills the tempest's roar.

2 O Father, You are sovereign
in all affairs of man;
no powers of death or darkness
can thwart Your perfect plan.

All chance and change transcending,
supreme in time and space,
You hold Your trusting children
secure in Your embrace.

3 O Father, You are sovereign,
the Lord of human pain,
transmuting earthly sorrows
to gold of heavenly gain.
All evil overruling,
as none but Conqueror could,
Your love pursues its purpose –
our soul's eternal good.

4 O Father, You are sovereign!
We see You dimly now,
but soon before Your triumph
earth's every knee shall bow.
With this glad hope before us
our faith springs up anew:
our sovereign Lord and Saviour,
we trust and worship You!

Margaret Clarkson, b. 1915

114 Based on PSALM 9

Our God almighty be adored,
eternal, all-sufficient Lord!
This righteous Lord forever reigns;
justice and truth He still maintains.

2 The sovereign judge prepares His throne,
and will His awesome power make known
to vindicate the righteous cause,
if mortals dare defy His laws.

3 Awake our noblest powers to bless
the God of ages – God of peace;
yet by a dearer title known –
Father and God of Christ His Son.

4 Through every age His gracious ear
is open to His servant's prayer;
nor can one humble soul complain,
that it has sought the Lord in vain.

5 To You our souls in faith arise,
to You we lift expectant eyes;
and boldly through this desert tread,
for You will guard where You shall lead.

Philip Doddridge, 1702-51

115 PSALM 90

Our God, our help in ages past,
our hope for years to come,
our shelter from the stormy blast,
and our eternal home;

2 Beneath the shadow of Thy throne
Thy saints have dwelt secure;
sufficient is Thine arm alone,
and our defence is sure.

3 Before the hills in order stood,
or earth received her frame,
from everlasting Thou art God,
to endless years the same.

4 A thousand ages in Thy sight
are like an evening gone,
short as the watch that ends the night
before the rising sun.

5 Time, like an ever-rolling stream,
bears all its sons away;
they fly forgotten, as a dream
dies at the opening day.

6 Our God, our help in ages past,
our hope for years to come,
be Thou our guard while troubles last,
and our eternal home.

Isaac Watts, 1674-1748

116

Sometimes a light surprises
the Christian while he sings;
it is the Lord who rises
with healing in His wings:
when comforts are declining,
He grants the soul again
a season of clear shining,
to cheer it after rain.

2 In holy contemplation,
we sweetly then pursue
the theme of God's salvation,
and find it ever new.
Set free from present sorrow,
we cheerfully can say,
'Then let the unknown morrow
bring with it what it may –

3 'It can bring with it nothing
but He will bear us through;
who gives the lilies clothing
will clothe His people too:
beneath the spreading heavens
no creature but is fed;
and He who feeds the ravens
will give His children bread.'

4 Though vine nor fig-tree neither
their looked-for fruit should bear,
though all the field should wither,
nor flocks nor herds be there,
yet God the same abiding,
His praise shall tune my voice;
for while in Him confiding,
I cannot but rejoice.

William Cowper, 1731-1800

117

The Lord Jehovah reigns;
His throne is built on high,
the garments He assumes
are light and majesty:
His glories shine with beams so bright,
no mortal eye can bear the sight.

2 The thunders of His hand
keep the wide world in awe;
His wrath and justice stand
to guard His holy law;
and where His love resolves to bless,
His truth confirms and seals the grace.

3 Through all His mighty works
amazing wisdom shines,
confounds the powers of hell,
and breaks their dark designs;
strong is His arm, and shall fulfil
His great decrees and sovereign will.

4 And will this mighty King
of glory condescend?
And will He write His name
my Father and my Friend?
I love His name, I love His Word,
join all my powers to praise the Lord.

Isaac Watts, 1674-1748

118

Psalm 99:1-5

The Lord our God shall reign,
though nations fear and quake;
He sits enthroned in majesty,
and causes earth to shake.

2 In Zion God is great,
exalted over all;
with fear and trembling, praise His name,
and on your faces fall.

3 For our eternal King
is clothed with power and might;
with justice shall He rule the world,
upholding what is right.

4 So praise the Lord your God,
and greet Him with acclaim;
before His footstool come with joy,
and bless His holy Name.

Graham D S Deans, b. 1953

119

PSALM 34

Through all the changing scenes of life,
in trouble and in joy,
the praises of my God shall still
my heart and tongue employ

2 Of His deliverance I will boast,
till all that are distressed
from my example comfort take,
and charm their griefs to rest.

3 O magnify the Lord with me,
with me exalt His Name;
when in distress to Him I called,
He to my rescue came.

4 The hosts of God encamp around
the dwellings of the just;
deliverance He provides to all
who make His Name their trust.

5 O make but trial of His love,
experience will decide
how blessed are they, and only they,
who in His truth confide.

6 Fear Him, you saints, and you will then
have nothing else to fear;
make you His service your delight,
your wants shall be His care.

Nahum Tate, 1652-1715
and Nicholas Brady, 1659-1726*

120

Through faith we understand
the things we cannot know –
the hidden pattern God has planned
and why each thread is so.
We trace life's vast design
and lose God's golden strand;
but when our wills with His entwine,
through faith we understand.

2 Through faith we understand
what mind and heart find dim,
and still Love's strong, all-knowing hand
leads those who trust in Him.
Ours not to know the way,
but bow to His command;
and when our childlike hearts obey,
through faith we understand.

Margaret Clarkson, b. 1915

121

When all Thy mercies, O my God,
my rising soul surveys,
transported with the view, I'm lost
in wonder, love, and praise.

2 Unnumbered comforts on my soul
Thy tender care bestowed,
before my infant heart conceived
from whom those comforts flowed.

3 When worn with sickness, oft hast Thou
with health renewed my face;
and when in sins and sorrows sunk,
revived my soul with grace.

4 Ten thousand thousand precious gifts
my daily thanks employ;
nor is the least a cheerful heart,
that tastes those gifts with joy.

5 Through every period of my life
Thy goodness I'll pursue,
and after death in distant worlds
the glorious theme renew.

6 Through all eternity to Thee
a joyful song I'll raise;
but O! eternity's too short
to utter all Thy praise!
Joseph Addison, 1672-1719

122

God of salvation, we adore
Your saving love, Your saving power,
and to our utmost stretch of thought
hail the redemption You have wrought.

2 We love the stroke that breaks our chain,
the sword by which our sins are slain;
and while abased in dust we bow,
we sing the grace that lays us low.

3 Perish each thought of human pride,
let God alone be magnified;
His glory let the heavens resound,
shouted from earth's remotest bound.

4 Saints who His full salvation know,
saints who but taste it here below,
join with the angelic choir to raise
enraptured songs of deathless praise.
Philip Doddridge, 1702-51

Redemption

123

All my hope on God is founded;
all my trust He shall renew;
He, my guide through changing order,
only good and only true:
God unknown,
He alone
calls my heart to be His own.

2 Human pride and earthly glory,
sword and crown betray His trust;
what with care and toil we fashion,
tower and temple, fall to dust;
but God's power,
hour by hour,
is my temple and my tower.

3 God's great goodness lasts for ever,
deep His wisdom, passing thought;
splendour, light and life attend Him,
beauty springing out of nought;
evermore
from His store
countless stars rise and adore.

4 Day by day the almighty Giver
grants to us His gifts of love;
in His will our souls find pleasure,
leading to our home above:
love shall stand
at His hand,
joy shall wait on His command.

5 Still from man to God eternal
sacrifice of praise be done;
high above all praises praising
for the gift of Christ His Son:
hear Christ's call,
one and all –
those who follow shall not fall.
*Robert Seymour Bridges**, 1844-1930;
from Joachim Neander, 1650-80

124

PSALM 22:23-26,31

All you that fear Jehovah's name,
His glory tell, His praise proclaim;
you children of His chosen race,
stand now in awe before His face,
stand now in awe before His face.

2 The suff'ring One He has not spurned,
who unto Him for help has turned;
from Him He has not hid His face,
but answered His request in grace,
but answered His request in grace.

3 O Lord, Your goodness makes me raise
amid Your people songs of praise;
before all them that fear You, now
I worship You and pay my vow,
I worship You and pay my vow.

4 For all the meek You will provide;
they shall be fed and satisfied;
all they that seek the Lord shall live,
and never ending praises give,
and never ending praises give.

5 The Lord's unfailing righteousness
all generations shall confess;
from age to age shall men be taught
what wondrous works the Lord has wrought,
what wondrous works the Lord has wrought.

THE PSALTER, 1912*

125

From heaven's eternal throne there came
a word of strong decree:
Light up the world with grace and truth
and set the captives free!

2 Forth from the courts of heavenly bliss
down to this world of shame,
the Son of God with light and life
in glad obedience came.

3 The Word made flesh in human form
entered the world He made;
the darkness fled and glory shone
around where He was laid.

4 While circling years in time revealed
the plan of God in grace,
the Son of man unfurled the truth
prophets had learned to trace.

5 Borne to a cross by cruel hands
of men in darkness held,
judgment and death eclipsed the Son,
whilst lies deceived the world.

6 Out from a tomb of dark despair
the Prince of light arose;
the truth prevails and grace abounds,
in all the world it flows.

7 Now fix your gaze, O sons of light,
on heaven's exalted King!
The Lamb of God will soon return
and full salvation bring.

Paul Eric Graham Cook, b. 1932

126 PSALM 89:1-6,34-37

My song forever shall record
the tender mercies of the Lord;
Your faithfulness will I proclaim,
and every age shall know Your name.

2 I sing of mercies that endure,
for ever built both firm and sure,
of faithfulness that never dies,
established changeless in the skies.

3 Behold God's truth and grace displayed,
for He has faithful covenant made,
and sworn that David's greater Son
shall ever sit upon His throne.

4 Who in the heavenly dwellings fair
can with the Lord Himself compare?
Or who among the mighty shares
the likeness that our Saviour bears?

5 God's promise is for ever sure,
the Saviour's people shall endure;
His throne for ever firm shall stay
when sun and moon have passed away.

THE PSALTER, 1912

127

Nature with open volume stands
to spread her Maker's praise abroad,
and every labour of His hands
shows something worthy of a God.

2 But in the grace that rescued man
His brightest form of glory shines;
here on the cross 'tis fairest drawn
in precious blood and crimson lines.

3 Here His whole Name appears complete;
nor mind can guess, nor reason prove,
which of the letters best is writ,
the power, the wisdom, or the love.

4 Here I behold His inmost heart,
where grace and vengeance strangely join,
piercing His Son with sharpest smart,
to make the purchased pleasures mine.

5 O the sweet wonders of that cross
where God the Saviour loved and died!
Her noblest life my spirit draws
from His dear wounds and bleeding side.

6 I would for ever speak His Name
in sounds to mortal ears unknown;
with angels join to praise the Lamb,
and worship at His Father's throne.

Isaac Watts, 1674-1748

128

Great God of wonders! all Thy ways
are matchless, godlike, and divine;
but the fair glories of Thy grace,
more godlike and unrivalled shine:

Who is a pardoning God like Thee?
Or who has grace so rich and free?

2 Such dire offences to forgive,
such guilty, daring worms to spare:
this is Thy grand prerogative,
and in the honour none shall share:

3 Angels and men, resign your claim
to pity, mercy, love, and grace:
these glories crown Jehovah's Name
with an incomparable blaze:

4 In wonder lost, with trembling joy,
we take the pardon of our God,
pardon for sins of deepest dye,
a pardon sealed with Jesus' blood:

5 O may this strange, this matchless grace,
this godlike miracle of love,
fill the wide earth with grateful praise
and all the angelic hosts above:

Samuel Davies, 1723-61

129

O Lord, enlarge our scanty thought,
to know the wonders Thou hast wrought;
unloose our stammering tongues to tell
Thy love immense, unsearchable.

2 What are our works but sin and death,
till Thou Thy quickening Spirit breathe;
until we strength from Thee derive
and in communion with Thee live?

3 How can it be, Thou heavenly King,
that Thou shouldst us to glory bring;
make slaves the partners of Thy throne,
decked with a never-fading crown?

4 Our hearts then melt, our eyes o'erflow,
our words are lost, nor will we know,
nor will we think of aught beside,
my Lord, my Love, is crucified!

5 First-born of many brethren Thou;
to Thee, lo! all our souls we bow;
to Thee our hearts and hands we give:
Thine may we die, Thine may we live!

Nicolaus Ludwig von Zinzendorf, 1700-60, *v. 1;*
Johann Nitschmann, 1712-83, *vv.* 2-4;
Anna Nitschmann, 1715-60, *v.* 5;
tr. by John Wesley, 1703-91

130

My hope is fixed on God alone –
the God of sovereign grace,
whose heart conceived a glorious plan
of mercy for rebellious man:
for Adam's fallen race.

2 My hope is fixed on God alone –
the God of holiness.
'The soul that sins will surely die':
this word He never will deny
but act in righteousness.

3 My hope is fixed on God alone –
the God whose promise stands.
His Son will crush the serpent's head,
will die and, rising from the dead,
meet all the law's demands.

4 My hope is fixed on God alone –
the God whose mighty Word
opens deaf ears and blinded eyes,
says to the prisoner, 'Come, arise!
and make your happy choice.'

5 My hope is fixed on God alone –
the God who cannot fail.
His Word and Spirit lead me on,
He is Himself my shield and song,
with Him I shall prevail.

6 My hope is fixed on God alone,
He'll keep me to the end.
My life is hid with Christ on high,
I know on Him I can rely,
My Saviour and my friend.

Colin P Goldsworthy, b. 1927

131

PSALM 103:8-18

My soul, repeat His praise
whose mercies are so great,
whose anger is so slow to rise,
so ready to abate.

2 High as the heavens are raised
above the ground we tread,
so far the riches of His grace
our highest thoughts exceed.

3 His power subdues our sins;
and His forgiving love,
far as the east is from the west,
does all our guilt remove.

4 The pity of the Lord
to those that fear His Name
is such as tender parents feel;
He knows our feeble frame.

5 Our days are as the grass,
or like the morning flower;
if one sharp blast sweep o'er the field,
it withers in an hour.

6 But Your compassions, Lord,
to endless years endure;
and children's children ever find
Your words of promise sure.

Isaac Watts, 1674-1748

132

O God of our fathers, Creator and Lord!
Majestic in glory, by heaven adored;
to first generations Your promise revealed,
Your fullness, in Jesus, declared.

2 O God of my own heart, redeemer and king!
My crucified Saviour, Your glories I sing;
in dying You loved me: Your own life laid down
to save me, forever, from sin.

3 O God for whose coming in glory we long!
Your gospel of hope shall be ever our song:
of rescue from judgement, and life without end,
for all who to Jesus belong.

William J U Philip, b. 1967

133

PSALM 103:1-5

O thou my soul, bless God the Lord,
and all that in me is
be stirrèd up His holy Name
to magnify and bless.

2 Bless, O my soul, the Lord thy God,
and not forgetful be
of all His gracious benefits
He hath bestowed on thee.

3 All thine iniquities who doth
most graciously forgive;
who thy diseases all and pains
doth heal, and thee relieve.

4 Who doth redeem thy life, that thou
to death may'st not go down;
who thee with lovingkindness doth
and tender mercies crown.

5 Who with abundance of good things
doth satisfy thy mouth,
so that, even as the eagle's age,
renewèd is thy youth.

SCOTTISH PSALTER, 1650

134

O love of God, how strong and true;
eternal, and yet ever new;
uncomprehended and unbought,
beyond all knowledge and all thought!

2 O love of God, how deep and great,
far deeper than man's deepest hate;
self-fed, self-kindled like the light,
changeless, eternal, infinite!

3 O heavenly love, how precious still,
in days of weariness and ill,
in nights of pain and helplessness,
to heal, to comfort, and to bless!

4 O wide-embracing, wondrous love,
we read you in the sky above;
we read you in the earth below,
in seas that swell and streams that flow.

5 We read you best in Him who came
to bear for us the cross of shame,
sent by the Father from on high,
our life to live, our death to die.

6 We read your power to bless and save,
e'en in the darkness of the grave;
still more in resurrection light
we read the fulness of your might.

7 O love of God, our shield and stay
through all the perils of our way;
eternal love, in you we rest,
for ever safe, for ever blest.

Horatius Bonar, 1808-89

135

O what matchless condescension
the eternal God displays,
claiming our supreme attention
to His boundless works and ways;
His own glory
He reveals in gospel days.

2 In the person of the Saviour
all His majesty is seen,
love and justice shine for ever;
and without a veil between,
we approach Him,
and rejoice in His dear name.

3 Would we view His highest glory,
here it shines in Jesus' face;
sing and tell the pleasing story,
O you sinners saved by grace;
and with pleasure,
bid the guilty Him embrace.

4 In His highest work, redemption,
see His glory in a blaze;
beyond mortal comprehension
higher than an angel's praise;
grace and justice
here unite to endless days.

5 True, 'tis sweet and solemn pleasure,
God to view in Christ the Lord;
here He smiles, and smiles for ever;
may my soul His name record,
praise and bless Him,
and His wonders spread abroad.

*William Gadsby**, 1773-1844

136

Sing praise to God who reigns above,
the God of all creation,
the God of wonders, power, and love,
the God of our salvation.
With healing balm my soul He fills,
the God who every sorrow stills –
to God all praise and glory!

2 What God's almighty power hath made
His gracious mercy keepeth;
by morning dawn or evening shade
His watchful eye ne'er sleepeth;
within the kingdom of His might,
lo, all is just and all is right –
to God all praise and glory!

3 I cried to Him in time of need:
Lord God, O hear my calling!
For death He gave me life indeed
and kept my feet from falling.
For this my thanks shall endless be;
O thank Him, thank our God, with me –
to God all praise and glory!

4 The Lord forsaketh not His flock,
His chosen generation;
He is their refuge and their rock,
their peace and their salvation.
As with a mother's tender hand
He leads His own, His chosen band –
to God all praise and glory!

5 Then come before His presence now
and banish fear and sadness;
to your Redeemer pay your vow
and sing with joy and gladness:
though great distress my soul befell,
the Lord, my God, did all things well –
to God all praise and glory!

Johann Jakob Schütz, 1640-90;
tr. by Frances Elizabeth Cox, 1812-97

137

To God be the glory! great things He has done!
So loved He the world that He gave us His Son;
who yielded His life an atonement for sin,
and opened the life-gate that all may go in.

Praise the Lord! praise the Lord! Let the earth hear His voice!
Praise the Lord! praise the Lord! Let the people rejoice!
O come to the Father through Jesus the Son:
and give Him the glory! great things He has done!

2 O perfect redemption, the purchase of blood!
To every believer the promise of God;
the vilest offender who truly believes,
that moment from Jesus a pardon receives.

3 Great things He has taught us, great things He has done,
and great our rejoicing through Jesus the Son;
but purer and higher and greater will be
our wonder, our rapture, when Jesus we see!

Frances Jane Van Alstyne, 1820-1915

138

We believe in God almighty,
who the heavens and earth has made,
Father, who in power created
all things hidden and displayed.
We believe in one Lord Jesus,
God's unique and only Son,
God from God, not made – begotten,
with the Father truly one.

2 He through whom all things have being,
He who was when time began,
He came down to earth from heaven,
by the Spirit born as man.
For us men and our salvation
entered He the virgin's womb,
for our sake the cross He suffered,
died, was laid within the tomb.

3 We believe He rose the third day,
as the Scriptures testified,
He ascended to the Father,
sat to reign at His right side.
He who once did come in weakness
will in glory come again;
He shall judge both dead and living
and as King eternal reign.

4 We believe in God the Spirit,
giver of all life, the Lord,
equal with the Son and Father,
who through prophets spoke His Word.
In one holy church believing,
once baptized, our sins forgiven,
one great hope sustains and feeds us –
we shall rise and live in heaven.

Andrew King, b. 1961

GOD THE SON

Glory and praise

139

All glory, praise, and honour
to Thee, Redeemer, King,
to whom the lips of children
made sweet hosannas ring!
Thou art the King of Israel,
Thou David's royal Son,
who in the Lord's name comest,
the King and blessèd One.

2 The company of angels
are praising Thee on high,
and mortal men and all things
created make reply.
The people of the Hebrews
with palms before Thee went;
our praise and prayer and anthems
before Thee we present.

3 To Thee before Thy passion
they sang their hymns of praise;
to Thee now high exalted
our melody we raise.
Thou didst accept their praises;
accept the prayers we bring,
who in all good delightest,
Thou good and gracious King.

Theodulph of Orleans, c. 750-821;
tr. by John Mason Neale, 1818-66

140

All hail the power of Jesus' Name!
Let angels prostrate fall;
bring forth the royal diadem
to crown Him Lord of all.

2 Crown Him, ye martyrs of our God,
who from His altar call;
extol the stem of Jesse's rod,
and crown Him Lord of all.

3 Ye seed of Israel's chosen race,
ye ransomed from the fall,
hail Him who saves you by His grace,
and crown Him Lord of all.

4 Ye Gentile sinners, ne'er forget
the wormwood and the gall;
go spread your trophies at His feet,
and crown Him Lord of all.

5 Let every kindred, every tribe,
on this terrestrial ball,
to Him all majesty ascribe,
and crown Him Lord of all.

6 O that with yonder sacred throng
we at His feet may fall,
join in the everlasting song,
and crown Him Lord of all!

Edward Perronet, 1726-92,
and John Rippon, 1751-1836

141

All heaven declares
the glory of the risen Lord.
Who can compare
with the beauty of the Lord?
Forever He will be
the Lamb upon the throne.
I gladly bow the knee
and worship Him alone.

2 I will proclaim
the glory of the risen Lord,
who once was slain
to reconcile man to God.
Forever You will be
the Lamb upon the throne.
I gladly bow the knee
and worship You alone.

Noel Richards, b. 1955,
and Tricia Richards, b. 1960

142 Based on REVELATION 5:11-13

Come, let us join our cheerful songs
with angels round the throne;
ten thousand thousand are their tongues,
but all their joys are one.

2 'Worthy the Lamb that died', they cry,
'to be exalted thus!'
'Worthy the Lamb', our lips reply,
'for He was slain for us!'

3 Jesus is worthy to receive
honour and power divine;
and blessings, more than we can give,
be, Lord, for ever Thine.

4 Let all that dwell above the sky,
and air, and earth, and seas,
conspire to lift Thy glories high,
and speak Thine endless praise.

5 The whole creation join in one,
to bless the sacred Name
of Him that sits upon the throne,
and to adore the Lamb.

Isaac Watts, 1674-1748

143 Based on REVELATION 1

At Your feet we fall, mighty risen Lord,
as we come before Your throne to worship You.
By Your Spirit's power You now draw our hearts,
and we hear Your voice in triumph ringing clear:

'I am He that liveth,
that liveth and was dead,
behold, I am alive
for evermore.'

2 There we see you stand, mighty risen Lord,
clothed in garments pure and holy, shining bright,
eyes of flashing fire, feet like burnished bronze,
and the sound of many waters in Your voice:

3 Like the shining sun in its noonday strength,
we now see the glory of Your wondrous face.
Once that face was marred, but now You're glorified,
and Your words like a two-edged sword have mighty power:

David Fellingham, b. 1945

144

All my days I will sing this song of gladness,
give my praise to the Fountain of delights;
for in my helplessness You heard my cry
and waves of mercy poured down on my life.

2 I will trust in the cross of my Redeemer,
I will sing of the blood that never fails,
of sins forgiven, of conscience cleansed,
of death defeated and life without end.

Beautiful Saviour, Wonderful Counsellor,
clothed in majesty, Lord of history,
You're the Way, the Truth, the Life.
Star of the morning, glorious in holiness,
You're the risen One, heaven's champion,
and You reign, You reign over all!

3 I long to be where the praise is never-ending,
yearn to dwell where glory never fades,
where countless worshippers will share one song
and cries of 'Worthy' will honour the Lamb!

Stuart Townend, b. 1963

145

Brethren, let us join to bless
Christ, the Lord our Righteousness;
let our praise to Him be given,
high at God's right hand in heaven.

2 Son of God, to Thee we bow,
Thou art Lord, and only Thou;
Thou the blessèd virgin's Seed,
glory of Thy church, and Head.

3 Thee the angels ceaseless sing,
Thee we praise, our Priest and King;
worthy is Thy Name of praise,
full of glory, full of grace.

4 Thou hast the glad tidings brought
of salvation by Thee wrought;
wrought to set Thy people free,
wrought to bring our souls to Thee.

5 May we follow and adore
Thee, our Saviour, more and more;
guide and bless us with Thy love,
till we join Thy saints above.

John Cennick, 1718-55

146

Crown Him with many crowns,
the Lamb upon His throne;
hark! how the heavenly anthem drowns
all music but its own.
Awake, my soul, and sing
of Him who died for thee,
and hail Him as thy chosen King
through all eternity.

2 Crown Him the Son of God,
before the worlds began:
and ye, who tread where He hath trod,
crown Him the Son of man:
who every grief hath known
that wrings the human breast,
and takes and bears them for His own,
that all in Him may rest.

3 Crown Him the Lord of love!
Behold His hands and side,
those wounds, yet visible above,
in beauty glorified:
no angel in the sky
can fully bear that sight,
but downward bends his burning eye
at mysteries so bright.

4 Crown Him the Lord of life,
who triumphed o'er the grave,
and rose victorious in the strife
for those He came to save:
His glories now we sing
who died, and rose on high;
who died eternal life to bring,
and lives that death may die.

5 Crown Him the Lord of peace,
whose power a sceptre sways
from pole to pole, that wars may cease,
and all be prayer and praise:
His reign shall know no end,
and round His piercèd feet
fair flowers of paradise extend
their fragrance ever sweet.

6 Crown Him the Lord of years,
the potentate of time,
creator of the rolling spheres,
ineffably sublime!
All hail, Redeemer, hail!
for Thou hast died for me:
Thy praise shall never, never fail
throughout eternity.

Matthew Bridges, 1800-94
and Godfrey Thring, 1823-1903

147

Fairest Lord Jesus,
Lord of creation,
Son of God and Mary's Son,
You only will I love,
You only will I praise,
my soul's delight, my joy my crown!

2 Fair are the meadows,
fairer the forests
clothed in the loveliness of spring;
Jesus is fairer,
Jesus is purer,
who makes our broken hearts to sing.

3 Fair is the sunshine,
fairer the moonlight,
with all its stars in vast array;
Jesus shines fairer,
Jesus shines purer,
than all angelic hosts on high.

4 Nothing in all the earth,
nothing in heaven above
can with His loveliness compare.
Now shall my heart's desire
to Him alone aspire,
my Jesus, Lord and King most fair.

Münster Gesangbuch, 1677;
translated and adapted
by John D Manton, b. 1930

148

Glory to God on high!
Let earth to heaven reply,
'Praise to His Name!'
Angels His love adore,
who all our sorrows bore;
and saints cry evermore,
'Worthy the Lamb!'

2 All they around the throne
cheerfully join in one,
praising His Name;
we, who have felt His blood
sealing our peace with God,
sound His dear Name abroad,
'Worthy the Lamb!'

3 Join, all the ransomed race,
our Lord and God to bless:
'Praise to His Name!'
In Him we will rejoice,
making a cheerful noise,
shouting with heart and voice,
'Worthy the Lamb!'

4 Though we must change our place,
yet shall we never cease
praising His Name!
To Him we'll tribute bring,
hail Him our gracious King,
and without ceasing sing,
'Worthy the Lamb!'

James Allen, 1734-1804

149

God of glory, God of grace,
we adore You!
God now seen in Jesus' face
we adore You!
Known are all Your works of old,
glories that cannot be told;
gracious Shepherd of one fold,
we adore You,
we adore You.

2 Judah's Lion strong to save,
we adore You!
Mighty victor of the grave,
we adore You!
Final Adam, second Man,
lowly Jesus, great I AM;
God's true servant, man's pure Lamb,
we adore You,
we adore You.

3 Heaven's costliest, fairest Son,
we adore You!
Given for a world undone,
we adore You!
Broken for us on the cross,
counting all the shame but dross
our great gain at Your great cost,
we adore You,
we adore You.

4 Risen, reigning, conquering Son,
we adore You!
Prince of Peace, eternal one,
we adore You!
Thanks we give, with hearts aflame,
for each virtue of Your name,
Jesus, evermore the same,
we adore You,
we adore You.

5 Soon with all the blood-bought throng,
we'll adore You;
sing the new eternal song,
and adore You.
Falling down before Your face,
all your ways of love we'll trace;
for the glory of Your grace,
we'll adore You,
we'll adore You.

6 Then, through Your eternal reign,
we'll adore You.
Praise with hearts that know no stain,
and adore You.
Then from every ransomed voice,
saved by an eternal choice,
with one heart we will rejoice,
and adore You,
yes, adore You!

Colin P Goldsworthy, b. 1927

150

Great is the gospel of our glorious God,
where mercy met the anger of God's rod;
a penalty was paid and pardon bought,
and sinners lost at last to Him were brought:

O let the praises of my heart be Thine,
for Christ has died that I may call Him mine,
that I may sing with those who dwell above,
adoring, praising Jesus, King of love.

2 Great is the mystery of godliness,
great is the work of God's own holiness;
it moves my soul, and causes me to long
for greater joys than to the earth belong:

3 The Spirit vindicated Christ our Lord,
and angels sang with joy and sweet accord;
the nations heard, a dark world flamed with light –
when Jesus rose in glory and in might:

William Vernon Higham, b. 1926

151

Hail, Thou once despisèd Jesus!
Hail, Thou Galilean King!
Thou didst suffer to release us;
Thou didst free salvation bring.
Hail, Thou agonizing Saviour,
bearer of our sin and shame!
By Thy merits we find favour;
life is given through Thy Name.

2 Paschal Lamb, by God appointed,
all our sins on Thee were laid;
by almighty love anointed,
Thou hast full atonement made:
all Thy people are forgiven
through the virtue of Thy blood;
opened is the gate of heaven;
peace is made for man with God.

3 Jesus, hail! enthroned in glory,
there for ever to abide;
all the heavenly hosts adore Thee,
seated at Thy Father's side:
there for sinners Thou art pleading,
there Thou dost our place prepare,
ever for us interceding,
till in glory we appear.

4 Worship, honour, power, and blessing,
Thou art worthy to receive;
loudest praises without ceasing,
meet it is for us to give.
Help, ye bright, angelic spirits!
Bring your sweetest, noblest lays;
help to sing our Saviour's merits,
help to chant Immanuel's praise!

John Bakewell, 1721-1819;
altd. by Augustus Montague Toplady, 1740-78

152

How sweet the name of Jesus sounds
in a believer's ear!
It soothes his sorrows, heals his wounds,
and drives away his fear.

2 It makes the wounded spirit whole,
and calms the troubled breast;
'tis manna to the hungry soul,
and to the weary rest.

3 Dear name! the rock on which I build,
my shield and hiding-place,
my never-failing treasury filled
with boundless stores of grace.

4 Jesus! my Shepherd, Brother, Friend,
my Prophet, Priest and King,
my Lord, my Life, my Way, my End,
accept the praise I bring.

5 Weak is the effort of my heart,
and cold my warmest thought;
but when I see Thee as Thou art,
I'll praise Thee as I ought.

6 Till then I would Thy love proclaim
with every fleeting breath;
and may the music of Thy name
refresh my soul in death!

John Newton, 1725-1807

153

I greet Thee who my sure Redeemer art,
my only trust and Saviour of my heart,
who pain didst undergo for my poor sake:
I pray Thee from our hearts all cares to take.

2 Thou art the King of mercy and of grace,
reigning omnipotent in every place:
so come, O King, and our whole being sway;
shine on us with the light of Thy pure day.

3 Thou art the Life, by which alone we live,
and all our substance and our strength receive;
O comfort us in death's approaching hour,
strong-hearted then to face it by Thy power.

4 Thou hast the true and perfect gentleness,
no harshness hast Thou, and no bitterness;
O grant to us the grace we find in Thee,
that we may dwell in perfect unity.

5 Our hope is in no other save in Thee;
our faith is built upon Thy promise free;
come, give us peace, make us so strong and sure,
that we may conquerors be, and ills endure.

STRASBOURG PSALTER, 1545;
*tr. by Elizabeth Lee Smith**, 1817-98

154

Immortal honours rest on Jesus' head,
my God, my portion, and my living bread;
in Him I live, upon Him cast my care;
He saves from death, destruction and despair.

2 He is my refuge in each deep distress,
the Lord my strength and glorious righteousness.
Through floods and flames He leads me safely on,
and daily makes His sovereign goodness known.

3 My every need He richly will supply,
nor will His mercy ever let me die;
in Him there dwells a treasure all divine,
and matchless grace has made that treasure mine.

4 O that my soul could love and praise Him more,
His beauties trace, His majesty adore,
live near His heart, upon His bosom lean,
obey His voice and all His will esteem.

William Gadsby, 1773-1844

155

I will sing of my Redeemer,
and His wondrous love to me;
on the cruel cross He suffered,
from the curse to set me free.

Sing, O sing of my Redeemer!
With His blood He purchased me,
on the cross He sealed my pardon,
paid the debt and made me free.

2 I will tell the wondrous story,
how my lost estate to save,
in His boundless love and mercy,
He the ransom freely gave.

3 I will praise my dear Redeemer,
His triumphant power I'll tell,
how the victory He giveth
over sin and death and hell.

4 I will sing of my Redeemer,
and His heavenly love to me;
He from death to life hath brought me,
Son of God, with Him to be.

Philipp Paul Bliss, 1838-76

156

I've found the pearl of greatest price,
my heart does sing for joy;
and sing I must, for Christ is mine,
Christ shall my song employ.

2 Christ is my Prophet, Priest, and King:
my Prophet full of light,
my great High Priest before the throne,
my King of heavenly might.

3 For He indeed is Lord of lords,
and He the King of kings;
He is the Sun of righteousness,
with healing in His wings.

4 Christ is my peace; He died for me,
for me He gave His blood;
and as my wondrous sacrifice,
offered Himself to God.

5 Christ Jesus is my all-in-all,
my comfort and my love;
my life below; and He shall be
my joy and crown above.

John Mason, c. 1646-94

157

It passes knowledge, that dear love of Thine,
my Saviour, Jesus, yet this soul of mine
would of Thy love, in all its breadth and length,
its height and depth, its everlasting strength,
know more and more.

2 It passes telling, that dear love of Thine,
my Saviour, Jesus, yet these lips of mine
would fain proclaim to sinners, far and near,
a love which can remove all guilty fear,
and love beget.

3 It passes praises, that dear love of Thine,
my Saviour, Jesus, yet this heart of mine
would sing that love, so full, so rich, so free,
which brings a rebel sinner, such as me,
nigh unto God.

4 But though I cannot sing, or tell, or know
the fulness of Thy love while here below,
my empty vessel I may freely bring:
O Thou who art of love the living spring,
my vessel fill.

5 O fill me, Jesus, Saviour, with Thy love!
Lead, lead me to the living fount above;
thither may I, in simple faith, draw nigh,
and never to another fountain fly,
but unto Thee.

6 And when my Jesus face to face I see,
when at His lofty throne I bow the knee,
then of His love, in all its breadth and length,
its height and depth, its everlasting strength,
my soul shall sing!

Mary Shekleton, 1827-83

158

Jesus, the glories of Your face
my songs of praise record:
I sing the overflowing grace
of my belovèd Lord.

2 You are the Father's chief delight:
Your beauty angels view:
You are all fair in Zion's sight,
and my Belovèd too.

3 Of You the ancient prophets wrote:
of You let Israel sing;
and heaven's vast choir, in every note,
praise my belovèd King.

4 Your precious name shall joy impart
to all that are Your own:
in life and death, O may my heart
be my Belovèd's throne.

Joseph Irons, 1785-1852

159

Jesus is the name we honour;
Jesus is the name we praise.
Majestic name above all other names,
the highest heaven and earth proclaim
that Jesus is our God.

We will glorify,
we will lift Him high,
we will give Him honour and praise.
We will glorify…

2 Jesus is the name we worship;
Jesus is the name we trust.
He is the King above all other kings,
let all creation stand and sing
that Jesus is our God.
We will glorify…

3 Jesus is the Father's splendour;
Jesus is the Father's joy.
He will return to reign in majesty,
and every eye at last will see
that Jesus is our God.
We will glorjfy…

Phil Lawson Johnston, b. 1950

160

Jesus is Lord! Creation's voice proclaims it,
for by His power each tree and flower
was planned and made.
Jesus is Lord! The universe declares it,
sun, moon and stars in heaven
cry, 'Jesus is Lord!'

Jesus is Lord! Jesus is Lord!
Praise Him with Hallelujahs,
for Jesus is Lord!

2 Jesus is Lord! Yet from His throne eternal
in flesh He came to die in pain
on Calvary's tree.
Jesus is Lord! From Him all life proceeding,
yet gave His life a ransom
thus setting us free.

3 Jesus is Lord! O'er sin the mighty conqueror,
from death He rose, and all His foes
shall own His name.
Jesus is Lord! God sent His Holy Spirit
to show by works of power
that Jesus is Lord.

David J Mansell, b. 1936

161

Jesus! the sinner's friend,
we hide ourselves in Thee!
God looks upon Thy sprinkled blood;
it is our only plea.

2 He hears Thy precious Name;
we plead Thy Name alone;
the Father must accept and bless
His well-belovèd Son.

3 He sees Thy spotless robe;
it covers all our sin;
the golden gates have welcomed Thee,
and we may enter in.

4 Thou hast fulfilled the law,
and we are justified;
ours is the blessing, Thine the curse:
we live, for Thou hast died.

5 Jesus! the sinner's friend,
we cannot speak Thy praise:
no mortal voice can sing the song
that ransomed hearts would raise.

6 But when before the throne,
upon the glassy sea,
clothed in our blood-washed robes of white,
we stand complete in Thee,

7 Jesus! we'll give Thee then
such praises as are meet,
and cast ten thousand golden crowns,
adoring, at Thy feet!

Catherine Pennefather, 1818-93

162

Jesus, the very thought of Thee
with sweetness fills my breast;
but sweeter far Thy face to see,
and in Thy presence rest.

2 Nor voice can sing, nor heart can frame,
nor can the memory find
a sweeter sound than Thy blest name,
O Saviour of mankind!

3 O hope of every contrite heart,
O joy of all the meek,
to those who fall how kind Thou art!
How good to those who seek!

4 But what to those who find? Ah! this
nor tongue nor pen can show:
the love of Jesus, what it is
none but His loved ones know.

5 Jesus, our only joy be Thou,
as Thou our prize shall be;
Jesus, be Thou our glory now,
and through eternity.

Bernard of Clairvaux (?), 1091-1153;
tr. by Edward Caswall, 1814-78

163

Jesus, Thou everlasting King,
accept the tribute which we bring;
accept the well-deserved renown,
and wear our praises as Thy crown.

2 Let every act of worship be
like our espousals, Lord, to Thee;
like the dear hour when from above
we first received Thy pledge of love.

3 The gladness of that happy day –
our hearts would wish it long to stay;
nor let our faith forsake its hold,
nor comfort sink, nor love grow cold.

4 Each following minute as it flies,
increase Thy praise, improve our joys,
till we are raised to sing Thy Name
at the great supper of the Lamb.

5 O that the months would roll away
and bring that coronation day!
The King of grace shall fill the throne,
His Father's glory all His own.

Isaac Watts, 1674-1748

164

Jesus, Thou joy of loving hearts,
Thou fount of life, Thou light of men,
from the best bliss that earth imparts,
we turn unfilled to Thee again.

2 Thy truth unchanged hath ever stood;
Thou savest those that on Thee call;
to them that seek Thee Thou art good,
to them that find Thee, all in all.

3 We taste Thee, O Thou living bread,
and long to feast upon Thee still;
we drink of Thee, the fountain-head,
and thirst our souls from Thee to fill.

4 Our restless spirits yearn for Thee
where'er our changeful lot is cast;
glad, when Thy gracious smile we see;
blest, when our faith can hold Thee fast.

5 O Jesus, ever with us stay;
make all our moments calm and bright;
chase the dark night of sin away;
shed o'er our souls Thy holy light.

Bernard of Clairvaux (?), 1091-1153;
tr. by Ray Palmer, 1808-87

165

Join all the glorious names
of wisdom, love, and power,
that ever mortals knew,
that angels ever bore;
all are too mean to speak His worth,
too mean to set my Saviour forth.

2 Great Prophet of my God,
my tongue would bless Your Name:
by You the joyful news
of our salvation came;
the joyful news of sins forgiven,
of hell subdued, and peace with heaven.

3 Jesus, my great High Priest,
offered His blood and died;
my guilty conscience seeks
no sacrifice beside;
His powerful blood did once atone,
and now it pleads before the throne.

4 My Saviour and my Lord,
my conqueror and my King,
Your sceptre and Your sword,
Your reigning grace I sing;
Yours is the power: behold, I sit
in willing bonds beneath Your feet.

5 Now let my soul arise,
and tread the tempter down:
my captain leads me forth
to conquest and a crown:
a feeble saint shall win the day,
though death and hell obstruct the way.

6 Should all the hosts of death,
and powers of hell unknown,
put their most dreadful forms
of rage and malice on,
I shall be safe, for Christ displays
superior power and guardian grace.

Isaac Watts, 1674-1748

166

Light of the world, for ever, ever shining,
there is no change in Thee;
true Light of life, all joy and health enshrining,
Thou canst not fade nor flee.

2 Thou hast arisen, but Thou declinest never;
today shines as the past;
all that Thou wast Thou art, and shalt be ever,
brightness from first to last.

3 Night visits not Thy sky, nor storm, nor sadness;
day fills up all its blue,
unfailing beauty and unfaltering gladness,
and love for ever new!

4 Light of the world! undimming and unsetting,
O shine each mist away!
Banish the fear, the falsehood and the fretting;
be our unchanging day.

Horatius Bonar, 1808-89

167

Meekness and majesty,
manhood and Deity,
in perfect harmony,
the Man who is God.
Lord of eternity
dwells in humanity,
kneels in humility
and washes our feet.

O what a mystery,
meekness and majesty,
bow down and worship,
for this is your God,
this is your God.

2 Father's pure radiance,
perfect in innocence,
yet learns obedience
to death on a cross:
suffering to give us life,
conquering through sacrifice,
and, as they crucify,
prays 'Father, forgive.'

3 Wisdom unsearchable,
God the invisible,
Love indestructible
in frailty appears.
Lord of infinity,
stooping so tenderly,
lifts our humanity
to the heights of His throne.

Graham Kendrick, b. 1950

168

Mighty Christ from time eternal,
mighty, He man's nature takes,
mighty, when on Calv'ry dying,
mighty, death itself He breaks.
See His might,
infinite,
King of heaven and earth by right!

2 Mighty was He in heaven's purpose,
mighty, in the pledge to save,
mighty, from His birth to Calv'ry,
mighty, bursting from the grave.
Still will He
mighty be
when things hidden now we see.

3 Great my Jesus in His Person,
great as God and man is He,
great His comeliness and beauty,
white and ruddy, fair to see.
Great that sight,
sovereign Might,
throned secure on heaven's height!

vv. 1 & 3, Titus Lewis, 1773-1811;
v. 2, Anonymous;
tr. by Graham Stuart Harrison, b. 1935

4 From the highest throne in glory,
to the cross of deepest woe,
all to ransom guilty captives:
flow, my praise, for ever flow!
Go, return, immortal Saviour!
Leave Your footstool, take Your throne;
thence return, and reign for ever,
be the kingdom all Your own!

Robert Robinson, 1735-90

169

Mighty God, while angels bless You,
may a mortal lisp Your name?
Lord of men, as well as angels,
You are every creature's theme.
Lord of every land and nation,
ancient of eternal days,
sounded through the wide creation
be Your just and lawful praise.

2 For the grandeur of Your nature,
grand beyond a seraph's thought;
for created works of power,
works with skill and kindness wrought;
for Your providence, that governs
through Your empire's wide domain,
wings an angel, guides a sparrow;
blessèd be Your gentle reign.

3 But Your rich, Your free redemption,
dark through brightness all along –
thought is poor, and poor expression –
who dare sing that wondrous song?
Brightness of the Father's glory,
shall Your praise unuttered lie?
Fly, my tongue, such guilty silence!
Sing the Lord who came to die.

170

O the deep, deep love of Jesus!
Vast, unmeasured, boundless, free,
rolling as a mighty ocean
in its fulness over me.
Underneath me, all around me,
is the current of Thy love;
leading onward, leading homeward,
to my glorious rest above.

2 O the deep, deep love of Jesus!
Spread His praise from shore to shore,
how He loveth, ever loveth,
changeth never, nevermore;
how He watches o'er His loved ones,
died to call them all His own;
how for them He intercedeth,
watcheth o'er them from the throne.

3 O the deep, deep love of Jesus!
Love of every love the best;
'tis an ocean vast of blessing,
'tis a haven sweet of rest.
O the deep, deep love of Jesus!
'Tis a heaven of heavens to me;
and it lifts me up to glory,
for it lifts me up to Thee.

Samuel Trevor Francis, 1834-1925

171

Jesus! the Name high over all,
in hell, or earth, or sky;
angels and men before it fall,
and devils fear and fly.

2 Jesus! the Name to sinners dear,
the Name to sinners given;
it scatters all their guilty fear,
it turns their hell to heaven.

3 Jesus! the prisoner's fetters breaks,
and bruises Satan's head;
power into strengthless souls it speaks,
and life into the dead.

4 O that the world might taste and see
the riches of His grace;
the arms of love that compass me
would all mankind embrace.

5 His only righteousness I show,
His saving truth proclaim;
'tis all my business here below
to cry, 'Behold the Lamb!'

6 Happy, if with my latest breath
I may but gasp His Name;
preach Him to all, and cry in death,
'Behold, behold the Lamb!'

Charles Wesley, 1707-88

172

My song shall bless the Lord of all,
my praise shall climb to His abode;
Thee, Saviour, by that name I call,
the great supreme, the mighty God.

2 Without beginning or decline,
object of faith and not of sense;
eternal ages saw Him shine,
He shines eternal ages hence.

3 As much when in the manger laid
almighty ruler of the sky,
as when the six days' work He made
filled all the morning stars with joy.

4 Of all the crowns Jehovah wears,
salvation is His dearest claim;
that gracious sound, well pleased, He hears,
and owns Emmanuel for His name.

5 A cheerful confidence I feel,
my well-placed hopes with joy I see;
my spirit burns with heavenly zeal,
to worship Him who died for me.

6 As man, He pities my complaint,
His power and truth are all divine;
He will not fail, He cannot faint;
salvation's sure, and must be mine.

William Cowper, 1731-1800

173

Now to the Lord a noble song!
Awake, my soul! awake, my tongue!
Hosanna to the eternal Name,
and all His boundless love proclaim.

2 See where it shines in Jesus' face,
the brightest image of His grace;
God, in the person of His Son,
has all His mightiest works outdone.

3 The spacious earth and spreading flood
proclaim the wise and powerful God;
and Your rich glories from afar
sparkle in every rolling star.

4 But in His looks a glory stands,
the noblest labour of Your hands;
the pleasing lustre of His eyes
outshines the wonders of the skies.

5 Grace! 'tis a sweet, a charming theme;
my thoughts rejoice at Jesus' name:
you angels, dwell upon the sound!
you heavens, reflect it to the ground!

6 O may I live to reach the place
where He unveils His lovely face;
there all His beauties to behold,
and sing His name to harps of gold!

Isaac Watts, 1674-1748

174

O Jesus, King most wonderful,
Thou conqueror renowned,
Thou sweetness most ineffable,
in whom all joys are found!

2 When once Thou visitest the heart,
then truth begins to shine;
then earthly vanities depart,
then kindles love divine.

3 O Jesus, light of all below,
Thou fount of life and fire,
surpassing all the joys we know,
and all we can desire:

4 May every heart confess Thy Name,
and ever Thee adore;
and, seeking Thee, itself inflame
to seek Thee more and more.

5 Thee may our tongues for ever bless,
Thee may we love alone,
and ever in our lives express
the image of Thine own.

6 Grant us, while here on earth we stay,
Thy love to feel and know;
and when from hence we pass away,
to us Thy glory show.

Bernard of Clairvaux (?), 1091-1153;
tr. by Edward Caswall, 1814-78

175

Name of Jesus! highest name!
Name that earth and heaven adore!
From the heart of God it came,
leads me to God's heart once more.

2 Name of Jesus! living tide!
Days of drought for me are past;
how much more than satisfied
are the thirsty lips at last!

3 Name of Jesus! dearest name!
Bread of heaven, and balm of love:
oil of gladness, surest claim
to the treasures stored above.

4 Jesus gives forgiveness free,
Jesus cleanses all my stains;
Jesus gives His life to me,
Jesus always He remains.

5 Only Jesus! fairest name!
Life, and rest, and peace, and bliss,
Jesus, evermore the same,
He is mine, and I am His.

Gerhard Tersteegen, 1697-1769;
tr. by Emma Frances Bevan, 1827-1909

176

O thou, my soul, forget no more
the Friend who all thy misery bore;
let every idol be forgot,
but, O my soul, forget Him not.

2 Jesus for thee a body takes,
thy guilt assumes, thy fetters breaks,
discharging all thy dreadful debt:
and canst thou e'er such love forget?

3 Renounce thy works and ways with grief,
and fly to this most sure relief;
nor Him forget who left His throne,
and for thy life gave up His own.

4 Infinite truth and mercy shine
in Him, and He Himself is thine;
and canst thou, then, with sin beset,
such charms, such matchless charms,
forget?

5 Ah no! till life itself depart,
His Name shall cheer and warm my heart;
and lisping this, from earth I'll rise,
and join the chorus of the skies.

6 Ah no! when all things else expire,
and perish in the general fire,
this Name all others shall survive,
and through eternity shall live.

Krishna Pal, 1764-1822;
tr. by Joshua Marshman, 1768-1837

177

Praise the Saviour, you who know Him!
Who can tell how much we owe Him?
Gladly let us render to Him
all we have and are.

2 Jesus is the name that charms us,
He for conflict fits and arms us;
nothing moves, and nothing harms us,
when we trust in Him.

3 Trust in Him, you saints, for ever;
He is faithful, changing never;
neither force nor guile can sever
those He loves from Him.

4 Keep us, Lord, O keep us cleaving
to Yourself, and still believing,
till the hour of our receiving
promised joys in heaven.

5 Then we shall be where we would be,
then we shall be what we should be,
that which is not now, nor could be,
then shall be our own.

Thomas Kelly, 1769-1855

178

One day when heaven was filled with His praises,
one day when sin was as vile as
could be,
Jesus came forth to be born of a virgin –
dwelt amongst men, my example is He!

*Living, He loved me; dying, He saved
me;
buried, He carried my sins far away!
Rising, He justified freely for ever;
one day He's coming – O glorious
day!*

2 One day they led Him up Calvary's
mountain,
one day they nailed Him to die on
the tree;
suffering anguish, despised and rejected;
bearing our sins, my Redeemer is He!

3 One day they left Him alone in the garden,
one day He rested, from suffering free;
angels came down o'er His tomb to
keep vigil;
hope of the hopeless, my Saviour is He!

4 One day the grave could conceal Him
no longer,
one day the stone rolled away from
the door;
He had arisen, o'er death He had
conquered;
now is ascended, my Lord evermore!

5 One day the trumpet will sound for His
coming,
one day the skies with His glory will
shine;
wonderful day, His belovèd ones bringing;
glorious Saviour, this Jesus is mine!

J Wilbur Chapman, 1859-1918

179

Praise Him, praise Him! Jesus, our blessèd Redeemer;
sing, O earth, His wonderful love proclaim!
Hail Him, hail Him! highest archangels in glory,
strength and honour give to His holy Name.
Like a shepherd, Jesus will guard His children,
in His arms He carries them all day long;
O ye saints that dwell in the mountains of Zion,
praise Him, praise Him! ever in joyful song.

2 Praise Him, praise Him! Jesus, our blessèd Redeemer;
for our sins He suffered and bled and died.
He, our rock, our hope of eternal salvation,
hail Him, hail Him! Jesus the crucified.
Loving Saviour, meekly enduring sorrow,
crowned with thorns that cruelly pierced His brow;
once for us rejected, despised, and forsaken,
Prince of glory, ever triumphant now.

3 Praise Him, praise Him! Jesus, our blessèd Redeemer;
heavenly portals loud with hosannas ring!
Jesus, Saviour, reigneth for ever and ever,
crown Him, crown Him! Prophet and Priest and King!
Death is vanquished, tell it with joy, ye faithful!
Where is now thy victory, boasting grave?
Jesus lives, no longer thy portals are cheerless;
Jesus lives, the mighty and strong to save.

Frances Jane Van Alstyne, 1820-1915

180

One there is, above all others
well deserves the name of friend;
His is love beyond a brother's,
costly, free, and knows no end:
they who once His kindness prove,
find it everlasting love.

2 Which of all our friends, to save us,
could, or would, have shed his blood?
but the Saviour died to have us
reconciled in Him to God:
this was boundless love indeed;
Jesus is a friend in need.

3 When He lived on earth abasèd
'Friend of sinners' was His name;
now, above all glory raisèd,
He rejoices in the same;
still He calls them brothers, friends,
and to all their wants attends.

4 Could we bear from one another
what He daily bears from us?
Yet this glorious friend and brother
loves us though we treat Him thus;
though for good we render ill,
He accounts us brethren still.

5 O for grace our hearts to soften!
teach us, Lord, at length to love:
we, alas! forget too often
what a friend we have above;
but, when home our souls are brought,
we shall love You as we ought.

John Newton, 1725-1807

181

There is a name I love to hear;
I love to sing its worth;
it sounds like music in mine ear,
the sweetest name on earth.

Oh how I love the Saviour's name,
Oh how I love the Saviour's name,
Oh how I love the Saviour's name,
the sweetest name on earth.

2 It tells me of a Saviour's love,
who died to set me free;
it tells me of His precious blood,
the sinner's perfect plea.

3 It tells of One whose loving heart
can feel my deepest woe,
who in my sorrow bears a part
that none can bear below.

4 Jesus, the name I love so well,
the name I love to hear:
no saint on earth its worth can tell,
no heart conceive how dear.

5 This name shall shed its fragrance still
along life's thorny road,
shall sweetly smooth the rugged hill
that leads me up to God.

6 And there, with all the blood-bought throng,
from sin and sorrow free,
I'll sing the new eternal song
of Jesus' love to me.

Frederick Whitfield, 1829-1904

182

Thou art the everlasting Word,
the Father's only Son;
God manifestly seen and heard,
and heaven's belovèd One.

Worthy, O Lamb of God, art Thou,
that every knee to Thee should bow!

2 In Thee, most perfectly expressed,
the Father's glories shine:
of the full deity possessed,
eternally divine:

3 True image of the Infinite,
whose essence is concealed;
brightness of uncreated light;
the heart of God revealed:

4 But the high mysteries of Thy Name
an angel's grasp transcend:
the Father only – glorious claim! –
the Son can comprehend:

5 Throughout the universe of bliss
the centre Thou, and sun,
the eternal theme of praise is this,
to heaven's belovèd One:

Josiah Conder, 1789-1855

183

Thou art the Way; to Thee alone
from sin and death we flee:
and he who would the Father seek
must seek Him, Lord, by Thee.

2 Thou art the Truth; Thy Word alone
true wisdom can impart;
Thou only canst inform the mind,
and purify the heart.

3 Thou art the Life; the rending tomb
proclaims Thy conquering arm;
and those who put their trust in Thee
nor death nor hell shall harm.

4 Thou art the Way, the Truth, the Life;
grant us that Way to know,
that Truth to keep, that Life to win,
whose joys eternal flow.

George Washington Doane, 1799-1859

184

Thou art worthy, Thou art worthy,
Thou art worthy, O Lord;
Thou art worthy, to receive glory,
glory and honour and power.
For Thou hast created, hast all things
created,
for Thou hast created all things;
and for Thy pleasure they are created:
Thou art worthy, O Lord.

2 Thou art worthy, Thou art worthy,
Thou art worthy, O Lamb;
Thou art worthy, to receive glory
and power at the Father's right hand.
For Thou hast redeemed us, hast
ransomed and cleaned us,
by Thy blood setting us free;
in white robes arrayed us, kings and
priests made us,
and we are reigning with Thee.

v. 1, Pauline Michael Mills, 1898-1992;
v. 2, Tom Smail

185

To the Name of our salvation,
praise and honour let us pay,
which for many a generation
hid in God's foreknowledge lay,
but with holy exultation
we may sing aloud today.

2 Jesus is the Name we treasure,
Name beyond what words can tell;
Name of gladness, Name of pleasure,
ear and heart delighting well;
Name of sweetness, passing measure,
saving us from sin and hell.

3 Jesus is the Name exalted
over every other name;
in this Name, whene'er assaulted,
we can put our foes to shame;
strength to them who else had halted,
eyes to blind, and feet to lame.

4 Therefore we, in love adoring,
this most blessèd Name revere:
holy Jesus, Thee imploring
so to write it in us here,
that, hereafter heavenward soaring,
we may sing with angels there.

Anonymous, 15th cent.;
tr. by John Mason Neale, 1818-66

186

'Tis the church triumphant singing,
Worthy the Lamb!
Heaven throughout with praises
ringing,
Worthy the Lamb!
Thrones and powers before Him
bending,
incense sweet with voice ascending
swell the chorus never ending,
Worthy the Lamb!

2 Every kindred, tongue and nation –
Worthy the Lamb!
Join to sing the great salvation;
Worthy the Lamb!
Loud as mighty thunders roaring,
floods of mighty waters pouring,
prostrate at His feet adoring,
Worthy the Lamb!

3 Harps and songs for ever sounding
Worthy the Lamb!
Mighty grace o'er sin abounding;
Worthy the Lamb!
By His blood He dearly bought us;
wandering from the fold He sought us;
and to glory safely brought us:
Worthy the Lamb!

4 Sing with blest anticipation,
Worthy the Lamb!
Through the vale of tribulation,
Worthy the Lamb!
Sweetest notes, all notes excelling,
on the theme for ever dwelling,
still untold, though ever telling,
Worthy the Lamb!

John Kent, 1766-1843

187

We know, by faith we surely know,
the Son of God is come,
is manifested here below,
and makes our hearts His home:
to us He has, in gracious love,
an understanding given,
to recognize Him from above,
the Lord of earth and heaven.

2 The self-existing God supreme,
our Saviour we adore,
fountain of life eternal, Him
we worship evermore:
out of His plenitude receive
ineffable delight,
and shall through endless ages live
triumphant in His sight.

Charles Wesley, 1707-88

188

Within a crib my Saviour lay,
a wooden manger filled with hay,
come down for love on Christmas Day:
All glory be to Jesus!

2 Upon a cross my Saviour died,
to ransom sinners, crucified,
His loving arms still open wide:
All glory be to Jesus!

3 A victor's crown my Saviour won,
His work of love and mercy done,
the Father's high-ascended Son:
All glory be to Jesus!

Timothy Dudley-Smith, b. 1926

189

What kind of greatness can this be
that chose to be made small,
exchanging untold majesty
for a world so pitiful?
That God should come as one of us,
I'll never understand.
The more I hear the story told,
the more amazed I am.

Oh what else can I do
but kneel and worship You
and come just as I am,
my whole life an offering?

2 The One in whom we live and move
in swaddling clothes lies bound.
The voice that cried, 'Let there be light,'
asleep without a sound.
The One who strode among the stars
and called each one by name,
lies helpless in His mother's arms
and must learn to walk again.

3 What greater love could He have shown
to shamed humanity?
Yet human pride hates to believe
in such deep humility.
But nations now may see His grace
and know that He is near,
when His meek heart, His words, His works
are incarnate in us here.

Graham Kendrick, b. 1950

190

When oceans vast their depths reveal
and moons have ceased to wane,
the Lamb who died and rose again,
on Zion's hill shall reign.

2 His glorious Name must long endure
when suns have ceased to shine,
and through eternity the saints
will sing His praise divine.

3 As countless as the drops of dew,
or sand upon the shore,
are blessings which the ransomed have
in Him for evermore.

4 Let every other name recede,
His Name alone extol;
in none but Him, there is the grace
to satisfy my soul.

Morgan Rhys, 1716-79;
tr. by Edward Mason Powell, 1852-1928

191

With harps and with vials there stand a great throng
in the presence of Jesus, and sing this new song:

Unto Him who has loved us and washed us from sin,
unto Him be the glory for ever! Amen.

2 All these once were sinners, defiled in His sight,
now arrayed in pure garments in praise they unite:

3 He makes of the rebel a priest and a king,
He has bought us, and taught us this new song to sing:

4 How helpless and hopeless we sinners had been
if He never had loved us till cleansed from our sin!

5 Aloud in His praises our voices shall ring,
so that others, believing, this new song shall sing:

Arthur Tappan Pierson, 1837-1911

192

Ye servants of God,
your Master proclaim,
and publish abroad
His wonderful Name:
the Name all-victorious
of Jesus extol;
His kingdom is glorious,
and rules over all.

2 God ruleth on high,
almighty to save;
and still He is nigh,
His presence we have;
the great congregation
His triumph shall sing,
ascribing salvation
to Jesus our King.

3 Salvation to God
who sits on the throne!
Let all cry aloud,
and honour the Son:
the praises of Jesus
the angels proclaim,
fall down on their faces,
and worship the Lamb.

4 Then let us adore,
and give Him His right,
all glory and power,
all wisdom and might,
all honour and blessing,
with angels above,
and thanks never-ceasing,
and infinite love.

Charles Wesley, 1707-88

193

You're the Word of God the Father,
from before the world began;
every star and every planet
has been fashioned by Your hand.
All creation holds together
by the power of Your voice:
let the skies declare Your glory,
let the land and seas rejoice!

You're the Author of creation,
You're the Lord of every man;
and Your cry of love rings out
across the lands.

2 Yet You left the gaze of angels,
came to seek and save the lost,
and exchanged the joy of heaven
for the anguish of a cross.
With a prayer You fed the hungry
with a word You stilled the sea;
yet how silently You suffered
that the guilty may go free.

3 With a shout You rose victorious,
wrestling victory from the grave,
and ascended into heaven
leading captives in Your wake.
Now You stand before the Father
interceding for Your own.
From each tribe and tongue and nation
You are leading sinners home.

Stuart Townend, b. 1963,
and Keith Getty

Incarnation

194

All my heart this night rejoices,
as I hear, far and near,
sweetest angel voices:
'Christ is born!' their choirs are singing,
till the air, everywhere,
now with joy is ringing.

2 Hark! a voice from yonder manger,
soft and sweet, doth entreat:
'Flee from woe and danger;
brethren, come: from all that grieves you
you are freed; all you need
I will surely give you.'

3 Come, then, let us hasten yonder;
here let all, great and small,
kneel in awe and wonder;
love Him who with love is yearning;
hail the star that from far
bright with hope is burning.

4 Ye who pine in weary sadness,
weep no more, for the door
now is found of gladness;
cling to Him, for He will guide you
where no cross, pain or loss
can again betide you.

5 Thee, dear Lord, with heed I'll cherish,
live to Thee, and with Thee
dying, shall not perish,
but shall dwell with Thee for ever
far on high, in the joy
that can alter never.

Paul Gerhardt, 1607-76;
tr. by Catherine Winkworth, 1827-78

then haste we to show Him;
the praises we owe Him;
our service He ne'er can despise;
whose love still is able
to show us that stable,
where softly in manger He lies.

Traditional Welsh carol, 'O deued pob Cristion';
tr. by Katharine Emily Roberts, 1877-1962,
and William Thomas Pennar Davies, 1911-96

195

All poor men and humble,
all lame men who stumble,
come haste ye, nor feel ye afraid;
for Jesus, our treasure,
with love past all measure,
in lowly poor manger was laid.
Though wise men who found Him
laid rich gifts around Him,
yet oxen they gave Him their hay:
and Jesus in beauty
accepted their duty;
contented in manger He lay.
Then haste we to show Him
the praises we owe Him;
our service He ne'er can despise:
whose love still is able
to show us that stable
where softly in manger He lies.

2 The Christ child will lead us,
the good shepherd feed us
and with us abide till His day.
Then hatred He'll banish;
then sorrow will vanish,
and death and despair flee away.
And He shall reign ever,
and nothing shall sever
from us the great love of our King;
His peace and His pity
shall bless His fair city;
His praises we ever shall sing;

196

Angels from the realms of glory,
wing your flight o'er all the earth;
ye who sang creation's story,
now proclaim Messiah's birth;

Come and worship
Christ, the new-born King:
come and worship,
worship Christ the new-born King.

2 Shepherds, in the field abiding,
watching o'er your flocks by night,
God with man is now residing;
yonder shines the infant light;

3 Sages, leave your contemplations;
brighter visions beam afar;
seek the great Desire of nations;
ye have seen His natal star;

4 Saints, before the altar bending,
watching long in hope and fear,
suddenly the Lord, descending,
in His temple shall appear;

5 Sinners, wrung with true repentance,
doomed for guilt to endless pains,
justice now revokes the sentence,
mercy calls you – break your chains;

James Montgomery, 1771-1854

(When sung to the tune Triumph,
omit the words of line 2 of chorus.)

197

As with gladness men of old
did the guiding star behold,
as with joy, they hailed its light,
leading onward, beaming bright –
so, most gracious Lord, may we
evermore be led to Thee.

2 As with joyful steps they sped,
Saviour, to Thy lowly bed,
there to bend the knee before
Thee, whom heaven and earth adore –
so may we with willing feet
ever seek the mercy-seat.

3 As they offered gifts most rare
at Thy cradle rough and bare –
so may we with holy joy,
pure, and free from sin's alloy,
all our costliest treasures bring,
Christ, to Thee, our heavenly King.

4 Holy Jesus, every day
keep us in the narrow way;
and, when earthly things are past,
bring our ransomed souls at last
where they need no star to guide,
where no clouds Thy glory hide.

5 In the heavenly country bright
need they no created light;
Thou its light, its joy, its crown,
Thou its sun which goes not down;
there for ever may we sing
hallelujahs to our King.

William Chatterton Dix, 1837-98

198

Behold, the great Creator makes
Himself a house of clay:
a robe of human flesh He takes
which He will wear for aye.

2 Hark, hark, the wise eternal Word
like a weak infant cries!
In form of servant is the Lord,
and God in cradle lies.

3 This wonder struck the world amazed,
it shook the starry frame;
squadrons of spirits stood and gazed,
then down in troops they came.

4 Glad shepherds ran to view the sight;
a choir of angels sings,
and eastern sages with delight
adore this King of kings.

5 Join then, all hearts that are not stone,
and all our voices prove,
to celebrate this Holy One,
the God of peace and love.

Thomas Pestel, c.1584 - c.1659

199

Brightest and best of the sons of the morning,
dawn on our darkness, and lend us your aid;
star of the east, the horizon adorning;
guide where our infant Redeemer is laid.

2 Cold on His cradle the dew-drops are shining;
low lies His head with the beasts of the stall;
angels adore Him in slumber reclining,
maker, and monarch, and Saviour of all.

3 Say, shall we yield Him, in costly
devotion,
perfumes of Edom, and offerings
divine,
gems of the mountain and pearls of the
ocean,
myrrh from the forest or gold from
the mine?

4 Vainly we offer each ample oblation,
vainly with gifts would His favour
secure;
richer by far is the heart's adoration,
dearer to God are the prayers of the
poor.

5 Brightest and best of the sons of the
morning,
dawn on our darkness, and lend us
your aid;
star of the east, the horizon adorning,
guide where our infant Redeemer is
laid.

Reginald Heber, 1783-1826

200

Child in the manger,
infant of Mary;
outcast and stranger,
Lord of all!
Child who inherits
all our transgressions,
all our demerits
on Him fall.

2 Once the most holy
child of salvation,
gently and lowly
lived below;
now as our glorious
mighty Redeemer,
see Him victorious
over each foe.

3 Prophets foretold Him,
infant of wonder;
angels behold Him
on His throne;
worthy our Saviour
of all their praises;
happy for ever
are His own.

Mary Macdonald, 1789-1872;
tr. by Lachlan Macbean, 1853-1931

201

**Christians, awake! salute the
happy morn,**
on which the Saviour of the world was
born;
rise to adore the mystery of love
which hosts of angels chanted from
above:
with them the joyful tidings first begun
of God incarnate, and the virgin's Son.

2 Then to the watchful shepherds it was
told,
who heard the angelic herald's voice,
'Behold,
I bring good tidings of a Saviour's birth
to you and all the nations upon earth;
this day has God fulfilled His promised
word,
this day is born a Saviour, Christ the
Lord.'

3 He spoke; and straightway the celestial
choir
in hymns of joy unknown before
conspire;
the praises of redeeming love they sang,
and heaven's whole orb with
hallelujahs rang;
God's highest glory was their anthem
still,
'Peace upon earth, and unto men
goodwill.'

4 O may we keep and ponder in our mind
God's wondrous love in saving lost mankind;
trace we the babe who has retrieved our loss
from His poor manger to His bitter cross;
tread in His steps, assisted by His grace,
till man's first heavenly state again takes place.

5 Then may we hope, the angelic hosts among,
to sing, redeemed, a glad triumphal song:
He that was born upon this joyful day
around us all His glory shall display;
saved by His love, incessant we shall sing
eternal praise to heaven's almighty King.

John Byrom, 1692-1763

202

Christ is come! Let earth adore Him;
God appears in mortal frame.
Saints and angels bow before Him,
praise His high and holy Name.
Word of our salvation's story,
helpless babe of human birth,
Christ has laid aside His glory,
born for us a child of earth.

2 Christ is come and calls us to Him;
here by faith behold your King;
with the shepherds kneel to view Him,
with the wise your treasures bring.
Child today and man tomorrow,
by His cross and crown of thorn
He shall vanquish sin and sorrow,
sing we then that Christ is born.

3 Christ is come! Let all enthrone Him,
every tongue declare His praise;
every heart rejoice to own Him
King of everlasting days.
Christ is come, our sure salvation,
Christ the ransomed sinner's friend,
so with all His new creation
sing the song that knows no end.

Timothy Dudley-Smith, b. 1926

203

Earth was waiting, spent and restless,
with a mingled hope and fear;
and the faithful few were sighing,
'Surely, Lord, the day is near;
the Desire of all the nations,
it is time He should appear.'

2 In the sacred courts of Zion,
where the Lord had His abode,
there the money-changers trafficked,
and the sheep and oxen trod;
and the world, because of wisdom,
knew not either Lord or God.

3 Then the Spirit of the Highest
on a virgin meek came down,
and He burdened her with blessing,
and He pained her with renown;
for she bore the Lord's Anointed,
for His cross and for His crown.

4 Earth for Him had groaned and travailed
since the ages first began;
for in Him was hid the secret
that through all the ages ran –
Son of Mary, Son of David,
Son of God, and Son of Man.

Walter Chalmers Smith, 1824-1908

204

Glory be to God on high,
and peace on earth descend:
God comes down, He bows the sky,
and shows Himself our friend:
God the invisible appears:
God, the blest, the great I AM,
sojourns in this vale of tears,
and Jesus is His name.

2 Him the angels all adored,
their maker and their King;
tidings of their humbled Lord
they now to mortals bring.
Emptied of His majesty,
of His dazzling glories shorn,
being's source begins to be,
and God Himself is born!

3 See the eternal Son of God
a mortal Son of man;
dwelling in an earthly clod,
whom heaven cannot contain.
Stand amazed, ye heavens, at this!
See the Lord of earth and skies;
humbled to the dust He is,
and in a manger lies.

4 We, the sons of men, rejoice,
the Prince of Peace proclaim;
with heaven's host lift up our voice,
and shout Immanuel's name:
knees and hearts to Him we bow;
of our flesh and of our bone,
Jesus is our brother now,
and God is all our own.

Charles Wesley, 1707-88

205

Hark, the glad sound! the Saviour comes,
the Saviour promised long;
let every heart prepare a throne,
and every voice a song.

2 He comes the prisoners to release,
in Satan's bondage held;
the gates of brass before Him burst,
the iron fetters yield.

3 He comes to clear the darkened mind,
to drive the night away,
and on the eyeballs of the blind
to pour celestial day.

4 He comes the broken heart to bind,
the bleeding soul to cure,
and with the treasures of His grace
to enrich the humble poor.

5 Our glad hosannas, Prince of Peace,
Your welcome shall proclaim,
and heaven's eternal arches ring
with Your belovèd name.

Philip Doddridge,* 1702-51

206

Hark! the herald angels sing
glory to the new-born King,
peace on earth, and mercy mild,
God and sinners reconciled.
Joyful, all ye nations, rise,
join the triumph of the skies;
with the angelic host proclaim,
'Christ is born in Bethlehem.'

Hark! the herald angels sing
glory to the new-born King.

2 Christ, by highest heaven adored,
Christ, the everlasting Lord,
late in time behold Him come,
offspring of a virgin's womb.
Veiled in flesh the Godhead see!
Hail, the incarnate Deity!
Pleased as Man with men to dwell,
Jesus, our Immanuel.

3 Hail, the heaven-born Prince of Peace!
Hail, the Sun of righteousness!
Light and life to all He brings,
risen with healing in His wings.
Mild, He lays His glory by,
born that man no more may die,
born to raise the sons of earth,
born to give them second birth.

4 Come, Desire of nations, come,
fix in us Thy humble home;
rise, the woman's conquering seed,
bruise in us the serpent's head.
Now display Thy saving power,
ruined nature now restore;
now in mystic union join
Thine to ours, and ours to Thine!

Charles Wesley, 1707-88

207

Infant holy,
infant lowly,
for His bed a cattle stall;
oxen lowing,
little knowing
Christ the babe is Lord of all.
Swift are winging
angels singing,
nowells ringing,
tidings bringing,
Christ the babe is Lord of all,
Christ the babe is Lord of all.

2 Flocks were sleeping,
shepherds keeping
vigil till the morning new,
saw the glory,
heard the story,
tidings of a gospel true.
Thus rejoicing,
free from sorrow,
praises voicing,
greet the morrow,
Christ the babe was born for you!
Christ the babe was born for you!

from a Polish Carol;
tr. by E M G Reed, 1885-1933

208

Let earth and heaven combine,
angels and men agree,
to praise in songs divine,
the incarnate Deity,
our God contracted to a span,
incomprehensibly made man.

2 He laid His glory by,
he wrapped Him in our clay;
unmarked by human eye,
the latent Godhead lay;
infant of days He here became,
and bore the mild Immanuel's name.

3 Unsearchable the love
that has the Saviour brought;
the grace is far above
or man or angel's thought:
suffice for us that God, we know,
our God, is manifest below.

4 He deigns in flesh to appear,
widest extremes to join;
to bring our vileness near,
and make us all divine:
and we the life of God shall know,
for God is manifest below.

5 Made perfect by His love,
and sanctified by grace,
we shall from earth remove,
and see His glorious face:
then shall His love be fully showed,
and man shall then be lost in God.

Charles Wesley, 1707-88

209

O come, all ye faithful,
joyful and triumphant,
O come ye, O come ye to Bethlehem;
come and behold Him,
born the King of angels:

O come, let us adore Him,
O come, let us adore Him,
O come, let us adore Him, Christ the Lord!

2 God of God,
Light of Light,
lo, He abhors not the virgin's womb;
very God,
begotten, not created:

3 Sing, choirs of angels,
sing in exultation,
sing, all ye citizens of heaven above;
'Glory to God
in the highest!'

4 Yea, Lord, we greet Thee,
born this happy morning,
Jesus, to Thee be glory given;
Word of the Father,
now in flesh appearing:

Latin, 17th cent.;
*tr. by Frederick Oakeley**, 1802-80

210

Once in royal David's city
stood a lowly cattle-shed,
where a mother laid her baby
in a manger for His bed.
Mary was that mother mild,
Jesus Christ her little child.

2 He came down to earth from heaven
who is God and Lord of all,
and His shelter was a stable,
and His cradle was a stall.
With the poor, and mean, and lowly
lived on earth our Saviour holy.

3 And through all His wondrous childhood
He would honour and obey,
love, and watch the lowly mother
in whose gentle arms He lay.
Christian children all must be
mild, obedient, good as He.

4 For He is our childhood's pattern:
day by day like us He grew;
He was little, weak, and helpless;
tears and smiles like us He knew;
and He feeleth for our sadness,
and He shareth in our gladness.

5 And our eyes at last shall see Him,
through His own redeeming love;
for that child so dear and gentle
is our Lord in heaven above;
and He leads His children on
to the place where He is gone.

6 Not in that poor lowly stable,
with the oxen standing by,
we shall see Him, but in heaven,
set at God's right hand on high;
when like stars His children crowned
all in white shall wait around.

Cecil Frances Alexander, 1818-95

211

O little town of Bethlehem,
how still we see thee lie!
Above thy deep and dreamless sleep
the silent stars go by:
yet in thy dark street shineth
the everlasting Light;
the hopes and fears of all the years
are met in thee tonight.

2 O morning stars, together
proclaim the holy birth,
and praises sing to God the King,
and peace to men on earth;
for Christ is born of Mary;
and, gathered all above,
while mortals sleep, the angels keep
their watch of wondering love.

3 How silently, how silently,
the wondrous gift is given!
So God imparts to human hearts
the blessings of His heaven.
No ear may hear His coming;
but in this world of sin,
where meek souls will receive Him, still
the dear Christ enters in.

4 O holy Child of Bethlehem,
descend to us, we pray;
cast out our sin, and enter in;
be born in us today.
We hear the Christmas angels
the great glad tidings tell;
O come to us, abide with us,
Our Lord Immanuel.

Phillips Brooks, 1835-93

212

See, amid the winter's snow,
born for us on earth below,
see, the Lamb of God appears,
promised from eternal years.

Hail, thou ever-blessèd morn!
Hail, redemption's happy dawn!
Sing through all Jerusalem:
Christ is born in Bethlehem!

2 Lo, within a manger lies
He who built the starry skies,
He who, throned in height sublime,
sits amid the cherubim.

3 Say, ye holy shepherds, say,
what your joyful news today;
wherefore have ye left your sheep
on the lonely mountain steep?

4 As we watched at dead of night,
lo, we saw a wondrous light:
angels, singing peace on earth,
told us of the Saviour's birth.

5 Sacred Infant, all divine,
what a tender love was Thine,
thus to come from highest bliss
down to such a world as this!

6 Teach, O teach us, holy Child,
by Thy face so meek and mild,
teach us to resemble Thee
in Thy sweet humility.

Edward Caswall, 1814-78

213

Silent night! holy night!
all is calm, all is bright
round yon virgin mother and Child,
holy Infant so tender and mild –
sleep in heavenly peace!

2 Silent night! holy night!
shepherds quake at the sight.
Glories stream from heaven afar,
heavenly hosts sing hallelujah;
Christ the Saviour is born!

3 Silent night! holy night!
Son of God, love's pure light
radiant beams from Thy holy face,
with the dawn of redeeming grace,
Jesus, Lord, at Thy birth.

Joseph Mohr, 1792-1848;
translator unknown

214

See He lies there in the manger
who once made the earth and sky.
Down from heaven He's come, a
stranger;
newly born, yet born to die.
Hands almighty, now lie helpless
round His mother's finger curled;
lips so gracious, now yet speechless,
soon will speak to all the world.

2 Shepherds hasten to adore Him,
wise men offer gifts so rare.
See the lowly maiden rocks Him
gently, with a mother's care.
Made a man for man's salvation,
yet eternal God is He;
born to save from every nation,
from their chains to set men free.

3 Now they worship and adore Him
as they hear the baby's cries;
but the crowds will mock and scorn
Him
as He helpless hangs and dies.
Christ incarnate, come to save us,
rid our hearts of wretched pride;
reign alone as Sovereign o'er us –
You are worthy! You have died!

4 Well might angels sing in wonder
as they herald forth His birth;
even they can scarcely ponder
why God's Son came down to earth.
See Him now, enthroned in glory,
earth awaiting His return.
While our hearts recount His story
may these hearts within us burn.

Graham Stuart Harrison, b. 1935

215

There was no room in Bethlehem
for Him who left His throne
to seek the lost at countless cost
and make their griefs His own;
but there was room at Calvary
upon a cross of shame
for Him to die, uplifted high,
and bear the sinner's blame.

2 There was no room in Bethlehem,
and in the world today
man will not give Him room to live
but bids Him turn away;
but there is room at Calvary,
and there He stands to give
a home to all who heed His call
and look to Him and live.

3 There was no room in Bethlehem
for Christ, the Prince of heaven,
come down to earth in human birth
that man might be forgiven;
but there is room at Calvary
for sinners to abide,
and all who come will find a home
in Jesus crucified.

Margaret Clarkson, b. 1915

216

Thou didst leave Thy throne
and Thy kingly crown,
when Thou camest to earth for me;
but in Bethlehem's home
was there found no room
for Thy holy nativity:
O come to my heart, Lord Jesus!
there is room in my heart for Thee.

2 Heaven's arches rang
when the angels sang,
proclaiming Thy royal degree;
but of lowly birth
cam'st Thou, Lord, on earth,
and in great humility:
O come to my heart, Lord Jesus!
there is room in my heart for Thee.

3 The foxes found rest,
and the birds their nest,
in the shade of the cedar tree;
but the earth was the bed
for Thy weary head,
in the deserts of Galilee:
O come to my heart, Lord Jesus!
there is room in my heart for Thee.

4 Thou camest, O Lord,
with the living word,
that should set Thy people free;
but, with mocking scorn,
and with crown of thorn,
they bore Thee to Calvary:
O come to my heart, Lord Jesus!
Thy cross is my only plea.

5 When heaven's arches ring,
and her choirs shall sing,
at Thy coming to victory,
let Thy voice call me home,
saying, 'Yet there is room,
there is room at My side for thee!'
And my heart shall rejoice, Lord
Jesus,
when Thou comest and callest for me.

*Emily Elizabeth Steele Elliott**, 1836-97

217

Thou who wast rich beyond all splendour,
all for love's sake becamest poor;
thrones for a manger didst surrender,
sapphire-paved courts for stable floor.
Thou who wast rich beyond all
splendour,
all for love's sake becamest poor.

2 Thou who art God beyond all praising,
all for love's sake becamest man;
stooping so low, but sinners raising
heavenwards by Thine eternal plan.
Thou who art God beyond all praising,
all for love's sake becamest man.

3 Thou who art love beyond all telling,
Saviour and King, we worship Thee.
Immanuel, within us dwelling,
make us what Thou wouldst have us
be.
Thou who art love beyond all telling,
Saviour and King, we worship Thee.

Frank Houghton, 1894-1972

218

Based on ISAIAH 9:2-7

To us a child of hope is born,
to us a Son is given,
Him shall the tribes of earth obey,
Him all the hosts of heaven.

2 His name shall be the Prince of Peace,
for evermore adored;
the Wonderful, the Counsellor,
the great and mighty Lord.

3 His power increasing still shall spread,
His reign no ending know;
justice shall guard His throne above,
and peace abound below.

4 The race that long in darkness pined
have seen a glorious Light;
the people dwell in day, who dwelt
in death's surrounding night.

5 To us a child of hope is born,
to us a Son is given,
the Wonderful, the Counsellor,
the mighty Lord of heaven.

*John Morison**, 1750-98

219

To us a Child of royal birth,
heir of the promises, is given:
the Invisible appears on earth,
the Son of man, the God of heaven.

2 A Saviour born, in love supreme
He comes our fallen souls to raise;
He comes His people to redeem
with all His plenitude of grace.

3 The Christ, by raptured seers foretold,
filled with the eternal Spirit's power,
Prophet, and Priest, and King behold,
and Lord of all the worlds adore.

4 The Lord of hosts, the God most high,
who quits His throne on earth to live,
with joy we welcome from the sky,
with faith into our hearts receive.

Charles Wesley, 1707-88

220

While shepherds watched their flocks by night,
all seated on the ground,
the angel of the Lord came down,
and glory shone around.

2 'Fear not!' said he, for mighty dread
had seized their troubled mind;
'Glad tidings of great joy I bring
to you and all mankind.

3 'To you, in David's town, this day
is born, of David's line,
a Saviour, who is Christ the Lord;
and this shall be the sign:

4 'The heavenly babe you there shall find
to human view displayed,
all meanly wrapped in swaddling bands,
and in a manger laid.'

5 Thus spake the seraph, and forthwith
appeared a shining throng
of angels praising God, and thus
addressed their joyful song:

6 'All glory be to God on high,
and to the earth be peace:
goodwill henceforth from heaven to men
begin and never cease.'

Nahum Tate, 1652-1715

Life and ministry

221

And didst Thou love the race that loved not Thee?
And didst Thou take to heaven a human brow?
Dost plead with man's voice by the marvellous sea?
Art Thou his kinsman now?

2 O God, O kinsman, loved, but not enough!
O Man, with eyes majestic after death!
whose feet have toiled along our pathways rough,
whose lips drawn human breath!

3 By that one likeness which is ours and Thine,
by that one nature which doth hold us kin,
by that high heaven where, sinless, Thou dost shine,
to draw us sinners in;

4 By Thy last silence in the judgment hall,
by long foreknowledge of the deadly tree,
by darkness, by the wormwood and the gall,
I pray Thee, visit me.

5 Come, lest this heart should, cold and cast away,
die ere the Guest adored she entertain –
lest eyes that never saw Thine earthly day
should miss Thy heavenly reign.

Jean Ingelow, 1820-97

222

How sweetly flowed the gospel's sound
from lips of gentleness and grace;
when listening thousands gathered round
and joy and reverence filled the place.

2 From heaven He came, of heaven He spoke,
to heaven He led His followers' way;
dark clouds of gloomy night He broke,
unveiling an immortal day.

3 'Come, wanderers, to my Father's home;
come, all you weary ones, and rest.'
Yes! gracious Saviour, we will come,
obey You, love You, and be blest.

John Bowring, 1792-1872

223

My dear Redeemer and my Lord,
I read my duty in Your Word;
but in Your life the law appears
drawn out in living characters.

2 Such was Your truth, and such Your zeal,
such deference to Your Father's will,
such love, and meekness so divine,
I would transcribe and make them mine.

3 Cold mountains and the midnight air
witnessed the fervour of Your prayer;
the desert Your temptations knew,
Your conflict, and Your victory too.

4 Be then my pattern: make me bear
more of Your gracious image here;
then God the Judge shall own my name
amongst the followers of the Lamb.

Isaac Watts, 1674-1748

224

What grace, O Lord, and beauty shone
around Your steps below!
What patient love was seen in all
Your life and death of woe!

2 For ever on Your burdened heart
a weight of sorrow hung,
yet no ungentle, murmuring word
escaped Your silent tongue.

3 Your foes might hate, despise, revile,
Your friends unfaithful prove:
unwearied in forgiveness still,
Your heart could only love.

4 O give us hearts to love like You,
like You, O Lord, to grieve
far more for others' sins than all
the wrongs that we receive.

5 One with Yourself, may every eye
in us, Your brethren, view
that gentleness and grace that spring
from union, Lord, with You.

Edward Denny, 1796-1889

225

I have a friend whose faithful love
is more than all the world to me,
'tis higher than the heights above,
and deeper than the soundless sea;
so old, so new, so strong, so true;
before the earth received its frame,
He loved me – blessèd be His Name!

2 He held the highest place above,
adored by all the sons of flame,
yet, such His self-denying love,
He laid aside His crown and came
to seek the lost, and, at the cost
of heavenly rank and earthly fame,
He sought me – blessèd be His
Name!

3 It was a lonely path He trod,
from every human soul apart,
known only to Himself and God
was all the grief that filled His heart:
yet from the track He turned not back
till where I lay in want and shame
He found me – blessèd be His Name!

4 Then dawned at last that day of dread
when, desolate but undismayed,
with wearied frame and thorn-crowned
head
He, now forsaken and betrayed,
went up for me to Calvary,
and dying there in grief and shame
He saved me – blessèd be His Name!

5 Long as I live my song shall tell
the wonders of His matchless love:
and when at last I rise to dwell
in the bright home prepared above,
my joy shall be His face to see,
and bowing then with loud acclaim,
I'll praise Him – blessèd be His
Name!

C A Tydeman

226

Who is He in yonder stall,
at whose feet the shepherds fall?

'Tis the Lord! O wondrous story!
'tis the Lord, the King of glory!
at His feet we humbly fall;
crown Him, crown Him Lord of all!

*2 Who is He in deep distress,
fasting in the wilderness?

3 Who is He to whom they bring
all the sick and sorrowing?

*4 Who is He that stands and weeps
at the grave where Lazarus sleeps?

5 Lo, at midnight, who is He
prays in dark Gethsemane?

6 Who is He on yonder tree
dies in grief and agony?

7 Who is He that from the grave
comes to rescue, help and save?

*8 Who is He that from His throne
rules through all the worlds alone?

Benjamin Russell Hanby, 1833-67

* *These verses may be omitted.*

227

Who is this, so weak and helpless,
child of lowly Hebrew maid,
humbly in a stable sheltered,
coldly in a manger laid?
'Tis the Lord of all creation,
who this wondrous path has trod;
He is God from everlasting,
and to everlasting God.

2 Who is this, a Man of Sorrows,
walking sadly life's hard way,
homeless, weary, sighing, weeping
over sin and Satan's sway?
'Tis our God, our glorious Saviour,
rules above the starry sky;
now for us a place preparing,
where no tear can dim the eye.

3 Who is this? behold Him shedding
drops of blood upon the ground!
Who is this, despised, rejected,
mocked, insulted, beaten, bound?
'Tis our God, who gifts and graces
on His church is pouring down;
who shall smite in righteous judgment
all His foes beneath His throne.

4 Who is this that hangs there dying,
while the cruel world scoffs and scorns;
numbered with the malefactors,
torn with nails, and crowned with thorns?
'Tis our God who lives for ever
'mid the shining ones on high,
in the glorious golden city
reigning everlastingly.

William Walsham How, 1823-97

Suffering and death

228

Alas! and did my Saviour bleed
and did my Sovereign die?
Would He devote that sacred head
for such a worm as I?

2 Was it for crimes that I had done,
He groaned upon the tree?
Amazing pity! grace unknown!
and love beyond degree!

3 Well might the sun in darkness hide,
and shut his glories in,
when God, the mighty Maker, died
for man, the creature's sin.

4 Thus might I hide my blushing face
while His dear cross appears;
dissolve my heart in thankfulness,
and melt my eyes to tears.

5 But drops of grief can ne'er repay
the debt of love I owe:
here, Lord, I give myself away;
'tis all that I can do.

Isaac Watts, 1674-1748

229

All you that pass by,
to Jesus draw nigh;
to you is it nothing that Jesus should die?
Your ransom and peace,
your surety He is,
come, see if there ever was sorrow like His.

2 He dies to atone
for sins not His own;
your debt He has paid, and your work
He has done.
You all may receive
the peace He did leave,
who made intercession, 'My Father,
forgive!'

3 For you and for me
He prayed on the tree:
the prayer is accepted, the sinner is free.
That sinner am I
who on Jesus rely,
and come for the pardon God cannot
deny.

4 His death is my plea;
my Advocate see,
and hear the blood speak that has
answered for me;
He purchased the grace
which now I embrace;
O Father, You know He has died in my
place.

Charles Wesley, 1707-88

230

And did the Holy and the Just,
the Sovereign of the skies,
stoop down to wretchedness and dust,
that guilty worms might rise?

2 Yes; the Redeemer left His throne,
His radiant throne on high –
surprising mercy! love unknown! –
to suffer, bleed and die.

3 He took the dying traitor's place,
and suffered in his stead:
for man – O miracle of grace! –
for man the Saviour bled!

4 Dear Lord, what heavenly wonders dwell
in Thy atoning blood!
By this are sinners snatched from hell,
and rebels brought to God.

5 Jesus, my soul adoring bends
to love so full, so free;
and may I hope that love extends
its sacred power to me?

6 What glad return can I impart
for favours so divine?
O take my all, this worthless heart,
and make it only Thine.

Anne Steele, 1717-78

231

And was it for my sin
that Jesus suffered so,
when moved by His all-powerful love
He came to earth below?

2 Your holy law fulfilled,
atonement now is made,
and our great debt, too great for us,
He now has fully paid.

3 He suffered pain and death,
when on the hill brought low;
His blood will wash the guilty clean,
as pure and white as snow.

4 For in His death our death
died with Him on the tree,
and great the number by His blood
will go to heaven made free.

5 When Jesus bowed His head
and, dying, took our place,
the veil was rent, a way was found
to that pure home of grace.

6 He conquered blackest hell;
He trod the serpent down;
a host from fetters He'll set free
by grace to be God's own.

John Elias, 1774-1841;
tr. by Noel Gibbard, b. 1932

232

Awake, my soul, and rise
amazed, and yonder see
how hangs the mighty Saviour God
upon a cursèd tree!

2 How gloriously fulfilled
is that most ancient plan,
conceived in the eternal mind
before the world began.

3 Here depths of wisdom shine,
which angels cannot trace;
the highest rank of cherubim
still lost in wonder gaze.

4 Here free salvation reigns,
and carries all before;
and this shall for the guilty race
be refuge evermore.

5 Now hell in all her strength,
her rage, and boasted sway,
can never snatch a wandering sheep
from Jesus' arms away.

William Williams, 1717-91

233

Behold the amazing sight!
the Saviour lifted high;
the Son of God, His soul's delight,
expires in agony.

2 For whom, for whom, my heart,
were all those sorrows borne?
Why did He feel that piercing smart,
and wear that crown of thorn?

3 For us in love He bled,
for us in anguish died;
'twas love that bowed His sacred head,
and pierced His precious side.

4 We see, and we adore,
we trust that dying love;
we feel its strong attractive power
to lift our souls above.

5 Behold the amazing sight!
nor trace His griefs alone,
but from the cross pursue our flight
to His triumphant throne.

Philip Doddridge, 1702-51

234

Behold the immortal Lamb
on Calvary's altar slain,
behold the crown of shame,
His agony of pain;

Let all adore! O may our souls
sing Jesus's praise for evermore!

2 Behold this sacrifice
was purposed by our God,
for He prepared the cross,
the life to be outpoured.

3 Behold, for from that place
God's love and justice shine,
that glory might be His,
that pardon might be mine.

4 Behold the life He gave,
but finished now His pains;
the Saviour lives to save,
the Lord of glory reigns!

5 Behold His throne of grace,
no longer need we fear;
with joy we see His face,
with confidence draw near.

Alan Charles Clifford, b. 1941

235

Give me a sight, O Saviour,
of Your wondrous love to me,
of the love that brought You down to earth,
to die on Calvary.

O make me understand it,
help me to take it in,
what it meant to You, the Holy One,
to bear away my sin.

2 Was it the nails, O Saviour,
that bound You to the tree?
No, 'twas Your everlasting love,
Your love for me, for me.

3 O wonder of all wonders,
that through Your death for me
my open sins, my secret sins,
can all forgiven be!

4 Then melt my heart, O Saviour,
bend me, yes, break me down,
until I own You conqueror,
and Lord and Sovereign crown.

Katharine Agnes May Kelly, 1869-1942

236

Come and see, come and see,
come and see the King of love,
see the purple robe and crown of thorns He wears.
Soldiers mock, rulers sneer,
as He lifts the cruel cross,
lone and friendless now He climbs towards the hill.

We worship at Your feet
where wrath and mercy meet
and a guilty world is washed by love's pure stream.
For us He was made sin;
O help me take it in.
Deep wounds of love cry out, 'Father, forgive!'
I worship, I worship
the Lamb who was slain.

2 Come and weep, come and mourn
for your sin that pierced Him there;
so much deeper than the wounds of thorn and nail.
All our pride, all our greed,
all our fallenness and shame:
and the Lord has laid the punishment on Him.
We worship at Your feet...

3 Man of heaven, born to earth
to restore us to Your heaven,
here we bow in awe beneath Your searching eyes.
From Your tears comes our joy,
from Your death our life shall spring;
by Your resurrection power we shall rise.
We worship at Your feet...

Graham Kendrick, b. 1950

237

Glory be to Jesus,
who, in bitter pains,
poured for me the life-blood
from His sacred veins.

2 Grace and life eternal
in that blood I find;
blest be His compassion,
infinitely kind!

3 Blest through endless ages
be the precious stream,
which from endless torments
did the world redeem.

4 Abel's blood for vengeance
pleaded to the skies;
but the blood of Jesus
for our pardon cries.

5 Oft as it is sprinkled
on our guilty hearts,
Satan in confusion
terror-struck departs.

6 Oft as earth exulting
wafts its praise on high,
angel-hosts rejoicing
make their glad reply.

7 Lift ye then your voices;
swell the mighty flood;
louder still and louder
praise the Lamb of God.

Italian, c. 1815;
tr. by Edward Caswall, 1814-78

238

Glory to Jesus, Son of God most high,
the crucified!
Glory to Jesus, throned above the sky,
for me He died;
high on Your throne, Your ear, Lord Jesus, bend
as grateful hearts now to Yourself ascend.

2 Deep were Your sorrows, Lord, when heaven frowned –
Gethsemane!
Bloodlike Your sweat, Lord, falling to the ground –
so heavily;
dark was the earth; the heavens were darker still,
O Christ my God! is this the Father's will?

3 Thorns wreathed Your brow when hanging on the tree –
man's cruelty!
Why lavish love like this, O Lord on me?
Such love on me!
Would that my soul could understand its length,
its breadth, depth, height, and everlasting strength!

4 Your precious blood was freely shed for me –
on Calvary,
to save me now and for eternity,
to set me free.
Nor death, nor hell, nor things below – above
can sever me from Your eternal love.

5 Like shoreless seas, Your love can know no bound,
on me outpoured,
vast, wide, immense, unfathomed and profound;
I love you, Lord!
And when above, my crown is at Your feet,
I'll praise You still for Calvary's mercy seat.

Edward C Quine, 1857-1942

239

Glory, glory everlasting
be to Him who bore the cross!
who redeemed our souls, by tasting
death, the death deserved by us:
spread His glory,
who redeemed His people thus.

2 His is love, 'tis love unbounded,
without measure, without end;
human thought is here confounded,
'tis too vast to comprehend:
praise the Saviour!
magnify the sinner's friend.

3 While we hear the wondrous story
of the Saviour's cross and shame,
sing we 'Everlasting glory
be to God, and to the Lamb!'
Saints and angels,
glory give to His great name!

Thomas Kelly, 1769-1855

240

Great High Priest, we view Thee stooping
with our names upon Thy breast,
in the garden groaning, drooping,
to the ground with horrors pressed;
holy angels stood confounded,
to behold their Maker thus;
and can we remain unmovèd,
when we know 'twas all for us?

2 On the cross Thy body broken
cancels every penal tie;
tempted souls, produce this token,
all demands to satisfy.
All is finished; do not doubt it,
but believe your dying Lord;
never reason more about it,
only trust His sacred Word.

3 Lord, we fain would trust Thee solely;
'twas for us Thy blood was spilt;
bruisèd Bridegroom, take us wholly,
take, and make us what Thou wilt.
Thou hast borne the bitter sentence
passed on man's accursèd race;
true belief and true repentance
are Thy gifts, Thou God of grace.

Joseph Hart, 1712-68

241

Hark! the voice of love and mercy
sounds aloud from Calvary;
see, it rends the rocks asunder,
shakes the earth and veils the sky:
'It is finished!'
Hear the dying Saviour cry.

2 'It is finished!' What assurance
do the wondrous words afford!
Heavenly blessings without measure
flow to us from Christ the Lord:
'It is finished!'
Saints the dying words record.

3 Finished all the types and shadows
of the ceremonial law,
finished all that God had promised;
death and hell dismay no more.
'It is finished!'
Saints, from hence your comfort draw.

4 Saints and angels shout His praises,
His great finished work proclaim;
all on earth and all in heaven
join to bless Immanuel's name:
Hallelujah!
Endless glory to the Lamb!

Jonathan Evans, 1749-1809

242

Here is love, vast as the ocean,
lovingkindness as the flood,
when the Prince of life, our ransom,
shed for us His precious blood.
Who His love will not remember?
Who can cease to sing His praise?
He can never be forgotten
throughout heaven's eternal days.

2 On the mount of crucifixion
fountains opened deep and wide;
through the floodgates of God's mercy
flowed a vast and gracious tide.
Grace and love, like mighty rivers,
poured incessant from above,
and heaven's peace and perfect justice
kissed a guilty world in love.

William Rees, 1802-83;
tr. by William Edwards, 1848-1929

243 Based on ISAIAH 53:5-8

He was pierced for our transgressions
and bruised for our iniquities;
and to bring us peace He was punished,
and by His stripes we are healed.

2 He was led like a lamb to the slaughter,
although He was innocent of crime;
and cut off from the land of the living,
He paid for the guilt that was mine.

We like sheep have gone astray,
turned each one to his own way,
and the Lord has laid on Him
the iniquity of us all.

(descant on repeat of chorus)

Like a lamb, like a lamb
to the slaughter He came,
and the Lord laid on Him
the iniquity of us all.

Maggi Dawn, b. 1959

244

His hands were pierced, the hands that made
the mountain range and everglade;
that washed the stains of sin away
and changed earth's darkness into day.

2 His feet were pierced, the feet that trod
the furthest shining star of God;
and left their imprint deep and clear
on every winding pathway here.

3 His heart was pierced, the heart that burned
to comfort every heart that yearned;
and from it flowed a cleansing flood,
the river of redeeming blood.

4 His hands and feet and heart, all three,
were pierced for me on Calvary;
and here and now, to Him I bring
my hands, feet, heart, an offering.

D Wood, b. 1913

245

I stand amazed in the presence
of Jesus the Nazarene,
and wonder how He could love me,
a sinner, condemned, unclean.

How marvellous! how wonderful!
and my song shall ever be:
how marvellous! how wonderful
is my Saviour's love to me!

2 For me it was in the garden
He prayed – 'Not My will, but Thine';
He had no tears for His own griefs,
but sweat drops of blood for mine.

3 In pity angels beheld Him,
and came from the world of light
to comfort Him in the sorrows
He bore for my soul that night.

4 He took my sins and my sorrows,
He made them His very own;
He bore the burden to Calvary,
and suffered and died alone.

5 When with the ransomed in glory
His face I at last shall see,
'twill be my joy through the ages
to sing of His love for me.

Charles Homer Gabriel, 1856-1932

246

Jesus was slain for me,
at Calvary;
crownèd with thorns was He
at Calvary.
There He in anguish died,
there from His opened side
poured forth the crimson tide,
at Calvary.

2 Pardoned is all my sin,
at Calvary;
cleansed is my heart within,
at Calvary.
Now robes of praise I wear,
gone are my grief and care,
Christ bore my burdens there,
at Calvary.

3 Wondrous His love for me,
at Calvary;
glorious His victory,
at Calvary.
Vanquished are death and hell,
O let His praises swell,
ever my tongue shall tell
of Calvary.

George Perfect, 1882-1958

247

King of my life, I crown Thee now,
Thine shall the glory be;
lest I forget Thy thorn-crowned brow,
lead me to Calvary.

Lest I forget Gethsemane,
lest I forget Thine agony,
lest I forget Thy love for me,
lead me to Calvary.

2 Show me the tomb where Thou wast
laid,
tenderly mourned and wept:
angels in robes of light arrayed
guarded Thee whilst Thou slept.

3 Let me, like Mary, hear the voice
that called her by her name,
and bade her mourning heart rejoice
and her dear Master claim.

4 May I be willing, Lord, to bear
daily my cross for Thee;
even Thy cup of grief to share –
Thou hast borne all for me.

5 Fill me, O Lord, with Thy desire
for all who know not Thee;
then touch my lips with holy fire,
to speak of Calvary.

Jennie Evelyn Hussey, 1874-1958

248

Man of sorrows! what a name
for the Son of God, who came
ruined sinners to reclaim!
Hallelujah! what a Saviour!

2 Bearing shame and scoffing rude,
in my place condemned He stood;
sealed my pardon with His blood:
Hallelujah! what a Saviour!

3 Guilty, vile, and helpless, we;
spotless Lamb of God was He:
full atonement! – can it be?
Hallelujah! what a Saviour!

4 Lifted up was He to die,
'It is finished!' was His cry;
now in heaven exalted high:
Hallelujah! what a Saviour!

5 When He comes, our glorious King,
all His ransomed home to bring,
then anew this song we'll sing:
Hallelujah! what a Saviour!

Philipp Paul Bliss, 1838-76

249

Never further than Thy cross,
never higher than Thy feet;
here earth's precious things seem dross,
here earth's bitter things grow sweet.

2 Gazing thus our sin we see,
learn Thy love while gazing thus;
sin which laid the cross on Thee,
love which bore the cross for us.

3 Here we learn to serve and give,
and, rejoicing, self deny;
here we gather love to live,
here we gather faith to die.

4 Symbols of our liberty
and our service here unite;
captives, by Thy cross set free,
soldiers of Thy cross, we fight.

5 Pressing onwards as we can,
still to this our hearts must tend;
where our earliest hopes began,
there our last aspirings end.

6 Till amid the hosts of light
we, in Thee redeemed, complete,
through Thy cross made pure and white,
cast our crowns before Thy feet.

Elisabeth Charles, 1828-96

250

O Christ, what burdens bowed Thy head!
our load was laid on Thee;
Thou stoodest in the sinner's stead,
didst bear all ill for me.
A victim led, Thy blood was shed!
Now there's no load for me.

2 Death and the curse were in our cup:
O Christ, 'twas full for Thee!
But Thou hast drained the last dark drop,
'tis empty now for me:
That bitter cup, love drank it up,
now blessing's draught for me.

3 Jehovah lifted up His rod:
O Christ, it fell on Thee!
Thou wast sore stricken of Thy God;
There's not one stroke for me.
Thy tears, Thy blood beneath it flowed;
Thy bruising healeth me.

4 For me, Lord Jesus, Thou hast died,
and I have died in Thee:
Thou'rt risen – my bands are all untied;
and now Thou liv'st in me;
when purified, made white and tried,
Thy glory then for me.

Anne Ross Cousin, 1824-1906

251

My Lord, what love is this
that pays so dearly,
that I, the guilty one
may go free!

Amazing love! O what sacrifice,
the Son of God given for me!
My debt He pays
and my death He dies
that I might live,
that I might live.

2 And so they watched Him die,
despised, rejected.
But O, the blood He shed
flowed for me!

3 And now this love of Christ
shall flow like rivers.
Come wash your guilt away,
live again!

Graham Kendrick, b. 1950

252

My song is love unknown,
my Saviour's love to me,
love to the loveless shown,
that they might lovely be.
O who am I,
that for my sake
my Lord should take
frail flesh, and die?

2 He came from His blest throne,
salvation to bestow:
but men made strange, and none
the longed-for Christ would know.
But O, my friend!
my friend indeed,
who at my need
His life did spend!

3 Sometimes they strew His way,
and His sweet praises sing;
resounding all the day
hosannas to their king.
Then 'Crucify!'
is all their breath,
and for His death
they thirst and cry.

4 They rise and needs will have
my dear Lord made away;
a murderer they save;
the Prince of life they slay.
Yet steadfast He
to suffering goes,
that He His foes
from thence might free.

5 In life, no house, no home
my Lord on earth might have;
in death, no friendly tomb
but what a stranger gave.
What may I say?
Heaven was His home:
but mine the tomb
wherein He lay.

6 Here might I stay and sing,
no story so divine;
never was love, dear King,
never was grief like Thine!
This is my friend,
in whose sweet praise
I all my days
could gladly spend.

Samuel Crossman, 1624-83

253

O Love divine! what have You done?
The immortal God has died for me!
The Father's co-eternal Son
bore all my sins upon the tree;
the immortal God for me has died!
my Lord, my Love is crucified.

2 Behold Him, you that pass Him by,
the bleeding Prince of life and peace!
Come, sinners, see your Maker die,
and say, was ever grief like His?
Come, feel with me His blood applied:
my Lord, my Love is crucified:

3 Is crucified for me and you,
to bring us rebels back to God:
believe, believe the record true,
you now are bought with Jesus' blood,
pardon for sin flows from His side:
my Lord, my Love is crucified.

4 Then let us sit beneath His cross,
and gladly catch the healing stream,
all things for Him account but loss,
and give up all our hearts to Him;
of nothing think or speak beside:
my Lord, my Love is crucified.

Charles Wesley, 1707-88

254

O perfect life of love!
all, all is finished now,
all that He left His throne above
to do for us below.

2 No work is left undone
of all the Father willed;
His toil and sorrows, one by one,
the Scriptures have fulfilled.

3 No pain that we can share
but He has felt its smart;
all forms of human grief and care
have pierced that tender heart.

4 And on His thorn-crowned head,
and on His sinless soul,
our sins in all their guilt were laid,
that He might make us whole.

5 In perfect love He dies:
for me He dies, for me!
O all-atoning sacrifice,
I cling by faith to Thee.

6 In every time of need,
before the judgment throne,
Thy work, O Lamb of God, I'll plead,
Thy merits, not my own.

7 Yet work, O Lord, in me
as Thou for me hast wrought;
and let my love the answer be
to grace Thy love has brought.

Henry Williams Baker, 1821-77

255

O sacred head! sore wounded,
with grief and shame bowed down,
how scornfully surrounded
with thorns, Thine only crown!
How pale art Thou with anguish,
with sore abuse and scorn!
How does that visage languish
which once was bright as morn!

2 Thy grief and bitter passion
were all for sinners' gain:
mine, mine was the transgression,
but Thine the deadly pain:
lo! here I fall, my Saviour;
'tis I deserve Thy place;
look on me with Thy favour,
and grant to me Thy grace.

3 What language shall I borrow
to thank Thee, dearest friend,
for this Thy dying sorrow,
Thy pity without end?
O make me Thine for ever;
and should I fainting be,
Lord, let me never, never
outlive my love to Thee!

4 Be near me when I'm dying;
O show Thy cross to me;
Thy death, my hope supplying,
from death shall set me free.
These eyes, new faith receiving,
from Jesus shall not move;
for he who dies believing
dies safely through Thy love.

Paul Gerhardt, 1607-76;
from SALVE CAPUT CRUENTATUM.
Attributed to Bernard of Clairvaux, 1091-1153;
*tr. by James Waddell Alexander**, 1804-59

256

O Son of Man, O Son of God,
eternal grace Thy painful path had planned,
a heavy cross and agony of shame –
the way ordained.

2 O death of Christ, O blood divine,
O perfect life He lived, all for our gain,
fulfilling all the law's demands, and more,
He did attain.

3 O bitter cup, O costly task,
to meet the wrath of God's own holiness!
The Saviour stood, and in my stead He died,
my soul to bless.

4 O love of God, O wondrous grace,
that such an angry death of anguish sore
should pay my penalty and make me whole –
O boundless store!

5 O wondrous flood of grace and love,
both mingled in the blood as He implored:
can this be so, all this for me, my Lord?
Thou art adored.

6 Peace through the blood of Christ alone,
peace with my God and peace within my soul,
peace in that day when He will come at last,
my all in all.

William Vernon Higham, b. 1926

257

On the cross, on the cross,
where the King of glory died.
Here is grace, here is love,
flowing from that wounded side.
Amazing mystery,
that He should die for me,
as a perfect sacrifice.
On the cross, on the cross,
Love incarnate on the cross.

2 At the cross, at the cross,
all my sin on Jesus laid.
Mine the debt, His the cost,
by His blood the price is paid.
And through His suffering,
that fragrant offering,
arms of love are opened wide.
At the cross, at the cross,
there is healing at the cross.

3 To the cross, to the cross,
Spirit lead me to the cross.
Bowed in awe, at His feet,
richest gain I count as loss.
Nothing compares with this,
to share His righteousness,
and be called a child of God.
To the cross, to the cross,
Spirit lead me to the cross.

Geoff Baker

258

Ride on! ride on in majesty!
Hark! all the tribes 'Hosanna' cry;
O Saviour meek, pursue Your road
with palms and scattered garments
strowed.

2 Ride on, ride on in majesty!
In lowly pomp ride on to die;
O Christ, Your triumphs now begin
o'er captive death and conquered sin.

3 Ride on, ride on in majesty!
The angel armies of the sky
look down with sad and wondering
eyes
to see the approaching sacrifice.

4 Ride on, ride on in majesty!
Your last and fiercest strife is nigh:
the Father on His sapphire throne
awaits His own anointed Son.

5 Ride on! ride on in majesty!
In lowly pomp ride on to die;
bow Your meek head to mortal pain,
then take, O God, Your power, and
reign.

Henry Hart Milman, 1791-1868

259

The enormous load of human guilt
was on my Saviour laid;
with woes as with a garment He
for sinners was arrayed.

2 And in the fearful pangs of death
He wept, He prayed for me;
loved and embraced my guilty soul
when nailèd to the tree.

3 O love amazing! love beyond
the reach of human tongue;
love which shall be the subject of
an everlasting song.

4 Eternity, though infinite,
is short enough to trace
the virtues of His healing wounds,
the wonders of His grace.

5 Let men rejoice in Jesu's blood,
let angels join our lays;
in one harmonious endless choir
sing His eternal praise.

William Williams, 1717-91

260

There is a fountain filled with blood
drawn from Immanuel's veins;
and sinners, plunged beneath that flood,
lose all their guilty stains.

2 The dying thief rejoiced to see
that fountain in his day;
and there have I, though vile as he,
washed all my sins away.

3 Dear dying Lamb, Thy precious blood
shall never lose its power,
till all the ransomed church of God
be saved to sin no more.

4 E'er since, by faith, I saw the stream
Thy flowing wounds supply,
redeeming love has been my theme,
and shall be till I die.

5 Then in a nobler, sweeter song
I'll sing Thy power to save,
when this poor lisping, stammering
tongue
lies silent in the grave.

William Cowper, 1731-1800

261

There is a green hill far away,
outside a city wall,
where the dear Lord was crucified
who died to save us all.

2 We may not know, we cannot tell
what pains He had to bear;
but we believe it was for us
He hung and suffered there.

3 He died that we might be forgiven,
He died to make us good,
that we might go at last to heaven,
saved by His precious blood.

4 There was no other good enough
to pay the price of sin;
He only could unlock the gate
of heaven, and let us in.

5 O dearly, dearly has He loved,
and we must love Him too,
and trust in His redeeming blood,
and try His works to do.

Cecil Frances Alexander, 1818-95

262

We sing the praise of Him who died,
of Him who died upon the cross;
the sinner's hope let men deride,
for this we count the world but loss.

2 Inscribed upon the cross we see,
in shining letters, 'God is love';
He bears our sins upon the tree;
He brings us mercy from above.

3 The cross! it takes our guilt away;
it holds the fainting spirit up;
it cheers with hope the gloomy day,
and sweetens every bitter cup.

4 It makes the coward spirit brave,
and nerves the feeble arm for fight;
it takes the terror from the grave,
and gilds the bed of death with light;

5 The balm of life, the cure of woe,
the measure and the pledge of love,
the sinner's refuge here below,
the angels' theme in heaven above.

Thomas Kelly, 1769-1855

263

When I survey the wondrous cross,
on which the Prince of glory died,
my richest gain I count but loss,
and pour contempt on all my pride.

2 Forbid it, Lord, that I should boast
save in the death of Christ my God:
all the vain things that charm me most,
I sacrifice them to His blood.

3 See, from His head, His hands, His feet,
sorrow and love flow mingled down;
did e'er such love and sorrow meet,
or thorns compose so rich a crown?

4 His dying crimson, like a robe,
spreads o'er His body on the tree:
then am I dead to all the globe,
and all the globe is dead to me.

5 Were the whole realm of nature mine,
that were an offering far too small;
love so amazing, so divine,
demands my soul, my life, my all.

Isaac Watts, 1674-1748

Resurrection

264

All shall be well!
for on our Easter skies
see Christ the Sun
of Righteousness arise.

2 All shall be well!
the sacrifice is made;
the sinner freed,
the price of pardon paid.

3 All shall be well!
the cross and passion past;
dark night is done,
bright morning come at last.

4 All shall be well!
within our Father's plan
death has no more
dominion over man.

5 Jesus alive!
rejoice and sing again,
'All shall be well
for evermore, Amen!'

Timothy Dudley-Smith, b. 1926

265

Hallelujah! Hallelujah!
hearts to heaven and voices raise;
sing to God a hymn of gladness,
sing to God a hymn of praise;
He who on the cross a victim
for the world's salvation bled,
Jesus Christ, the King of glory,
now is risen from the dead.

2 Christ is risen, Christ the first-fruits
of the holy harvest field,
which will all its full abundance
at His second coming yield;
then the golden ears of harvest
will their heads before Him wave,
ripened by His glorious sunshine
from the furrows of the grave.

3 Christ is risen, we are risen:
shed upon us heavenly grace,
rain and dew and gleams of glory
from the brightness of Thy face;
that we, with our hearts in heaven,
here on earth may fruitful be,
and by angel hands be gathered,
and be ever, Lord, with Thee.

4 Hallelujah! Hallelujah!
glory be to God on high;
hallelujah to the Saviour
who has gained the victory;
hallelujah to the Spirit,
fount of love and sanctity;
Hallelujah! Hallelujah!
to the triune Majesty!

Christopher Wordsworth, 1807-85

266

Christ is risen! Hallelujah!
risen our victorious head!
Sing His praises! Hallelujah!
Christ is risen from the dead.
Gratefully our hearts adore Him
as His light once more appears,
bowing down in joy before Him,
rising up from grief and tears.

Christ is risen! Hallelujah!
risen our victorious Head!
Sing His praises! Hallelujah!
Christ is risen from the dead.

2 Christ is risen! all the sadness
of His earthly life is o'er;
through the open gates of gladness
He returns to life once more;
death and hell before Him bending,
He is risen, the victor now,
angels on His steps attending,
glory round His wounded brow.

3 Christ is risen! henceforth never
death or hell shall us enthral;
we are Christ's, in Him for ever
we have triumphed over all;
all the doubting and dejection
of our trembling hearts have ceased;
'tis His day of resurrection,
let us rise and keep the feast.

John Samuel Bewley Monsell, 1811-75

267

Christ, the Lord, is risen today,
Hallelujah!
Sons of men and angels say:
raise your joys and triumphs high;
sing, O heavens, and earth reply.

2 Love's redeeming work is done;
fought the fight, the battle won.
Lo! our Sun's eclipse is o'er;
lo! He sets in blood no more.

3 Vain the stone, the watch, the seal;
Christ has burst the gates of hell;
death in vain forbids Him rise;
Christ has opened paradise.

4 Lives again our glorious King!
'Where, O death, is now your sting?'
Once He died our souls to save;
'Where's your victory, boasting grave?'

5 Soar we now where Christ has led,
following our exalted head;
made like Him, like Him we rise;
ours the cross, the grave, the skies.

6 King of glory! Soul of bliss!
Everlasting life is this,
You to know, Your power to prove,
thus to sing, and thus to love.

Charles Wesley, 1707-88

268

Jesus Christ is risen today
Hallelujah !
our triumphant holy day,
who did once, upon the cross,
suffer to redeem our loss.

2 Hymns of praise then let us sing
unto Christ, our heavenly King,
who endured the cross and grave,
sinners to redeem and save.

3 But the pains which He endured
our salvation has procured;
now above the sky He's King,
where the angels ever sing.

LYRA DAVIDICA, 1708
and Supplement to the New Version, c. 1816

269

Come, you saints, look here and wonder,
see the place where Jesus lay;
He has burst His bands asunder,
He has borne our sins away.
Joyful tidings!
Yes, the Lord is risen today.

2 Jesus triumphs! O sing praises!
By His death He overcame:
thus the Lord His glory raises;
thus He fills His foes with shame.
O sing praises!
praises to the Victor's name.

3 Jesus triumphs! angel voices
celebrate their conquering king:
all His ransomed church rejoices
as we join His praise to sing.
Songs eternal
shall through heaven's high arches
ring.

*Thomas Kelly**, 1769-1855

270

I know that my Redeemer lives:
what joy the blest assurance gives!
He lives, He lives, who once was dead;
He lives, my everlasting head.

2 He lives, triumphant from the grave;
He lives, eternally to save;
He lives, all glorious in the sky;
He lives, exalted there on high.

3 He lives to bless me with His love,
and still He pleads for me above;
He lives to raise me from the grave,
and me eternally to save.

4 He lives, my kind, wise, constant friend,
who still will keep me to the end;
He lives, and while He lives I'll sing,
Jesus, my Prophet, Priest, and King.

5 He lives my mansion to prepare;
and He will bring me safely there;
He lives, all glory to His name!
Jesus, unchangeably the same!

Samuel Medley, 1738-99

271

He dies! He dies! the lowly Man of sorrows;
on whom were laid our many griefs
and woes;
He bore our sins, endured our rightful
judgement
and He has triumphed over all our foes.

*Jesus, the first, the last, who once
was dead;
now lives again, for death is captive
led!*

2 He lives! He lives! what glorious
consolation!
exalted at His Father's own right hand;
He pleads for us, and by His intercession
His saints forever by His grace shall
stand!

3 He comes! He comes! O blest
anticipation!
true to His ever sure and faithful Word;
to call His bride to share His exaltation,
caught up to be forever with the Lord!

Charles Russell Hurditch, 1839-1908

272

In the tomb so cold they laid Him,
death its victim claimed.
Powers of hell, they could not hold Him,
back to life He came!

*Christ is risen!
death has been conquered!
Christ is risen!
He shall reign for ever!*

2 Hell had spent its fury on Him,
left Him crucified:
yet by blood He boldly conquered,
sin and death defied!

3 Now the fear of death is broken,
love has won the crown:
prisoners of the darkness – listen,
walls are tumbling down.

4 Raised from death, to heaven ascending,
love's exalted King:
let His song of joy unending
through the nations ring!

Graham Kendrick, b. 1950

273

Jesus lives! your terrors now
can, O grave, no more appal us;
Jesus lives! by this we know
death itself cannot enthral us.
Hallelujah!

2 Jesus lives! henceforth is death
but the gate of life immortal;
this shall calm our trembling breath,
when we pass its gloomy portal.

3 Jesus lives! for us He died;
then, alone to Jesus living,
pure in heart may we abide,
glory to our Saviour giving.

4 Jesus lives! our hearts know well
nought from us His love shall sever;
life, nor death, nor powers of hell
tear us from His keeping ever.

5 Jesus lives! to Him the throne
over all the world is given;
may we go where He is gone,
rest and reign with Him in heaven.

Christian Fürchtegott Gellert, 1715-69;
tr. by Frances Elizabeth Cox, 1812-97

274

The strife is o'er, the battle done;
the victory of life is won;
the song of triumph has begun:
Hallelujah!

2 The powers of death have done their worst,
but Christ their legions has dispersed;
let shouts of holy joy outburst:

3 The three sad days have quickly sped;
He rises glorious from the dead;
all glory to our risen head:

4 He broke the bonds of death and hell;
the bars from heaven's high portals fell;
let hymns of praise His triumph tell:

5 Lord, by the stripes which wounded Thee,
from death's dread sting Thy servants free,
that we may live and sing to Thee:

Latin, c. 12th cent.;
tr. by Francis Pott, 1832-1909

275

Jesus, Prince and Saviour,
Lord of life who died,
Christ, the friend of sinners,
mocked and crucified;
for a world's salvation
He His body gave,
lay at last death's victim
lifeless in the grave.

Lord of life triumphant,
risen now to reign!
King of endless ages,
Jesus lives again!

2 In His power and Godhead
every victory won,
pain and passion ended,
all His purpose done:
Christ the Lord is risen!
sighs and sorrows past,
death's dark night is over,
morning comes at last!

3 Resurrection morning,
sinners' bondage freed!
Christ the Lord is risen,
He is risen indeed!
Jesus, Prince and Saviour,
Lord of life who died,
Christ the King of glory
now is glorified!

Timothy Dudley-Smith, b. 1926

276

Low in the grave He lay,
Jesus, my Saviour!
waiting the coming day,
Jesus, my Lord!

Up from the grave He arose,
with a mighty triumph o'er His foes;
He arose a victor from the dark domain,
and He lives for ever with His saints to reign:
He arose! He arose!
Hallelujah! Christ arose!

2 Vainly they watch His bed,
Jesus, my Saviour!
Vainly they seal the dead,
Jesus, my Lord!

3 Death cannot keep his prey,
Jesus, my Saviour!
He tore the bars away,
Jesus, my Lord!

Robert Lowry, 1826-99

277

Led like a lamb to the slaughter,
in silence and shame,
there on Your back
You carried a world
of violence and pain,
bleeding, dying,
bleeding, dying.

You're alive, You're alive,
You have risen! Alleluia!
And the power and the glory is given,
Alleluia! Jesus, to You.

2 At break of dawn, poor Mary,
still weeping she came,
when through her grief
she heard Your voice,
now speaking her name.
Mary! Master!
Mary! Master!

3 At the right hand of the Father,
now seated on high,
You have begun
Your eternal reign
of justice and joy.
Glory, glory,
Glory, glory.

Graham Kendrick, b. 1950

278

Our Saviour has risen!
the tempter is foiled;
His legions are scattered,
His strongholds are spoiled.
O sing hallelujah! O sing hallelujah!
O sing hallelujah, be joyful and sing,
our great foe is baffled and Jesus is King!

2 O sin, you are vanquished,
your long reign is done,
though still you may grieve us,
your lordship is gone.
O sing hallelujah! O sing hallelujah!
O sing hallelujah, be joyful and sing,
who now can condemn us, our Jesus is King!

3 O death, we defy you,
a stronger is here;
who entered your palace
and banished our fear.
O sing hallelujah! O sing hallelujah!
O sing hallelujah, be joyful and sing,
the grave cannot scare us, Christ Jesus is King!

4 Our Saviour has risen!
The day breaks at last;
the long night of weeping
is now nearly past.
O sing hallelujah! O sing hallelujah!
O sing hallelujah, be joyful and sing,
our foes are all conquered, Christ Jesus is King!

William Conyngham Plunket, 1828-97

279

See Christ the victor raised
in resurrection life,
the mighty arm of God displayed,
who ends the strife.
He is the Lord of all,
whose arm is shortened not;
see devils' flight, and Satan's fall,
and hell their lot.

2 The sting of death is sin,
the power of law declares;
but Jesus Christ the Son doth win,
our guilt He bears.
Behold, ye sinners, now,
and look to Christ alone;
behold the blood upon His brow –
He did atone.

3 Immortal is my dress,
corruption fled away,
now robed in Him, yes, nothing less,
in bright array.
O death, where is thy sting?
O grave, thy victory?
The living Christ on mercy's wing
grants peace to me.

William Vernon Higham, b. 1926

280

The happy morn is come;
triumphant o'er the grave,
the Saviour leaves the tomb,
omnipotent to save:

Captivity is captive led,
for Jesus lives, who once was dead.

2 Who now accuses them
for whom their surety died?
Or who shall those condemn
whom God has justified?

3 Christ has the ransom paid;
the glorious work is done;
on Him our help is laid,
by Him our victory won:

4 All hail triumphant Lord!
the Resurrection Thou;
all hail incarnate Word!
before Thy throne we bow:

Thomas Haweis, 1733-1820

281

Thine be the glory, risen,
conquering Son,
endless is the victory Thou o'er death
hast won;
angels in bright raiment rolled the stone
away,
kept the folded grave-clothes, where
Thy body lay.

Thine be the glory, risen, conquering
Son,
endless is the victory Thou o'er death
hast won!

2 Lo! Jesus meets us, risen from the tomb;
lovingly He greets us, scatters fear and
gloom;
let the church with gladness hymns of
triumph sing,
for her Lord now liveth, death hath lost
its sting.

3 No more we doubt Thee, glorious
Prince of life;
life is nought without Thee: aid us in
our strife;
make us more than conquerors,
through Thy deathless love;
bring us safe through Jordan to Thy
home above.

Edmond Louis Budry, 1854-1932;
tr. by Richard Birch Hoyle, 1875-1939

282

You humble souls that seek the
Lord,
chase all your fears away;
and bow with rapture down to see
the place where Jesus lay.

2 So low the Lord of life was brought,
such wonders love can do;
so cold in death that heart once lay,
which throbbed and bled for you.

3 But raise your eyes, and tune your
songs;
the Saviour lives again:
not all the bolts and bars of death
the conqueror could detain.

4 High o'er the angelic bands He rears
His once dishonoured head;
and through unnumbered years He
reigns,
who dwelt among the dead.

5 With joy like His shall every saint
His vacant tomb survey;
then rise with his ascending Lord
to realms of endless day.

Philip Doddridge, 1702-51

283

Yes, the Redeemer rose,
the Saviour left the dead,
and o'er our hellish foes
high raised His conquering head;
in wild dismay
the guards around
fell to the ground
and sunk away.

2 Lo! the angelic bands
in full assembly meet,
to wait His high commands
and worship at His feet;
joyful they come,
and wing their way
from realms of day
to Jesus' tomb.

3 Then back to heaven they fly,
and the glad tidings bear;
hark! as they soar on high,
what music fills the air!
Their anthems say,
'Jesus, who bled,
has left the dead,
He rose today.'

4 O mortals, catch the sound,
redeemed by Him from hell,
and send the echo round
the globe on which you dwell;
transported cry,
'Jesus, who bled,
has left the dead,
no more to die.'

5 All hail, triumphant Lord,
who saves us with Your blood!
Wide be Your name adored,
our risen, reigning God!
With You we rise,
with You we reign,
and kingdoms gain
beyond the skies.

Philip Doddridge, 1702-51

284

The final triumph won,
the full atonement made,
salvation's work is done,
redemption's price is paid:
the morning breaks, the dark is fled,
for Christ is risen from the dead!

2 The tomb in which He lay
lies empty now and bare;
the stone is rolled away,
no lifeless form is there:
the sting is drawn from death and
grave,
for Christ is risen, strong to save!

3 For us the Saviour died,
with us He lives again,
to God the Father's side
exalted now to reign:
to throne and crown by right
restored,
for Christ is risen, Christ is Lord!

4 As one with Him we rise
to seek the things above,
in life that never dies,
in righteousness and love:
let praise unite our ransomed powers,
for Christ is risen, Christ is ours!

Timothy Dudley-Smith, b. 1926

Ascension and exaltation

285

Conquering Prince and Lord of glory,
majesty enthroned in light;
all the heavens are bowed before Thee,
far beyond them spreads Thy might;
shall not I fall at Thy feet,
and my heart with rapture beat,
now Thy glory is displayed,
Thine ere yet the worlds were made?

2 As I watch Thee far ascending
to the right hand of the throne,
see the host before Thee bending,
praising Thee in sweetest tone;
shall not I too at Thy feet
here the angels' strain repeat,
and rejoice that heaven doth ring
with the triumph of my King?

3 Power and Spirit are o'erflowing,
on me also be they poured;
every hindrance overthrowing,
make Thy foes Thy footstool, Lord!
Yea, let earth's remotest end
To Thy righteous sceptre bend,
make Thy way before Thee plain,
o'er all hearts and spirits reign.

4 Lo! Thy presence now is filling
all Thy church in every place;
fill my heart too; make me willing
in this season of Thy grace;
come, Thou King of glory, come,
deign to make my heart Thy home,
there abide and rule alone,
as upon Thy heavenly throne!

Gerhard Tersteegen, 1697-1769;
tr. by Catherine Winkworth, 1827-78

286

Golden harps are sounding,
angel voices sing,
gates of pearl are opened,
opened for the King;
Christ, the King of glory,
Jesus, King of love,
is gone up in triumph
to His throne above.

All His work is ended,
joyfully we sing;
Jesus has ascended!
Glory to our King!

2 He who came to save us,
He who bled and died,
now is crowned with glory
at His Father's side;
never more to suffer,
never more to die,
Jesus, King of glory,
has gone up on high.

3 Praying for His children
in that blessèd place,
calling them to glory,
sending them His grace;
His bright home preparing,
faithful ones, for you;
Jesus ever liveth,
ever loveth too.

Frances Ridley Havergal, 1836-79

287

Rejoice and be glad! the Redeemer has come:
go, look on His cradle, His cross, and His tomb.

Sound His praises, tell the story of
Him who was slain;
Sound His praises, tell with gladness
He now lives again.

2 Rejoice and be glad! it is sunshine at last;
the clouds have departed, the shadows are past.

3 Rejoice and be glad! for the blood has been shed;
redemption is finished, the price has been paid.

4 Rejoice and be glad! now the pardon is free;
the Just for the unjust has died on the tree.

5 Rejoice and be glad! for the Lamb that was slain
o'er death is triumphant, and now lives again.

6 Rejoice and be glad! for our King is on high;
He pleads now for us on His throne in the sky.

7 Rejoice and be glad! He is coming again;
He is coming in glory, the Lamb that was slain.

Horatius Bonar, 1808-89

288

Hail the day that sees Him rise,
Hallelujah!
to His throne above the skies;
Christ, awhile to mortals given,
reascends His native heaven.

2 There the glorious triumph waits;
lift your heads, eternal gates!
Christ has vanquished death and sin;
take the King of glory in!

3 Though high heaven its Lord receives,
still He loves the earth He leaves;
though returning to His throne,
still He calls mankind His own.

4 Now for us He intercedes;
His prevailing death He pleads;
near Himself prepares our place,
first-fruits of the human race.

5 Lord, though parted from our sight,
far above the starry height,
lift our hearts that we might rise,
following You beyond the skies.

*Charles Wesley**, 1707-88

When sung to Ephraim *or* Monkland *omit Hallelujahs after each line.*

289

Look, ye saints! the sight is glorious;
see the Man of sorrows now,
from the fight returned victorious,
every knee to Him shall bow:
Crown Him! Crown Him!
Crowns become the victor's brow.

2 Crown the Saviour! angels, crown Him!
rich the trophies Jesus brings;
in the seat of power enthrone Him,
while the vault of heaven rings:
Crown Him! Crown Him!
Crown the Saviour King of kings!

3 Sinners in derision crowned Him,
mocking thus the Saviour's claim;
saints and angels throng around Him,
own His title, praise His name:
Crown Him! Crown Him!
Spread abroad the victor's fame!

4 Hark, those bursts of acclamation!
Hark, those loud triumphant chords!
Jesus takes the highest station:
O what joy the sight affords!
Crown Him! Crown Him!
King of kings, and Lord of lords!

Thomas Kelly, 1769-1855

290

Our mighty Prince of peace arose,
the victor over all His foes;
ascended now to His repose –
the crown is on His head!

2 Fling open wide the gates of heaven!
Let eager shouts of joy be given,
like surging waves by thunder riven –
the crown is on His head!

3 The glorious triumph now is won.
Seraphs and angels, hail the Son!
His time of suffering now is done –
the crown is on His head!

4 Famous the victory He has gained!
Sinners' salvation He attained,
cleansing with blood those once so stained –
the crown is on His head!

5 Christ is enthroned in heaven on high;
before Him all shall prostrate lie,
raising the glad triumphant cry –
the crown is on His head!

6 Sing praises then, you heavenly host,
to echo to earth's furthest coast;
praise Father, Son and Holy Ghost –
the crown is on His head!

Graham Stuart Harrison, b. 1935

291 Based on Psalm 47

Clap your hands, you people all,
praise the God on whom you call;
lift your voice and shout His praise,
triumph in His sovereign grace!

2 Glorious is the Lord most high,
terrible in majesty;
He His sovereign sway maintains,
king o'er all the earth He reigns.

3 Jesus is gone up on high,
takes His seat above the sky:
shout the angel-choirs aloud,
echoing to the trump of God.

4 Sons of earth, the triumph join:
praise Him with the host divine;
emulate the heavenly powers;
their victorious Lord is ours.

5 Shout the God enthroned above,
trumpet forth His conquering love;
praises to our Jesus sing,
praises to our glorious King!

6 Power is all to Jesus given,
power o'er hell, and earth, and heaven;
power He now to us imparts:
praise Him with believing hearts.

7 Wonderful in saving power,
Him let all our hearts adore;
earth and heaven repeat the cry –
'Glory be to God most high!'

Charles Wesley, 1707-88

292

The head that once was crowned with thorns
is crowned with glory now;
a royal diadem adorns
the mighty victor's brow.

2 The highest place that heaven affords
is His by sovereign right,
the King of kings, and Lord of lords,
and heaven's eternal Light.

3 The joy of all who dwell above,
the joy of all below,
to whom He manifests His love,
and grants His name to know.

4 To them the cross, with all its shame,
with all its grace, is given:
their name an everlasting name,
their joy the joy of heaven.

5 They suffer with their Lord below,
they reign with Him above;
their profit and their joy to know
the mystery of His love.

6 The cross He bore is life and health,
though shame and death to Him;
His people's hope, His people's wealth,
their everlasting theme.

Thomas Kelly, 1769-1855

293

PSALM 24:7-10

Ye gates, lift up your heads on high;
ye doors that last for aye,
be lifted up, that so the King
of glory enter may!
But who of glory is the King?
The mighty Lord is this,
e'en that same Lord that great in might
and strong in battle is.

2 Ye gates, lift up your heads; ye doors,
doors that do last for aye,
be lifted up, that so the King
of glory enter may!
But who is He that is the King
of glory? Who is this?
The Lord of hosts, and none but He,
the King of glory is.

Coda
Hallelujah! Hallelujah!
Hallelujah! Hallelujah! Hallelujah!
Amen, Amen, Amen.

SCOTTISH PSALTER, 1650

Heavenly priesthood

294

A good High Priest is come,
supplying Aaron's place,
and taking up his room,
dispensing life and grace,
the law by Aaron's priesthood came,
but grace and truth by Jesus' name.

2 He once temptations knew,
of every sort and kind,
that He might succour show
to every tempted mind:
in every point the Lamb was tried
like us, and then for us He died.

3 He died; but lives again,
and by the throne He stands,
there shows how He was slain,
opening His piercèd hands:
our Priest abides and pleads the cause
of us who have transgressed His laws.

4 I other priests disclaim,
and laws and offerings too;
none but the bleeding Lamb
the mighty work can do:
He shall have all the praise; for He
has loved, and lived, and died for me.

John Cennick, 1718-55

295

Done is the work that saves,
once and for ever done;
finished the righteousness
that clothes the unrighteous one.
The love that blesses us below
is flowing freely to us now.

2 The sacrifice is made,
the veil is rent in twain,
the mercy-seat is red
with blood of victim slain;
why stand ye then without, in fear?
The blood divine invites us near.

3 The gate is open wide;
the new and living way
is clear and free and bright
with love and peace and day.
Into the holiest now we come,
our present and our endless home.

4 Upon the mercy-seat
the High Priest sits within;
the blood is in His hand
which makes and keeps us clean.
With boldness let us now draw near;
that blood has banished every fear.

5 Then to the Lamb once slain
be glory, praise and power,
who died and lives again,
who liveth evermore,
who loved and washed us in His blood,
who makes us kings and priests to God.

Horatius Bonar, 1808-89

296

Before the throne of God above
I have a strong, a perfect plea,
a great High Priest, whose name is Love,
who ever lives and pleads for me.

2 My name is graven in His hands,
my name is written on His heart;
I know that, while in heaven He stands,
no tongue can bid me thence depart.

3 When Satan tempts me to despair,
and tells me of the guilt within,
upward I look, and see Him there
who made an end of all my sin.

4 Because the sinless Saviour died,
my sinful soul is counted free;
for God the Just is satisfied
to look on Him, and pardon me.

5 Behold Him there! the risen Lamb!
my perfect, spotless righteousness,
the great unchangeable I AM,
the King of glory and of grace!

6 One with Himself, I cannot die,
my soul is purchased by His blood;
my life is hid with Christ on high,
with Christ, my Saviour and my God.

Charitie Lees De Chenez, 1841-1923

When sung to the tune Before the Throne, *this hymn is sung as three eight-line verses with the last line repeated.*

297

How may I, holy God, draw near,
and bow myself before Your face?
How in Your purer eyes appear?
What shall I bring to gain Your grace?

2 What have I now in which to trust?
I nothing have, I nothing am;
excluded is my every boast,
my glory swallowed up in shame.

3 Guilty I stand before Your face,
on me I feel Your wrath abide;
'tis just the sentence should take place;
'tis just – but O Your Son has died!

4 See where before the throne He stands,
and pours the all-prevailing prayer,
points to His side, and lifts His hands,
and shows that I am graven there.

5 He ever lives for me to pray;
He prays that I with Him may reign:
'Amen' to what my Lord will say!
Jesus, You cannot pray in vain.

Charles Wesley, 1707-88

298

The Saviour to glory is gone;
His sufferings and sorrows are past;
His work is completed and done,
and shall to eternity last.
For ever He lives to bestow
the blessings He purchased so dear;
our hearts with true gratitude glow,
whilst to Him, by faith, we draw near.

2 Expecting from Him to receive
all fulness of glory and grace,
rejoicing in hope, we believe,
His promises thankful embrace.
Our King shall protect us from harms,
our Advocate make our plea good;
our Shepherd will bear in His arms
the sheep which He bought with His blood.

3 Our Prophet will point out the way
which leads to the mansions above;
our Priest all our ransom shall pay,
our Friend of unchangeable love.
But whilst to the Lamb on His throne
our hearts and our voices we raise,
His glory exalted we own
above all our blessing and praise.

Thomas Haweis, 1733-1820

299

The veil is rent: see! Jesus stands
before the throne of grace;
and clouds of incense from His hands
fill all that glorious place.

2 His precious blood is sprinkled there,
before and on the throne;
and His own wounds in heaven declare
His work on earth is done.

3 ''Tis finished!' on the cross, He said,
in agonies and blood;
''Tis finished!' now He lives to plead
before the face of God.

4 ''Tis finished!' here our souls can rest,
His work can never fail;
by Him, our sacrifice and priest,
we enter through the veil.

5 Within the holiest of all,
cleansed by His precious blood,
before Your throne Your children fall,
and worship You, our God.

James George Deck, 1802-84

300

Where high the heavenly temple stands,
the house of God not made with hands,
a great High Priest our nature wears,
the Saviour of mankind appears.

2 He who for men their surety stood,
and poured on earth His precious blood,
pursues in heaven His mighty plan,
the Saviour and the friend of man.

3 Though now ascended up on high,
He bends on earth a brother's eye;
partaker of the human name,
He knows the frailty of our frame.

4 Our fellow-sufferer yet retains
a fellow-feeling of our pains,
and still remembers in the skies
His tears, His agonies, and cries.

5 In every pang that rends the heart,
the Man of sorrows had a part;
He sympathizes with our grief,
and to the sufferer sends relief.

6 With boldness, therefore, at the throne
let us make all our sorrows known;
and ask the aid of heavenly power
to help us in the evil hour.

*Michael Bruce**, 1746-67

301

With joy we meditate the grace
of our High Priest above;
His heart is made of tenderness,
and overflows with love.

2 Touched with a sympathy within,
He knows our feeble frame;
He knows what sore temptations mean,
for He has felt the same.

3 But spotless, innocent, and pure,
the great Redeemer stood,
while Satan's fiery darts He bore,
and did resist to blood.

4 He in the days of feeble flesh
poured out His cries and tears;
and, though exalted, feels afresh
what every member bears.

5 He'll never quench the smoking flax,
but raise it to a flame;
the bruisèd reed He never breaks,
nor scorns the lowest name.

6 Then let our humble faith address
His mercy and His power:
we shall obtain delivering grace
in the distressing hour.

Isaac Watts, 1674-1748

302

Jesus is King and I will extol Him,
give Him the glory and honour His
name.
He reigns on high, enthroned in the
heavens,
Word of the Father, exalted for us.

2 We have a hope that is steadfast and
certain,
gone through the curtain and touching
the throne.
We have a Priest who is there
interceding,
pouring His grace on our lives day by
day.

3 We come to Him, our Priest and
Apostle,
clothed in His glory and bearing His
name,
laying our lives with gladness before
Him;
filled with His Spirit we worship the
King:

4 'O Holy One, our hearts do adore You;
thrilled with Your goodness we give You
our praise.'
Angels in light with worship surround
Him,
Jesus, our Saviour, for ever the same.

Wendy Churchill

Reign and power

303

Come, Thou long-expected Jesus,
born to set Thy people free;
from our fears and sins release us,
let us find our rest in Thee.

2 Israel's strength and consolation,
hope of all the earth Thou art;
dear desire of every nation,
joy of every longing heart.

3 Born Thy people to deliver,
born a child, and yet a king;
born to reign in us for ever,
now Thy gracious kingdom bring.

4 By Thine own eternal Spirit
rule in all our hearts alone;
by Thine all-sufficient merit
raise us to Thy glorious throne.

Charles Wesley, 1707-88

304

At the name of Jesus
every knee shall bow,
every tongue confess Him
King of glory now.
'Tis the Father's pleasure
we should call Him Lord,
who from the beginning
was the mighty Word.

2 Humbled for a season,
to receive a name
from the lips of sinners
unto whom He came;
faithfully He bore it
spotless to the last,
brought it back victorious
when from death He passed.

3 Name Him, brothers, name Him,
with love strong as death,
but with awe and wonder,
and with bated breath;
He is God the Saviour,
He is Christ the Lord,
ever to be worshipped,
trusted, and adored.

4 In your hearts enthrone Him;
there let Him subdue
all that is not holy,
all that is not true;
crown Him as your captain
in temptation's hour;
let His will enfold you
in its light and power.

5 Brothers, this Lord Jesus
shall return again
with His Father's glory,
with His angel train;
for all wreaths of empire
meet upon His brow,
and our hearts confess Him
King of glory now.

Caroline Maria Noel, 1817-77

305

Christ triumphant, ever reigning,
Saviour, Master, King,
Lord of heaven, our lives sustaining,
hear us as we sing:

Yours the glory and the crown,
the high renown,
the eternal name.

2 Word incarnate, truth revealing,
Son of Man on earth!
Power and majesty concealing
by Your humble birth:

3 Suffering servant, scorned, ill-treated,
victim crucified!
Death is through the cross defeated,
sinners justified:

4 Priestly king, enthroned for ever
high in heaven above!
Sin and death and hell shall never
stifle hymns of love:

5 So our hearts and voices raising
through the ages long,
ceaselessly upon You gazing,
this shall be our song:

Michael Saward, b. 1932

306

God is gone up on high,
with a triumphant noise;
the clarions of the sky
proclaim the angelic joys!

Join all on earth, rejoice and sing;
glory ascribe to glory's King.

2 God in the flesh below,
for us He reigns above:
let all the nations know
our Jesu's conquering love!

3 All power to our great Lord
is by the Father given;
by angel hosts adored,
He reigns supreme in heaven:

4 High on His holy seat
He bears the righteous sway;
His foes beneath His feet
shall sink and die away:

5 His foes and ours are one,
Satan, the world, and sin;
but He shall tread them down,
and bring His kingdom in:

6 Till all the earth, renewed
in righteousness divine,
with all the hosts of God
in one great chorus join:

Charles Wesley, 1707-88

307

Hark! the song of jubilee,
loud as mighty thunders roar,
or the fulness of the sea,
when it breaks upon the shore.
Hallelujah! for the Lord
God omnipotent shall reign:
Hallelujah! let the word
echo round the earth again.

2 Hallelujah! hark! the sound
from the depths unto the skies,
wakes above, beneath, around,
all creation's harmonies;
see Jehovah's banner furled:
sheathed His sword; He speaks – 'tis done:
and the kingdoms of this world
are the kingdoms of His Son.

3 He shall reign from pole to pole
with illimitable sway:
He shall reign, when, like a scroll,
yonder heavens have passed away;
then the end – beneath His rod
man's last enemy shall fall;
Hallelujah! Christ in God,
God in Christ, is all in all.

James Montgomery, 1771-1854

308

Hear the sound of angels singing –
Jesus Christ is Lord!
Heaven's courts with joy are ringing
Jesus Christ is Lord!
Saints triumphant tell the story,
sinners, saved by grace in glory,
bow in worship and adore Thee –
Jesus Christ is Lord!

2 Down on earth the battle rages,
Jesus Christ is Lord!
as Thy church the foe engages,
Jesus Christ is Lord!
Fearful that our cause must perish,
pain and wounds we cannot relish,
but one certain hope we cherish –
Jesus Christ is Lord!

3 Be the warfare soon completed,
Jesus Christ is Lord!
Soon the enemy defeated,
Jesus be adored!
Then to see Him! Gladdest meeting!
Oh what joy to hear His greeting!
Then for evermore repeating –
Jesus Christ is Lord!

Gordon T Booth, b. 1922

309

Jesus, immortal King, go on;
the glorious day will soon be won;
Thine enemies prepare to flee,
and leave the conquered world to Thee.

2 Gird on Thy sword, victorious Chief!
the captive sinner's sole relief;
cast the usurper from his throne,
and make the universe Thine own.

3 Then shall contending nations rest,
for love shall reign in every breast;
weapons, for war designed, shall cease,
or then be implements of peace.

4 Thy footsteps, Lord, with joy we trace,
and mark the conquests of Thy grace;
finish the work Thou hast begun,
and let Thy will on earth be done.

5 Hark! how the hosts triumphant sing,
'The Lord omnipotent is King!'
Let all the saints rejoice at this,
the kingdoms of the world are His!

Thomas Kelly, 1769-1855

310 Psalm 72

Jesus shall reign where'er the sun
does his successive journeys run;
His kingdom stretch from shore to shore,
till moons shall wax and wane no more.

2 To Him shall endless prayer be made,
and praises throng to crown His head;
His Name, like sweet perfume, shall rise
with every morning sacrifice.

3 People and realms of every tongue
dwell on His love with sweetest song;
and infant voices shall proclaim
their early blessings on His Name.

4 Blessings abound where'er He reigns:
the prisoner leaps to lose his chains;
the weary find eternal rest,
and all the sons of want are blest.

5 Where He displays His healing power,
death and the curse are known no more;
in Him the tribes of Adam boast
more blessings than their father lost.

6 Let every creature rise and bring
their highest honours to our King;
angels descend with songs again,
and earth repeat the loud 'Amen'.

Isaac Watts, 1674-1748

311 Based on Psalm 98

Joy to the world! the Lord is come!
let earth receive her King;
let every heart prepare Him room,
and heaven and nature sing.

2 Joy to the earth! the Saviour reigns!
let men their songs employ;
while fields and floods, rocks, hills and plains,
repeat the sounding joy.

3 No more let sins and sorrows grow,
nor thorns infest the ground;
He comes to make His blessings flow
far as the curse is found.

4 He rules the world with truth and grace,
and makes the nations prove
the glories of His righteousness,
the wonders of His love.

Isaac Watts, 1674-1748

312

Lamb of God, You now are seated
high upon Your Father's throne,
all Your gracious work completed,
all Your mighty victory won;
every knee in heaven is bending
to the Lamb for sinners slain;
every voice and harp is swelling –
worthy is the Lamb to reign!

2 Lord, in all Your power and glory,
still Your thoughts and eyes are here;
watching o'er Your ransomed people,
to Your gracious heart so dear;
You for them are interceding –
everlasting is Your love –
and a blessèd rest preparing
in our Father's house above.

3 Lamb of God, You soon in glory
will to this sad earth return;
all Your foes shall quake before You,
all that now despise You, mourn:
then Your saints shall rise to meet You,
with You in Your kingdom reign;
Yours the praise and Yours the glory,
Lamb of God for sinners slain.

James George Deck, 1802-84

313

Name of all majesty,
fathomless mystery,
King of the ages
by angels adored;
power and authority,
splendour and dignity,
bow to His mastery,
Jesus is Lord!

2 Child of our destiny,
God from eternity,
love of the Father
on sinners outpoured;
see now what God has done,
sending His only Son,
Christ the belovèd One,
Jesus is Lord!

3 Saviour of Calvary,
costliest victory,
darkness defeated
and Eden restored;
born as a man to die,
nailed to a cross on high,
cold in the grave to lie,
Jesus is Lord!

4 Source of all sovereignty,
light, immortality,
life everlasting
and heaven assured;
so with the ransomed, we
praise Him eternally,
Christ in His majesty,
Jesus is Lord!

Timothy Dudley-Smith, b. 1926

314

Rejoice, the Lord is King!
Your Lord and King adore;
mortals, give thanks and sing
and triumph evermore:

Lift up your heart, lift up your voice;
Rejoice, again I say, Rejoice.

2 Jesus the Saviour reigns,
the God of truth and love:
when He had purged our stains,
He took His seat above:

3 His kingdom cannot fail;
He rules o'er earth and heaven;
the keys of death and hell
are to our Jesus given:

4 He sits at God's right hand
till all His foes submit,
and bow to His command,
and fall beneath His feet:

5 Rejoice in glorious hope;
Jesus the Judge shall come,
and take His servants up
to their eternal home:

We soon shall hear the archangel's voice;
the trump of God shall sound, Rejoice!

Charles Wesley, 1707-88

Second coming

315

Day of judgment! day of wonders!
Hark! the trumpet's aweful sound,
louder than a thousand thunders,
shakes the vast creation round:
how the summons
will the sinner's heart confound!

2 See the Judge, our nature wearing,
clothed in majesty divine;
you who long for His appearing
then shall say, 'This God is mine!'
Gracious Saviour,
own me in that day for Thine.

3 At His call the dead awaken,
rise to life from earth and sea;
all the powers of nature, shaken
by His look, prepare to flee;
careless sinner,
what will then become of thee?

4 But to those who have confessèd,
loved and served the Lord below,
He will say, 'Come near, you blessèd,
see the kingdom I bestow;
you for ever
shall my love and glory know.'

John Newton, 1725-1807

316

In hope our hearts rejoice,
the hope of Christ's appearing;
by faith we see His throne,
and know His hour is nearing
when He shall come to reign,
His joy at last complete;
all glory round His head,
all foes beneath His feet.

2 He comes to claim His own
on that long-promised morrow,
to wipe earth's tears away,
and banish sin and sorrow.
Then we shall see His face,
and know as we are known,
set free to serve our God,
and worship Him alone.

3 Now all the good we know
is marred by sin and sadness;
on earth we only sip
God's fount of heavenly gladness.
What then shall be our bliss
in unimagined spheres,
to drink eternal joys
through everlasting years!

4 And so we walk by faith
the path His love ordains us;
we trust His sovereign grace;
His Word of truth sustains us.
'O come, Lord Jesus, come!'
we pray with heart and voice:
till that triumphant hour
in hope our hearts rejoice.

Margaret Clarkson, b. 1915

317

Lead, Lord Jesus, my frail spirit
to that Rock so strong and high,
standing sure midst surging tempest,
safe when pounding waves are nigh:
in the Rock of Ages hiding,
come there flood or fiery blaze,
when the whole creation crumbles,
Rock of Ages, Thee I'll praise.

2 When earth's rocks are cleft asunder
by the terror of that day,
when, as cruel storms beat on them,
strong men cringe in fear away,
that sure Rock will still be standing,
midst the waters, midst the blaze;
there on heaven's eternal ocean,
Rock of Ages, Thee I'll praise.

Samuel Jonathan Griffith, 1850-93;
tr. by Graham Stuart Harrison, b. 1935

318

Lo! He comes with clouds descending,
once for favoured sinners slain;
thousand thousand saints attending
swell the triumph of His train:
Hallelujah!
God appears on earth to reign.

*2 Every eye shall now behold Him
robed in dreadful majesty;
those who set at nought and sold Him,
pierced and nailed Him to the tree,
deeply wailing,
shall the true Messiah see.

*3 Every island, sea, and mountain,
heaven and earth, shall flee away;
all who hate Him must, confounded,
hear the trump proclaim the day;
come to judgment!
come to judgment! come away!

4 Now redemption, long expected,
see in solemn pomp appear!
All His saints, by man rejected,
now shall meet Him in the air:
Hallelujah!
See the day of God appear!

5 Yea, Amen! let all adore Thee,
high on Thine eternal throne!
Saviour, take the power and glory;
claim the kingdom for Thine own:
O come quickly!
Hallelujah! come, Lord, come!

John Cennick, 1718-55,
and Charles Wesley, 1707-88

* *These verses may be omitted.*

319

Now to the Lord that makes us know
the wonders of His dying love,
be humble honours paid below,
and strains of nobler praise above.

2 For He has cleansed our foulest sins,
and washed us in His richest blood;
and He has made us priests and kings,
and brought us rebels near to God.

3 To Jesus, our atoning Priest,
to Jesus, our superior King,
be everlasting power confessed,
and every tongue His glory sing.

4 Behold! on flying clouds He comes,
and all earth's nations then shall see
the glorious face of Him from whom
both heaven and earth away shall
flee.

5 The unbelieving world shall wail,
while we rejoice to see the day;
come, Lord, nor let Your promise fail,
nor let Your chariots long delay!

Isaac Watts, 1674-1748

320

Rejoicing in hope
we wait for our King:
His coming is sure,
His conquest we sing.
His hour of returning
draws daily more near;
with hearts hushed and burning
we see Him appear.

2 He comes with a shout,
and music's glad sound,
the ransomed of earth
encircling Him round.
The dead and the living
shall meet in the air,
in deathless thanksgiving
His glories declare.

3 Redeemed by His blood,
renewed by His grace,
we long to adore
our Lord face to face:
our eyes shall behold Him
in light unsurpassed;
our love shall enfold Him
in worship at last.

4 Our King shall arise,
His purpose complete,
and cast His last foe
far under His feet;
His total creation,
released from sin's pain,
in perfect salvation
shall share in His reign.

5 And so we endure
the wounds of the way,
rejoicing in hope
of Christ's crowning day.
With angels in wonder
His triumph we'll sing,
in praises like thunder
hail Jesus our King!

Margaret Clarkson, b. 1915

4 Bring near Your great salvation,
O Lamb for sinners slain;
fill up the roll of Your elect,
then take Your power and reign;
appear, Desire of nations,
Your exiles long for home;
show in the heavens Your promised sign;
O Prince and Saviour, come.

Henry Alford, 1810-71

321

Ten thousand times ten thousand,
in sparkling raiment bright,
the armies of the ransomed saints
throng up the steeps of light;
'tis finished, all is finished,
their fight with death and sin;
fling open wide the golden gates,
and let the victors in.

2 What rush of hallelujahs
fills all the earth and sky!
What ringing of a thousand harps
proclaims the triumph nigh!
O day for which creation
and all its tribes were made!
O joy, for all its former woes
a thousand-fold repaid!

3 O then what raptured greetings
on Canaan's happy shore,
what knitting severed friendships up
where partings are no more!
Then eyes with joy shall sparkle
that brimmed with tears of late;
orphans no longer fatherless,
nor widows desolate.

322

The King shall come, when morning dawns
and light triumphant breaks;
when beauty gilds the eastern hills
and life to joy awakes.

2 He who was born a little child
to suffer and to die
shall come with glory, like the sun
that lights the morning sky.

3 Far brighter than the rising morn
when He, victorious, rose
and left the lonesome place of death
despite the rage of foes.

4 Far brighter than the glorious morn
shall this fair morning be,
when Christ our King in beauty comes,
and we His face shall see!

5 The King shall come, when morning dawns,
and light and beauty brings.
'Hail, Christ the Lord!' Your people pray,
'Come quickly, King of kings.'

Greek Anonymous;
tr. by John Brownlie, 1857-1925

323

Great Judge of quick and dead,
before whose bar severe,
with holy joy, or guilty dread,
we all shall soon appear;
our cautioned souls prepare
for that tremendous day,
and fill us now with watchful care,
and stir us up to pray –

2 To pray, and wait the hour,
that aweful hour unknown,
when, robed in majesty and power,
You shall from heaven come down,
the immortal Son of Man,
to judge the human race,
with all Your Father's dazzling train,
with all Your glorious grace.

3 O may we thus be found
obedient to His Word,
attentive to the trumpet's sound,
and looking for our Lord!
So help us to ensure
a lot among the blest;
and watch a moment to secure
an everlasting rest!

Charles Wesley, 1707-88

GOD THE HOLY SPIRIT

324

Away with our fears,
our troubles and tears:
the Spirit is come,
the witness of Jesus returned to His home.

2 The pledge of our Lord
to His heaven restored
is sent from the sky,
and tells us our Head is exalted on high.

3 Our Advocate there
by His blood and His prayer
the gift has obtained,
for us He has prayed, and the Comforter gained.

4 Our glorified Head
His Spirit has shed,
with His people to stay,
and never again will He take Him away.

5 Our heavenly guide
with us shall abide,
His comforts impart,
and set up His kingdom of love in the heart.

6 The heart that believes
His kingdom receives,
His power and His peace,
His life, and His joy's everlasting increase.

Charles Wesley, 1707-88

325

Breathe on me, Breath of God;
fill me with life anew,
that I may love what Thou dost love,
and do what Thou wouldst do.

2 Breathe on me, Breath of God,
until my heart is pure,
until with Thee I will one will,
to do and to endure.

3 Breathe on me, Breath of God,
till I am wholly Thine,
until this earthly part of me
glows with Thy fire divine.

4 Breathe on me, Breath of God;
so shall I never die,
but live with Thee the perfect life
of Thine eternity.

Edwin Hatch, 1835-89

326

Come down, O Love divine,
and seek this soul of mine,
and visit it with Your own ardour glowing;
O Comforter, draw near,
within my heart appear,
and kindle it, Your holy flame bestowing.

2 O let it freely burn,
till earthly passions turn
to dust and ashes, in its heat consuming;
and let Your glorious light
shine ever on my sight,
and clothe me round, the while my path illuming.

3 Let holy charity
my outward garment be,
and lowliness become my inner clothing;
true lowliness of heart,
which takes the humbler part,
and o'er its own shortcomings weeps with loathing.

4 And so the yearning strong,
with which the soul will long,
shall far outpass the power of human telling;
for none can guess its grace,
till he become the place
wherein the Holy Spirit makes His dwelling.

Bianco da Siena, c. 1350-1434;
tr. by Richard Frederick Littledale, 1833-90

327

Come, Holy Ghost, all-quickening fire,
come, and in me delight to rest;
drawn by the lure of strong desire,
O come and consecrate my breast;
the temple of my soul prepare,
and fix Thy sacred presence there.

2 Eager for Thee I ask and pant;
so strong, the principle divine
carries me out, with sweet constraint,
till all my hallowed soul is Thine;
plunged in the Godhead's deepest sea,
and lost in Thine immensity.

3 My peace, my life, my comfort Thou,
my treasure and my all Thou art;
true witness of my sonship, now
engraving pardon on my heart,
seal of my sins in Christ forgiven,
earnest of love, and pledge of heaven.

4 Come then, my God, mark out Thine heir,
of heaven a larger earnest give;
with clearer light Thy witness bear,
more feelingly within me live;
let all my powers Thine entrance feel,
and deeper stamp Thyself the seal.

Charles Wesley, 1707-88

328

Come, gracious Spirit, heavenly dove,
with light and comfort from above,
be now our guardian, be our guide,
o'er every thought and step preside.

2 The light of truth to us display,
and make us know and choose Your way;
plant holy fear in every heart,
that we from God may ne'er depart.

3 Lead us to Christ, the living way,
nor let us from His pastures stray;
lead us to holiness, the road
that we must take to dwell with God.

4 Lead us to heaven, that we may share
fulness of joy for ever there;
lead us to God, our final rest,
to be with Him for ever blest.

Simon Browne, 1680-1732

329

Come Holy Spirit, come,
let Thy bright beams arise;
dispel the sorrow from our minds,
the darkness from our eyes.

2 Cheer our desponding hearts,
Thou heavenly Paraclete;
give us to lie with humble hope
at our Redeemer's feet.

3 Revive our drooping faith,
our doubts and fears remove,
and kindle in our breasts the flame
of never-dying love.

4 Convince us of our sin,
then lead to Jesus' blood;
and to our wondering view reveal
the secret love of God.

5 'Tis Thine to cleanse the heart,
to sanctify the soul,
to pour fresh life in every part,
and new create the whole.

6 Dwell, therefore, in our hearts;
our minds from bondage free:
then shall we know, and praise, and love,
the Father, Son, and Thee.

Joseph Hart,* 1712-68

330

Come, Thou everlasting Spirit,
bring to every thankful mind
all the Saviour's dying merit,
all His sufferings for mankind.

2 True recorder of His passion,
now the living faith impart,
now reveal His great salvation,
preach His gospel to our heart.

3 Come, Thou witness of His dying;
come, remembrancer divine!
Let us feel Thy power, applying
Christ to every soul, and mine!

Charles Wesley, 1707-88

331

Come, Holy Ghost, our hearts inspire,
let us Thine influence prove,
source of the old prophetic fire,
fountain of light and love.

2 Come, Holy Ghost, for moved by Thee
the prophets wrote and spoke;
unlock the truth, Thyself the key,
unseal the sacred book.

3 Expand Thy wings, celestial dove,
brood o'er our nature's night;
on our disordered spirits move,
and let there now be light.

4 God, through Himself, we then shall know,
if Thou within us shine,
and sound, with all Thy saints below,
the depths of love divine.

Charles Wesley, 1707-88

332

Come, Holy Spirit, God and Lord!
be all Thy graces now outpoured
on the believer's mind and soul,
to strengthen, save, and make us whole.

2 Thou strong defence, Thou holy light,
teach us to know our God aright,
and call Him Father from the heart
the word of life and truth impart;

3 That we may love no stranger's creed,
nor follow other teacher's lead,
but Jesus for our master own,
and put our trust in Him alone.

4 From every error keep us free;
let none but Christ our master be,
that we in living faith abide,
in Him with all our might confide.

Martin Luther, 1483-1546;
tr. by Catherine Winkworth, 1827-78

333

Come, Holy Spirit, like a dove descending,
rest now upon us while we meet to pray;
show us the Saviour His great love revealing;
lead us to Him, the life, the truth, the way.

2 Come, Holy Spirit, every cloud dispelling;
fill us with gladness through the Master's name:
bring to our memory words that He has spoken;
then shall our tongues His wondrous grace proclaim.

3 Come, Holy Spirit, sent from God the Father,
true friend and teacher, comforter and guide;
our thoughts directing, keep us close to Jesus,
and in our hearts for evermore abide.

Robert Bruce,
in NEW SONGS AND SOLOS, 1888

334

Father of everlasting grace,
Thy goodness and Thy truth we praise,
Thy goodness and Thy truth we prove;
Thou hast, in honour of Thy Son,
the gift unspeakable sent down,
the Spirit of life, and power, and love.

2 Send us the Spirit of Thy Son,
to make the depths of Godhead known,
to make us share the life divine;
send Him the sprinkled blood to apply,
send Him our souls to sanctify,
and show and seal us ever Thine.

3 So shall we pray, and never cease,
so shall we thankfully confess
Thy wisdom, truth, and power, and love;
with joy unspeakable adore,
and bless and praise Thee evermore,
and serve Thee as Thy hosts above:

4 Till, added to that heavenly choir,
we raise our songs of triumph higher,
and praise Thee in a bolder strain,
out-soar the first-born seraph's flight,
and sing, with all our friends in light,
Thy everlasting love to man.

Charles Wesley, 1707-88

335

Gracious Spirit, dove divine,
let Thy light within me shine;
all my guilty fears remove,
fill me full of heaven and love.

2 Speak Thy pardoning grace to me,
set the burdened sinner free;
lead me to the Lamb of God,
wash me in His precious blood.

3 Life and peace to me impart,
seal salvation on my heart;
breathe Thyself into my breast,
earnest of immortal rest.

4 Let me never from Thee stray,
keep me in the narrow way;
fill my soul with joy divine,
keep me, Lord, for ever Thine.

John Stocker, 1777

336

Holy Ghost, dispel our sadness,
pierce the clouds of sinful night:
come, true source of sweetest gladness,
breathe Your life, and spread Your light.

2 From the height which knows no measure,
as a gracious shower descend;
bringing down the richest treasure
man can wish or God can send.

3 Author of the new creation,
come, with unction and with power;
make our hearts Your habitation,
on our souls Your graces shower.

4 Come, O best of all donations
God can give, or we implore;
having Your sweet consolations
we need wish for nothing more.

Paul Gerhardt, 1607-76;
tr. by John Christian Jacobi, 1670-1750;
altd by Augustus Montague Toplady, 1740-78

337

Lord God the Holy Ghost,
in this accepted hour,
as on the day of Pentecost,
descend in all Your power.

2 We meet with one accord
in our appointed place,
and wait the promise of our Lord,
the Spirit of all grace.

3 Like mighty rushing wind
upon the waves beneath,
move with one impulse every mind,
one soul, one feeling breathe.

4 The young, the old, inspire
with wisdom from above;
and give us hearts and tongues of fire,
to pray and praise and love.

5 Spirit of light, explore,
and chase our gloom away,
with lustre shining more and more,
unto the perfect day.

James Montgomery, 1771-1854

338

For Your gift of God the Spirit,
power to make our lives anew,
pledge of life and hope of glory,
Saviour, we would worship You.
Crowning gift of resurrection
sent from Your ascended throne,
fullness of the very Godhead,
come to make Your life our own.

2 He who in creation's dawning
brooded on the lifeless deep,
still across our nature's darkness
moves to wake our souls from sleep,
moves to stir, to draw, to quicken,
thrusts us through with sense of sin;
brings to birth and seals and fills us –
saving Advocate within.

3 He, Himself the living Author,
wakes to life the sacred Word,
reads with us its holy pages
and reveals our risen Lord.
He it is who works within us,
teaching rebel hearts to pray;
He whose holy intercessions
rise for us both night and day.

4 He, the mighty God, indwells us;
His to strengthen, help, empower;
His to overcome the tempter,
ours to call in danger's hour.
In His strength we dare to battle
all the raging hosts of sin,
and by Him alone we conquer
foes without and foes within.

Margaret Clarkson, b. 1915

339

O Spirit of the living God,
in all Thy plenitude of grace,
where'er the foot of man has trod,
descend on our apostate race.

2 Give tongues of fire and hearts of love
to preach the reconciling word;
give power and unction from above,
whene'er the joyful sound is heard.

3 Be darkness, at Thy coming, light;
confusion, order in Thy path;
souls without strength inspire with might
bid mercy triumph over wrath.

4 O Spirit of the Lord, prepare
all the round earth her God to meet;
breathe Thou abroad like morning air,
till hearts of stone begin to beat.

5 Baptize the nations; far and nigh
the triumphs of the cross record;
the name of Jesus glorify
till every kindred call Him Lord.

6 God from eternity has willed
all flesh shall His salvation see;
so be the Father's love fulfilled,
the Saviour's sufferings crowned
through Thee.

James Montgomery, 1771-1854

340

O Breath of God, breathe on us now,
and move within us while we pray;
the spring of our new life art Thou,
the very light of our new day.

2 O strangely art Thou with us Lord,
neither in height nor depth to seek:
in nearness shall Thy voice be heard;
Spirit to spirit Thou dost speak.

3 Christ is our advocate on high;
Thou art our advocate within:
O plead the truth, and make reply
to every argument of sin.

4 But ah, this faithless heart of mine!
the way I know; I know my guide:
forgive me, O my Friend divine,
that I so often turn aside.

5 Be with me when no other friend
the mystery of my heart can share;
and be Thou known, when fears
transcend,
by Thy best name of Comforter.

Alfred Henry Vine, 1845-1917

341

O Holy Spirit, come,
and Jesus' love declare:
O tell us of our heavenly home,
and guide us safely there.

2 Our unbelief remove
by Your almighty breath:
O work the wondrous work of love,
the mighty work of faith.

3 Come with resistless power,
come with almighty grace,
come with the long-expected shower,
and fall upon this place.

Oswald Allen, 1816-78

342

Spirit of God, descend upon my heart;
wean it from earth; through all its
pulses move;
stoop to my weakness, mighty as Thou
art,
and make me love Thee as I ought to
love.

2 Hast Thou not bid me love Thee, God and King –
all, all Thine own, soul, heart and strength and mind?
I see Thy cross – there teach my heart to cling:
O let me seek Thee, and O let me find!

3 Teach me to feel that Thou art always nigh;
teach me the struggles of the soul to bear,
to check the rising doubt, the rebel sigh;
teach me the patience of unanswered prayer.

4 Teach me to love Thee as Thine angels love,
one holy passion filling all my frame –
the baptism of the heaven-descended Dove,
my heart an altar, and Thy love the flame.

George Croly, 1780-1860

343

Our blest Redeemer, ere He breathed
His tender last farewell,
a Guide, a Comforter, bequeathed
with us to dwell.

2 He came in semblance of a dove,
with sheltering wings outspread,
the holy balm of peace and love
on earth to shed.

3 He came in tongues of living flame,
to teach, convince, subdue;
all-powerful as the wind He came,
as viewless too.

4 He came sweet influence to impart,
a gracious willing guest,
while He can find one humble heart
wherein to rest.

5 And His that gentle voice we hear,
soft as the breath of even,
that checks each fault, that calms each fear,
and speaks of heaven.

6 And every virtue we possess,
and every conquest won,
and every thought of holiness,
are His alone.

7 Spirit of purity and grace,
our weakness, pitying, see:
O make our hearts Thy dwelling-place,
and worthier Thee.

Henriette Auber, 1773-1862

344

Spirit divine, attend our prayers,
and make our hearts Your home;
descend with all Your gracious powers,
O come, great Spirit, come!

2 Come as the light, to us reveal
our emptiness and woe;
and lead us in those paths of life
where all the righteous go.

3 Come as the fire, and purge our hearts
like sacrificial flame;
let our whole soul an offering be
to our Redeemer's name.

4 Come as the dew, and sweetly bless
this consecrated hour;
may barrenness rejoice to own
Your fertilizing power.

5 Come as the dove, and spread Your wings,
the wings of peaceful love;
and let Your church on earth become
blest as the church above.

6 Come as the wind, with rushing sound
and Pentecostal grace;
that all of woman born may see
the glory of Your face.

7 Spirit divine, attend our prayers;
make a lost world Your home;
descend with all Your gracious powers,
O come, great Spirit, come!

Andrew Reed, 1787-1862

345

Spirit of faith, come down,
reveal the things of God;
and make to us the Godhead known,
and witness with the blood.
'Tis Yours the blood to apply,
and give us eyes to see
who did for guilty sinners die
has surely died for me.

2 No man can truly say
that Jesus is the Lord,
unless You take the veil away,
and breathe the living word;
then, only then, we feel
our interest in His blood,
and cry, with joy unspeakable:
You are my Lord, my God!

3 O that the world might know
the all-atoning Lamb!
Spirit of faith, descend, and show
the virtue of His name;
the grace which all may find,
the saving power impart;
and testify to all mankind,
and speak in every heart.

4 Inspire the living faith,
which whosoe'er receives,
the witness in himself he has,
and consciously believes;
the faith that conquers all,
and does the mountain move,
and saves whoe'er on Jesus call
and perfects them in love.

Charles Wesley, 1707-88

346

Why should the children of a King
go mourning all their days?
Great Comforter, descend, and bring
some tokens of Your grace.

2 Do You not dwell in all Your saints,
and seal the heirs of heaven?
When will You banish my complaints,
and show my sins forgiven?

3 Assure my conscience of its part
in the Redeemer's blood,
and bear Your witness with my heart
that I am born of God.

4 You are the earnest of His love,
the pledge of joys to come,
and Your soft wings, celestial Dove,
will safe convey me home.

Isaac Watts, 1674 -1748

THE HOLY SCRIPTURES

347

Almighty God, Your word is cast
like seed into the ground;
now let the dew of heaven descend,
and righteous fruits abound.

2 Let not the foe of Christ and man
this holy seed remove,
but give it root in every heart
to bring forth fruits of love.

3 Let not the world's deceitful cares
the rising plant destroy,
but let it yield a hundredfold
the fruits of peace and joy..

4 Oft as the precious seed is sown,
Your quickening grace bestow,
that all whose souls the truth receive
its saving power may know.

John Cawood, 1775-1852

348

Father of mercies, in Your Word
what endless glory shines!
For ever be Your Name adored
for these celestial lines.

2 Here may the blind and hungry come,
and light and food receive;
here shall the lowliest guest have room,
and taste and see and live.

3 Here springs of consolation rise
to cheer the fainting mind,
and thirsting souls receive supplies,
and sweet refreshment find.

4 Here the Redeemer's welcome voice
spreads heavenly peace around;
and life and everlasting joys
attend the blissful sound.

5 O may these heavenly pages be
my ever dear delight;
and still new beauties may I see,
and still increasing light!

6 Divine Instructor, gracious Lord,
O be for ever near;
teach me to love Your sacred Word,
and view my Saviour there.

Anne Steele, 1717-78

349

PSALM 19

God's law is perfect, and converts
the soul in sin that lies;
God's testimony is most sure,
and makes the simple wise.

2 The statutes of the Lord are right,
and do rejoice the heart;
the Lord's command is pure, and doth
light to the eyes impart.

3 Unspotted is the fear of God,
and doth endure for ever;
the judgments of the Lord are true
and righteous altogether.

4 Moreover, they Thy servant warn
how he his life should frame;
a great reward provided is
for them that keep the same.

5 The words which from my mouth
proceed,
the thoughts sent from my heart,
accept, O Lord, for Thou my strength
and my Redeemer art.

SCOTTISH PSALTER, 1615

350

Blessèd Jesus, at Your word
we are gathered all to hear You;
let our minds and wills be stirred
now to seek and love and fear You;
by Your teachings true and holy,
drawn from earth to love You solely.

2 All our knowledge, sense and sight,
lie in deepest darkness shrouded,
till Your Spirit breaks our night
with the beams of truth unclouded;
You alone to God can win us;
You must work all good within us.

3 Glorious Lord, Yourself impart,
Light of Light, from God proceeding,
open now our mind and heart,
help us by Your Spirit's pleading.
Hear the cry Your church now raises;
Lord, accept our prayers and praises.

Tobias Clausnitzer, 1619-84;
tr. by Catherine Winkworth, 1827-78

351

Break Thou the Bread of Life,
dear Lord, to me,
as Thou didst break the bread
beside the sea.
Beyond the sacred page
I seek Thee, Lord;
my spirit longs for Thee,
O living Word!

2 Thou art the Bread of Life,
O Lord, to me,
Thy holy Word the truth
that saveth me.
Give me to eat and live
with Thee above;
teach me to love Thy truth,
for Thou art love.

3 O send Thy Spirit, Lord,
now unto me,
that He may touch my eyes,
and make me see.
Show me the truth concealed
within Thy Word,
that in Thy book revealed
I see Thee, Lord.

4 Bless Thou the Bread of Life
to me, to me,
as Thou didst bless the loaves
by Galilee;
then shall all bondage cease,
all fetters fall;
and I shall find my peace,
my all in all.

Mary Artemisia Lathbury, 1841-1913;
v. 2, Alexander Groves, 1842-1909

352

God has spoken by His prophets,
spoken His unchanging Word;
each from age to age proclaiming
God the One, the righteous Lord!
Mid the world's despair and turmoil
one firm anchor holding fast,
God is on His throne eternal,
He alone the first and last.

2 God has spoken by Christ Jesus,
Christ, the everlasting Son,
brightness of the Father's glory,
with the Father ever one;
spoken by the Word incarnate,
God of God ere time began,
Light of Light, to earth descending,
Man, revealing God to man.

3 God is speaking by His Spirit
speaking to the hearts of men,
in the age-long Word declaring
God's own message, now as then.
Through the rise and fall of nations
one sure faith is standing fast:
God abides, His Word unchanging,
God alone the first and last.

George Wallace Briggs, 1875-1959

353

How sure the Scriptures are!
God's vital, urgent Word,
as true as steel, and far
more sharp than any sword:
so deep and fine,
at His control
they pierce where soul
and spirit join.

2 They test each human thought,
refining like a fire;
they measure what we ought
to do and to desire:
for God knows all –
exposed it lies
before His eyes
to whom we call.

3 Let those who hear His voice
confronting them today,
reject the tempting choice
of doubting or delay:
for God speaks still –
His word is clear,
so let us hear
and do His will!

Christopher Idle, b. 1938

354

How precious is the book divine,
by inspiration given!
Bright as a lamp its doctrines shine,
to guide our souls to heaven.

2 Its light, descending from above,
our gloomy world to cheer,
displays a Saviour's boundless love,
and brings His glories near.

3 It shows to man his wandering ways,
and where his feet have trod;
and brings to view the matchless grace
of a forgiving God.

4 When once it penetrates the mind
it conquers every sin;
the enlightened soul begins to find
the path of peace divine.

5 It sweetly cheers our heavy hearts,
in this dark vale of tears;
life, light, and joy it still imparts,
and quells our rising fears.

6 This lamp through all the tedious night
of life shall guide our way,
till we behold the clearer light
of an eternal day.

John Fawcett, 1740-1817

355

Lamp of our feet, whereby we trace
our path when apt to stray;
stream from the fount of heavenly grace,
brook by the traveller's way;

2 Bread of our souls, whereon we feed;
true manna from on high;
our guide and chart, wherein we read
of realms beyond the sky;

3 Pillar of fire, through watches dark,
and radiant cloud by day;
when waves would whelm our tossing bark,
our anchor and our stay;

4 Word of the ever-living God,
will of His glorious Son –
without thee how could earth be trod,
or heaven itself be won?

5 Lord, grant us all aright to learn
the wisdom it imparts,
and to its heavenly teaching turn
with simple, childlike hearts.

*Bernard Barton**, 1784-1849

356

Lord, Thy Word abideth,
and our footsteps guideth;
who its truth believeth
light and joy receiveth.

2 When our foes are near us,
then Thy Word doth cheer us,
word of consolation,
message of salvation.

3 When the storms are o'er us,
and dark clouds before us,
then its light directeth,
and our way protecteth.

4 Who can tell the pleasure,
who recount the treasure,
by Thy Word imparted,
to the simple-hearted?

5 Word of mercy, giving
succour to the living;
Word of life, supplying
comfort to the dying!

6 O that we, discerning
its most holy learning,
Lord, may love and fear Thee,
evermore be near Thee!

Henry Williams Baker, 1821-77

357

O Word of God incarnate,
O wisdom from on high,
O truth unchanged, unchanging,
O light of our dark sky,
we praise Thee for the radiance
that from the hallowed page,
a lantern to our footsteps,
shines on from age to age.

2 The church from her dear Master
received the gift divine,
and still that light she lifteth,
o'er all the earth to shine.
It is the golden casket
where gems of truth are stored;
it is the heaven-drawn picture
of Christ, the living Word.

3 It floateth like a banner
before God's host unfurled;
it shineth like a beacon
above the darkened world;
it is the chart and compass
that, o'er life's surging sea,
'mid mists and rocks and quicksands
still guides, O Christ, to Thee.

4 O make Thy church, dear Saviour,
a lamp of burnished gold,
to bear before the nations
Thy true light, as of old.
O teach Thy wandering pilgrims
by this their path to trace,
till, clouds and darkness ended,
they see Thee face to face.

William Walsham How, 1823-97

358

Speak, Lord, in the stillness,
speak Your Word to me;
help me now to listen
in expectancy.

2 Speak, O gracious Master,
in this quiet hour;
let me see Your face, Lord,
feel Your touch of power.

3 For the words You give me,
they are life indeed;
living bread from heaven,
now my spirit feed.

4 Speak, Your servant listens –
I await Your Word;
let me know Your presence,
let Your voice be heard!

5 Fill me with the knowledge
of Your glorious will;
all Your own good pleasure
in my life fulfil.

Emily May Crawford, 1864-1927

359 PSALM 19

The heavens declare Thy glory, Lord,
in every star Thy wisdom shines;
but when our eyes behold Thy Word,
we read Thy Name in fairer lines.

2 The rolling sun, the changing light,
and night and day, Thy power confess;
but the blest volume Thou hast writ
reveals Thy justice and Thy grace.

3 Sun, moon and stars convey Thy praise
round the whole earth, and never stand:
so when Thy truth began its race,
it touched and glanced on every land.

4 Nor shall Thy spreading gospel rest
till through the world Thy truth has run;
till Christ has all the nations blest,
that see the light, or feel the sun.

5 Great Sun of righteousness, arise,
bless the dark world with heavenly light:
Thy gospel makes the simple wise;
Thy laws are pure, Thy judgments right.

6 Thy noblest wonders here we view,
in souls renewed, and sins forgiven:
Lord cleanse my sins, my soul renew,
and make Thy Word my guide to heaven.

Isaac Watts, 1674-1748

360 PSALM 19:7-10

The law of the Lord is perfect,
converting the soul;
the testimony of the Lord is sure,
making wise the simple.

More to be desired are they than gold,
yea than much fine gold,
sweeter also than honey and the honeycomb.

2 The statutes of the Lord are right,
rejoicing the heart;
the commandment of the Lord is pure,
enlightening the eyes.

3 The fear of the Lord is clean,
enduring for ever;
the judgements of the Lord are true
and righteous altogether.

Author unknown

361

The Spirit breathes upon the Word,
and brings the truth to sight;
precepts and promises afford
a sanctifying light.

2 A glory gilds the sacred page,
majestic, like the sun;
it gives a light to every age;
it gives, but borrows none.

3 The hand that gave it still supplies
the gracious light and heat;
its truths upon the nations rise;
they rise, but never set.

4 Let everlasting thanks be Thine,
for such a bright display,
as makes a world of darkness shine
with beams of heavenly day.

5 My soul rejoices to pursue
the steps of Him I love,
till glory breaks upon my view,
in brighter worlds above.

William Cowper, 1731-1800

362

Based on REVELATION 22:17-20

Words of eternal life to me,
O may my faith receive the whole!
Your holy precepts, let them be
hid in the secret of my soul.

2 Though heaven and earth shall pass away,
these words of prophecy are sure,
unchangeable amidst decay
and pure as God Himself is pure.

3 If any add a single word
or with one sacred word dispense,
no part to him will God afford,
His arm shall be His truth's defence.

4 Firm in the truth that we abide
till Christ our Lord appear again:
'Come', say the Spirit and the Bride,
'Lord Jesus, quickly come and reign.'

*James Montgomery**, 1771-1854

THE CHRISTIAN CHURCH

Character and privileges

363 Based on Psalm 66:8

All thanks to the Lamb, who calls us to meet!
His love we proclaim, His praises repeat;
we own Him our Jesus, continually near
to pardon and bless us, and perfect us here.

2 In Him we have peace, in Him we have power,
preserved by His grace throughout the dark hour.
In all our temptation He keeps us to prove
His utmost salvation, His fulness of love.

3 Through pride and desire unhurt we have gone,
through water and fire in Him we went on;
the world and the devil through Him we o'ercame,
our Saviour from evil, for ever the same.

4 O what shall we do our Saviour to love?
To make us anew, come, Lord, from above!
The fruit of Your passion, Your holiness give,
give us the salvation of all that believe.

5 Come, Jesus, and loose the hesitant tongue,
and teach even us the spiritual song;
let us without ceasing give thanks for Your grace,
and glory, and blessing, and honour and praise.

Charles Wesley, 1707-88

364 1 John 3:1-4

Behold the amazing gift of love
the Father has bestowed
on us, the sinful sons of men,
to call us sons of God.

2 Concealed as yet this honour lies,
by this dark world unknown,
a world that knew not, when He came,
even God's eternal Son.

3 High is the rank we now possess,
but higher we shall rise;
though what we shall hereafter be
is hid from mortal eyes.

4 Our souls, we know, when He appears,
shall bear His image bright;
for all His glory, full disclosed,
shall open to our sight.

5 A hope so great and so divine
may trials well endure,
and purge the soul from sense and sin,
as Christ Himself is pure.

Scottish Paraphrases, 1781

365 Psalm 1

Happy the people who refuse
to walk the way the wicked choose,
who will not stand where sinners meet,
nor with the scornful take their seat:
the Word of God is their delight,
their meditation day and night.

2 Trees set along the waterside
shall yield their fruit at harvest-tide;
though parched the landscape, bare the sky,
their leaves will never fade or die:
so prosper those who daily draw
upon the Lord's eternal law.

3 Not so the wicked! What are they
but winnowed chaff that blows away?
When judgement comes, they shall not stand
among the just at God's right hand:
the Lord protects his people's path,
but godless ways must end in wrath.

David G Preston, b. 1949

366

Glorious things of thee are spoken,
Zion, city of our God!
He whose word cannot be broken,
formed thee for His own abode.
On the Rock of Ages founded,
what can shake thy sure repose?
With salvation's walls surrounded,
thou may'st smile at all thy foes.

2 See! the streams of living waters,
springing from eternal love,
well supply thy sons and daughters,
and all fear of want remove:
who can faint while such a river
ever flows their thirst to assuage –
grace which, like the Lord the giver,
never fails from age to age?

3 Round each habitation hovering,
see! the cloud and fire appear,
for a glory and a covering,
showing that the Lord is near:
blest inhabitants of Zion,
washed in the Redeemer's blood –
Jesus, whom their souls rely on,
makes them kings and priests to God.

4 Saviour, if of Zion's city
I through grace a member am,
let the world deride or pity,
I will glory in Thy name:
fading is the worldling's pleasure,
all his boasted pomp and show;
solid joys and lasting treasure
none but Zion's children know.

John Newton, 1725-1807

367 PSALM 84

How lovely are Thy dwellings fair!
O Lord of hosts, how dear
the pleasant tabernacles are,
where Thou dost dwell so near!

2 My soul doth long and almost die
Thy courts O Lord, to see;
my heart and flesh aloud do cry,
O living God, for Thee.

3 Happy who in Thy house reside,
where Thee they ever praise!
Happy whose strength in Thee doth bide,
and in their hearts Thy ways!

4 They journey on from strength to strength
with joy and gladsome cheer,
till all before our God at length
in Zion do appear.

5 For God, the Lord, both sun and shield,
gives grace and glory bright;
no good from them shall be withheld
whose ways are just and right.

6 Lord God of hosts who reigns on high,
that man is truly blest
who only on Thee doth rely,
and in Thee only rest.

John Milton, 1608-74

368

PSALM 122

How pleased and blest was I
to hear the people cry,
'Come, let us seek our God today!'
Yes, with a cheerful zeal
we haste to Zion's hill,
and there our vows and honours pay.

2 Zion, thrice happy place,
adorned with wondrous grace,
and walls of strength embrace you round;
in you our tribes appear,
to pray, and praise, and hear
the sacred gospel's joyful sound.

3 There David's greater Son
has fixed His royal throne,
He sits for grace and judgment there;
He bids the saint be glad,
He makes the sinner sad,
and humble souls rejoice with fear.

4 May peace attend your gate,
and joy within you wait,
to bless the soul of every guest!
The man that seeks your peace,
and wishes your increase,
a thousand blessings on him rest!

5 My tongue repeats her vows,
peace to this sacred house!
For there my friends and kindred dwell;
and, since my glorious God
makes you His blest abode,
my soul shall ever love you well!

Isaac Watts, 1674-1748

369

PSALM 84

Lord of the worlds above,
how pleasant and how fair
the dwellings of Thy love,
Thine earthly temples, are!
To Thine abode
my heart aspires,
with warm desires
to see my God.

2 O happy souls that pray
where God delights to hear!
O happy men that pay
their constant service there!
They praise Thee still,
and happy they
who love the way
to Zion's hill!

3 They go from strength to strength,
through this dark vale of tears,
till each arrives at length,
till each in heaven appears:
O glorious seat!
Thou, God our King,
shalt thither bring
our willing feet!

4 To spend one sacred day
where God and saints abide,
affords diviner joy
than thousand days beside;
where God resorts,
I love it more
to keep the door
than shine in courts.

5 God is our sun and shield,
our light and our defence;
with gifts His hands are filled,
we draw our blessings thence:
He shall bestow
on Jacob's race
His special grace
and glory too.

6 The Lord His people loves;
His hand no good withholds
from those His heart approves,
from holy, humble souls:
thrice happy he
O God of hosts,
whose spirit trusts
alone in Thee!
Isaac Watts, 1674-1748

370

The church's one foundation
is Jesus Christ her Lord;
she is His new creation
by water and the Word;
from heaven He came and sought her
to be His holy bride;
with His own blood He bought her,
and for her life He died.

2 Elect from every nation,
yet one o'er all the earth;
her charter of salvation –
one Lord, one faith, one birth;
one holy Name she blesses,
partakes one holy food;
and to one hope she presses,
with every grace endued.

3 Though with a scornful wonder
men see her sore oppressed,
by schisms rent asunder,
by heresies distressed,
yet saints their watch are keeping,
their cry goes up, 'How long?'
And soon the night of weeping
shall be the morn of song.

4 'Mid toil and tribulation,
and tumult of her war,
she waits the consummation
of peace for evermore;
till with the vision glorious
her longing eyes are blest,
and the great church victorious
shall be the church at rest.

5 Yet she on earth has union
with those whose rest is won,
and mystic sweet communion
with God the Three in One.
O happy ones and holy!
Lord, give us grace that we,
like them, the meek and lowly,
on high may dwell with Thee!
Samuel John Stone, 1839-1900

371

We love the place, O God,
wherein Your honour dwells;
the joy of Your abode
all earthly joy excels.

2 It is the house of prayer,
in which Your servants meet;
and You, O Lord, are there,
Your chosen flock to greet.

3 We love the Word of life,
the Word that tells of peace,
of comfort in the strife
and joys that never cease.

4 We love to sing below
for mercies freely given;
but O we long to know
the triumph song of heaven!

5 Lord Jesus, give us grace,
on earth to love You more,
in heaven to see Your face,
and with Your saints adore.
William Bullock, 1798-1874
and Henry Williams Baker, 1821-77

Fellowship and love

372 John 13:34-35

A new commandment I give unto you,
that you love one another as I have loved you,
that you love one another as I have loved you.

2 By this shall all men know that you are My disciples,
if you have love one for another.
By this shall all men know that you are My disciples,
if you have love one for another.

373

All praise to our redeeming Lord,
who joins us by His grace,
and bids us, each to each restored,
together seek His face.

2 He bids us build each other up;
and, gathered into one,
to our high calling's glorious hope
we hand in hand go on.

3 The gift which He on one bestows,
we all delight to prove;
the grace through every vessel flows,
in purest streams of love.

4 Even now we think and speak the same,
and cordially agree;
united all, through Jesu's name,
in perfect harmony.

5 We all partake the joy of one,
the common peace we feel,
a peace to earthly minds unknown,
a joy unspeakable.

6 And if our fellowship below
in Jesus be so sweet,
what heights of rapture shall we know
when round His throne we meet!

Charles Wesley, 1707-88

374

God be with you till we meet again,
by His counsels guide, uphold you,
with His sheep securely fold you:
God be with you till we meet again.

Till we meet, till we meet,
till we meet at Jesus' feet,
till we meet, till we meet,
God be with you till we meet again.

2 God be with you till we meet again,
'neath His wings protecting hide you,
daily manna still provide you:
God be with you till we meet again.

3 God be with you till we meet again,
when life's perils thick confound you,
put His arms unfailing round you:
God be with you till we meet again.

4 God be with you till we meet again,
keep love's banner floating o'er you,
smite death's threatening wave before you:
God be with you till we meet again!

Jeremiah Eames Rankin, 1828-1904

375

And are we yet alive,
and see each other's face?
Glory and praise to Jesus give
for His redeeming grace!

2 Preserved by power divine
to full salvation here,
again in Jesu's praise we join,
and in His sight appear.

3 What troubles have we seen,
what conflicts have we passed,
fightings without, and fears within,
since we assembled last!

4 But out of all the Lord
has brought us by His love;
and still He does His help afford,
and hides our life above.

5 Then let us make our boast
of His redeeming power,
which saves us to the uttermost,
till we can sin no more:

6 Let us take up the cross,
till we the crown obtain;
and gladly reckon all things loss,
so we may Jesus gain.

Charles Wesley, 1707-88

376

Blest be the tie that binds
our hearts in Christian love;
the fellowship of kindred minds
is like to that above.

2 Before our Father's throne
we pour our ardent prayers;
our fears, our hopes, our aims are one,
our comforts and our cares.

3 We share our mutual woes,
our mutual burdens bear;
and often for each other flows
the sympathizing tear.

4 When for awhile we part,
this thought will soothe our pain,
that we shall still be joined in heart,
and hope to meet again.

5 This glorious hope revives
our courage by the way,
while each in expectation lives,
and longs to see the day.

6 From sorrow, toil, and pain,
and sin we shall be free;
and perfect love and friendship reign
through all eternity.

John Fawcett, 1740-1817

377

I love Your kingdom, Lord,
the house of Your abode,
the church our blest Redeemer saved
with His own precious blood.

2 I love Your church, O God:
her walls before You stand,
dear as the apple of Your eye,
and graven on Your hand.

3 For her my tears shall fall,
for her my prayers ascend;
to her my cares and toils be given,
till toils and cares shall end.

4 Beyond my highest joy
I prize her heavenly ways,
her sweet communion, solemn vows,
her hymns of love and praise.

5 Jesus our Friend divine,
our Saviour and our King,
Your hand from every snare and foe
shall great deliverance bring.

6 Sure as Your truth shall last,
to Zion shall be given
the brightest glories earth can yield,
and brighter bliss of heaven.
Timothy Dwight, 1752-1817

378

'Forgive our sins as we forgive',
You taught us, Lord, to pray;
but You alone can grant us grace
to live the words we say.

2 How can Your pardon reach and bless
the unforgiving heart
that broods on wrongs and will not let
old bitterness depart?

3 In blazing light Your cross reveals
the truth we dimly know;
what trivial debts are owed to us,
how great our debt to You!

4 Lord, cleanse the depths within our souls
and bid resentment cease;
then, bound to all in bonds of love,
our lives will spread Your peace.
Rosamund Herklots, 1905-87
By permission of Oxford University Press

379

1 Corinthians 13

Gracious Spirit, Holy Ghost,
taught by You, we covet most,
of Your gifts at Pentecost,
holy, heavenly love.

2 Faith that mountains could remove,
tongues of earth or heaven above,
knowledge, all things, empty prove
without heavenly love.

3 Though I as a martyr bleed,
give my goods the poor to feed,
all is vain if love I need;
therefore give me love.

4 Love is kind and suffers long,
love is meek, and thinks no wrong,
love than death itself more strong;
therefore give us love.

5 Prophecy will fade away,
melting in the light of day;
love will ever with us stay;
therefore give us love.

6 Faith, and hope, and love we see,
joining hand in hand, agree;
but the greatest of the three,
and the best, is love.
Christopher Wordsworth, 1807-85

380

Psalm 133

How beautiful the sight
of brethren who agree
in friendship to unite,
and bonds of charity!
'Tis like the precious ointment shed
o'er all his robes from Aaron's head.

2 'Tis like the dews that fill
the cups of Hermon's flowers;
or Zion's fruitful hill,
bright with the drops of showers,
when mingling odours breathe around,
and glory rests on all the ground.

3 For there the Lord commands
blessings, a boundless store,
from His unsparing hands,
yea, life for evermore:
thrice happy they who meet above
to spend eternity in love!
James Montgomery, 1771-1854

381

Based on Psalm 133

How good a thing it is,
how pleasant to behold,
when all God's people live at one,
the law of love uphold!

2 As perfume, by its scent,
breathes fragrance all around,
so life itself will sweeter be
where unity is found.

3 And like refreshing dew
that falls upon the hills,
true union sheds its gentle grace,
and deeper love instils.

4 God grants the choicest gifts
to those who live in peace;
to them His blessings shall abound
and evermore increase.

James Edward Seddon, 1915-83

382

In Thy Name, O Lord, assembling,
we, Thy people, now draw near;
teach us to rejoice with trembling;
speak, and let Thy servants hear;
hear with meekness,
hear Thy Word with godly fear.

2 Grant us, Lord, some gracious token
of Thy love before we part;
crown Thy Word which will be spoken,
life and peace to each impart,
and all blessings
which will sanctify the heart.

3 While our days on earth are lengthened,
may we give them, Lord, to Thee;
cheered by hope, and daily strengthened,
may we run, nor weary be,
till Thy glory
without cloud in heaven we see.

4 There, in worship purer, sweeter,
Thee Thy people shall adore,
tasting of enjoyment greater
far than thought conceived before:
full enjoyment,
full, unmixed and evermore.

Thomas Kelly, 1769-1855

383

Jesus, Lord, we look to Thee,
let us in Thy Name agree;
show Thyself the Prince of peace;
bid all strife for ever cease.

2 By Thy reconciling love
every stumbling-block remove;
each to each unite, endear,
come, and spread Thy banner here.

3 Make us of one heart and mind,
courteous, pitiful, and kind,
lowly, meek, in thought and word,
altogether like our Lord.

4 Let us for each other care,
each the other's burden bear,
to Thy church the pattern give,
show how true believers live.

5 Free from anger and from pride,
let us thus in God abide;
all the depths of love express,
all the heights of holiness.

6 Let us then with joy remove
to the family above;
on the wings of angels fly,
show how true believers die.
Charles Wesley, 1707-88

384

Lord from whom all blessings flow,
perfecting the church below,
steadfast may we cleave to Thee,
love, the mystic union be;
join our faithful spirits, join
each to each, and all to Thine;
lead us through the paths of peace
on to perfect holiness.

2 Move and actuate and guide;
various gifts to each divide;
placed according to Thy will,
let us all our work fulfil;
never from our calling move;
needful to each other prove;
use the grace on each bestowed,
tempered by the art of God.

3 Sweetly may we all agree,
touched with softest sympathy;
there is neither bond nor free,
great nor servile, Lord, in Thee:
love, like death, has all destroyed,
rendered all distinctions void;
names and sects and parties fall,
Thou, O Christ, art All in all.
Charles Wesley, 1707-88

385

Thou God of truth and love,
we seek Thy perfect way,
ready Thy choice to approve,
Thy providence to obey:
enter into Thy wise design,
and sweetly lose our will in Thine.

2 Surely Thou dost unite
our kindred spirits here,
that all hereafter might
before Thy throne appear;
meet at the marriage of the Lamb,
and all Thy glorious love proclaim.

3 Then let us ever bear
the blessèd end in view,
and join, with mutual care,
to fight our passage through;
and kindly help each other on,
till all receive the starry crown.

4 O may Thy Spirit seal
our souls unto that day,
with all Thy fulness fill,
and then transport away –
away to our eternal rest,
away to our Redeemer's breast!
Charles Wesley, 1707-88

386

We come unto our fathers' God;
their rock is our salvation;
the eternal arms, their dear abode,
we make our habitation;
we bring Thee, Lord, the praise they brought,
we seek Thee as Thy saints have sought
in every generation.

2 The fire divine their steps that led
still goeth bright before us;
the heavenly shield around them spread
is still high holden o'er us;
the grace those sinners that subdued,
the strength those weaklings that renewed,
doth vanquish, doth restore us.

3 The cleaving sins that brought them low
are still our souls oppressing;
the tears that from their eyes did flow
fall fast, our shame confessing;
as with Thee, Lord, prevailed their cry,
so our strong prayer ascends on high
and bringeth down Thy blessing.

4 Their joy unto their Lord we bring;
their song to us descendeth;
the Spirit who in them did sing
to us His music lendeth;
His song in them, in us, is one;
we raise it high, we send it on –
the song that never endeth!

5 Ye saints to come, take up the strain,
the same sweet theme endeavour;
unbroken be the golden chain,
keep on the song for ever!
Safe in the same dear dwelling-place,
rich with the same eternal grace,
bless the same boundless giver!

Thomas Hornblower Gill, 1819-1906

387

We covenant with hand and heart,
to follow Christ our Lord,
with world and sin and self to part,
and to obey His Word:
to love each other heartily,
in truth and in sincerity,
and under cross, reproach and shame
to glorify His name.

Samuel Traugott Benade, 1746-1839

Conflict and triumph

388

A mighty fortress is our God,
a sure defence and weapon;
He orders all things for our good,
frees us from all oppression.
Our ancient, evil foe
is bent on working woe.
His craft and power are great,
and armed with cruel hate,
on earth is not his equal.

2 Our human power will not avail –
we soon should be defeated,
did not that one true Man prevail,
by God Himself elected.
Who then, you ask, is this?
His name is Jesus Christ,
the mighty Lord of Hosts;
He, as the one true God,
must triumph in the battle!

3 And though this world with devils filled
should threaten to devour us,
we will not fear, for God has willed
that nought shall overpower us.
The ruler of this age
may clothe himself with rage;
to us he'll do no harm –
God has pronounced his doom;
the merest word can fell him!

4 God's Word shall stand. Do what they may,
men shall bow down before it.
The Lord will help us win the day
with His good gifts and Spirit.
Then let them take our life,
goods, honour, children, wife;
we will relinquish all;
they profit not at all –
ours the abiding kingdom!

Martin Luther, 1483-1546;
tr. by John D Manton, b. 1930;
v. 1 (part), Frederick H Hedge, 1805-90

389

A safe stronghold our God is still,
a trusty shield and weapon;
He'll help us clear from all the ill
that hath us now o'ertaken.
The ancient prince of hell
hath risen with purpose fell;
strong mail of craft and power
he weareth in this hour;
on earth is not his fellow.

2 With force of arms we nothing can,
full soon were we down-ridden;
but for us fights the proper Man,
whom God Himself hath bidden.
Ask ye, Who is this same?
Christ Jesus is His Name,
the Lord Sabaoth's Son;
He, and no other one,
shall conquer in the battle.

3 And were this world all devils o'er,
and watching to devour us,
we lay it not to heart so sore;
not they can overpower us.
And let the prince of ill
look grim as e'er he will,
he harms us not a whit:
for why? his doom is writ;
a word shall quickly slay him.

4 God's Word, for all their craft and force,
one moment will not linger,
but, spite of hell, shall have its course;
'tis written by His finger.
And though they take our life,
goods, honour, children, wife,
yet is their profit small:
these things shall vanish all;
the city of God remaineth.

Martin Luther, 1483-1546;
tr. by Thomas Carlyle, 1795-1881

390

Come, let us join our friends above
that have obtained the prize,
and on the eagle wings of love
to joys celestial rise:
let saints below in concert sing
with those to glory gone;
for all the servants of our King
in earth and heaven are one.

2 One family we dwell in Him,
one church above, beneath,
though now divided by the stream,
the narrow stream of death:
one army of the living God,
to His command we bow;
part of His host have crossed the flood,
and part are crossing now.

3 Our spirits too shall quickly join
with theirs in glory crowned,
and shout to see our Captain's sign,
to hear His trumpet sound.
O that we now might grasp our guide!
O that the word were given!
Come, Lord of hosts, the waves divide,
and land us all in heaven.

Charles Wesley, 1707-88

391

For all the saints who from their labours rest,
who Thee by faith before the world confessed,
Thy name, O Jesus, be for ever blest.
Hallelujah! Hallelujah!

2 Thou wast their rock, their fortress, and their might;
Thou, Lord, their captain in the well-fought fight;
Thou, in the darkness drear, their one true light.
Hallelujah! Hallelujah!

3 O may Thy soldiers, faithful, true, and bold,
fight as the saints who nobly fought of old,
and win with them, the victor's crown of gold.
Hallelujah! Hallelujah!

4 O blest communion, fellowship divine!
we feebly struggle, they in glory shine;
yet all are one in Thee, for all are Thine.
Hallelujah! Hallelujah!

5 And when the strife is fierce, the warfare long,
steals on the ear the distant triumph-song,
and hearts are brave again, and arms are strong.
Hallelujah! Hallelujah!

6 The golden evening brightens in the west;
soon, soon to faithful warriors cometh rest,
sweet is the calm of paradise the blest.
Hallelujah! Hallelujah!

7 But lo! there breaks a yet more glorious day;
the saints triumphant rise in bright array;
the King of glory passes on His way.
Hallelujah! Hallelujah!

8 From earth's wide bounds, from ocean's farthest coast,
through gates of pearl streams in the countless host,
singing to Father, Son, and Holy Ghost.
Hallelujah! Hallelujah!

William Walsham How, 1823-97

392

'Forward!' be our watchword,
steps and voices joined;
seek the things before us,
not a look behind;
burns the fiery pillar
at our army's head;
who shall dream of shrinking,
by our Captain led?
Forward through the desert,
through the toil and fight:
Jordan flows before us,
Zion beams with light.

2 Forward, flock of Jesus,
salt of all the earth,
till each yearning purpose
spring to glorious birth.
Sick, they ask for healing,
blind, they grope for day;
pour upon the nations
wisdom's loving ray.
Forward out of error,
leave behind the night;
forward through the darkness,
forward into light.

3 Glories upon glories
has our God prepared,
by the souls that love Him
one day to be shared;
eye has not beheld them,
ear has never heard,
nor of these has uttered
thought or speech a word.
Forward, marching forward,
clad in armour bright,
till the veil be lifted,
till our faith be sight.

Henry Alford, 1810-71

393

Lord of our life, and God of our salvation,
star of our night, and hope of every nation,
hear and receive Thy church's supplication,
Lord God Almighty!

2 See round Thine ark the hungry billows curling;
see how Thy foes their banners are unfurling;
Lord, while their darts envenomed they are hurling,
Thou canst preserve us.

3 Lord, Thou canst help when earthly armour faileth;
Lord, Thou canst save when deadly sin assaileth;
Lord, o'er Thy church nor death nor hell prevaileth:
grant us Thy peace, Lord.

4 Peace in our hearts, our evil thoughts assuaging,
peace in Thy church, where brothers are engaging,
peace, when the world its busy war is waging:
calm Thy foes' raging.

5 Grant us Thy help till backward they are driven;
grant them Thy truth, that they may be forgiven;
grant peace on earth, and after we have striven,
peace in Thy heaven.

Philip Pusey, 1799-1855;
based on Matthäus Apelles von Löwenstern, 1594-1648

Revival and restoration

394

All glory to God in the sky,
and peace upon earth be restored!
O Jesus, exalted on high,
appear our omnipotent Lord!
Who, meanly in Bethlehem born,
did stoop to redeem a lost race,
once more to Your creatures return,
and reign in Your kingdom of grace.

2 When You in our flesh did appear,
all nature acknowledged Your birth;
arose the acceptable year,
and heaven was opened on earth:
receiving its Lord from above,
the world was united to bless
the giver of concord and love,
the Prince and the Author of peace.

3 O may You again be made known!
Again in Your Spirit descend,
and set up in each of Your own
a kingdom that never shall end.
You only are able to bless,
and make the glad nations obey,
and bid the dire enmity cease,
and bow the whole world to Your sway.

4 Come then to Your servants again,
who long Your appearing to know,
Your quiet and peaceable reign
in mercy establish below;
all sorrow before You shall fly,
and anger and hatred be o'er,
and envy and malice shall die,
and discord afflict us no more.

Charles Wesley, 1707-88

395

Here from the world we turn,
Jesus to seek;
here may His loving voice
tenderly speak.
Jesus, our dearest friend,
while at Thy feet we bend,
O let Thy smile descend!
'Tis Thee we seek.

2 Come, Holy Comforter,
presence divine,
now in our longing hearts
graciously shine;
O for Thy mighty power!
O for a blessèd shower,
filling this hallowed hour
with joy divine!

3 Saviour, Thy work revive,
here may we see
those who are dead in sin
quickened by Thee.
Come to our hearts' delight,
make every burden light,
cheer Thou our waiting sight;
we long for Thee.

Frances Jane Van Alstyne, 1820-1915

396

Come, Holy Spirit, heavenly dove,
with all Your quickening powers;
kindle a flame of sacred love
in these cold hearts of ours.

2 In vain we tune our formal songs,
in vain we strive to rise;
hosannas languish on our tongues,
and our devotion dies.

3 And shall we then for ever live
at this poor dying rate?
Our love so faint, so cold to You,
and Yours to us so great?

4 Come, Holy Spirit, heavenly dove,
with all Your quickening powers;
come, shed abroad the Saviour's love,
and that shall kindle ours.

Isaac Watts, 1674-1748

397

Hosea 6:1-4

Come, let us to the Lord our God
with contrite hearts return;
our God is gracious, nor will leave
the desolate to mourn.

2 His voice commands the tempest forth,
and stills the stormy wave;
and though His arm be strong to smite,
'tis also strong to save.

3 Long has the night of sorrow reigned;
the dawn shall bring us light;
God shall appear, and we shall rise
with gladness in His sight.

4 Our hearts, if God we seek to know,
shall know Him and rejoice;
His coming like the morn shall be,
like morning songs His voice.

5 As dew upon the tender herb,
diffusing fragrance round;
as showers that usher in the spring,
and cheer the thirsty ground:

6 So shall His presence bless our souls,
and shed a joyful light;
that hallowed morn shall chase away
the sorrows of the night.

Scottish Paraphrases, 1781

398

O Breath of Life, come sweeping through us,
revive Your church with life and power,
O Breath of Life, come, cleanse, renew us,
and fit Your church to meet this hour.

2 O Wind of God, come, bend us, break us,
till humbly we confess our need;
then in Your tenderness remake us,
revive, restore; for this we plead.

3 O Breath of Love, come, breathe within us,
renewing thought and will and heart:
come, love of Christ, afresh to win us,
revive Your church in every part.

4 Revive us, Lord! is zeal abating
while harvest fields are vast and white?
Revive us, Lord, the world is waiting,
equip Your church to spread the light.

Elizabeth Ann Head, 1850-1936

399

Revive Thy work, O Lord,
Thy mighty arm make bare;
speak with the voice that wakes the dead,
and make Thy people hear!

2 Revive Thy work, O Lord,
disturb the sleep of death;
quicken the smouldering embers now
by Thine almighty breath!

3 Revive Thy work, O Lord,
create soul-thirst for Thee;
and hungering for the Bread of Life,
O may our spirits be!

4 Revive Thy work, O Lord,
exalt Thy precious Name;
and, by the Holy Ghost, our love
for Thee and Thine inflame!

5 Revive Thy work, O Lord:
give power unto Thy Word;
and may its pure and sacred truth
in living faith be heard.

6 Revive Thy work, O Lord,
and give refreshing showers;
the glory shall be all Thine own,
the blessing, Lord, be ours!

Albert Midlane, 1825-1909

400

Our God! our God! shine on us here;
Your own this latter day:
to us Your radiant steps appear;
we watch Your glorious way.

2 Not only olden ages felt
the presence of the Lord;
not only with the fathers dwelt
Your Spirit and Your Word.

3 Does not the Spirit still descend
and bring the heavenly fire?
Does not He still Your church extend,
and waiting souls inspire?

4 Come, Holy Ghost, in us arise;
be this Your mighty hour,
and make Your willing people wise
to know Your day of power.

5 Bear us aloft, more glad, more strong
on Your celestial wing;
and grant us grace to look and long
for our returning King.

Thomas Hornblower Gill, 1819-1906

401

Our Jesus is gone up on high,
for us the blessing to receive;
it now comes streaming from the sky,
the Spirit comes, and sinners live.

2 Lord, we believe to us and ours
the apostolic promise given;
we wait the Pentecostal powers,
the Holy Ghost sent down from heaven.

3 Ah! leave us not to mourn below,
or long for Your return to pine;
now, Lord, the Comforter bestow,
and fix in us the guest divine.

4 Assembled here with one accord,
calmly we wait the promised grace,
the purchase of our dying Lord:
come, Holy Ghost, and fill the place.

5 If every one that asks may find,
if still You do on sinners fall,
come as a mighty rushing wind;
great grace be now upon us all.

Charles Wesley, 1707-88

402

Restore, O Lord,
the honour of Your name,
in works of sovereign power
come, shake the earth again,
that men may see
and come with reverent fear
to the living God,
whose kingdom shall outlast the years.

2 Restore, O Lord,
in all the earth Your fame,
and in our time revive
the church that bears Your name.
And in Your anger,
Lord, remember mercy,
O living God,
whose mercy shall outlast the years.

3 Bend us, O Lord,
where we are hard and cold,
in Your refiner's fire
come, purify the gold.
Though suffering comes
and evil crouches near,
still our living God is reigning,
He is reigning here.

4 Restore, O Lord,
the honour of Your name,
in works of sovereign power
come, shake the earth again,
that men may see
and come with reverent fear
to the living God,
whose kingdom shall outlast the years.

Graham Kendrick, b. 1950,
& Chris Rolinson, b. 1958

403

Thou glorious Sovereign of the skies,
and wilt Thou bow Thy gracious ear?
While feeble mortals raise their cries,
wilt Thou, the great Jehovah, hear?

2 How shall Thy servants give Thee rest,
till Zion's mouldering walls Thou raise?
till Thine own power shall stand confessed,
and make Jerusalem a praise?

3 On all our souls let grace descend,
like heavenly dew in copious showers,
that we may call our God our friend,
that we may hail salvation ours.

4 Then shall each age and rank agree
united shouts of joy to raise;
and Zion, made a praise by Thee,
to Thee shall render back the praise.

Philip Doddridge, 1702-51

404

PSALM 126

When in His might the Lord
arose to set us free,
and Zion was restored
from her captivity,
in transports then of joy and mirth
we praised the Lord of all the earth.

2 The nations saw with fear
the might of God displayed,
when He at last drew near
to give His people aid;
great things for us the Lord has wrought,
and gladness to our hearts has brought.

3 Again refresh us, Lord,
with Your reviving love,
and be Your blessing poured
in mercy from above;
by grace revive our hearts again,
as streams refreshed by copious rain.

4 Although with bitter tears
the sower bears His seed,
when harvest time appears
He shall be glad indeed;
for they that in the sowing weep
shall yet in joy and gladness reap.

THE PSALTER*, 1912

The life of prayer

405

Come, my soul, thy plea prepare,
Jesus loves to answer prayer;
He Himself has bid thee pray,
therefore will not say thee nay.

2 Thou art coming to a King,
large petitions with thee bring;
for His grace and power are such,
none can ever ask too much.

3 With my burden I begin:
Lord, remove this load of sin;
let Thy blood, for sinners spilt,
set my conscience free from guilt.

4 Lord, I come to Thee for rest;
take possession of my breast;
there Thy blood-bought right maintain,
and without a rival reign.

5 While I am a pilgrim here,
let Thy love my spirit cheer;
as my guide, my guard, my friend,
lead me to my journey's end.

6 Show me what I have to do;
every hour my strength renew;
let me live a life of faith;
let me die Thy people's death.

John Newton, 1725-1807

406

Approach, my soul, the mercy-seat,
where Jesus answers prayer;
there humbly fall before His feet,
for none can perish there.

2 Thy promise is my only plea;
with this I venture nigh;
Thou callest burdened souls to Thee,
and such, O Lord, am I!

3 Bowed down beneath a load of sin,
by Satan sorely pressed,
by war without, and fears within,
I come to Thee for rest.

4 Be Thou my shield and hiding-place,
that, sheltered near Thy side,
I may my fierce accuser face,
and tell him Thou hast died.

5 O wondrous love! to bleed and die,
to bear the cross and shame,
that guilty sinners, such as I,
might plead Thy gracious Name!

John Newton, 1725-1807

407

Behold the throne of grace,
the promise calls us near;
there Jesus shows a smiling face,
and waits to answer prayer.

2 That rich atoning blood,
which sprinkled round we see,
provides for those who come to God
an all-prevailing plea.

3 Beyond our utmost wants
His love and power can bless;
to praying souls He always grants
more than they can express.

4 Thine image, Lord, bestow,
Thy presence and Thy love;
we ask to serve Thee here below,
and reign with Thee above.

5 Abiding in Thy faith,
our will conformed to Thine,
let us victorious be in death,
and then in glory shine.

John Newton, 1725-1807

408

From every stormy wind that blows,
from every swelling tide of woes,
there is a calm, a safe retreat;
'tis found beneath the mercy-seat.

2 There is a place where Jesus sheds
the oil of gladness on our heads,
a place than all beside more sweet;
it is the blood-stained mercy-seat.

3 There is a spot where spirits blend,
where friend holds fellowship with friend;
though sundered far, by faith we meet
around one common mercy-seat.

4 There, there on eagle wing we soar,
and time and sense seem all no more,
and heaven comes down our souls to
greet,
and glory crowns the mercy-seat.

5 O let my hands forget their skill,
my tongue be silent, cold, and still,
this bounding heart forget to beat,
if I forget the mercy-seat!

Hugh Stowell, 1799-1865

409

God of pity, God of grace,
when we humbly seek Thy face,
bend from heaven, Thy dwelling-place;
hear, forgive, and save.

2 When we in Thy temple meet,
spread our wants before Thy feet,
pleading at Thy mercy-seat,
look from heaven and save.

3 When Thy love our hearts shall fill,
and we long to do Thy will,
turning to Thy holy hill,
Lord, accept and save.

4 Should we wander from Thy fold,
and our love to Thee grow cold,
with a pitying eye behold;
Lord, forgive and save.

5 Should the hand of sorrow press,
earthly care and want distress,
may our souls Thy peace possess;
Jesus, hear and save.

6 And whate'er our cry may be,
when we lift our hearts to Thee,
from our burden set us free;
hear, forgive, and save.

Eliza Frances Morris, 1821-74

410

Great Shepherd of Your people, hear;
Your presence now display;
as You have given a place for prayer,
so give us hearts to pray.

2 Show us some token of Your love,
our fainting hope to raise;
and pour Your blessings from above,
that we may render praise.

3 Within these walls let holy peace,
and love and concord dwell;
here give the troubled conscience ease,
the wounded spirit heal.

4 May we in faith receive Your Word,
in faith present our prayers,
and in the presence of our Lord
unburden all our cares.

5 The hearing ear, the seeing eye,
the contrite heart bestow:
and shine upon us from on high,
that we in grace may grow.

John Newton, 1725-1807

411

Head of the church and Lord of all,
hear from Thy throne our suppliant call:
we come the promised grace to seek,
of which aforetime Thou didst speak.

2 'Lo, I am with you' – that sweet word,
Lord Jesus, meekly be it heard,
and stamped with all-inspiring power
on our weak souls this favoured hour.

3 Without Thy presence, King of saints,
our purpose fails, our spirit faints;
Thou must our wavering faith renew,
ere we can yield Thee service true.

4 Thy consecrating might we ask –
or vain the toil, unblest the task;
and impotent of fruit will be
love's holiest effort wrought for Thee.

5 'Lo, I am with you' – even so,
Thy joy our strength, we fearless go:
and praise shall crown the suppliant's call,
head of the church, and Lord of all!

Joseph Tritton, 1819-87

412

Jesus! stand among us
in Your risen power,
let this time of worship
be a hallowed hour.

2 Breathe Your Holy Spirit
into every heart,
bid the fears and sorrows
from each soul depart.

3 Thus with quickened footsteps,
we'll pursue our way,
watching for the dawning
of eternal day.

William Pennefather, 1816-73

413

Jesus, Thou sovereign Lord of all,
the same through one eternal day,
attend Thy feeblest followers' call,
and O instruct us how to pray!
Pour out the supplicating grace,
and stir us up to seek Thy face.

2 We cannot think a gracious thought,
we cannot feel a good desire,
till Thou, who call'dst a world from
nought,
the power into our hearts inspire;
and then we in Thy Spirit groan,
and then we give Thee back Thine own.

3 Jesus, regard the joint complaint
of all Thy tempted followers here,
and now supply the common want,
and send us down the Comforter;
the Spirit of ceaseless prayer impart,
and fix Thy Agent in our heart.

4 To help our soul's infirmity,
to heal Thy sin-sick people's care,
to urge our God-commanding plea,
and make our hearts a house of
prayer,
the promised Intercessor give,
and let us now Thyself receive.

5 Come in Thy pleading Spirit down
to us who for Thy coming stay;
of all Thy gifts we ask but one,
we ask the constant power to pray:
indulge us, Lord, in this request;
Thou canst not then deny the rest.

Charles Wesley, 1707-88

414

Jesus, where'er Thy people meet,
there they behold Thy mercy-seat;
where'er they seek Thee Thou art found,
and every place is hallowed ground.

2 For Thou, within no walls confined,
inhabitest the humble mind;
such ever bring Thee where they come,
and going, take Thee to their home.

3 Dear Shepherd of Thy chosen few,
Thy former mercies here renew;
here to our waiting hearts proclaim
the sweetness of Thy saving name.

4 Here may we prove the power of
prayer,
to strengthen faith and sweeten care,
to teach our faint desires to rise,
and bring all heaven before our eyes.

5 Lord, we are few, but Thou art near,
nor short Thine arm, nor deaf Thine ear;
O rend the heavens, come quickly down,
and make a thousand hearts Thine own!

William Cowper, 1731-1800

415

**Lord Jesus Christ, we seek Thy
face;**
within the veil we bow the knee;
O let Thy glory fill the place,
and bless us while we wait on Thee.

2 We thank Thee for the precious blood
that purged our sins and brought us nigh,
all cleansed and sanctified to God,
Thy holy name to magnify.

3 Shut in with Thee, far, far above
the restless world that wars below,
we seek to learn and prove Thy love,
Thy wisdom and Thy grace to know.

4 The brow that once with thorns was bound,
Thy hands, Thy side, we now would see;
draw near, Lord Jesus, glory-crowned,
and bless us while we wait on Thee.

Alexander Stewart, 1843-1923

416

Lord, teach us how to pray aright,
with reverence and with fear;
though dust and ashes in Your sight,
we may, we must draw near.

2 We perish if we cease from prayer;
O grant us power to pray!
And when to meet You we prepare,
O meet us by the way.

3 Burdened with guilt, convinced of sin,
in weakness, want and woe,
fightings without, and fear within;
Lord, whither shall we go?

4 God of all grace, we come to You
with broken, contrite hearts;
give what Your eye delights to view,
truth in the inward parts.

5 Give deep humility; the sense
of godly sorrow give;
a strong, desiring confidence
to hear Your voice and live.

6 Faith in the only sacrifice
that can for sin atone;
to cast our hopes, to fix our eyes,
on Christ, on Christ alone.

7 Patience to watch and wait and weep,
though mercy long delay;
courage, our fainting souls to keep,
and trust You though You slay.

8 Give these, and then Your will be done;
thus strengthened with Your might,
we by Your Spirit and Your Son
shall pray, and pray aright.

James Montgomery, 1771-1854

417

Mercy in our time of failure,
grace to help in time of need:
this sure promise of our Saviour
is a word that we may plead.

2 He has passed into the heavens,
He is seated on the throne,
ever for us interceding,
always caring for His own.

3 There is none He will not welcome,
no request He cannot meet;
let us not be slow to ask Him,
lay our burdens at His feet.

4 We can never come too often,
never with a need too great,
never with a prayer too simple;
only fear to come too late!

5 Daily on our pilgrim journey
praise Him for His matchless grace,
live for His immortal glory
till in heaven we see His face.

Leith Samuel, 1915-99

418

O Thou by whom we come to God,
the Life, the Truth, the Way,
the path of prayer Thyself hast trod;
Lord, teach us how to pray.

2 Prayer is the soul's sincere desire,
uttered or unexpressed;
the motion of a hidden fire
that trembles in the breast.

3 Prayer is the burden of a sigh,
the falling of a tear;
the upward glancing of an eye,
when none but God is near.

4 Prayer is the simplest form of speech
that infant lips can try;
prayer the sublimest strains that reach
the Majesty on high.

5 Prayer is the contrite sinner's voice,
returning from his ways;
while angels in their songs rejoice,
and cry, 'Behold, he prays!'

6 Prayer is the Christian's vital breath,
the Christian's native air;
his watchword at the gates of death;
he enters heaven with prayer.

7 Nor prayer is made on earth alone,
the Holy Spirit pleads,
and Jesus, on the eternal throne,
for sinners intercedes.

8 O Thou by whom we come to God,
the Life, the Truth, the Way,
the path of prayer Thyself hast trod;
Lord, teach us how to pray.

James Montgomery, 1771-1854

419

Our heavenly Father calls,
and Christ invites us near;
with both, our friendship shall be sweet,
and our communion dear.

2 God pities all our griefs;
He pardons every day;
almighty to protect our souls,
and wise to guide our way.

3 How large His bounties are!
what various stores of good,
diffused with our Redeemer's hand,
and purchased with His blood!

4 Jesus, our living head,
we bless Your faithful care;
our advocate before the throne,
and our forerunner there.

5 Here fix, my wand'ring heart!
here wait, my warmest love!
till the communion be complete
in nobler scenes above.

Philip Doddridge, 1702-51

420

Shepherd divine, our wants relieve
in this our evil day,
to all Thy tempted followers give
the power to watch and pray.

2 Long as our fiery trials last,
long as the cross we bear,
O let our souls on Thee be cast
in never-ceasing prayer!

3 The Spirit of interceding grace
give us in faith to claim;
to wrestle till we see Thy face,
and know Thy hidden Name.

4 Till Thou Thy perfect love impart,
till Thou Thyself bestow,
be this the cry of every heart:
I will not let Thee go –

5 I will not let Thee go, unless
Thou tell Thy Name to me,
with all Thy great salvation bless,
and make me all like Thee.

6 Then let me on the mountain-top
behold Thy open face,
where faith in sight is swallowed up,
and prayer in endless praise.

Charles Wesley, 1707-88

421

What various hindrances we meet
in coming to the mercy-seat;
yet who, that knows the worth of prayer,
but wishes to be often there!

2 Prayer makes the darkened cloud withdraw,
prayer climbs the ladder Jacob saw,
gives exercise to faith and love,
brings every blessing from above.

3 Restraining prayer we cease to fight;
prayer makes the Christian's armour bright;
and Satan trembles when he sees
the weakest saint upon his knees.

4 When Moses stood with arms spread wide,
success was found on Israel's side;
but when through weariness they failed,
that moment Amalek prevailed.

5 Have you no words? ah, think again!
words flow apace when you complain,
and fill your fellow-creature's ear
with the sad tale of all your care.

6 Were half the breath thus vainly spent
to heaven in supplication sent,
your cheerful song would oftener be –
'Hear what the Lord has done for me.'

William Cowper, 1731-1800

422

What a friend we have in Jesus,
all our sins and griefs to bear!
What a privilege to carry
everything to God in prayer!
O what peace we often forfeit,
O what needless pain we bear,
all because we do not carry
everything to God in prayer!

2 Have we trials and temptations?
Is there trouble anywhere?
We should never be discouraged:
take it to the Lord in prayer.
Can we find a friend so faithful,
who will all our sorrows share?
Jesus knows our every weakness:
take it to the Lord in prayer.

3 Are we weak and heavy-laden,
burdened with a load of care?
Precious Saviour, still our refuge:
take it to the Lord in prayer.
Do your friends despise, forsake you?
Take it to the Lord in prayer;
in His arms He'll take and shield you,
you will find a solace there.

Joseph Medlicott Scriven, 1819-86

The Ordinances

(1) Baptism

423

Baptized in water for our Lord,
we follow and obey His word.
In Him we die, in Him we rise
to reign with Him beyond the skies.

2 Baptized into the triune name,
the Father's promises we claim;
forgiveness through Christ's blood alone
and access to the heavenly throne.

3 Baptized in Christ and with Him one,
a transformed life is here begun;
now dead to sins we used to love,
our minds are set on things above.

4 Baptized, filled with the Spirit's power;
His presence with us hour by hour;
to demonstrate through our new birth
God's living presence on this earth.

5 Baptized to show what God has done
by saving sinners through His Son;
in Him we die, in Him we rise
to reign with Him beyond the skies.

Paul Sayer, b. 1934

424

Come, Holy Spirit, dove divine,
on these baptismal waters shine,
and teach our hearts in highest strain
to praise the Lamb for sinners slain.

2 We love Your Name, we love Your laws,
and joyfully embrace Your cause,
we love Your cross, the shame, the pain,
O Lamb of God, for sinners slain.

3 And as we rise with You to live,
O let the Holy Spirit give
the sealing unction from above,
the breath of life, the fire of love.

Adoniram Judson, 1788-1850

425

Hast Thou said, exalted Jesus,
'Take thy cross and follow Me'?
Shall the word with terror seize us?
Shall we from the burden flee?
Lord, I'll take it,
and, rejoicing, follow Thee.

2 Sweet the sign that here reminds me,
Saviour, of Thy love for me;
sweeter still the love that binds me
in its deathless bond to Thee:
O what pleasure,
buried with my Lord to be!

3 Then, baptized in love and glory,
Lamb of God, Thy praise I'll sing;
loudly with the immortal story
all the harps of heaven shall ring:
saints and angels
sound it loud from every string.

John Eustace Giles, 1805-75

426

Jesus, our Lord and King,
to Thee our praises rise;
to Thee our bodies we present,
a living sacrifice.

2 Now justified by grace
and made alive to God,
formed for Thyself, to show Thy praise,
we sound Thy love abroad.

3 As dead indeed to sin,
from its dominion free,
henceforth, as not our own, but Thine,
we follow only Thee.

4 Baptized into Thy death,
with Thee again we rise,
to newness of a life of faith,
to new and endless joys.

Anonymous

5 The servants of God are baptized,
they rise up with Christ to new life;
come, Spirit, abide in their hearts
for days of temptation and strife.

6 The servants of God are baptized,
with Christians made visibly one;
come, Spirit, and rest on us now
to worship God's glorious Son.

Nick Needham, b. 1959

427

The servants of God are baptized,
with Jesus made visibly one;
come, Spirit, and clothe them with power,
the world and its pleasures to shun.

2 The servants of God are baptized,
salvation revealed and displayed;
come, Spirit, and seal on their minds
the sacrifice Jesus has made.

3 The servants of God are baptized,
united with Christ in His death;
come, Spirit, descend on their souls
and fill with Your life-giving breath.

4 The servants of God are baptized,
immersed in the tomb with their Lord;
come, Spirit, and open their eyes
to walk in the light of God's Word.

428

Witness, you men and angels now,
before the Lord we speak;
to Him we make our solemn vow,
a vow we dare not break;

2 That, long as life itself shall last,
ourselves to Christ we yield;
nor from His cause will we depart,
or ever quit the field.

3 We trust not in our native strength,
but on His grace rely,
that, with returning wants, the Lord
will all our need supply.

4 O guide our doubtful feet aright,
and keep us in Your ways;
and while we turn our vows to prayers,
Lord turn our prayers to praise.

Benjamin Beddome, 1717-95

The Ordinances

(2) The Lord's Supper

429

According to Thy gracious Word,
in meek humility,
this will I do, my dying Lord,
I will remember Thee.

2 Thy body, broken for my sake,
my bread from heaven shall be;
Thy covenantal cup I take,
and thus remember Thee.

3 Gethsemane can I forget?
Or there Thy conflict see,
Thine agony and bloody sweat,
and not remember Thee?

4 When to the cross I turn my eyes,
and rest on Calvary,
O Lamb of God, my sacrifice!
I must remember Thee:

5 Remember Thee, and all Thy pains,
and all Thy love to me:
yes, while a breath, a pulse remains,
will I remember Thee.

6 And when these failing lips grow dumb,
and mind and memory flee,
when Thou shalt in Thy kingdom come,
Jesus, remember me.

James Montgomery, 1771-1854

430

Amidst us our Belovèd stands,
and bids us view His piercèd hands;
points to His wounded feet and side,
blest emblems of the crucified.

2 What food luxurious loads the board,
when at His table sits the Lord!
The wine how rich, the bread how sweet,
when Jesus deigns the guests to meet!

3 If now, with eyes defiled and dim,
we see the signs, but see not Him,
O may His love the scales displace,
and bid us see Him face to face!

4 Our past delights we now recount,
when with Him in the holy mount,
these cause our souls to thirst anew
His marred but lovely face to view.

5 O glorious Bridegroom of our hearts,
Your present smile a heaven imparts;
O lift the veil, if veil there be,
let every saint Your beauties see!

Charles Haddon Spurgeon, 1834-92

431

Be known to us in breaking bread,
but do not then depart;
Saviour, abide with us, and spread
Your table in our heart.

2 There sup with us in love divine;
Your body and Your blood,
that living bread, that heavenly wine,
be our immortal food.

3 We would not live by bread alone,
but by Your Word of grace,
in strength of which we travel on
to our abiding place.

vv. 1 & 2, James Montgomery, 1771-1854;
v. 3, Anonymous

432

Beneath Your cross I lay me down,
and mourn to see Your thorny crown;
love drops in blood from every vein,
love is the spring of all Your pain.

2 Here, Jesus, I shall ever stay,
and spend my longing hours away,
think on Your bleeding wounds and
pain,
and contemplate Your woes again.

3 The rage of Satan and of sin,
of foes without and fears within,
shall ne'er my conquering soul remove,
or from Your cross, or from Your love.

4 Secured from harm beneath Your shade,
here death and hell shall ne'er invade;
nor Sinai, with its thundering noise,
shall e'er disturb my happier joys.

5 O unmolested, happy rest,
where inward fears are all suppressed!
Here I shall love and live secure,
and patiently my cross endure.

William Williams, 1717-91

433

By Christ redeemed, in Christ restored,
we keep the memory adored,
and show the death of our dear Lord
until He come.

2 His body broken in our stead
is seen in this memorial bread,
and so our feeble love is fed
until He come.

3 The drops of His dread agony,
His life-blood shed for us, we see;
the wine shall tell the mystery
until He come.

4 And thus that dark betrayal-night
with the last advent we unite,
by one blest chain of loving rite,
until He come:

5 Until the trump of God be heard,
until the ancient graves be stirred,
and with the great commanding word
the Lord shall come.

6 O blessèd day! O glad estate!
Let not our hearts be desolate,
but, strong in faith, in patience wait
until He come.

*George Rawson**, 1807-89

434

For ever here my rest shall be,
close to Thy bleeding side;
this all my hope, and all my plea,
for me the Saviour died!

2 My dying Saviour, and my God,
fountain for guilt and sin,
sprinkle me ever with Thy blood,
and cleanse, and keep me clean.

3 Wash me, and make me thus Thine own,
wash me, and mine Thou art,
wash me, but not my feet alone,
my hands, my head, my heart.

4 The atonement of Thy blood apply,
till faith to sight improve,
till hope in full fruition die,
and all my soul be love.

Charles Wesley, 1707-88

435

For mercies countless as the sands,
which daily I receive
from Jesus, my Redeemer's hands,
my soul, what can you give?

2 Alas! from such a heart as mine
what can I bring Him forth?
My best is stained and dyed with sin,
my all is nothing worth.

3 Yet this acknowledgment I'll make,
for all He has bestowed:
salvation's sacred cup I'll take,
and call upon my God.

John Newton, 1725-1807

436

He lovèd me, and gave Himself for me;
amazing love, amazing sacrifice!
I'll take my harp down from the willow tree,
and bid its note in praise of Jesus rise.

2 He lovèd me, and gave Himself for me;
and surely I myself to Him will give;
none, Jesus will I ever love like Thee,
and to Thy glory only will I live.

3 O when I stand 'mid yonder shining throng,
and on fair Canaan's coast my Saviour see,
I'll add this chorus to the swelling song,
'He lovèd me, and gave Himself for me.'

Fergus Ferguson, 1824-97

437

He gave His life in selfless love,
for sinful man He came;
He had no stain of sin Himself
but bore our guilt and shame:
He took the cup of pain and death,
His blood was freely shed;
we see His body on the cross,
we share the living bread.

2 He did not come to call the good
but sinners to repent;
it was the lame, the deaf, the blind
for whom His life was spent:
to heal the sick, to find the lost –
it was for such He came,
and round His table all may come
to praise His holy name.

3 They heard Him call His Father's name –
then 'Finished!' was His cry;
like them we have forsaken Him
and left Him there to die:
the sins that crucified Him then
are sins His blood has cured;
the love that bound Him to a cross
our freedom has ensured.

4 His body broken once for us
is glorious now above;
the cup of blessing we receive,
a sharing of His love;
as in His presence we partake,
His dying we proclaim
until the hour of majesty
when Jesus comes again.

Christopher Porteous, b. 1935

438

PART 1

Here, O my Lord, I see Thee face to face;
here would I touch and handle things unseen,
here grasp with firmer hand the eternal grace,
and all my weariness upon Thee lean.

2 Here would I feed upon the bread of God,
here drink with Thee the royal wine of heaven;
here would I lay aside each earthly load,
here taste afresh the calm of sin forgiven.

3 Mine is the sin, but Thine the righteousness;
mine is the guilt, but Thine the cleansing blood!
here is my robe, my refuge and my peace –
Thy blood, Thy righteousness, O Lord my God.

4 This is the hour of banquet and of song;
this is the heavenly table spread for me;
here let me feast, and, feasting, still prolong
the brief, bright hour of fellowship with Thee.

PART 2

5 Too soon we rise; the symbols disappear;
the feast, though not the love, is past and gone;
the bread and wine remove, but Thou art here,
nearer than ever, still my shield and sun.

6 I have no help but Thine; nor do I need
another arm save Thine to lean upon;
it is enough, my Lord, enough indeed;
my strength is in Thy might, Thy might alone.

7 Feast after feast thus comes and passes by,
yet, passing, points to the glad feast above,
giving sweet foretaste of the festive joy,
the Lamb's great bridal feast of bliss and love.

Horatius Bonar, 1808-89

439

I hunger and I thirst;
Jesus, my manna be;
ye living waters, burst
out of the rock for me.

2 Thou bruised and broken bread,
my life-long wants supply;
as living souls are fed,
O feed me, or I die.

3 Thou true life-giving vine,
let me Thy sweetness prove;
renew my life with Thine,
refresh my soul with love.

4 Rough paths my feet have trod,
since first their course began;
feed me, Thou bread of God;
help me, Thou Son of Man.

5 For still the desert lies
my thirsting soul before;
O living waters, rise
within me evermore.

John Samuel Bewley Monsell, 1811-75

440

In memory of the Saviour's love,
we keep the sacred feast,
where every humble contrite heart
is made a welcome guest.

2 By faith we take the bread of life,
with which our souls are fed;
and drink the token of His blood
that was for sinners shed.

3 Under His banner here we sing
the wonders of His love,
and so anticipate by faith
the heavenly feast above.

Thomas Cotterill,* 1779-1823

441

Jesus invites His saints
to meet around His board;
here pardoned rebels sit and hold
communion with their Lord.

2 This holy bread and wine
maintain our fainting breath,
by union with our living Lord,
and interest in His death.

3 Our heavenly Father calls
Christ and His members one;
we the young children of His love,
and He the first-born Son.

4 We are but several parts
of the same broken bread;
one body has its several limbs,
but Jesus is the Head.

5 Let all our powers be joined
His glorious Name to raise;
pleasure and love fill every mind,
and every voice be praise.

Isaac Watts, 1674-1748

442

Jesus calls us to His table
as He did before He died;
called His friends so frail and faithless,
on the night He was denied.
Son of God yet friend of sinners,
breaking bread and sharing wine:
tokens of Your costly passion,
signs and seals of love divine.

2 'Take and eat, this is My body
broken on the cross for you;
gone the weight of your transgression,
by My death you are made new.
Feast upon the bread of heaven,
eat in faith that you are Mine,
foretaste of the kingdom banquet
where the ransomed church shall dine.

3 'Take and drink, this is My lifeblood
shed and offered in your place,
flowing from My piercèd body,
wounds of sin, yet fount of grace.
Judgment's cup has now been emptied,
cup of life to you I bring:
taste and see that God forgives you,
in His faithful, stricken King.'

4 Christ, we come now to Your table,
come to take what here You give;
come in thanks and awe and wonder,
come to eat and drink and live.
Wash me, cleanse me, feed me, fill me,
pour Your Spirit from on high,
so we may proclaim the mystery
that You came to earth to die.

Andrew J Goddard, b. 1967

443

Jesus, we thus obey
Thy last and kindest word;
here in Thine own appointed way
we come to meet our Lord.

2 Our hearts we open wide,
to make the Saviour room;
and lo! the Lamb, the crucified,
the sinner's friend is come.

3 Thus we remember Thee,
and take this bread and wine
as Thine own dying legacy,
and our redemption's sign.

4 With high and heavenly bliss
Thou dost our spirits cheer;
Thy house of banqueting is this,
and Thou hast brought us here.

5 Thy presence makes the feast;
now let our spirits feel
the glory not to be expressed,
the joy unspeakable.

6 Now let our souls be fed
with manna from above,
and over us Thy banner spread
of everlasting love.

Charles Wesley, 1707-88

444

Lord, in this blest and hallowed hour
reveal Your presence and Your power;
show to my faith Your hands and side,
my Lord and God, the crucified!

2 Gladly I find a calm retreat
from vain distractions near Your feet;
and, borne above all earthly care,
be joyful in Your house of prayer.

3 Or let me through the opening skies
catch one bright glimpse of paradise,
and realize, with raptured awe,
the vision dying Stephen saw.

4 But, if unworthy of such joy,
still shall Your love my heart employ;
for, of Your favoured children's fare,
what bliss the very crumbs to share!

5 Yet never can my soul be fed
with less than You, the living bread;
Yourself unto my soul impart,
and with Your presence fill my heart.

Josiah Conder, 1789-1855

445

Not worthy, Lord, to gather up the crumbs
with trembling hand that from Thy table fall,
a weary heavy-laden sinner comes
to plead Thy promise and obey Thy call.

2 I am not worthy to be thought Thy child,
nor sit the lowest at Thy table Lord;
too long a wanderer, and too oft beguiled,
I only ask one reconciling word.

3 One word from Thee, my Lord, one smile, one look,
and I could face the cold, rough world again;
and with that treasure in my heart could brook
the wrath of devils and the scorn of men.

4 I hear Thy voice: Thou bidd'st me come and rest;
I come, I kneel, I clasp Thy piercèd feet;
Thou bidd'st me take my place, a welcome guest,
among Thy saints, and of Thy banquet eat.

5 My praise can only breathe itself in prayer,
my prayer can only lose itself in Thee;
dwell Thou for ever in my heart, and there,
Lord, let me sup with Thee: sup Thou with me.

Edward Henry Bickersteth, 1825-1906

446

My God, and is Thy table spread?
And does Thy cup with love o'erflow?
Thither be all Thy children led,
and let them all its sweetness know.

2 Why are these emblems still in vain
before unwilling hearts displayed?
Was not for you the Victim slain?
Are you forbid the children's bread?

3 O let Thy table honoured be,
and furnished well with joyful guests;
and may each soul salvation see,
that here its sacred pledges tastes.

4 Revive Thy dying churches, Lord,
and bid our drooping graces live;
and more, that energy afford
a Saviour's grace alone can give.

Philip Doddridge, 1702-51

447

Sweet feast of love divine!
'Tis grace that makes us free
to feed upon this bread and wine,
in memory, Lord, of Thee.

2 Here every welcome guest
waits, Lord, from Thee to learn
the secrets of Thy Father's breast,
and all Thy grace discern.

3 Here conscience ends its strife,
and faith delights to prove
the sweetness of the bread of life,
the fulness of Thy love.

4 The blood that flowed for sin,
in symbol here we see,
and feel the blessèd pledge within
that we are loved of Thee.

5 O if this glimpse of love
is so divinely sweet,
what will it be, O Lord, above,
Thy gladdening smile to meet!

6 To see Thee face to face,
Thy perfect likeness wear,
and all Thy ways of wondrous grace
through endless years declare!

Edward Denny, 1796-1889

448

Sweet the moments, rich in blessing,
which before the cross I spend,
life and health, and peace possessing
from the sinner's dying friend!

2 Here I rest, in wonder viewing
all my sins on Jesus laid,
and a full redemption flowing
from the sacrifice He made.

3 Here I find my hope of heaven,
while upon the Lamb I gaze;
loving much, and much forgiven,
let my heart o'erflow in praise.

4 Love and grief my heart dividing,
with my tears His feet I'll bathe,
constant still in faith abiding,
life deriving from His death.

5 Lord, in ceaseless contemplation
fix my thankful heart on Thee!
till I taste Thy full salvation,
and Thine unveiled glory see.

William Walter Shirley, 1725-86, *and others;*
based on James Allen, 1734-1804

449

The Lord is here!
His promised word
is evermore the same,
Himself to be
where two or three
are gathered in His Name.

2 The Lord is here!
Where Christ is come
His Spirit too is there,
with all who raise
the song of praise
or breathe the voice of prayer.

3 The Lord is here!
He comes in peace
with blessings from above,
by pledge and sign
of bread and wine
to fold us in His love.

4 The Lord is here!
To every soul
this gift of grace be given,
to walk the way
of Christ today,
and share the life of heaven.

Timothy Dudley-Smith, b. 1926

450

To Calvary, Lord, in spirit now
our weary souls repair,
to dwell upon Thy dying love,
and taste its sweetness there.

2 Sweet resting-place of every heart
that feels the plague of sin,
yet knows that deep mysterious joy,
the peace of God within.

3 There through Thine hour of deepest woe,
Thy suffering spirit passed;
grace there its wondrous victory gained,
and love endured its last.

4 Dear suffering Lamb! Thy bleeding wounds,
with cords of love divine,
have drawn our willing hearts to Thee,
and linked our life with Thine.

5 Why linger then? Come, Saviour, come,
responsive to our call;
come, claim Thy ancient power and reign,
the heir and Lord of all.

Edward Denny, 1796-1889

451

To His table richly spread
Christ invites His people near;
but I see His hands, His side
scarred by nail wounds and the spear.

2 Shamed with conscious guilt I come,
grieving as I learn to trace
all that my redemption cost
written on His patient face.

3 How may I partake the feast,
I, who daily still offend?
How may I who caused His pain
call the Son of God my friend?

4 Mercy shines within His eyes,
mercy rests upon His face,
mercy cancels all my debt,
by the merits of His grace.

5 Penitent I gladly come
to His feast – a welcome guest –
drink of Christ and share His life,
leaning on His kindly breast.

6 Till at last I heavenward rise,
all the work of grace complete,
taste of glory's better wine,
love and worship at His feet.

Faith Cook, b. 1937

452

A parting hymn we sing
around Your table, Lord;
again our grateful tribute bring,
our solemn vows record.

2 Here have we seen Your face,
and felt Your presence near;
so may the savour of Your grace
in word and life appear.

3 In self-forgetting love
be our communion shown,
until we join the church above,
and know as we are known.

Aaron Robarts Wolfe, 1821-1902

453

O Saviour, I have nought to plead,
in earth beneath, or heaven above,
but just my own exceeding need,
and Your exceeding love.

2 The need will soon be past and gone,
exceeding great, but quickly o'er;
Your love unbought is all Your own,
and lasts for evermore.

Jane Crewdson, 1809-63

454

When on Calvary I rest,
God in flesh made manifest
shines in my Redeemer's face,
full of beauty, truth and grace.

2 Here I would for ever stay,
weep and gaze my soul away;
you are heaven on earth to me,
lovely, mournful Calvary.

James Montgomery, 1771-1854

The ministry

455

Father of mercies, bow Thine ear,
attentive to our earnest prayer;
we plead for those who plead for
Thee;
successful pleaders may they be!

2 How great their work, how vast their
charge!
Do Thou their anxious souls enlarge:
their best acquirements are our
gain;
we share the blessings they obtain.

3 Clothe, then, with energy divine,
their words, and let those words be Thine;
to them Thy sacred truth reveal,
suppress their fear, inflame their zeal.

4 Teach them to sow the precious seed,
teach them Thy chosen flock to feed;
teach them immortal souls to gain,
souls that will well reward their pain.

5 Let thronging multitudes around
hear from their lips the joyful sound,
in humble strains Thy grace implore,
and feel Thy new-creating power.

Benjamin Beddome, 1717-95

456

Give me the faith which can remove
and sink the mountain to a plain;
give me the child-like praying love,
which longs to build Thy house again;
Thy love, let it my heart o'erpower,
and all my simple soul devour.

2 I want an even strong desire,
I want a calmly fervent zeal,
to save poor souls out of the fire,
to snatch them from the verge of hell,
and turn them to a pardoning God,
and quench the brands in Jesu's blood.

3 I would the precious time redeem,
and longer live for this alone,
to spend, and to be spent, for them
who have not yet my Saviour known;
fully on these my mission prove,
and only breathe, to breathe Thy love.

4 My talents, gifts, and graces, Lord,
into Thy blessèd hands receive;
and let me live to preach Thy Word,
and let me to Thy glory live;
my every sacred moment spend
in publishing the sinners' friend.

5 Enlarge, inflame, and fill my heart
with boundless charity divine!
So shall I all my strength exert,
and love them with a zeal like Thine;
and lead them to Thy open side,
the sheep for whom their Shepherd died.

Charles Wesley, 1707-88

457

Lord of the church, we humbly pray
for those who guide us in Your way,
and speak Your holy word;
with love divine their hearts inspire,
and touch their lips with hallowed fire,
and needful grace afford.

2 Help them to preach the truth of God,
redemption through the Saviour's blood;
nor let Your Spirit cease
on all the church His gifts to shower –
to them, a messenger of power,
to us, of life and peace.

3 So may they live to You alone;
then hear the welcome word 'Well done!'
and take their crown above;
enter into their Master's joy,
and all eternity employ
in praise and bliss and love!

Edward Osler, 1798-1863

458

Pour out Thy Spirit from on high,
Lord, Thine ordainèd servants bless;
graces and gifts to each supply,
and clothe them with Thy righteousness.

2 Within Thy temple when they stand,
to teach the truth, as taught by Thee,
Saviour, like stars in Thy right hand
the angels of the churches be!

3 Wisdom and zeal and faith impart,
firmness with meekness, from above,
to bear Thy people on their heart,
and love the souls whom Thou dost love;

4 To watch and pray, and never faint,
by day and night strict guard to keep,
to warn the sinner, cheer the saint,
nourish Thy lambs and feed Thy sheep;

5 Then, when their work is finished here,
and they in hope their charge resign,
when the chief Shepherd shall appear,
may they, O God, in glory shine!

James Montgomery, 1771-1854

459

The means of grace are in my hand,
the blessing is at God's command,
who must the work fulfil;
and though I read, and watch and pray,
yet here the Lord directs my way,
and worketh all things still.

2 I cannot speak a proper word,
nor think aright, but from the Lord
preparing heart and tongue;
in nature I can see no good,
but all my good proceeds from God,
and does to grace belong.

3 I see it now, and do confess
my utter need of Jesus' grace,
and of His Spirit's light;
I beg His kind and daily care;
O Lord, my heart and tongue prepare
to think and speak aright.

4 Prepare my heart to love Thee well,
and love Thy truth which doth excel,
and love Thy children dear;
instruct me how to live by faith,
and feel the virtue of Thy death,
and find Thy presence near.

5 Prepare my tongue to pray and praise,
to speak of providential ways,
and heavenly truth unfold;
to strengthen well a feeble soul,
correct the wanton, rouse the dull,
and silence sinners bold.

John Berridge, 1716-93

The kingdom of Christ on earth

460

'For My sake and the gospel's, go
and tell redemption's story';
His heralds answer, 'Be it so,
and Yours, Lord, all the glory!'
They preach His birth, His life, His cross,
the love of His atonement,
for whom they count the world but loss,
His Easter, His enthronement.

2 Hark, hark, the trump of jubilee
proclaims to every nation,
from pole to pole, by land and sea,
glad tidings of salvation.
As nearer draws the day of doom,
while still the battle rages,
the heavenly Day-spring through the gloom
breaks on the night of ages.

3 Still on and on the anthems spread
of hallelujah voices,
in concert with the holy dead
the warrior church rejoices;
their snow-white robes are washed in blood,
their golden harps are ringing;
earth and the paradise of God
one triumph-song are singing.

4 He comes, whose advent-trumpet drowns
the last of time's evangels,
Immanuel crowned with many crowns,
the Lord of saints and angels:
O Life, Light, Love, the great I AM,
triune, who changes never,
the throne of God and of the Lamb
is Yours, and Yours for ever!

Edward Henry Bickersteth, 1825-1906

461

Based on ISAIAH 2:1-5

Behold, the mountain of the Lord
in latter days shall rise
on mountain tops above the hills,
and draw the wondering eyes.

2 To this the joyful nations round,
all tribes and tongues, shall flow;
Up to the hill of God, they'll say,
and to His house we'll go.

3 The beam that shines from Zion's hill
shall lighten every land;
the King who reigns in Salem's towers
shall all the world command.

4 Among the nations He shall judge;
His judgments truth shall guide;
His sceptre shall protect the just,
and quell the sinner's pride.

5 No strife shall rage, nor hostile feuds
disturb those peaceful years;
to ploughshares men shall beat their swords,
to pruning-hooks their spears.

6 Come then, O come from every land,
to worship at His shrine;
and, walking in the light of God,
with holy beauties shine.

Michael Bruce, 1746-67

462

Father, let Your kingdom come,
let it come with living power!
Speak at length the final word,
usher in the triumph hour.

2 As it came in days of old,
in the deepest hearts of men,
when Your martyrs died for You,
let it come, O God, again!

3 O what long, sad years have gone,
since Your church was taught this prayer!
O what eyes have watched and wept
for the dawning everywhere!

4 Break, triumphant day of God!
break at last, our hearts to cheer;
throbbing souls and holy songs
wait to hail Your dawning here.

5 Empires, temples, sceptres, thrones –
may they all for God be won;
and, in every human heart,
Father, let Your kingdom come!

John Page Hopps, 1834-1911

463

Go quickly, for the fading hours
with haste are sinking to the west;
exert with zeal your ransomed powers,
nor think it yet the time for rest.

2 Go quickly, for the sons of time
are journeying to a hopeless grave,
and tell to earth's remotest clime
of Him who came to seek and save.

3 Go quickly to the realms of sin;
invite as many as you find;
and welcome all to enter in –
the poor, the maimed, the lame, the blind.

4 Go quickly with the living Word
sent to the nations from above,
till every heart on earth has heard
the tidings of redeeming love.

William Wileman, 1848-1944

464

Go forth and tell! O Church of God, awake!
God's saving news to all the nations take;
proclaim Christ Jesus, Saviour, Lord and King,
that all the world His worthy praise may sing.

2 Go forth and tell! God's love embraces all;
He will in grace respond to all who call:
how shall they call if they have never heard
the gracious invitation of His word?

3 Go forth and tell where still the darkness lies;
in wealth or want, the sinner surely dies:
give us, O Lord, concern of heart and mind,
a love like Yours which cares for all mankind.

4 Go forth and tell! The doors are open wide;
share God's good gift – let no one be denied;
live out your life as Christ your Lord shall choose,
your ransomed powers for His sole glory use.

5 Go forth and tell! O Church of God, arise!
Go in the strength which Christ your Lord supplies;
go till all nations His great name adore
and serve Him, Lord and King for evermore.

James Edward Seddon, 1915-83

465 Psalm 67

God in mercy grant us blessing,
lift on us His radiant face;
may all earth, His ways confessing,
know the power of saving grace:
let the peoples' voices raise,
Lord, to You their hymns of praise.

2 Let them all with jubilation
sing of Your transcendent worth,
justly ruling every nation,
sovereign Lord of all the earth:
let the peoples' voices raise,
Lord, to You their hymns of praise.

3 See the blessing God has granted
on our labours in the field!
May His word in hearts implanted
worldwide harvests duly yield:
so shall all the nations raise
to our God their hymns of praise.

David G Preston, b. 1949

466

Based on Psalm 67

God of mercy! God of grace!
show the brightness of Your face;
shine upon us, Saviour, shine;
fill Your church with light divine;
and Your saving health extend
unto earth's remotest end.

2 Let the people praise You, Lord;
be by all that live adored:
let the nations shout and sing
glory to their Saviour King;
at Your feet their tribute pay,
and Your holy will obey.

3 Let the people praise You, Lord;
earth shall then her fruits afford;
God to man His blessing give;
man to God devoted live:
all below, and all above,
one in joy and light and love.

Henry Francis Lyte, 1793-1847

467

Based on Psalm 72

Hail to the Lord's anointed,
great David's greater Son!
Hail, in the time appointed,
His reign on earth begun!
He comes to break oppression,
to set the captive free,
to take away transgression,
and rule in equity.

2 He shall come down like showers
upon the fruitful earth,
and love, joy, hope, like flowers,
spring in His path to birth:
before Him on the mountains
shall peace, the herald, go;
and righteousness, in fountains,
from hill to valley flow.

3 Kings shall fall down before Him,
and gold and incense bring;
all nations shall adore Him,
His praise all people sing;
to Him shall prayer unceasing
and daily vows ascend;
His kingdom still increasing,
a kingdom without end.

4 He comes with solace speedy
to those who suffer wrong;
to help the poor and needy,
and bid the weak be strong;
to give them songs for sighing,
their darkness turn to light,
whose souls, condemned and dying,
were precious in His sight.

5 O'er every foe victorious,
He on His throne shall rest;
from age to age more glorious,
all-blessing and all-blest:
the tide of time shall never
His covenant remove;
His Name shall stand for ever,
His changeless Name of love.

James Montgomery, 1771-1854

468

In doubt and dread dismay,
midst superstition's gloom,
the godless grope their way,
and joyless reach the tomb:
no holy light,
no healing ray
of gospel day
has blessed their sight.

2 Rise Sun of righteousness,
and on Your gracious wing,
be pleased to heal and bless,
and Your salvation bring.

Let darkened minds
Your brightness see;
O set them free
from sin that blinds.

3 With searching beams explore
the dark strongholds of sin;
and on sin's prisoners pour
transforming light within:
bright Morning-star,
unveil Your face,
and shed Your grace
both near and far.

4 Lord Jesus, light of life!
arouse the world from sleep;
send love in place of strife,
and joy to those who weep:
great King of kings,
Your Spirit give,
that souls may live
beneath Your wings!

*William Henry Havergal**, 1793-1870

469

I cannot tell why He, whom angels worship,
should set His love upon the sons of men,
or why, as Shepherd, He should seek the wanderers,
to bring them back, they know not how or when.
But this I know, that He was born of Mary,
when Bethlehem's manger was His only home,
and that He lived at Nazareth and laboured,
and so the Saviour, Saviour of the world, is come.

2 I cannot tell how silently He suffered,
as with His peace He graced this place of tears,
or how His heart upon the cross was broken,
the crown of pain to three and thirty years.
But this I know, He heals the broken-hearted,
and stays our sin, and calms our lurking fear,
and lifts the burden from the heavy laden,
for yet the Saviour, Saviour of the world, is here.

3 I cannot tell how He will win the nations,
how He will claim His earthly heritage,
how satisfy the needs and aspirations
of east and west, of sinner and of sage.
But this I know, all flesh shall see His glory,
and He shall reap the harvest He has sown,
and some glad day His sun shall shine in splendour
when He the Saviour, Saviour of the world, is known.

4 I cannot tell how all the lands shall worship,
when, at His bidding, every storm is stilled,
or who can say how great the jubilation
when all the hearts of men with love are filled.
But this I know, the skies will thrill with rapture,
and myriad, myriad human voices sing,
and earth to heaven, and heaven to earth will answer:
'At last the Saviour, Saviour of the world, is King!'

William Young Fullerton, 1857-1932

470

Lord, for the years Your love has kept and guided,
urged and inspired us, cheered us on our way,
sought us and saved us, pardoned and provided,
Lord of the years, we bring our thanks today.

2 Lord, for that word, the word of life which fires us,
speaks to our hearts and sets our souls ablaze,
teaches and trains, rebukes us and inspires us,
Lord of the word, receive Your people's praise.

3 Lord, for our land, in this our generation,
spirits oppressed by pleasure, wealth and care:
for young and old, for commonwealth and nation,
Lord of our land, be pleased to hear our prayer.

4 Lord, for our world, when we disown and doubt Him,
loveless in strength, and comfortless in pain;
hungry and helpless, lost indeed without Him,
Lord of the world, we pray that Christ may reign.

5 Lord, for ourselves; in living power remake us,
self on the cross and Christ upon the throne;
past put behind us, for the future take us,
Lord of our lives, to live for Christ alone.

Timothy Dudley-Smith, b. 1926

471 Based on Psalm 45:1-6

O'er the gloomy hills of darkness
look, my soul; be still and gaze;
all the promises do travail
with a glorious day of grace:
blessed jubilee!
let your glorious morning dawn.

2 Kingdoms wide that sit in darkness,
grant them, Lord, Your glorious light;
and from eastern coast to western
may the morning chase the night;
and redemption,
freely purchased, win the day.

3 May the glorious day approaching
end their night of sin and shame,
and the everlasting gospel
spread abroad Your holy name
o'er the borders
of the great Immanuel's land!

4 Fly abroad, O mighty gospel,
win and conquer, never cease;
may your lasting wide dominion
multiply and still increase!
Sway Your sceptre,
Saviour, all the world around.

William Williams, 1717-91

472

Let us sing the King Messiah,
King of righteousness and peace;
hail Him, all His happy subjects,
never let His praises cease:
ever hail Him;
never let His praises cease.

2 How transcendent are Your glories,
fairer than the sons of men,
while Your blessèd mediation
brings us back to God again:
blest Redeemer,
how we triumph in Your reign!

3 Gird Your sword on, mighty hero!
Spread the Word of truth afar;
prosper in Your course majestic;
all success attend Your war!
Gracious victor,
let mankind before You bow!

4 Majesty combined with meekness,
righteousness and peace unite
to ensure Your blessèd conquests;
on, great Prince, assert Your right:
ride triumphant
all around the conquered globe.

5 Blest are all that touch Your sceptre;
blest are all that own Your reign,
freed from sin, that worst of tyrants,
rescued from its galling chain:
saints and angels,
all who know You bless Your reign.

John Ryland, 1753-1825

473

Lord, her watch Your church is keeping;
when shall earth Your rule obey?
When shall end the night of weeping?
When shall break the promised day?
See the whitening harvest languish,
waiting still the labourers' toil;
was it vain, Your Son's deep anguish?
Shall the strong retain the spoil?

2 Tidings, sent to every creature,
millions yet have never heard;
can they hear without a preacher?
Lord almighty, give the Word:
give the Word; in every nation
let the gospel trumpet sound,
witnessing a world's salvation
to the earth's remotest bound.

3 Then the end: Your church completed,
all Your chosen gathered in,
with their King in glory seated,
Satan bound, and banished sin;
gone for ever parting, weeping,
hunger, sorrow, death, and pain:
lo! her watch Your church is keeping;
come, Lord Jesus, come to reign!

Henry Downton, 1818-85

474

My heart and voice I raise,
to spread Messiah's praise;
Messiah's praise let all repeat;
the universal Lord,
by whose almighty word
creation rose in form complete.

2 A servant's form He wore,
and in His body bore
our dreadful curse on Calvary:
He like a victim stood,
and poured His precious blood,
to set the guilty captives free.

3 But soon the Victor rose
triumphant o'er His foes,
and led the vanquished host in chains:
He threw their empire down,
His foes compelled to own
o'er all the great Messiah reigns.

4 With mercy's mildest grace,
He governs all our race
in wisdom, righteousness and love.
Who to Messiah fly
shall find redemption nigh,
and all his great salvation prove.

5 Hail, Saviour, Prince of Peace!
Your kingdom shall increase,
till all the world Your glory see,
and righteousness abound
as the great deep profound,
and fill the earth with purity.

Benjamin Rhodes, 1743-1815

475

PSALM 45:1-4

My heart is full of Christ, and longs
its glorious matter to declare!
Of Him I make my loftier songs,
I cannot from His praise forbear;
my ready tongue makes haste to sing
the glories of my heavenly King.

2 Fairer than all the earth-born race,
perfect in comeliness Thou art;
replenished are Thy lips with grace,
and full of love Thy tender heart:
God ever blest! we bow the knee,
and own all fulness dwells in Thee.

3 Gird on Thy thigh the Spirit's sword,
and take to Thee Thy power divine;
stir up Thy strength, almighty Lord,
all power and majesty are Thine:
assert Thy worship and renown;
O all-redeeming God, come down!

4 Come and maintain Thy righteous cause,
and let Thy glorious toil succeed;
O spread the victory of Thy cross,
ride on, and prosper in Thy deed!
Through earth triumphantly ride on,
and reign in every heart alone.

Charles Wesley, 1707-88

476

O come, O come, Immanuel,
and ransom captive Israel,
that mourns in lonely exile here
until the Son of God appear.

Rejoice! rejoice! Immanuel
shall come to thee, O Israel!

2 O come, O come, Thou Lord of might,
who to Thy tribes, on Sinai's height,
in ancient times didst give the law
in cloud and majesty and awe.

3 O come, Thou Rod of Jesse, free
Thine own from Satan's tyranny;
from depths of hell Thy people save,
and give them victory o'er the grave.

4 O come, Thou Day-spring, come and cheer
our spirits by Thine advent here;
disperse the gloomy clouds of night,
and death's dark shadows put to flight.

5 O come, Thou Key of David, come,
and open wide our heavenly home;
make safe the way that leads on high,
and close the path to misery.

Latin, 12th cent.;
*tr. by John Mason Neale**, 1818-66

477

O Lord our God, arise!
the cause of truth maintain,
and wide o'er all the peopled world
extend her blessèd reign.

2 O Prince of life, arise!
nor let Your glory cease;
far spread the conquests of Your grace,
and bless the earth with peace.

3 O Holy Ghost, arise!
expand Your quickening wing,
and o'er a dark and ruined world
let light and order spring.

4 All on the earth, arise!
to God the Saviour sing;
from shore to shore, from earth to heaven,
let echoing anthems ring.

Ralph Wardlaw, 1779-1853

478

Onward march, all-conquering Jesus,
gird Thee on Thy mighty sword;
sinful earth can ne'er oppose Thee;
hell itself quails at Thy Word.
Thy great Name is so exalted,
every foe shrinks back in fear;
terror creeps through all creation,
when it knows that Thou art near.

2 Free my soul from sin's foul bondage;
hasten now the glorious dawn;
break proud Babel's gates in sunder;
let the massive bolts be drawn.
Forth, like ocean's heaving surges,
bring in myriads ransomed slaves,
host on host, with shouts of triumph,
endless, countless as the waves.

3 Even today I hear sweet music,
praises of a blood-freed throng;
full deliverance, glorious freedom,
are their themes for endless song;
whiter than the snow their raiment,
victor palms they wave on high,
as they pass, with fullest glory,
into life's felicity.

4 How my raptured soul rejoices
that the jubilee is near;
every word will be accomplished
spoken by our Saviour here.
North and south, in countless myriads,
from earth's darkest ends they come,
with the dance and gladsome music,
into heaven's eternal home.

William Williams, 1717-91;
tr. by William Howells, 1855-1932

479

See how great a flame aspires,
kindled by a spark of grace!
Jesu's love the nations fires,
sets the kingdoms on a blaze;
fire to bring on earth He came;
kindled in some hearts it is:
O that all might catch the flame,
all partake the glorious bliss!

2 When He first the work begun,
small and feeble was His day:
now the word does swiftly run,
now it wins its widening way;
more and more it spreads and grows,
ever mighty to prevail;
sin's strongholds it now o'erthrows,
shakes the trembling gates of hell.

3 Sons of God, your Saviour praise;
He the door has opened wide,
He has given the word of grace,
Jesu's word is glorified;
Jesus, mighty to redeem,
He alone the work has wrought;
worthy is the work of Him,
Him who spake a world from nought.

4 Saw ye not the cloud arise,
little as a human hand?
Now it spreads along the skies,
hangs o'er all the thirsty land;
lo! the promise of a shower
drops already from above;
but the Lord will shortly pour
all the Spirit of His love.

Charles Wesley, 1707-88

480

They shall come from the east,
they shall come from the west,
and sit down in the kingdom of God;
both the rich and the poor,
the despised, the distressed,
they'll sit down in the kingdom of God.
And none will ask what they have been
provided that their robes are clean;
they shall come from the east,
they shall come from the west,
and sit down in the kingdom of God.

2 They shall come from the east,
they shall come from the west,
and sit down in the kingdom of God;
to be met by their Father
and welcomed and blessed,
and sit down in the kingdom of God.
The black, the white, the dark, the fair,
your colour will not matter there;
they shall come from the east,
they shall come from the west,
and sit down in the kingdom of God.

3 They shall come from the east,
they shall come from the west,
and sit down in the kingdom of God;
out of great tribulation to triumph and rest
they'll sit down in the kingdom of God.
From every tribe and every race,
all men as brothers shall embrace;
they shall come from the east,
they shall come from the west,
and sit down in the kingdom of God.

John Gowans, b. 1934

481

Sing we the King who is coming to reign,
glory to Jesus, the Lamb that was slain.
Life and salvation His empire shall bring,
joy to the nations when Jesus is King.

Come let us sing: praise to our King.
Jesus our King, Jesus our King:
this is our song, who to Jesus belong:
glory to Jesus, to Jesus our King.

2 All men shall dwell in His marvellous light,
races long severed His love shall unite,
justice and truth from His sceptre shall spring,
wrong shall be ended when Jesus is King.

3 All shall be well in His kingdom of peace,
freedom shall flourish and wisdom increase,
foe shall be friend when His triumph we sing,
sword shall be sickle when Jesus is King.

4 Kingdom of Christ, for Your coming we pray,
hasten, O Father, the dawn of the day
when this new song Your creation shall sing:
'Satan is vanquished and Jesus is King!'

5 Souls shall be saved from the burden of sin;
doubt shall not darken His witness within;
hell has no terrors, and death has no sting,
love is victorious, when Jesus is King.

Charles Sylvester Horne, 1865-1914

482

Thou whose almighty word
chaos and darkness heard,
and took their flight,
hear us, we humbly pray,
and where the gospel day
sheds not its glorious ray,
let there be light!

2 Thou who didst come to bring
on Thy redeeming wing
healing and sight,
health to the sick in mind,
sight to the inly blind,
O now to all mankind
let there be light!

3 Spirit of truth and love,
life-giving, holy dove,
speed forth Thy flight;
move on the waters' face,
bearing the lamp of grace,
and in earth's darkest place
let there be light!

4 Blessèd and holy three,
glorious Trinity,
Wisdom, Love, Might;
boundless as ocean's tide
rolling in fullest pride,
through the world, far and wide,
let there be light!

John Marriott, 1780-1825

483

We have a gospel to proclaim,
good news for men in all the earth,
the gospel of a Saviour's name:
we sing His glory, tell His worth.

2 Tell of His birth at Bethlehem,
not in a royal house or hall
but in a stable dark and dim:
the Word made flesh, a light for all.

3 Tell of His death at Calvary,
hated by those He came to save;
in lonely suffering on the cross
for all He loved, His life He gave.

4 Tell of that glorious Easter morn:
empty the tomb, for He was free;
He broke the power of death and hell
that we might share His victory.

5 Tell of His reign at God's right hand,
by all creation glorified;
He sends His Spirit on His church
to live for Him, the Lamb who died.

6 Now we rejoice to name Him King –
Jesus is Lord of all the earth;
this gospel message we proclaim,
we sing His glory, tell His worth.

Edward J Burns, b. 1938

484

We have heard the joyful sound:
Jesus saves!
Spread the tidings all around:
Jesus saves!
Bear the news to every land,
climb the steeps and cross the waves.
Onward! 'tis our Lord's command:
Jesus saves!

2 Sing above the battle's strife:
Jesus saves!
By His death and endless life,
Jesus saves!
Sing it softly through the gloom,
when the heart for mercy craves;
sing in triumph o'er the tomb:
Jesus saves!

3 Give the winds a mighty voice:
Jesus saves!
Let the nations now rejoice:
Jesus saves!
Shout salvation full and free,
highest hills and deepest caves;
this our song of victory:
Jesus saves!

Priscilla Jane Owens, 1829-1907

485

Ye that know the Lord is gracious,
ye for whom a Corner-stone
stands, of God elect and precious,
laid that ye may build thereon,
see that on that sure foundation
ye a living temple raise,
towers that may tell forth salvation,
walls that may re-echo praise.

2 Living stones, by God appointed
each to his allotted place,
kings and priests, by God anointed,
shall ye not declare His grace?
Ye, a royal generation,
tell the tidings of your birth,
tidings of a new creation
to an old and weary earth.

3 Tell the praise of Him who called you
out of darkness into light,
broke the fetters that enthralled you,
gave you freedom, peace and sight:
tell the tale of sins forgiven,
strength renewed and hope restored,
till the earth, in tune with heaven,
praise and magnify the Lord!

Cyril Argentine Alington, 1872-1955

486

Great God of Abraham! hear our prayer;
let Abraham's seed Thy mercy share:
O may they now at length return
and look on Him they pierced, and mourn!

2 Remember Jacob's flock of old;
bring home the wanderers to Thy fold;
remember too Thy promised word,
'Israel at last shall seek the Lord.'

3 Though outcasts still, estranged from Thee,
cut off from their own olive-tree,
why should they longer such remain?
For Thou canst graft them in again.

4 Lord, put Thy law within their hearts,
and write it in their inward parts;
the veil of darkness rend in two,
which hides Messiah from their view.

5 O haste the day, foretold so long,
when Jew and Greek, a glorious throng,
one house shall seek, one prayer shall pour,
and one Redeemer shall adore!

Thomas Cotterill, 1779-1823

THE GOSPEL

Salvation by grace

487

Amazing grace! how sweet the sound,
that saved a wretch like me!
I once was lost, but now am found;
was blind, but now I see.

2 'Twas grace that taught my heart to fear,
and grace my fears relieved;
how precious did that grace appear
the hour I first believed!

3 Through many dangers, toils and snares
I have already come;
'tis grace has brought me safe thus far,
and grace will lead me home.

4 The Lord has promised good to me,
His Word my hope secures;
He will my shield and portion be
as long as life endures.

5 Yes, when this flesh and heart shall fail,
and mortal life shall cease,
I shall possess within the veil
a life of joy and peace.

6 The earth shall soon dissolve like snow,
the sun forbear to shine;
but God, who called me here below,
will be forever mine.

John Newton, 1725-1807

The following may be sung as an alternative final verse:

6 When I've been there a thousand years,
bright shining as the sun,
I've no less days to sing God's praise
than when I first begun.

From A COLLECTION OF SACRED BALLADS, 1790

488

And are our sins forgiven
if we in Jesus trust?
See where the nails through Him were driven,
the spear in Him was thrust.

2 And has His gospel still
its ancient power to save?
The One who died on Calvary's hill
still rescues from the grave.

3 And does He still baptise
His church with heavenly fire?
We yet shall see Him rend the skies
and meet our hearts' desire.

4 And is our Jesus Lord,
eternal and divine?
Angels and saints with one accord
acclaim their God and mine.

Eluned Harrison, b. 1934

489

Far before time, beyond creation's dawn,
before the sun and moon and stars were born,
salvation's way for sinners lost, undone,
was counselled forth by God the Three in One.

2 A store of grace unlimited was laid
in Jesus Christ before the seas were made;
and precious cov'nant mercies did abound
in floods of blessing all the world around.

3 The trumpet sounds the note of glad release
on Calvary, by God's atoning grace:
glad hymns of praise in every tongue shall be
for Jesu's blood and death that set us free.

Peter Jones, 1775-1845;
tr. by Edmund Tudor Owen, b. 1935

490

Father, 'twas Thy love that knew us
earth's foundations long before;
that same love to Jesus drew us
by its sweet constraining power,
and will keep us
safely now, and evermore.

2 Pause, my soul, adore and wonder!
ask, O why such love to me?
Grace hath put me in the number
of the Saviour's family.
Hallelujah,
thanks, eternal thanks, to Thee!

3 Since that love had no beginning,
and shall never, never cease;
keep, O keep me, Lord, from sinning,
guide me in the way of peace.
Make me walk in
all the paths of holiness.

4 God of love, our souls adore Thee!
We would still Thy grace proclaim,
till we cast our crowns before Thee,
and in glory praise Thy Name:
Hallelujah
be to God and to the Lamb!

vv. 1 & 4, James George Deck, 1802-84;
vv. 2 & 3, Anonymous

491

Grace, 'tis a charming sound,
harmonious to the ear;
heaven with the echo shall resound,
and all the earth shall hear.

2 Grace first contrived a way
to save rebellious man;
and all the steps that grace display,
which drew the wondrous plan.

3 Grace first inscribed my name
in God's eternal book;
'twas grace that gave me to the Lamb,
who all my sorrows took.

4 Grace turned my wandering feet
to tread the heavenly road;
and new supplies each hour I meet,
while pressing on to God.

5 Grace taught my soul to pray,
and made my eyes o'erflow;
'tis grace that kept me to this day,
and will not let me go.

6 Grace all the work shall crown,
through everlasting days;
it lays in heaven the topmost stone,
and well deserves the praise.

vv. 1, 2, 4 & 6, Philip Doddridge, 1702-51;
vv. 3 & 5, Augustus Montague Toplady, 1740-78

492

How heavy is the night
that hangs upon our eyes,
till Christ, with His reviving light,
over our souls arise!

2 Our guilty spirits dread
to meet the wrath of heaven;
but in His righteousness arrayed,
we see our sins forgiven.

3 Unholy and impure
are all our thoughts and ways:
His hands infected nature cure
with sanctifying grace.

4 The powers of hell agree
to hold our souls in vain;
He sets the sons of bondage free,
and breaks the accursèd chain.

5 Lord, we adore Your ways
to bring us near to God,
Your sovereign power, Your healing grace,
and Your atoning blood.

Isaac Watts, 1674-1748

493

How deep the Father's love for us,
how vast beyond all measure,
that He should give His only Son
to make a wretch His treasure.
How great the pain of searing loss;
the Father turns His face away,
as wounds which mar the chosen One
bring many sons to glory.

2 Behold the Man upon a cross,
my sins upon His shoulders;
ashamed, I hear my mocking voice
call out among the scoffers.
It was my sin that held Him there
until it was accomplished.
His dying breath has brought me life;
I know that it is finished.

3 I will not boast in anything,
no gifts, no power, no wisdom;
but I will boast in Jesus Christ,
His death and resurrection.
Why should I gain from His reward?
I cannot give an answer,
but this I know with all my heart,
His wounds have paid my ransom.

Stuart Townend, b. 1963

494

How vast the benefits divine
which we in Christ possess!
We are redeemed from sin and shame,
and called to holiness.
'Tis not for works that we have done,
these all to Him we owe;
but He of His electing love
salvation doth bestow.

2 To Thee, O Lord, alone is due
all glory and renown;
aught to ourselves we dare not take,
or rob Thee of Thy crown.
Thou wast Thyself our surety
in God's redemption plan;
in Thee His grace was given us,
long ere the world began.

3 Safe in the arms of sovereign love
we ever shall remain;
nor shall the rage of earth or hell
make Thy sure counsel vain.
Not one of all the chosen race
but shall to heaven attain;
here they will share abounding grace,
and there with Jesus reign.

Augustus Montague Toplady, 1740-78;
revised by Dewey Westra, 1899-1979

495

Lift up your heads, you mighty gates,
behold, the King of glory waits!
The King of kings is drawing near,
the Saviour of the world is here;
life and salvation will He bring,
wherefore rejoice and gladly sing.

2 The Lord is just, a helper tried,
mercy is ever at His side;
His kingly crown is holiness;
His sceptre, pity in distress;
the end of all our woe He brings,
wherefore the earth is glad and sings.

3 O blest the land, the city blest,
where Christ the ruler is confessed!
O happy hearts and happy homes,
to whom this King in triumph comes!
The cloudless Sun of joy He is,
who brings us pure delight and bliss.

4 Fling wide the portals of your heart,
make it a temple set apart
from earthly use, for heaven's employ,
adorned with prayer, and love, and joy;
so shall your Sovereign enter in,
and new and nobler life begin.

5 Redeemer, come, we open wide
our hearts to You; here, Lord, abide!
Your inner presence let us feel,
Your grace and love in us reveal,
Your Holy Spirit guide us on,
until the glorious goal is won!

Georg Weissel, 1590-1635;
tr. by Catherine Winkworth, 1827-78

496

PSALM 116:1-6

I love the Lord for He heard my voice;
He heard my cry for mercy.
Because He turned His ear to me,
I will call on Him as long as I live.

The cords of death entangled me,
the anguish of the grave came upon me,
I was overcome by trouble and sorrow.
Then I called on the name of the Lord.
O Lord, save me, O Lord, save me.

2 The Lord is gracious and righteous,
our God is full of compassion;
the Lord protects the simple-hearted.
When I was in great need He saved me.
The Lord saved me, the Lord saved me!

Psalm 116:1-6 taken from THE HOLY BIBLE,
NEW INTERNATIONAL VERSION®, NIV®

497

Now to the power of God supreme
be everlasting honours given;
He saves from hell – we bless His name;
He calls our wandering feet to heaven.

2 Not for our duties or deserts,
but of His own abounding grace
He works salvation in our hearts,
and forms a people for His praise.

3 'Twas His own purpose that begun
to rescue rebels doomed to die;
He gave us grace in Christ His Son
before He spread the starry sky.

4 Jesus the Lord appears at last,
and makes His Father's counsels
known;
declares the great transactions past,
and brings immortal blessings down.

5 He dies – and in that dreadful night
did all the powers of hell destroy;
rising, He brought our heaven to light,
and took possession of the joy.

Isaac Watts, 1674-1748

498

'Tis not that I did choose Thee,
for, Lord, that could not be;
this heart would still refuse Thee
hadst Thou not chosen me.
Thou from the sin that stained me
hast cleansed and set me free;
of old Thou hast ordained me,
that I should live to Thee.

2 'Twas sovereign mercy called me,
and taught my opening mind;
the world had else enthralled me,
to heavenly glories blind.
My heart owns none above Thee;
for Thy rich grace I thirst;
this knowing, if I love Thee,
Thou must have loved me first.

Josiah Conder, 1789-1855

499 Based on Titus 3:5-7

'Tis not by works of righteousness
which our own hands have done,
but we are saved by sovereign grace,
abounding through the Son.

2 'Tis from the mercy of our God
that all our hopes begin;
'tis by the water and the blood
our souls are washed from sin.

3 'Tis through the purchase of His death
who hung upon the tree,
the Spirit is sent down to breathe
on such dry bones as we.

4 Raised from the dead, we live anew;
and, justified by grace,
we shall appear in glory too,
and see our Father's face.

Isaac Watts, 1674-1748

500

O Christ, what love is this,
that all Your loved ones know:
that brought You down from highest bliss
to live in such a world as this,
the Father's will to do,
the Father's will to do.

2 O Christ, what burdens these,
You bore on Your own soul;
our guilt, our judgment and God's wrath:
the Man of sorrows died our death,
and all to make us whole,
and all to make us whole.

3 O Christ, what dread reproach!
The Holy One made sin,
the King of kings with thorns is crowned,
the Lord of heaven and earth disowned,
and sinners welcomed in,
and sinners welcomed in!

4 O Christ, what joy is this?
The joy of sins forgiven,
no condemnation now we have,
nor dark despair beyond the grave,
instead, the hope of heaven,
instead, the hope of heaven.

5 O Christ, what glory waits
the objects of Your love!
no eye has seen nor ear has heard,
what God in His great grace prepared,
in that blest world above,
in that blest world above.

Eric J Alexander, b. 1932

501

O how the grace of God
amazes me!
It loosed me from my bonds
and set me free.
What made it happen so?
'Twas His will, this much I know,
set me, as now I show,
at liberty.

2 My God has chosen me,
though one of nought,
to sit beside my King
in heaven's court.
Hear what my Lord has done!
O the love that made Him run
to meet His erring son!
This has God wrought.

3 Not for my righteousness,
for I have none,
but for His mercy's sake,
Jesus, God's Son,
suffered on Calvary's tree –
crucified with thieves was He –
great was his grace to me,
His wayward one.

4 And when I think of how,
at Calvary,
He bore sin's penalty
instead of me,
amazed, I wonder why
He, the sinless One, should die
for one so vile as I:
my Saviour He!

5 Now all my heart's desire,
is to abide
in Him, my Saviour dear,
in Him to hide;
my shield and buckler He,
covering and protecting me:
from Satan's darts I'll be
safe at His side.

6 Lord Jesus, hear my prayer;
Your grace impart;
when evil thoughts arise
through Satan's art,
O drive them all away
and, my God, from day to day,
keep me beneath Your sway,
King of my heart.

7 Come now, the whole of me,
eyes, ears and voice,
join me creation all,
with joyful noise:
praise Him who broke the chain
holding me in sin's domain,
and set me free again!
Sing and rejoice!

E T Sibomana, c. 1910-75;
tr. by Rosemary Guillebaud, 1915-2002

Slightly amended and modernised

502

O what riches and what virtue,
far beyond the thought of man,
are invested in our Saviour,
in the wonder of God's plan.
See in Jesus boundless treasure,
more than we can ever measure.

2 From the heights of glory moving
to this world of sin and night
came this gift of grace and mercy:
Christ the Word and Christ the Light.
See in Jesus hope and gladness,
banishing our grief and sadness.

3 On the cross He bore our judgement
pouring out His precious blood;
making a complete atonement,

reconciling us to God.
See in Jesus, bruised and broken,
God's great word of pardon spoken.

4 Into death He took His people,
raising them when He arose;
freeing them from death's dominion,
overcoming all their foes.
See in Jesus, God's new Man,
firstfruits of His glorious plan.

5 Many search for earthly riches
thinking they will satisfy,
while the pearl of greatest beauty
in the gospel record lies.
See in Jesus God's abundance,
blessing of eternal substance.

6 From the fulness of His riches
we may draw all needed grace;
King and Priest, He reigns forever,
mercy shining from His face.
See this Jesus, throned in glory,
live to tell salvation's story.

Colin P Goldsworthy, b. 1927

503

Only by grace can we enter,
only by grace can we stand;
not by our human endeavour
but by the blood of the Lamb.
Into Your presence You call us,
You call us to come,
into Your presence You draw us
and now by Your grace we come,
now by Your grace we come.

Lord, if You mark our transgressions
who will stand?
Thanks to Your grace we are cleansed
by the blood of the Lamb.
(repeat chorus)

Only by grace can we enter,
only by grace can we stand;
not by our human endeavour
but by the blood of the Lamb.
Into Your presence You call us,
You call us to come,
into Your presence you draw us
and now by Your grace we come,
now by Your grace we come.

Gerrit Gustafson

504

Sovereign grace o'er sin abounding,
ransomed souls, the tidings swell;
'tis a deep that knows no sounding;
who its breadth or length can tell?
On its glories
let my soul for ever dwell.

2 What from Christ that soul shall sever,
bound by everlasting bands?
Once in Him, in Him for ever,
thus the eternal cov'nant stands:
none shall pluck thee
from the Strength of Israel's hands.

3 Heirs of God, joint-heirs with Jesus,
long ere time its race begun;
to His name eternal praises;
O what wonders He has done!
One with Jesus,
by eternal union one.

4 On such love, my soul, still ponder,
love so great, so rich and free;
say, while lost in holy wonder,
'Why, O Lord, such love to me?'
Hallelujah!
Grace shall reign eternally.

John Kent, 1766-1843

505

The love of Christ who died for me
is more than mind can know,
His mercy measureless and free
to meet the debt I owe.

2 He came my sinful cause to plead,
He laid His glories by,
for me a homeless life to lead,
a shameful death to die.

3 My sins I only see in part,
my self-regarding ways;
the secret places of my heart
lie bare before His gaze.

4 For me the price of sin He paid;
my sins beyond recall
are all alike on Jesus laid,
He died to bear them all.

5 O living Lord of life, for whom
the heavens held their breath,
to see, triumphant from the tomb,
a love that conquers death,

6 Possess my heart that it may be
Your kingdom without end,
O Christ who died for love of me
and lives to be my friend.

Timothy Dudley-Smith, b. 1926

506

Based on PSALM 18

What kind of love is this,
that gave itself for me?
I am the guilty one,
yet I go free.
What kind of love is this?
A love I've never known.
I didn't even know His name,
what kind of love is this?

2 What kind of Man is this,
that died in agony?
He who had done no wrong
was crucified for me.
What kind of Man is this,
who laid aside His throne
that I may know the love of God?
What kind of Man is this?

3 By grace I have been saved;
it is the gift of God.
He destined me to be His son,
such is His love.
No eye has ever seen,
no ear has ever heard,
nor has the heart of man conceived
what kind of love is this.

Bryn & Sally Haworth, b. 1948

507

When love came down to earth
and made His home with men,
the hopeless found a hope,
the sinner found a friend.
Not to the powerful,
but to the poor He came,
and humble, hungry hearts
were satisfied again.

What joy, what peace
has come to us.
What hope, what help,
what love!

2 When every unclean thought,
and every sinful deed
was scourged upon His back,
and hammered through His feet,
the innocent is cursed,
the guilty are released;
the punishment of God
on God has brought me peace.

3 Come lay your heavy load
down at the Master's feet;
your shame will be removed,
your joy will be complete.
Come crucify your pride,
and enter as a child;
for those who bow down low
He'll lift up to His side.

Stuart Townend, b. 1963

508

Wonderful grace of Jesus,
greater than all my sin;
how shall my tongue describe it,
where shall its praise begin?
Taking away my burden,
setting my spirit free;
for the wonderful grace of Jesus
reaches me.

Wonderful the matchless grace of Jesus,
deeper than the mighty rolling sea;
higher than the mountain,
sparkling like a fountain,
all sufficient grace for even me;
broader than the scope of my
transgressions,
greater far than all my sin and shame;
O magnify the precious name of Jesus,
praise His name!

2 Wonderful grace of Jesus,
reaching to all the lost,
by it I have been pardoned,
saved to the uttermost;
chains have been torn asunder,
giving me liberty;
for the wonderful grace of Jesus
reaches me.

3 Wonderful grace of Jesus,
reaching the most defiled,
by its transforming power,
making me God's dear child,
purchasing peace and heaven,
for all eternity;
and the wonderful grace of Jesus
reaches me.

Haldor Lillenas, 1885-1959

Divine calling and new birth

509

And can it be that I should gain
an interest in the Saviour's blood?
Died He for me, who caused His pain?
For me, who Him to death pursued?
Amazing love! how can it be
that Thou, my God, shouldst die for me?

2 'Tis mystery all! the Immortal dies!
Who can explore His strange design?
In vain the first-born seraph tries
to sound the depths of love divine!
'Tis mercy all! let earth adore,
let angel minds inquire no more.

3 He left His Father's throne above –
so free, so infinite His grace –
emptied Himself of all but love,
and bled for Adam's helpless race:
'tis mercy all, immense and free;
for, O my God, it found out me!

4 Long my imprisoned spirit lay
fast bound in sin and nature's night;
Thine eye diffused a quickening ray,
I woke, the dungeon flamed with
light;
my chains fell off, my heart was free,
I rose, went forth, and followed Thee.

5 No condemnation now I dread;
Jesus, and all in Him, is mine!
Alive in Him, my living Head,
and clothed in righteousness divine,
bold I approach the eternal throne,
and claim the crown, through Christ my own.

Charles Wesley, 1707-88

510

Based on PSALM 18

Whom should we love like Thee,
our God, our guide, our King,
the tower to which we flee,
the rock to which we cling?
O for a thousand tongues to show
the mercies which to Thee we owe!

2 The storm upon us fell,
the floods around us rose;
the depths of death and hell
seemed on our souls to close;
to God we cried in strong despair;
He heard, and came to help our prayer.

3 He came, the King of kings,
He bowed the sable sky;
and on the tempest's wings
rode glorious down from high;
the earth before her Maker shook,
the mountains quaked at His rebuke.

4 Above the storm He stood,
and awed it to repose;
He drew us from the flood,
and scattered all our foes.
He set us in a spacious place,
and there upholds us by His grace.

5 Whom should we love like Thee,
our God, our guide, our King,
the tower to which we flee,
the rock to which we cling?
O for a thousand tongues to show
the mercies which to Thee we owe!

Henry Francis Lyte, 1793-1847

511

All that I was, my sin, my guilt,
my death, was all my own;
all that I am I owe to Thee,
my gracious God, alone.

2 The evil of my former state
was mine, and only mine;
the good in which I now rejoice
is Thine, and only Thine.

3 The darkness of my former state,
the bondage – all was mine;
the light of life in which I walk,
the liberty is Thine.

4 Thy grace first made me feel my sin,
and taught me to believe;
then, in believing, peace I found,
and now in Christ I live.

5 All that I am while here on earth,
all that I hope to be,
when Jesus comes and glory dawns,
I owe it, Lord, to Thee.

Horatius Bonar, 1808-89

512

Come, O Thou all-victorious Lord,
Thy power to us make known;
strike with the hammer of Thy Word,
and break these hearts of stone.

2 O that we all might now begin
our foolishness to mourn,
and turn at once from every sin,
and to our Saviour turn!

3 Give us ourselves and Thee to know,
in this our gracious day;
repentance unto life bestow,
and take our sins away.

4 Conclude us first in unbelief,
and freely then release;
fill every soul with sacred grief,
and then with sacred peace.

5 Impoverish, Lord, and then relieve,
and then enrich the poor;
the knowledge of our sickness give,
the knowledge of our cure.

6 That blessèd sense of guilt impart,
and then remove the load;
trouble, and wash the troubled heart
in the atoning blood.

7 Our desperate state through sin declare,
and speak our sins forgiven;
in perfect holiness prepare,
and take us up to heaven.

Charles Wesley, 1707-88

513

How sad our state by nature is!
our sin how deep it stains!
and Satan binds our captive minds
fast in his slavish chains.

2 But there's a voice of sovereign grace
sounds from the sacred Word –
Come, you despairing sinners, come,
and trust upon the Lord.

3 My soul obeys the almighty call,
and runs to this relief;
I would believe Your promise, Lord;
O help my unbelief!

4 To the dear fountain of Your blood,
incarnate God, I fly;
here let me wash my guilty soul
from crimes of deepest dye.

5 A guilty, weak and helpless wretch,
on Your kind arms I fall;
be now my strength and righteousness,
my Jesus and my all.

Isaac Watts, 1674-1748

514

Born by the Holy Spirit's breath,
loosed from the law of sin and death,
now cleared in Christ from every claim,
no judgment stands against our name.

2 In us the Spirit makes His home
that we in Him may overcome;
Christ's risen life, in all its powers,
its all-prevailing strength, is ours.

3 Children and heirs of God most High,
we by His Spirit 'Father' cry;
that Spirit with our spirit shares
to frame and breathe our wordless
prayers.

4 One is His love, His purpose one:
to form the likeness of His Son
in all who, called and justified,
shall reign in glory at His side.

5 Nor death nor life, nor powers unseen,
nor height nor depth can come between;
we know through peril, pain and sword,
the love of God in Christ our Lord.

Timothy Dudley-Smith, b. 1926

515

God calleth yet: at last shall I not heed?
How long shall I refuse the grace I need?
While pleasure fades, and time's swift moments fly,
still shall my soul in mortal peril lie?

2 God calleth yet: at length shall I not turn?
Dare I once more His faithful pleading spurn?
Though I have known full well what I should be,
my will rebelled: yet now He beckons me.

3 God calleth yet: alas, this stubborn heart!
I feared His yoke, shrank from the nobler part;
God and my soul how oft have I betrayed!
He draws me still: rise, heart, be not afraid.

4 Yield to Him now, once and for ever yield;
make God thy portion, and His grace thy shield.
What though the world its pleasures still display?
God calleth yet: O heart, do thou obey!

Gerhard Tersteegen, 1697-1769;
tr. by Howell Elvet Lewis, 1860-1953

516

I hear Thy welcome voice
that calls me, Lord, to Thee,
for cleansing in Thy precious blood
that flowed on Calvary.

I am coming, Lord,
coming now to Thee:
wash me, cleanse me, in the blood
that flowed on Calvary.

2 Though coming weak and vile,
Thou dost my strength assure;
Thou dost my vileness fully cleanse,
till spotless all and pure.

3 'Tis Jesus calls me on
to perfect faith and love,
to perfect hope and peace and trust,
for earth and heaven above.

4 'Tis Jesus who confirms
the blessèd work within,
by adding grace to welcomed grace,
where reigned the power of sin.

5 All hail, atoning blood!
All hail, redeeming grace!
All hail, the gift of Christ our Lord,
our strength and righteousness!

Lewis Hartsough, 1828-1919

517

Jesus! Redeemer, Saviour, Lord,
the weary sinner's friend,
come to my help, pronounce the word,
and bid my troubles end.

2 Deliverance to my soul proclaim,
and life, and liberty;
shed forth the virtue of Thy name,
and Jesus prove to me!

3 Faith to be healed Thou know'st I have,
for Thou that faith hast given;
Thou canst, Thou wilt the sinner save,
and make me meet for heaven.

4 Thou canst o'ercome this heart of mine,
Thou wilt victorious prove;
for everlasting strength is Thine,
and everlasting love.

5 Thy powerful Spirit shall subdue
unconquerable sin,
cleanse this foul heart, and make it new,
and write Thy law within.

6 Bound down with twice ten thousand
ties,
yet let me hear Thy call,
my soul in confidence shall rise,
shall rise and break through all.

Charles Wesley, 1707-88

518

In loving kindness Jesus came,
my soul in mercy to reclaim,
and from the depths of sin and shame
through grace He lifted me.

From sinking sands He lifted me;
with tender hand He lifted me;
from shades of night to plains of
light,
O praise His name, He lifted me!

2 He called me long before I heard,
before my sinful heart was stirred;
but when I took him at His word,
forgiven, He lifted me.

3 His brow was pierced with many a thorn,
His hands by cruel nails were torn,
when from my guilt and grief forlorn,
in love He lifted me.

4 Now on a higher plane I dwell,
and with my soul I know 'tis well;
yet how or why, I cannot tell,
He should have lifted me.

Charles Homer Gabriel, 1856-1932

519

I sought the Lord, and afterward I knew
He moved my soul to seek Him,
seeking me;
it was not I that found, O Saviour true;
no, I was found of Thee.

2 Thou didst reach forth Thy hand and
mine enfold;
I walked and sank not on the storm-
vexed sea –
'twas not so much that I on Thee took
hold,
as Thou dear Lord on me.

3 I find, I walk, I love, but O the whole
of love is but my answer, Lord, to Thee;
for Thou wert long beforehand with my
soul,
always Thou lovedst me.

Anonymous, 1878

520

Sometimes my eyes are blind,
I cannot read Your Word.
The light I need I cannot find,
nor can I see my Lord.

2 Remove the veil of sin,
that I may truly see.
Then, Holy Spirit, shine within,
reveal the truth to me.

3 Lord, open wide my eyes
and teach me more and more.
Show me those things that make me
wise –
the wonders of Your law.

Stephen Crowter, b. 1968

521

Jesus, my all, to heaven is gone,
He whom I fix my hopes upon:
His track I see, and I'll pursue
the narrow way till Him I view.

2 The way the holy prophets went,
the road that leads from banishment,
the King's highway of holiness,
I'll go, for all His paths are peace.

3 This is the way I long have sought,
and mourned because I found it not;
my grief and burden long have been,
because I could not cease from sin.

4 The more I fought against its power,
I sinned and stumbled but the more;
till late I heard my Saviour say,
'Come hither, soul, I am the Way!'

5 Lo! glad I come; and You, blest Lamb,
shall take me to You as I am!
Nothing but sin have I to give;
nothing but love shall I receive.

6 Now will I tell to sinners round
what a dear Saviour I have found!
I'll point to Your redeeming blood,
and say, 'Behold the way to God!'

John Cennick, 1718-55

522

Lord, I was blind! I could not see
in Thy marred visage any grace;
but now the beauty of Thy face
in radiant vision dawns on me.

2 Lord, I was deaf! I could not hear
the thrilling music of Thy voice;
but now I hear Thee and rejoice,
and all Thine uttered words are dear.

3 Lord, I was dumb! I could not speak
the grace and glory of Thy Name;
but now, as touched with living flame,
my lips Thine eager praises wake.

4 Lord, I was dead! I could not stir
my lifeless soul to come to Thee;
but now, since Thou hast quickened me,
I rise from sin's dark sepulchre.

5 Lord, Thou hast made the blind to see;
the deaf to hear, the dumb to speak,
the dead to live; and lo, I break
the chains of my captivity!

William Tidd Matson, 1833-99

523

My gracious Lord, Your love is vast,
eternal, full and free.
It reaches far beyond my thought,
and brings my foolish pride to naught.
How can such love seek me?

2 Yet You have sought me, holy Lord,
from heaven's throne above;
though lost and blind and dead in sin,
with rebel will defiled within,
You sought me in Your love.

3 Such love was Your design, O Lord,
before the worlds were framed,
that God the Father and the Son
in cov'nant formed a mighty plan,
my rebel heart to gain.

4 Your saving love has triumphed, Lord,
and conquered me by grace.
Now pardoned, cleansed, redeemed, restored,
I lift my heart in worship, Lord,
in songs of boundless praise.

Eric J Alexander, b. 1932

524

O Christ, in Thee my soul hath found,
and found in Thee alone,
the peace, the joy I sought so long,
the bliss till now unknown.

Now none but Christ can satisfy,
none other Name for me!
There's love and life and lasting joy,
Lord Jesus, found in Thee.

2 I sighed for rest and happiness,
I yearned for them, not Thee;
but, while I passed my Saviour by,
His love laid hold on me.

3 I tried the broken cisterns, Lord,
but, ah, the waters failed!
e'en as I stooped to drink they fled,
and mocked me as I wailed.

4 The pleasures lost I sadly mourned,
but never wept for Thee,
till grace the sightless eyes received
Thy loveliness to see.

Anonymous

525

O happy day, that fixed my choice
on You, my Saviour and my God!
Well may this glowing heart rejoice,
and tell its raptures all abroad.

2 O happy bond, that seals my vows
to Him who merits all my love!
Let cheerful anthems fill His house
while to that sacred place I move.

3 'Tis done! the great transaction's done!
I am my Lord's and He is mine;
He drew me, and I followed on,
charmed to confess the voice divine.

4 Now rest, my long-divided heart;
fixed on this blissful centre, rest;
with ashes who would grudge to part,
when called on angels' food to feast?

5 High heaven, that heard the solemn vow,
that vow renewed shall daily hear,
till in life's latest hour I bow,
and bless in death a bond so dear.

Philip Doddridge, 1702-51

Where this hymn is sung to 'O happy day', the following chorus is sung:

O happy day! O happy day!
when Jesus washed my sins away;
He taught me how to watch and pray,
and live rejoicing every day;
Happy day! O happy day!
when Jesus washed my sins away.

526

O Thou who hast redeemed of old,
and bidd'st me of Thy strength take hold,
and be at peace with Thee,
help me Thy benefits to own,
and hear me tell what Thou hast done,
O dying Lamb, for me.

2 Give me the eye of faith to see
the Man transfixed on Calvary,
to know Thee who Thou art –
the one eternal God and true;
and let the sight affect, subdue,
and break my stubborn heart.

3 Lover of souls, to rescue mine,
reveal the charity divine
that suffered in my stead;
that made Thy soul a sacrifice,
and quenched in death those gracious eyes,
and bowed that sacred head.

4 The veil of unbelief remove;
and by Thy manifested love,
and by Thy sprinkled blood,
destroy the love of sin in me,
and get Thyself the victory,
and bring me back to God.

Charles Wesley, 1707-88

527

O the bitter shame and sorrow,
that a time could ever be,
when I let the Saviour's pity
plead in vain, and proudly answered,
'All of self, and none of Thee!'

2 Yet He found me; I beheld Him
bleeding on the accursèd tree,
heard Him pray, 'Forgive them, Father!'
and my wistful heart said faintly,
'Some of self, and some of Thee!'

3 Day by day His tender mercy,
healing, helping, full and free,
sweet and strong, and ah! so patient,
brought me lower, while I whispered,
'Less of self, and more of Thee!'

4 Higher than the highest heavens,
deeper than the deepest sea,
Lord, Thy love at last has conquered;
grant me now my supplication –
'None of self, and all of Thee!'

Theodore Monod, 1836-1921

Invitation and response

528

And will the Judge descend?
and must the dead arise?
and not a single soul escape
His all-discerning eyes?

2 How will my heart endure
the terrors of that day,
when earth and heaven before His face
astonished shrink away?

3 But ere the trumpet shake
the mansions of the dead,
hark! from the gospel's cheering sound,
what joyful tidings spread!

4 O sinners, seek His grace,
whose wrath you cannot bear;
fly to the shelter of His cross,
and find salvation there!

5 So shall that curse remove
by which the Saviour bled,
and the last aweful day shall pour
His blessings on your head.

Philip Doddridge, 1702-51

529

Above the voices of the world around me,
my hopes and dreams, my cares and loves and fears,
the long-awaited call of Christ has found me,
the voice of Jesus echoes in my ears:
'I gave My life to break the cords that bind you,
I rose from death to set your spirit free;
turn from your sins and put your past behind you,
take up your cross and come and follow Me.'

2 What can I offer Him who calls me to Him?
Only the wastes of sin and self and shame;
a mind confused, a heart that never knew Him,
a tongue unskilled at naming Jesus' name.
Yet at Your call, and hungry for Your blessing,
drawn by that cross which moves a heart of stone,
now, Lord, I come, my tale of sin confessing,
and in repentance turn to You alone.

3 Lord, I believe; help now my unbelieving;
I come in faith because Your promise stands.
Your word of pardon and of peace receiving,
all that I am I place within Your hands.
Let me become what You shall choose to make me,
freed from the guilt and burden of my sins.
Jesus is mine, who never shall forsake me,
and in His love my new-born life begins.

Timothy Dudley-Smith, b. 1926

530

Arise, my soul, arise,
shake off your guilty fears;
the bleeding Sacrifice
in my behalf appears:
before the throne my Surety stands,
my name is written on His hands.

2 He ever lives above,
for me to intercede,
His all-redeeming love,
His precious blood, to plead;
His blood atoned for this our race,
and sprinkles now the throne of grace.

3 Five bleeding wounds He bears,
received on Calvary;
they pour effectual prayers,
they strongly speak for me:
Forgive him, O forgive! they cry,
nor let the ransomed sinner die!

4 The Father hears Him pray,
His dear Anointed One;
He cannot turn away
the presence of His Son:
His Spirit answers to the blood,
and tells me I am born of God.

5 My God is reconciled,
His pardoning voice I hear;
He owns me for His child,
I can no longer fear;
with confidence I now draw nigh,
and 'Father, Abba, Father!' cry.

Charles Wesley, 1707-88

531

Are you weary, are you languid,
are you sore distressed?
'Come to Me', says One, 'and, coming,
be at rest!'

2 Has He marks to lead me to Him,
if He be my guide?
In His feet and hands are wound-prints,
and His side.

3 Has He diadem as monarch
that His brow adorns?
Yes, a crown in very surety,
but of thorns!

4 If I find Him, if I follow,
what awaits me here?
Many a sorrow, many a labour,
many a tear.

5 If I still hold closely to Him,
what has He at last?
Sorrow vanquished, labour ended,
Jordan past.

6 If I ask Him to receive me,
will He say me nay?
Not till earth and not till heaven
pass away.

7 Finding, following, keeping, struggling,
is He sure to bless?
Saints, apostles, prophets, martyrs
answer: Yes!

John Mason Neale, 1818-66;
based on Stephen the Sabaite, 725-94

532

Christ, whose glory fills the skies,
Christ, the true, the only Light,
Sun of righteousness, arise,
triumph o'er the shades of night;
day-spring from on high, be near;
day-star, in my heart appear.

2 Dark and cheerless is the morn
unaccompanied by You;
joyless is the day's return,
till Your mercy's beams I view,
till they inward light impart,
glad my eyes, and warm my heart.

3 Visit then this soul of mine;
pierce the gloom of sin and grief;
fill me, Radiancy divine;
scatter all my unbelief;
more and more Yourself display,
shining to the perfect day.

Charles Wesley, 1707-88

533

Heal us, Immanuel; hear our prayer;
we wait to feel Your touch:
deep-wounded souls to You repair,
and, Saviour, we are such.

2 Our faith is feeble, we confess;
we faintly trust Your Word:
but will You pity us the less?
Be that far from You, Lord!

3 Remember him who once applied
with trembling for relief;
'Lord, I believe!' with tears he cried,
'O help my unbelief!'

4 She, too, who touched You in the press,
and healing virtue stole,
was answered: 'Daughter, go in peace;
your faith has made you whole.'

5 Like her, with hopes and fears we come,
to touch You, if we may:
O send us not despairing home,
send none unhealed away.

William Cowper, 1731-1800

534

Come to the Saviour now!
He gently calleth thee;
in true repentance bow,
before Him bend the knee.
He waiteth to bestow
salvation, peace and love,
true joy on earth below,
a home in heaven above.
Come, come, come!

2 Come to the Saviour now!
He suffered all for thee,
and in His merits thou
hast an unfailing plea.
No vain excuses frame,
for feelings do not stay;
none who to Jesus came
were ever sent away.
Come, come, come!

3 Come to the Saviour now,
ye who have wandered far;
renew your solemn vow,
for His by right you are.
Come like poor wandering sheep
returning to His fold;
His arm will safely keep,
His love will ne'er grow cold.
Come, come, come!

4 Come to the Saviour, all,
whate'er your burdens be;
hear now His loving call –
'Cast all your care on Me.'
Come, and for every grief,
in Jesus you will find
a sure and safe relief,
a loving friend and kind.
Come, come, come!

John Murch Wigner, 1844-1911

535

'Come unto Me, ye weary,
and I will give you rest.'
O blessèd voice of Jesus,
which comes to hearts oppressed!
It tells of benediction,
of pardon, grace, and peace,
of joy that hath no ending,
of love that cannot cease.

2 'Come unto Me, ye wanderers,
and I will give you light.'
O loving voice of Jesus,
which comes to cheer the night!
Our hearts were filled with sadness,
and we had lost our way;
but morning brings us gladness,
and songs the break of day.

3 'Come unto Me, ye fainting,
and I will give you life.'
O cheering voice of Jesus,
which comes to aid our strife!
The foe is stern and eager,
the fight is fierce and long;
but Thou hast made us mighty,
and stronger than the strong.

4 'And whosoever cometh
I will not cast him out.'
O welcome voice of Jesus,
which drives away our doubt,
which calls us, very sinners,
unworthy though we be
of love so free and boundless,
to come, dear Lord, to Thee!

William Chatterton Dix, 1837-98

536

Come to the waters, whoever is thirsty
drink from the Fountain that never runs dry.
Jesus, the Living One, offers you mercy,
life more abundant in boundless supply.

2 Come to the River that flows through the city,
forth from the throne of the Father and Son;
Jesus the Saviour says, 'Come and drink deeply.'
Drink from the pure, inexhaustible One.

3 Come to the Fountain without any
money;
buy what is given without any cost.
Jesus, the gracious One, welcomes the
weary;
Jesus, the selfless One, died for the lost.

4 Come to the Well of unmerited favour;
stretch out your hands, fill your cup to
the brim;
Jesus is such a compassionate Saviour;
draw from the grace that flows freely
from Him.

5 Come to the Saviour, the God of
salvation.
God has provided an end to sin's strife.
Why will you suffer the law's
condemnation?
Take the free gift of the water of life.

James Montgomery Boice, 1939-2000

537

**Come, let us sing of a wonderful
love,**
tender and true;
out of the heart of the Father above,
streaming to me and to you:
wonderful love
dwells in the heart of the Father above.

2 Jesus, the Saviour, this gospel to tell
joyfully came;
came with the helpless and hopeless to
dwell,
sharing their sorrow and shame;
seeking the lost,
saving, redeeming at measureless cost.

3 Jesus is seeking the wanderers yet;
why do they roam?
Love only waits to forgive and forget;
home! weary wanderer, home!
Wonderful love
dwells in the heart of the Father above.

4 Come to my heart, O Thou wonderful
love!
Come and abide,
lifting my life till it rises above
envy and falsehood and pride,
seeking to be
lowly and humble, a learner of Thee.

Robert Walmsley, 1831-1905

538

Come, sinners, to the gospel feast,
let every soul be Jesu's guest;
ye need not one be left behind,
for God hath bidden all mankind.

2 Sent by my Lord, on you I call,
the invitation is to all:
come, all the world; come, sinner, thou!
all things in Christ are ready now.

3 Come, all ye souls by sin oppressed,
ye restless wanderers after rest,
ye poor, and maimed, and lame, and
blind,
in Christ a hearty welcome find.

4 His love is mighty to compel;
His conquering love consent to feel,
yield to His love's resistless power,
and fight against your God no more.

5 See Him set forth before your eyes,
that precious, bleeding sacrifice!
His offered benefits embrace,
and freely now be saved by grace.

6 This is the time; no more delay!
this is the Lord's accepted day;
come in, this moment, at His call,
and live for Him who died for all.

Charles Wesley, 1707-88

539

Come, ye sinners, poor and wretched,
weak and wounded, sick and sore;
Jesus ready stands to save you,
full of pity joined with power;
He is able,
He is willing; doubt no more!

2 Come, ye needy, come and welcome;
God's free bounty glorify!
True belief and true repentance,
every grace that brings us nigh,
without money,
come to Jesus Christ and buy!

3 Let not conscience make you linger,
nor of fitness fondly dream;
all the fitness He requireth,
is to feel your need of Him:
this He gives you;
'tis the Spirit's rising beam!

4 Come, ye weary, heavy-laden,
bruised and broken by the fall;
if you tarry till you're better,
you will never come at all:
not the righteous –
sinners Jesus came to call!

5 View Him prostrate in the garden;
on the ground your Maker lies;
then on Calvary's tree behold Him,
hear Him cry, before He dies,
'It is finished!'
Sinner, will not this suffice?

6 Lo! the incarnate God, ascended,
pleads the merit of His blood;
venture on Him, venture wholly,
let no other trust intrude;
none but Jesus
can do helpless sinners good.

Joseph Hart, 1712-68

540

Come, ye souls by sin afflicted,
bowed with fruitless sorrow down,
by the broken law convicted,
through the cross behold the crown;
look to Jesus;
mercy flows through Him alone.

2 Blessèd are the eyes that see Him,
blest the ears that hear His voice;
blessèd are the souls that trust Him,
and in Him alone rejoice;
His commandments
then become their happy choice.

3 Sweet as home to pilgrims weary,
light to newly opened eyes,
flowing springs in deserts dreary,
is the rest the cross supplies;
all who taste it
shall to bliss immortal rise.

4 Take His easy yoke and wear it;
love will make obedience sweet;
Christ will give you strength to bear it,
while His wisdom guides your feet
safe to glory,
where His ransomed captives meet.

Joseph Swain, 1761-96

541

Did you hear the angels singing
in the skies of Bethlehem's town?
Did you know the Lord of glory
as an infant weak came down?
Did you hear a voice from heaven,
'This is my belovèd Son'?
Did you know that in His person
God and man were joined in one?

2 Did you hear the Saviour weeping
in the garden as He prayed?
Have you seen His love for sinners
which His suffering there displayed?
Then they stretched His hands above Him
and they nailed Him to the tree:
Have you felt the blood of cleansing
flowing there for you and me?

3 Have you heard the sound of weeping
as they laid Him in the tomb?
Have you felt your soul rejoicing
that He rose from out its gloom?
Did your soul ascend within you
when to heaven He returned?
Have you tasted of repentance?
Have you from your idols turned?

4 Will you hear the trumpet sounding
whether here or in your tomb?
When the Lord returns in glory
will He speak your lasting doom?
O, to Him you must be coming
while it yet is called Today;
For no sinner came to Jesus
that the Saviour turned away.

Eluned Harrison, b. 1934

542

Consider Christ,
the source of our salvation,
that He should pay
the penalty for me.
Though He was pure,
a lamb without a blemish,
He took my sins
and nailed them to the tree.

My Lord and God
You are so rich in mercy.
Mere words alone
are not sufficient thanks.
So take my life,
transform, renew and change me
that I might be
a living sacrifice.

2 Consider Christ,
that He could trust His Father
e'en in the garden
of Gethsemane.
Though full of dread
and fearful of the anguish;
He drank the cup
that was reserved for me.

3 Consider Christ,
for death He has defeated.
And He arose,
appeared for all to see.
And now He sits
at God's right hand in heaven;
where He prepares
a resting place for me.

Bryson Smith, b. 1958

543

Have you been to Jesus for the cleansing power?
Are you washed in the blood of the Lamb?
Are you fully trusting in His grace this hour?
Are you washed in the blood of the Lamb?

Are you washed in the blood,
in the soul-cleansing blood of the Lamb?
Are your garments spotless?
Are they white as snow?
Are you washed in the blood of the Lamb?

2 Are you walking daily by the Saviour's side?
Are you washed in the blood of the Lamb?
Do you rest each moment in the Crucified?
Are you washed in the blood of the Lamb?

3 When the Bridegroom cometh will your robes be white,
pure and white in the blood of the Lamb?
Will your soul be ready for the mansions bright,
and be washed in the blood of the Lamb?

4 Lay aside the garments that are stained by sin,
and be washed in the blood of the Lamb;
there's a fountain flowing for the soul unclean,
O be washed in the blood of the Lamb!

Elisha Albright Hoffman, 1839-1929

544

Have you heard the voice of Jesus
softly pleading with your heart?
Have you felt His presence glorious,
as He calls your soul apart,
with a love so true and loyal,
love divine that ever flows
from a Saviour, righteous, royal,
and a cross that mercy shows?

2 Have you heard the voice of mercy
granting peace and pardon pure?
Have you felt the balm of Calvary
binding all your wounds secure?
Was there ever such salvation,
was there ever care like this?
See the Saviour's grief and passion,
grace and mercy's gentle kiss.

3 Have you heard the Saviour calling
all to leave and follow Him?
Have you felt His person drawing
with compulsion lives to win?
Hearken to His invitation,
to the music of God's grace;
let the peace of God's salvation
fill your soul, and love embrace.

William Vernon Higham, b. 1926

545

Himself He could not save,
He on the cross must die,
or mercy cannot come
to ruined sinners nigh.
Yes, Christ, the Son of God, must bleed,
that sinners might from sin be freed.

2 Himself He could not save,
for justice must be done;
and sin's full weight must fall
upon a sinless One;
for nothing less can God accept
in payment for the fearful debt.

3 Himself He could not save,
for He the surety stood
for all who now rely
upon His precious blood;
He bore the penalty of guilt
when on the cross His blood was spilt.

4 Himself He could not save,
yet now a Saviour He:
come, sinner, to Him come,
He waits to welcome thee.
Believe in Him, and thou shalt prove
His saving power, His deathless love.

Albert Midlane, 1825-1909

546

I need Thee every hour, most gracious Lord;
no tender voice like Thine can peace afford.

I need Thee, O I need Thee!
every hour I need Thee;
O bless me now, my Saviour!
I come to Thee.

2 I need Thee every hour; stay Thou near by;
temptations lose their power when Thou art nigh.

3 I need Thee every hour, in joy or pain;
come quickly and abide, or life is vain.

4 I need Thee every hour; teach me Thy will,
and Thy rich promises in me fulfil.

5 I need Thee every hour, most Holy One;
O make me Thine indeed, Thou blessèd Son!

Annie Sherwood Hawks, 1835-1918

547

Jesus, the sinner's friend, to Thee,
lost and undone, for aid I flee,
weary of earth, myself, and sin;
open Thine arms, and take me in!

2 Pity, and heal my sin-sick soul;
'tis Thou alone canst make me whole;
fall'n, till in me Thine image shine,
and cursed I am, till Thou art mine.

3 At last I own it cannot be
that I should fit myself for Thee:
here then to Thee I all resign;
Thine is the work, and only Thine.

4 What shall I say Thy grace to move?
Lord, I am sin, but Thou art love:
I give up every plea beside –
Lord, I am lost, but Thou hast died!

Charles Wesley, 1707-88

548

I need Thee, precious Jesus!
for I am full of sin;
my soul is dark and guilty,
my heart is dead within:
I need the cleansing fountain,
where I can always flee,
the blood of Christ most precious,
the sinner's perfect plea.

2 I need Thee, precious Jesus!
for I am very poor;
a stranger and a pilgrim,
I have no earthly store:
I need the love of Jesus
to cheer me on my way,
to guide my doubting footsteps,
to be my strength and stay.

3 I need Thee, precious Jesus!
I need a friend like Thee;
a friend to soothe and comfort,
a friend to care for me:
I need the heart of Jesus
to feel each anxious care,
to tell my every trouble
and all my sorrows share.

4 I need Thee, precious Jesus!
and hope to see Thee soon,
encircled with the rainbow,
and seated on Thy throne;
there with Thy blood-bought children
my joy shall ever be,
to sing Thy praise, Lord Jesus,
to gaze, my Lord, on Thee.

Frederick Whitfield, 1829-1904

549

Based on PSALM 62:1,2,8

I rest in God alone,
from Him comes my salvation;
my soul finds rest in Him,
my fortress – I'll not be shaken.

My hope is in the Lord,
my honour and strength;
my refuge is in Him for ever,
my trust and all of my heart –
in Him alone my soul finds rest.

I rest in God alone…

2 O trust in Him, you people,
pour out your hearts,
for God is our refuge for ever,
my trust and all of my heart –
in Him alone my soul finds rest.

O trust in Him, you people…

John Daniels

550

Jesu, Lover of my soul,
let me to Thy bosom fly,
while the nearer waters roll,
while the tempest still is high:
hide me, O my Saviour, hide,
till the storm of life be past;
safe into the haven guide;
O receive my soul at last!

2 Other refuge have I none;
hangs my helpless soul on Thee;
leave, ah! leave me not alone,
still support and comfort me:
all my trust on Thee is stayed,
all my help from Thee I bring;
cover my defenceless head
with the shadow of Thy wing.

3 Thou, O Christ, art all I want;
more than all in Thee I find;
raise the fallen, cheer the faint,
heal the sick, and lead the blind:
just and holy is Thy Name,
I am all unrighteousness;
false and full of sin I am,
Thou art full of truth and grace.

4 Plenteous grace with Thee is found,
grace to cover all my sin;
let the healing streams abound,
make and keep me pure within:
Thou of life the fountain art,
freely let me take of Thee;
spring Thou up within my heart,
rise to all eternity.

Charles Wesley, 1707-88

551

Lord, I hear of showers of blessing
Thou art scattering, full and free,
showers the thirsty land refreshing;
let some drops now fall on me,
even me.

2 Pass me not, O gracious Father,
sinful though my heart may be!
Thou might'st leave me, but the rather
let Thy mercy light on me.

3 Pass me not, O tender Saviour!
let me love and cling to Thee;
I am longing for Thy favour,
when Thou comest, call for me.

4 Pass me not, O mighty Spirit!
Thou canst make the blind to see;
witness of the Saviour's merit!
speak the word of power to me.

5 Love of God so pure and changeless,
blood of Christ so rich and free,
grace of God so strong and boundless,
magnify them all in me!

Elizabeth Codner, 1824-1919

552

My faith looks up to Thee,
Thou Lamb of Calvary,
Saviour divine!
Now hear me while I pray;
take all my guilt away;
O let me from this day
be wholly Thine!

2 May Thy rich grace impart
strength to my fainting heart,
my zeal inspire;
as Thou hast died for me,
O may my love to Thee,
pure, warm and changeless be,
a living fire.

3 While life's dark maze I tread,
and griefs around me spread,
be Thou my guide;
bid darkness turn to day,
wipe sorrow's tears away,
nor let me ever stray
from Thee aside.

4 When ends life's transient dream,
when death's cold, sullen stream
shall o'er me roll,
blest Saviour, then, in love,
fear and distrust remove;
O bear me safe above,
a ransomed soul.

Ray Palmer, 1808-87

553

No blood, no altar now:
the sacrifice is o'er;
no flame, no smoke ascends on high,
the lamb is slain no more.
But richer blood has flowed from
nobler veins,
to purge the soul from guilt and cleanse
the reddest stains.

2 We thank You for the blood,
the blood of Christ, Your Son;
the blood by which our peace is
made,
the victory is won;
great victory o'er hell and sin and woe,
that needs no second fight and leaves
no second foe.

3 We thank You for the grace,
descending from above,
that overflows our widest guilt –
the eternal Father's love,
love of the Father's everlasting Son,
love of the Holy Ghost – Jehovah,
Three in One.

Horatius Bonar, 1808-89

554

Now may the gospel's conquering power
be felt by all assembled here;
so shall this prove a joyful hour,
and God's own arm of strength
appear.

2 Lord! let Thy mighty voice be heard;
speak in the Word, and speak with power;
so shall Thy glorious Name be feared
by those who never feared before.

3 O pity those who sleep in sin,
preserve them from the sinner's doom;
show them the ark, and take them in,
and save them from the wrath to come.

4 So shall Thy people joyful be,
and angels shall more loudly sing,
and both ascribe the praise to Thee,
to Thee, the everlasting King!

Thomas Kelly, 1769-1855

555

O teach me what it meaneth,
that cross uplifted high,
with One, the Man of sorrows,
condemned to bleed and die!
O teach me what it cost Thee
to make a sinner whole;
and teach me, Saviour, teach me
the value of a soul!

2 O teach me what it meaneth,
that sacred crimson tide,
the blood and water flowing
from Thine own wounded side.
Teach me that if none other
had sinned, but I alone,
yet still Thy blood, Lord Jesus,
Thine only, must atone.

3 O teach me what it meaneth,
Thy love beyond compare,
the love that reacheth deeper
than depths of self-despair!
Yes, teach me, till there gloweth
in this cold heart of mine
some feeble, pale reflection
of that pure love of Thine.

4 O teach me what it meaneth,
for I am full of sin,
and grace alone can reach me,
and love alone can win.
O teach me, for I need Thee,
I have no hope beside –
the chief of all the sinners
for whom the Saviour died!

5 O infinite Redeemer!
I bring no other plea;
because Thou dost invite me
I cast myself on Thee.
Because Thou dost accept me
I love and I adore;
because Thy love constraineth,
I'll praise Thee evermore!

Lucy Ann Bennett, 1850-1927

556

O for a thousand tongues to sing
my great Redeemer's praise,
the glories of my God and King,
the triumphs of His grace!

2 My gracious Master and my God,
assist me to proclaim,
to spread through all the earth abroad
the honours of Thy name.

3 Jesus! the name that charms our fears,
that bids our sorrows cease;
'tis music in the sinner's ears,
'tis life, and health, and peace.

4 He breaks the power of cancelled sin,
He sets the prisoner free;
His blood can make the foulest clean,
His blood availed for me.

5 He speaks, and, listening to His voice,
new life the dead receive,
the mournful, broken hearts rejoice,
the humble poor believe.

6 Hear Him, ye deaf; His praise, ye dumb,
your loosened tongues employ;
ye blind, behold your Saviour come,
and leap, ye lame, for joy.

7 Look unto Him, ye nations, own
your God, ye fallen race;
look, and be saved through faith alone,
be justified by grace.

Charles Wesley, 1707-88

557

O walk with Jesus, wouldst thou know
how deep, how wide His love can flow!
They only fail His love to prove
who in the ways of sinners rove.

2 Walk thou with Him; that way is light,
all other pathways end in night:
walk thou with Him; that way is rest;
all other pathways are unblest.

3 O walk with Jesus! to thy view
He will make all things sweet and new;
will bring new fragrance from each flower,
and hallow every passing hour.

4 Jesus, a great desire have we
to walk life's troubled path with Thee:
come to us now, in converse stay;
and O walk with us day by day!

Edwin Paxton Hood, 1820-85

558

PSALM 130

Out of the depths I cry to Thee;
Lord, hear me, I implore Thee;
if Thou shouldst mark iniquity,
who, Lord, shall stand before Thee?
O may Thine ear attend my cry!
Lord, bid me to Thyself draw nigh,
while now I call upon Thee.

2 'Tis Thee, O Lord, my soul doth seek,
upon Thy Word relying;
Thou art a God who aids the meek,
their every need supplying.
Lord, may I Thy forgiveness know,
that I to Thee due fear may show,
and humbly walk before Thee.

3 More doth my soul, Lord, for Thee wait
than those that long for morning,
who through the darkest hours of night
are watching for the dawning.
From every sin, Lord, set me free;
make my whole life bring praise to Thee,
for Thou alone art worthy.

4 Hope thou, my soul, then, in the Lord,
whose plentiful redemption
and mercy shall to thee afford
the promise of salvation.
They hope in vain who think they can
escape from sin by strength of man:
God only can deliver.

Graham Stuart Harrison, b. 1935

559

O what a Saviour that He died for me!
From condemnation He hath made me free;
'He that believeth on the Son', saith He,
'hath everlasting life.'

Verily, verily, I say unto you,
verily, verily, message ever new;
he that believeth on the Son, 'tis true,
hath everlasting life.

2 All my iniquities on Him were laid,
all my indebtedness by Him was paid;
all who believe on Him, the Lord hath said,
have everlasting life.

3 Though poor and needy I can trust my
Lord,
though weak and sinful I believe His
Word;
O glad message! every child of God
hath everlasting life.

4 Though all unworthy, yet I will not
doubt,
for him that cometh He will not cast out.
He that believeth, O the good news
shout,
hath everlasting life.

James McGranahan, 1840-1907

560

The Saviour calls, let every ear
attend the heavenly sound;
you doubting souls, dismiss your fear,
hope smiles reviving round.

2 For every thirsty, longing heart,
here streams of bounty flow;
and life and health and bliss impart,
to banish mortal woe.

3 O sinners, come, 'tis mercy's voice;
the gracious call obey;
mercy invites to heavenly joys,
and can you yet delay?

4 Dear Saviour, draw reluctant hearts,
to You let sinners fly,
and take the bliss Your love imparts,
and drink and never die.

Anne Steele, 1717-78

561

Pass me not, O gentle Saviour,
hear my humble cry;
while on others Thou art calling,
do not pass me by.

Saviour! Saviour!
hear my humble cry,
and while others Thou art calling,
do not pass me by.

2 Let me at a throne of mercy
find a sweet relief;
kneeling there in deep contrition,
help my unbelief.

3 Trusting only in Thy merit,
would I seek Thy face;
heal my wounded, broken spirit,
save me by Thy grace.

4 Thou the spring of all my comfort,
more than life to me,
whom have I on earth beside Thee,
whom in heaven but Thee?

Frances Jane Van Alstyne, 1820-1915

562

Tell me, have you seen my Saviour?
How my soul would with Him dwell!
He's the chief among ten thousand,
in Him truth and grace excel.
Who His love's great power can
measure?
Who its length and breadth can tell?
Many waters cannot quench it;
it shall vanquish death and hell.

2 Tell me, have you heard my Saviour?
Heard my own belovèd's voice?
He comes leaping on the mountains
and the echoing hills rejoice.
Have you heard Him come and call
you,
'Rise, my love and come away'?
With Him winter's past and over,
why with winter will you stay?

3 Tell me, do you know my Saviour?
Know Him dying on the tree?
Know your sins were laid upon Him,
know His power to set you free?
O that all might know my Saviour
in His love and power to save!
O, my soul, rise up and greet Him,
He is risen from the grave.

Eluned Harrison, b. 1934

563

Tell me the old, old story
of unseen things above,
of Jesus and His glory,
of Jesus and His love.
Tell me the story simply
as to a little child,
for I am weak and weary,
and helpless and defiled.

Tell me the old, old story,
tell me the old, old story,
tell me the old, old story,
of Jesus and His love.

2 Tell me the story slowly,
that I may take it in –
that wonderful redemption,
God's remedy for sin.
Tell me the story often,
for I forget so soon;
the early dew of morning
has passed away at noon.

3 Tell me the story softly,
with earnest tones and grave:
remember, I'm the sinner
whom Jesus came to save.
Tell me that story always,
if you would really be,
in any time of trouble,
a comforter to me.

4 Tell me the same old story
when you have cause to fear
that this world's empty glory
is costing me too dear.
Yes, and when that world's glory
is dawning on my soul,
tell me the old, old story –
Christ Jesus makes you whole.

Arabella Catherine Hankey, 1834-1911

564

The blood of Christ, Thy spotless Lamb,
O God, is all my plea:
nought else could for my sin atone,
I have no merit of my own
which I can bring to Thee.

2 No sacrifice save His who bore
my load upon the tree;
no other plea which lips could frame,
no other blood, no other name,
accepted is for me.

3 Since Christ has entered by His blood
the holiest on high;
by that same hallowed blood-stained track
Thou welcomest the wanderer back,
and biddest me draw nigh.

4 O wondrous cross! O precious blood!
O death by which I live!
The sinless One, for me made sin,
doth now His wondrous heart within
eternal refuge give!

5 By that blest cross, that cleansing blood,
I know His power to save;
the merits of His work confessed,
I stand in Him completely blest,
a conqueror o'er the grave.

William Samuel Warren Pond, 1858-1919

565

There is a path of pardon
in His blood;
there is a sure salvation
in His blood;
the law's full consummation,
a Father's approbation,
hear Zion's acclamation!
in His blood;
atonement and redemption
in His blood!

2 O come, ye sons of Adam,
and rejoice!
Now trust the God of Abraham
and rejoice!
O hasten, happy sinner,
to life in Christ for ever,
to bonds that nought can sever:
O rejoice!
In full and glad surrender,
come, rejoice!

William Williams, 1801-76;
tr. by William Vernon Higham, b. 1926

566

There is life for a look at the crucified One,
there is life at this moment for thee;
then look, sinner, look unto Him and be saved,
unto Him who was nailed to the tree.

Look, look, look and live!
There is life for a look at the crucified One,
there is life at this moment for thee.

2 It is not thy tears of repentance or prayers,
but the blood that atones for the soul;
on Him, then, who shed it, thou mayest at once
thy weight of iniquities roll.

3 His anguish of soul on the cross hast thou seen?
His cry of distress hast thou heard?
Then why, if the terrors of wrath He endured,
should pardon to thee be deferred?

4 Then doubt not thy welcome, since God has declared
there remaineth no more to be done;
that once in the end of the world He appeared
and completed the work He begun.

5 But take with rejoicing from Jesus at once
the life everlasting He gives;
and know with assurance thou never canst die,
since Jesus, thy righteousness, lives.

Amelia Matilda Hull, c. 1825-82

567

Weary souls, that wander wide
from the central point of bliss,
turn to Jesus crucified,
fly to those dear wounds of His:
sink into the cleansing flood;
rise into the life of God!

2 Find in Christ the way of peace,
peace unspeakable, unknown;
by His pain He gives you ease,
life by His expiring groan;
rise, exalted by His fall,
find in Christ your all in all.

3 O believe the record true:
God to you His Son has given!
You may now be happy too,
find on earth the life of heaven,
live the life of heaven above,
all the life of glorious love.

Charles Wesley, 1707-88

568

Will your anchor hold in the storms of life,
when the clouds unfold their wings of strife?
When the strong tides lift, and the cables strain,
will your anchor drift, or firm remain?

We have an anchor that keeps the soul
steadfast and sure while the billows roll;
fastened to the Rock which cannot move,
grounded firm and deep in the Saviour's love!

2 Will your anchor hold in the straits of fear,
when the breakers roar and the reef is near?
While the surges rave, and the wild winds blow,
shall the angry waves then your bark o'erflow?

3 Will your anchor hold in the floods of death,
when the waters cold chill your latest breath?
On the rising tide you can never fail,
while your anchor holds within the veil.

4 Will your eyes behold through the morning light
the city of gold and the harbour bright?
Will you anchor safe by the heavenly shore,
when life's storms are past for evermore?

Priscilla Jane Owens, 1829-1907

569

Today Thy mercy calls us
to wash away our sin,
however great our trespass,
whatever we have been;
however long from mercy
our hearts have turned away,
Thy blood, O Christ, can cleanse us
and make us pure today.

2 Today Thy gate is open,
and all who enter in
shall find a Father's welcome,
and pardon for their sin;
the past shall be forgotten,
a present joy be given,
a future grace be promised,
a glorious crown in heaven.

3 O all-embracing mercy!
O ever-open door!
What should we do without Thee
when heart and eye run o'er?
When all things seem against us,
to drive us to despair,
we know one gate is open,
one ear will hear our prayer.

Oswald Allen, 1816-78

Repentance, faith and justification

570

A Man there is, a real man,
who once on Calvary died.
His blood for guilty sinners ran
from hands and feet and side.

2 This wondrous Man, of whom we tell,
is true Almighty God;
He bought our souls from death and hell;
the price, His own heart's blood.

3 That human heart He still retains,
though throned in highest bliss;
and feels each tempted member's pains;
for our affliction's His.

4 Come then, repenting sinner, come;
approach with humble faith;
owe what you will, the total sum
is cancelled by His death!

5 His blood can cleanse the sin-stained soul,
and wash our guilt away;
He will present us sound and whole
in that tremendous day.

*Joseph Hart**, 1712-1768

571

At the cross of Jesus
I would take my place,
drawn by such a measure
of redeeming grace.
Fill my eyes with sorrow,
lift my eyes to see
Jesus Christ my Saviour
crucified for me.

2 At the cross of Jesus
patiently He bore
bitter shame and sorrow,
grief and anguish sore.
Through eternal ages
I shall never know
what He had to suffer,
why He loved me so.

3 At the cross of Jesus
even though I be
chief of all the sinners
there is hope for me.
Judged, condemned and guilty
I am lost indeed,
but the cross of Jesus
meets my deepest need.

4 At the cross of Jesus
pardon is complete:
love and justice mingle,
truth and mercy meet.
Though my sins condemn me
Jesus died instead:
there is full forgiveness
in the blood He shed.

5 At the cross of Jesus
liberty You gave;
so I come, dear Saviour,
glad to be Your slave.
Let Your love possess me,
so that all may see
what Your death accomplished
on the cross for me.

John Eddison, b. 1916

572

God made me for Himself, to serve Him here,
with love's pure service and in childlike fear;
to show His praise, for Him to labour now;
then see His glory where the angels bow.

2 All needful grace was mine through His dear Son,
whose life and death my full salvation won;
the grace that would have strengthened me, and taught;
grace that would crown me when my work was wrought.

3 And I, poor sinner, cast it all away;
lived for the toil or pleasure of each day;
as if no Christ had shed His precious blood,
as if I owed no homage to my God.

4 O Holy Spirit, with Your fire divine,
melt into tears this thankless heart of mine;
teach me to love what once I seemed to hate,
and live to God before it be too late.

Henry Williams Baker, 1821-71

573

Beneath the cross of Jesus
O may I take my stand,
the shadow of a mighty rock
within a weary land;
a home within the wilderness,
a rest upon the way,
from the burning of the noontide heat,
and the burden of the day.

2 O safe and happy shelter!
O refuge tried and sweet!
That awesome place where heaven's love
and heaven's justice meet!
As to the holy patriarch
that wondrous dream was given,
so seems my Saviour's cross to me
a ladder up to heaven.

3 There lies beneath its shadow,
but on the farther side,
the darkness of an awful grave
that gapes both deep and wide:
and there between us stands the cross,
two arms outstretched to save,
like a watchman set to guard the way
from that eternal grave.

4 Upon that cross of Jesus,
mine eye at times can see
the very dying form of One
who suffered there for me;
and from my stricken heart, with tears,
two wonders I confess –
the wonders of His glorious love,
and my own worthlessness.

5 I take, O cross, thy shadow,
for my abiding-place;
I ask no other sunshine than
the sunshine of His face;
content to let the world go by,
to know no gain nor loss –
my sinful self my only shame,
my glory all – the cross!

Elizabeth Cecilia Clephane, 1830-69

574

I bring my sins to Thee,
the sins I cannot count,
that all may cleansèd be
in Thy once-opened fount:
I bring them, Saviour, all to Thee;
the burden is too great for me.

2 My heart to Thee I bring,
the heart I cannot read,
a faithless wandering thing,
an evil heart indeed:
I bring it, Saviour, now to Thee,
that fixed and faithful it may be.

3 My life I bring to Thee,
I would not be my own;
O Saviour, let me be
Thine ever, Thine alone!
My heart, my life, my all, I bring
to Thee, my Saviour and my King.

Frances Ridley Havergal, 1836-79

575 Based on ROMANS 8:32-34

Blessèd be God, our God!
who gave for us His well-belovèd Son,
the gift of gifts, all other gifts in one –
blessèd be God, our God!

2 What will He not bestow,
who freely gave this mighty gift unbought,
unmerited, unheeded, and unsought –
what will He not bestow?

3 He sparèd not His Son!
'Tis this that silences each rising fear;
'tis this that bids the hard thought disappear –
He sparèd not His Son!

4 Who shall condemn us now?
Since Christ has died, and risen, and gone above,
for us to plead at the right hand of Love,
who shall condemn us now?

5 'Tis God that justifies!
Who shall recall the pardon or the grace,
or who the broken chain of guilt replace?
'Tis God that justifies!

6 The victory is ours!
For us in might came forth the Mighty One;
for us He fought the fight, the triumph won –
the victory is ours!

Horatius Bonar, 1808-89

576

From whence this fear and unbelief?
Hath not the Father put to grief
His spotless Son for me?
And will the righteous Judge of men
condemn me for that debt of sin
which, Lord, was charged on Thee?

2 Complete atonement Thou hast made,
and to the utmost Thou hast paid
whate'er Thy people owed;
how then can wrath on me take place,
if sheltered in Thy righteousness,
and sprinkled with Thy blood?

3 If Thou hast my discharge procured,
and freely in my room endured
the whole of wrath divine;
payment God cannot twice demand,
first at my bleeding Surety's hand,
and then again at mine.

4 Turn then, my soul, unto thy rest!
The merits of thy great High Priest
have bought thy liberty;
trust in His efficacious blood,
nor fear thy banishment from God,
since Jesus died for thee.

Augustus Montague Toplady, 1740-78

577

I am trusting Thee, Lord Jesus,
trusting only Thee,
trusting Thee for full salvation,
great and free.

2 I am trusting Thee for pardon,
at Thy feet I bow;
for Thy grace and tender mercy,
trusting now.

3 I am trusting Thee for cleansing
in the crimson flood;
trusting Thee to make me holy
by Thy blood.

4 I am trusting Thee to guide me:
Thou alone shalt lead,
every day and hour supplying
all my need.

5 I am trusting Thee for power;
Thine can never fail;
words which Thou Thyself shalt give me
must prevail.

6 I am trusting Thee, Lord Jesus;
never let me fall;
I am trusting Thee for ever,
and for all.

Frances Ridley Havergal, 1836-79

578

I once was a stranger to grace and to God;
I knew not my danger, and felt not my load;
though friends spoke in rapture of Christ on the tree,
Jehovah Tsidkenu was nothing to me.

2 Like tears from the daughters of Zion that roll,
I wept when the waters went over His soul!
Yet thought not that my sins had nailed to the tree
Jehovah Tsidkenu – 'twas nothing to me.

3 When free grace awoke me, by light from on high,
then legal fears shook me, I trembled to die;
no refuge, no safety in self could I see;
Jehovah Tsidkenu my Saviour must be.

4 My terrors all vanished before the sweet name;
my guilty fears banished, with boldness I came
to drink at the fountain, life-giving and free:
Jehovah Tsidkenu was all things to me.

5 E'en treading the valley, the shadow of death,
this watchword shall rally my faltering breath;
for, when from life's fever my God sets me free,
Jehovah Tsidkenu my death-song shall be.

Robert Murray M'Cheyne, 1813-43

Jehovah Tsidkenu *means 'The LORD our Righteousness' (Jer. 23:6; 33:16).*

579

I heard the voice of Jesus say,
'Come unto Me and rest;
lay down, thou weary one, lay down
thy head upon My breast!'
I came to Jesus as I was,
weary, and worn, and sad;
I found in Him a resting-place,
and He has made me glad.

2 I heard the voice of Jesus say,
'Behold, I freely give
the living water – thirsty one,
stoop down, and drink, and live!'
I came to Jesus, and I drank
of that life-giving stream;
my thirst was quenched, my soul revived,
and now I live in Him.

3 I heard the voice of Jesus say,
'I am this dark world's Light;
look unto Me, thy morn shall rise,
and all thy day be bright.'
I looked to Jesus, and I found
in Him my star, my sun;
and in that light of life I'll walk
till travelling days are done.

Horatius Bonar, 1808-89

580

In Eden – sad indeed that day –
my countless blessings fled away,
my crown fell in disgrace.
But on victorious Calvary
that crown was won again for me –
my life shall all be praise.

2 Faith, see the place, and see the tree
where heaven's Prince, instead of me,
was nailed to bear my shame.
Bruised was the dragon by the Son,
though two had wounds, there conquered One –
and Jesus was His name.

William Williams, 1717-91;
tr. by Robert Maynard Jones (Bobi Jones), b. 1929

581

None other Lamb, none other Name,
none other hope in heaven or earth or sea,
none other hiding-place from guilt and shame,
none beside Thee.

2 My faith burns low, my hope burns low;
only my heart's desire cries out in me,
by the deep thunder of its want and woe,
cries out to Thee.

3 Lord, Thou art life, though I be dead;
love's fire Thou art, however cold I be:
nor heaven have I, nor place to lay my head,
nor home, but Thee.

Christina Georgina Rossetti, 1830-94

582

In full and glad surrender
I give myself to Thee,
Thine utterly and only
and evermore to be.

2 O Son of God, who lov'st me,
I will be Thine alone;
and all I have and am, Lord,
shall henceforth be Thine own.

3 Reign over me, Lord Jesus;
O make my heart Thy throne!
It shall be Thine, dear Saviour,
it shall be Thine alone.

4 O come and reign, Lord Jesus;
rule over everything!
and keep me always loyal
and true to Thee, my King.

Frances Ridley Havergal, 1836-79

583

Jesus, Your blood and righteousness
my beauty are, my glorious dress;
midst flaming worlds, in these arrayed;
with joy shall I lift up my head.

2 Bold shall I stand in that great day,
for who aught to my charge shall lay?
Fully absolved through these I am,
from sin and fear, from guilt and shame.

3 The holy, meek, unspotted Lamb,
who from the Father's presence came,
who died for me, e'en me, to atone,
now for my Lord and God I own.

4 This spotless robe the same appears
when ruined nature sinks in years;
no age can change its glorious hue,
the robe of Christ is ever new.

5 When from the dust of death I rise
to claim my mansion in the skies,
e'en then shall this be all my plea,
Jesus has lived, has died for me!

6 O let the dead now hear Your voice!
Now bid Your banished ones rejoice!
Their beauty this, their glorious dress,
Jesus, the Lord our righteousness.

Nicolaus Ludwig von Zinzendorf, 1700-60;
tr. by John Wesley, 1703-91

584

Jesus, I will trust Thee,
trust Thee with my soul;
guilty, lost, and helpless,
Thou canst make me whole:
there is none in heaven
or on earth like Thee:
Thou hast died for sinners –
therefore, Lord, for me.

2 Jesus, I must trust Thee,
pondering Thy ways,
full of love and mercy
all Thine earthly days:
sinners gathered round Thee,
lepers sought Thy face;
none too vile or loathsome
for a Saviour's grace.

3 Jesus, I can trust Thee,
trust Thy written Word,
though Thy voice of pity
I have never heard:
when Thy Spirit teacheth,
to my taste how sweet!
Only may I hearken,
sitting at Thy feet.

4 Jesus, I do trust Thee,
trust without a doubt;
whosoever cometh
Thou wilt not cast out:
faithful is Thy promise,
precious is Thy blood:
these my soul's salvation,
Thou My Saviour God!

Mary Jane Walker, 1816-78

585

Just as I am, without one plea
but that Thy blood was shed for me,
and that Thou bidd'st me come to Thee,
O Lamb of God, I come.

2 Just as I am, and waiting not
to rid my soul of one dark blot,
to Thee, whose blood can cleanse each
spot,
O Lamb of God, I come.

3 Just as I am, though tossed about
with many a conflict, many a doubt,
fightings and fears within, without,
O Lamb of God, I come.

4 Just as I am, poor, wretched, blind:
sight, riches, healing of the mind,
yea, all I need, in Thee to find,
O Lamb of God, I come.

5 Just as I am, Thou wilt receive,
wilt welcome, pardon, cleanse, relieve;
because Thy promise I believe,
O Lamb of God, I come.

6 Just as I am – Thy love unknown
has broken every barrier down –
now to be Thine, yea, Thine alone,
O Lamb of God, I come.

7 Just as I am, of that free love
the breadth, length, depth, and height to prove,
here for a season, then above,
O Lamb of God, I come.

Charlotte Elliott, 1789-1871

586

My hope is built on nothing less
than Jesus' blood and righteousness;
I dare not trust the sweetest frame,
but wholly lean on Jesus' name.

On Christ, the solid rock, I stand;
all other ground is sinking sand.

2 When darkness veils His lovely face,
I rest on His unchanging grace;
in every high and stormy gale,
my anchor holds within the veil.

3 His oath, His cov'nant, and His blood,
support me in the whelming flood;
when all around my soul gives way,
He then is all my hope and stay.

4 When He shall come with trumpet sound,
O may I then in Him be found!
clothed in His righteousness alone,
faultless to stand before the throne.

Edward Mote, 1797-1874

587

Make me a captive, Lord,
and then I shall be free;
force me to render up my sword,
and I shall conqueror be.
I sink in life's alarms
when by myself I stand;
imprison me within Thine arms,
and strong shall be my hand.

2 My heart is weak and poor
until it master find;
it has no spring of action sure,
it varies with the wind:
it cannot freely move
till Thou hast wrought its chain;
enslave it with Thy matchless love,
and deathless it shall reign.

3 My will is not my own
till Thou hast made it Thine;
if it would reach the monarch's throne
it must its crown resign:
it only stands unbent,
amid the clashing strife,
when on Thy bosom it has leant,
and found in Thee its life.

George Matheson, 1842-1906

588

No more, my God, I boast no more
of all the duties I have done;
I quit the hopes I held before,
to trust the merits of Your Son.

2 Now for the love I bear His Name,
what was my gain I count my loss;
my former pride I call my shame,
and nail my glory to His cross.

3 Yes, and I must and will esteem
all things but loss for Jesus' sake:
O may my soul be found in Him,
and of His righteousness partake!

4 The best obedience of my hands
dares not appear before Your throne;
but faith can answer Your demands
by pleading what my Lord has done.

Isaac Watts, 1674-1748

589

Not all the blood of beasts,
on Jewish altars slain,
could give the guilty conscience peace
or wash away the stain.

2 But Christ, the heavenly Lamb,
takes all our sins away;
a sacrifice of nobler name,
and richer blood than they.

3 My faith would lay her hand
on that dear head of Thine,
while like a penitent I stand,
and there confess my sin.

4 My soul looks back to see
the burden Thou didst bear
when hanging on the cursèd tree,
and knows her guilt was there.

5 Believing, we rejoice
to see the curse remove;
we bless the Lamb with cheerful voice,
and sing His wondrous love.

Isaac Watts, 1674-1748

590

Not what these hands have done
can save this guilty soul;
not what this toiling flesh has borne
can make my spirit whole.

2 Not what I feel or do
can give me peace with God;
not all my prayers, and sighs, and tears
can bear my awful load.

3 Thy work alone, O Christ,
can ease this weight of sin;
Thy blood alone, O Lamb of God,
can give me peace within.

4 Thy love to me, O God,
not mine, O Lord, to Thee,
can rid me of this dark unrest,
and set my spirit free.

5 Thy grace alone, O God,
to me can pardon speak;
Thy power alone, O Son of God,
can this sore bondage break.

6 I bless the Christ of God,
I rest on love divine,
and with unfaltering lip and heart,
I call this Saviour mine.

Horatius Bonar, 1808-89

591

O my Saviour, lifted
from the earth for me,
draw me, in Thy mercy,
nearer unto Thee.

2 Lift my earth-bound longings,
fix them, Lord, above;
draw me with the magnet
of Thy mighty love.

3 And I come, Lord Jesus;
dare I turn away?
No! Thy love hath conquered,
and I come today.

4 Bringing all my burdens,
sorrow, sin, and care;
at Thy feet I lay them,
and I leave them there.

William Walsham How, 1823-97

592

Out of my bondage, sorrow and night,
Jesus, I come; Jesus, I come;
into Your freedom, gladness and light,
Jesus, I come to You.
Out of my sickness into Your health,
out of my want and into Your wealth,
out of my sin and into Yourself,
Jesus, I come to You.

2 Out of my shameful failure and loss,
Jesus, I come; Jesus, I come;
into the glorious gain of Your cross,
Jesus, I come to You.
Out of earth's sorrows into Your balm,
out of life's storm and into Your calm,
out of distress to jubilant psalm,
Jesus, I come to You.

3 Out of unrest and arrogant pride,
Jesus, I come; Jesus, I come;
into Your blessèd will to abide,
Jesus, I come to You.
Out of myself to dwell in Your love,
out of despair into raptures above,
upward ascend on wings like a dove,
Jesus, I come to You.

4 Out of the fear and dread of the tomb,
Jesus, I come; Jesus, I come;
into the joy and light of Your home,
Jesus, I come to You.
Out of the depths of ruin untold,
into the peace of Your sheltering fold,
ever Your glorious face to behold,
Jesus, I come to You.

William True Sleeper, 1819-1904

593

Rock of Ages, cleft for me,
let me hide myself in Thee;
let the water and the blood,
from Thy riven side which flowed,
be of sin the double cure,
cleanse me from its guilt and power.

2 Not the labours of my hands
can fulfil Thy law's demands;
could my zeal no respite know,
could my tears for ever flow,
all for sin could not atone:
Thou must save, and Thou alone.

3 Nothing in my hand I bring,
simply to Thy cross I cling;
naked, come to Thee for dress;
helpless, look to Thee for grace;
foul, I to the fountain fly;
wash me, Saviour, or I die.

4 While I draw this fleeting breath,
when my eyelids close in death,
when I soar to realms unknown,
see Thee on Thy judgment throne;
Rock of Ages, cleft for me,
let me hide myself in Thee.

Augustus Montague Toplady, 1740-78

594

PSALM 51

Show pity, Lord; O Lord, forgive;
let a repenting rebel live:
are not Thy mercies large and free?
May not a sinner trust in Thee?

2 A broken heart, my God, my King,
is all the sacrifice I bring;
the God of grace will ne'er despise
a broken heart for sacrifice.

3 My soul lies humbled in the dust,
and owns Thy dreadful sentence just;
look down, O Lord, with pitying eye,
and save the soul condemned to die.

4 Then will I teach the world Thy ways;
sinners shall learn Thy sovereign grace;
I'll lead them to my Saviour's blood,
and they shall praise a pardoning God.

5 O may Thy love inspire my tongue!
Salvation shall be then my song;
and all my powers shall join to bless
the Lord my strength and righteousness.

Isaac Watts, 1674-1748

595

Sinners Jesus will receive:
tell this word of grace to all
who the heavenly pathway leave,
all who linger, all who fall;
this can bring them back again:
Christ receiveth sinful men.

2 Shepherds seek their wandering sheep
o'er the mountains bleak and cold;
Jesus such a watch doth keep
o'er the lost ones of His fold,
seeking them o'er moor and fen:
Christ receiveth sinful men.

3 Sick and sorrowful and blind,
I with all my sins draw nigh;
O my Saviour, Thou canst find
help for sinners such as I;
speak that word of love again:
Christ receiveth sinful men.

4 Christ receiveth sinful men,
even me with all my sin;
openeth to me heaven again;
with Him I may enter in.
Death hath no more sting nor pain:
Christ receiveth sinful men.

Erdmann Neumeister, 1671-1756;
tr. by Emma Frances Bevan, 1827-1909

596

Thy works, not mine, O Christ,
speak gladness to this heart;
they tell me all is done,
they bid my fear depart.
To whom save Thee, who canst alone
for sin atone, Lord, shall I flee?

2 Thy wounds, not mine, O Christ,
can heal my bruisèd soul;
Thy stripes, not mine, contain
the balm that makes me whole.
To whom save Thee, who canst alone
for sin atone, Lord, shall I flee?

3 Thy cross, not mine, O Christ,
has borne the awful load
of sins that none could bear
but the incarnate God.
To whom save Thee, who canst alone
for sin atone, Lord, shall I flee?

4 Thy death, not mine, O Christ,
has paid the ransom due;
ten thousand deaths like mine
would have been all too few.
To whom save Thee, who canst alone
for sin atone, Lord, shall I flee?

5 Thy righteousness, O Christ,
alone can cover me;
no righteousness avails
save that which is of Thee.
To whom save Thee, who canst alone
for sin atone, Lord, shall I flee?

Horatius Bonar, 1808-89

597

Take up your cross, the Saviour said,
if you would My disciple be;
deny yourself, the world forsake,
and humbly follow after Me.

2 Take up your cross; let not its weight
fill your weak soul with vain alarm;
His strength shall bear your spirit up,
and brace your heart, and nerve your arm.

3 Take up your cross, nor heed the shame,
nor let your foolish pride rebel;
the Lord for you the cross endured
to save your soul from death and hell.

4 Take up your cross, then, in His strength,
and calmly every danger brave,
to guide you to a better home,
and lead to victory o'er the grave.

5 Take up your cross, and follow Christ,
nor think till death to lay it down;
for only he who bears the cross
may hope to wear the glorious crown.

Charles William Everest, 1814-77

598

With broken heart and contrite sigh,
a trembling sinner, Lord, I cry;
Your pardoning grace is rich and free,
O God, be merciful to me!

2 I smite upon my troubled breast,
with deep and conscious guilt oppressed;
Christ and His cross my only plea:
O God, be merciful to me!

3 Far off I stand with tearful eyes,
nor dare uplift them to the skies;
but You can all my anguish see;
O God, be merciful to me!

4 No deeds of kindness I have done
can for a single sin atone:
to Calvary alone I flee;
O God, be merciful to me!

5 And when, redeemed from sin and hell,
with all the ransomed throng I dwell,
my raptured song shall ever be:
God has been merciful to me!

Cornelius Elven, 1797-1873

599

The price is paid:
come, let us enter in
to all that Jesus died
to make our own.
For every sin
more than enough He gave,
and bought our freedom
from each guilty stain.

The price is paid, alleluia –
amazing grace,
so strong and sure!
And so with all my heart,
my life in every part,
I live to thank You
for the price You paid.

2 The price is paid:
see Satan flee away –
for Jesus, crucified,
destroys his power.
No more to pay!
Let accusation cease:
in Christ there is
no condemnation now!

3 The price is paid:
and by that scourging cruel,
He took our sicknesses
as if His own.
And by His wounds,
His body broken there,
His healing touch may now
by faith be known.

4 The price is paid:
'Worthy the Lamb!' we cry –
eternity shall never
cease His praise.
The Church of Christ
shall rule upon the earth:
in Jesus' name
we have authority!

Graham Kendrick, b. 1950

600

'Tis finished! the Messiah dies,
cut off for sins, but not His own;
accomplished is the sacrifice,
the great redeeming work is done.
'Tis finished! all the debt is paid;
justice divine is satisfied;
the grand and full atonement made;
God for a guilty world has died.

2 The veil is rent in Christ alone;
the living way to heaven is seen;
the middle wall is broken down,
and all mankind may enter in.
The types and figures are fulfilled;
exacted is the legal pain;
the precious promises are sealed;
the spotless Lamb of God is slain.

3 The reign of sin and death is o'er,
and all may live from sin set free;
Satan has lost his mortal power;
'tis swallowed up in victory.
Saved from the legal curse I am,
my Saviour hangs on yonder tree:
see there the meek, expiring Lamb!
'Tis finished! He expires for me.

4 Accepted in the Well-beloved,
and clothed in righteousness divine,
I see the bar to heaven removed,
and all Your merits, Lord, are mine.
Death, hell, and sin are now subdued;
all grace is now to sinners given;
and lo, I plead the atoning blood,
and in Your right I claim Your
heaven.

Charles Wesley, 1707-88

601

To heart and soul how sweet Thou art,
O great High Priest of God!
My heart brought nigh to God's own heart
by Thy most precious blood.

2 No more my countless sins shall rise
to fill me with dismay;
that precious blood before His eyes
has put them all away.

3 My soul draws near with trust secure,
with boldness glad and free;
what matters it that I am poor,
for I am rich in Thee.

4 Forgotten every stain and spot,
their memory past and gone,
for me, O God, Thou seest not,
Thou lookest on Thy Son.

5 Is all a dream? Thou canst not lie;
Thy Spirit and Thy blood
proclaim to sinners such as I
the boundless love of God.

6 They tell Thy love, so deep, so free,
they tell the Father's heart;
not what I am, or I must be,
they tell me what Thou art.

7 Come, weary sinners, great and small,
the open door stands wide,
the blessèd heart that welcomes all,
the Lamb of God, who died.

Gerhard Tersteegen, 1697-1769;
tr. by Emma Frances Bevan, 1827-1909

602

Weary of earth and laden with my sin,
I look at heaven and long to enter in;
but there no evil thing may find a home,
and yet I hear a voice that bids me come.

2 So vile I am, how dare I hope to stand
in the pure glory of that holy land,
before the whiteness of that throne appear?
Yet there are hands stretched out to draw me near.

3 For though my feet would tread the heavenly way,
evil is ever with me day by day;
yet on mine ears the gracious tidings fall:
'Repent, believe; you shall be loosed from all!'

4 It is the voice of Jesus that I hear,
His are the hands stretched out to draw me near,
and His the blood that can for all atone,
and set me faultless there before the throne.

5 O great Absolver, grant my soul may wear
the lowliest garb of penitence and prayer,
that in the Father's courts my glorious dress
may be the garment of Your righteousness!

6 Yes, You will answer for me, righteous Lord:
Yours all the merit, mine the great reward;
Yours the sharp thorns, and mine the golden crown;
mine the life won, and Yours the life laid down.

7 Nought can I bring, dear Lord, for all I owe;
yet let my full heart what it can bestow:
like ointment sweet, let my devotion prove,
forgiven greatly, how I greatly love.

Samuel John Stone, 1839-1900

603

Years I spent in vanity and pride,
caring not my Lord was crucified,
knowing not it was for me He died
on Calvary.

Mercy there was great and grace was free,
pardon there was multiplied to me,
there my burdened soul found liberty,
at Calvary.

2 By God's Word at last my sin I learned,
then I trembled at the law I'd spurned,
till my guilty soul imploring turned
to Calvary.

3 Now I've given to Jesus everything,
now I gladly own Him as my King,
now my raptured soul can only sing
of Calvary.

4 O the love that drew salvation's plan!
O the grace that brought it down to man!
O the mighty gulf that God did span
at Calvary!

William Reed Newell, 1868-1956

THE CHRISTIAN LIFE

Assurance and hope

604

Blessèd assurance, Jesus is mine:
O what a foretaste of glory divine!
Heir of salvation, purchase of God,
born of His Spirit, washed in His blood.

This is my story, this is my song,
praising my Saviour all the day long.

2 Perfect submission, perfect delight,
visions of rapture burst on my sight;
angels descending bring from above
echoes of mercy, whispers of love.

3 Perfect submission, all is at rest,
I in my Saviour am happy and blest;
watching and waiting, looking above,
filled with His goodness, lost in His love.

Frances Jane Van Alstyne, 1820-1915

605

A debtor to mercy alone,
of covenant mercy I sing;
nor fear, with Your righteousness on,
my person and offering to bring;
the terrors of law and of God
with me can have nothing to do;
my Saviour's obedience and blood
hide all my transgressions from view.

2 The work which His goodness began,
the arm of His strength will complete;
His promise is Yea and Amen,
and never was forfeited yet.
Things future, nor things that are now,
not all things below nor above,
can make Him His purpose forgo,
or sever my soul from His love.

3 My name from the palms of His hands
eternity will not erase;
impressed on His heart it remains,
in marks of indelible grace;
yes, I to the end shall endure,
as sure as the earnest is given;
more happy, but not more secure,
the glorified spirits in heaven.

Augustus Montague Toplady, 1740-78

606

A sovereign Protector I have,
unseen, yet for ever at hand,
unchangeably faithful to save,
almighty to rule and command.
He smiles, and my comforts abound;
His grace as the dew shall descend;
and walls of salvation surround
the soul He delights to defend.

2 Inspirer and hearer of prayer,
Thou shepherd and guardian of
Thine,
my all to Thy covenant care
I sleeping and waking resign.
If Thou art my shield and my sun,
the night is no darkness to me;
and fast as my moments roll on,
they bring me but nearer to Thee.

3 Kind author and ground of my hope,
Thee, Thee, for my God I avow;
my glad Ebenezer set up,
and own Thou hast helped me till now.
I muse on the years that are past,
wherein my defence Thou hast
proved;
nor wilt Thou relinquish at last
a sinner so signally loved!

Augustus Montague Toplady, 1740-78

607 Based on 1 John 3:1-4

Behold, what wondrous grace
the Father has bestowed
on sinners of a mortal race,
to call them sons of God.

2 'Tis no surprising thing
that we should be unknown;
the Jewish world knew not their King,
God's everlasting Son.

3 Nor does it yet appear
how great we must be made;
but when we see our Saviour here,
we shall be like our Head.

4 A hope so much divine
may trials well endure,
may purge our souls from sense and sin,
as Christ the Lord is pure.

5 If in our Father's love
we share a filial part,
send down Your Spirit like a dove
to rest upon each heart.

6 We would no longer lie
like slaves beneath Your throne;
our faith shall 'Abba, Father' cry,
and You the kindred own.

Isaac Watts, 1674-1748

608 Based on 1 Peter 1:3-5

Blest be the everlasting God,
the Father of our Lord!
Be His abounding mercy praised,
His majesty adored!

2 When from the dead He raised His Son,
and called Him to the sky,
He gave our souls a lively hope
that they should never die.

3 To an inheritance divine
He taught our hearts to rise;
'tis uncorrupted, undefiled,
unfading in the skies.

4 Saints by the power of God are kept,
till the salvation come;
we walk by faith as strangers here,
till Christ shall call us home.

Isaac Watts, 1674-1748

609

Come, Holy Ghost, my heart assure,
dispel my fears, that I no more
may doubt that mercy now is mine,
nor question promises divine;
impress the seal, Your image leave,
confirm in power that grace I have,
that I may run the heavenly race
with joy, beholding Jesus' face.

2 Come, blessèd Comforter divine,
relieve this doubting heart of mine;
banish the clouds of unbelief,
O liberate my soul from grief,
illumine me with heavenly light,
scatter the thoughts of darkest night!
With anxious sighs I look above,
longing to know my Saviour's love.

3 Come, promise of the Father's love,
abide within me, gentle Dove;
my soul assured, I then shall rest
on my Redeemer's tender breast
until I come to heaven at last,
with all my sins and troubles past;
truly to know that grace was sure,
happy to know, and doubt no more!

Alan Charles Clifford, b. 1941

610

Dear Saviour, Thou art mine,
how sweet the thought to me!
Let me repeat Thy name,
and lift my heart to Thee.

Mine! mine! mine! I know Thou art mine;
Saviour, dear Saviour, I know Thou art mine.

2 Thou art the sinner's friend,
so I Thy friendship claim,
a sinner saved by grace,
when Thy sweet message came.

3 My hardened heart was touched;
Thy pardoning voice I heard;
and joy and peace came in,
while listening to Thy Word.

4 So let me sing Thy praise,
so let me call Thee mine;
I cannot doubt Thy Word,
I know that I am Thine.

Anna Hudson

611

How gracious, kind and good,
my great High Priest, art Thou!
As Aaron in the holiest stood,
so Christ in heaven now.

2 When conscience would despair,
by reason of my sin,
Thy blood can banish all its care,
and peace restore within.

3 It gives the anxious mind
a confidence in Thee;
though nothing in ourselves we find,
but insufficiency.

4 Whene'er my footsteps slide,
and when my spirit fails,
I flee to Thy dear bleeding side,
and humble faith prevails.

5 Then feels my deepest smart
the soul-reviving power,
and gently rests my troubled heart
beneath the crimson shower.

Gerhard Tersteegen, 1697-1769;
tr. in Leifchild's ORIGINAL HYMNS, 1842

612

How firm a foundation, you saints of the Lord,
is laid for your faith in His excellent Word!
What more can He say than to you He has said –
you, who unto Jesus for refuge have fled?

2 In every condition – in sickness, in health,
in poverty's vale, or abounding in wealth;
at home or abroad, on the land, on the sea,
as days may demand, shall your strength ever be.

3 'Fear not, I am with you, O be not dismayed!
I, I am your God, and will still give you aid:
I'll strengthen you, help you, and cause you to stand,
upheld by My righteous, omnipotent hand.

4 'When through the deep waters I cause
you to go,
the rivers of grief shall not you overflow;
for I will be with you, your troubles to
bless,
and sanctify to you your deepest distress.

5 'When through fiery trials your pathway
shall lie,
my grace all-sufficient shall be your
supply;
the flame shall not hurt you: I only
design
your dross to consume, and your gold
to refine.

6 'The soul that on Jesus has leaned for
repose
I will not, I will not desert to its foes;
that soul, though all hell should
endeavour to shake,
I'll never, no never, no never forsake!'

'K' in Rippon's SELECTION, *1787*

613

I bless the Christ of God,
I rest on love divine,
and with unfaltering lip and heart
I call this Saviour mine.

2 His cross dispels each doubt;
I bury in His tomb
each thought of unbelief and fear,
each lingering shade of gloom.

3 I praise the God of grace,
I trust His truth and might;
He calls me His, I call Him mine,
my God, my joy, my light.

4 In Him is only good,
in me is only ill;
my ill but draws His goodness forth,
and me He loveth still.

5 'Tis He who saveth me,
and freely pardon gives;
I love because He loveth me,
I live because He lives,

6 My life with Him is hid,
my death has passed away,
my clouds have melted into light,
my midnight into day.

Horatius Bonar, 1808-89

614

I could not do without You,
O Saviour of the lost,
whose precious blood redeemed me
at such tremendous cost;
Your righteousness, Your pardon,
Your precious blood must be
my only hope and comfort,
my glory and my plea.

2 I could not do without You,
I cannot stand alone,
I have no strength or goodness,
no wisdom of my own;
but You, belovèd Saviour,
are all in all to me,
my power in every weakness,
my all-sufficiency

3 I could not do without You:
the years are fleeting fast,
and soon in solemn loneness
the river must be passed;
but You will never leave me,
and though the waves roll high,
I know You will be near me
and whisper, 'It is I.'

Frances Ridley Havergal, 1836-79

615

I know not why God's wondrous grace
to me has been made known,
nor why – unworthy as I am –
He claimed me for His own.

But 'I know whom I have believèd,
and am persuaded that He is able
to keep that which I've committed
unto Him against that day.'

2 I know not how this saving faith
to me He did impart,
or how believing in His Word
wrought peace within my heart.

3 I know not how the Spirit moves,
convincing men of sin,
revealing Jesus through the Word,
creating faith in Him.

4 I know not what of good or ill
may be reserved for me –
of weary ways or golden days
before His face I see.

5 I know not when my Lord may come;
I know not how, nor where;
if I shall pass the vale of death,
or meet Him in the air.

Daniel Webster Whittle, 1840-1901

616

I know that my Redeemer
lives crowned upon the throne;
Lord over earth and heaven,
He saves and He alone;
He conquered death by dying
upon the accursèd tree,
and from His death sprang glorious
eternal life for me.

2 I think upon my Saviour,
I trust His power to keep,
His mighty arm enfolds me
awaking and in sleep.
Christ is my rock, my courage;
Christ is my soul's true life;
and Christ – my heart still knows it –
will bear me through the strife.

3 In Jesus' name I'm living;
in Jesus' name I'll die;
I'll fear not, though life's vigour
from death's cold shadow fly.
O grave, where is your triumph?
O death, where is your sting?
My Saviour! He has conquered!
Secure in Him I sing.

Hallgrim Pjetursson, 1614-74;
tr. by Charles V Pilcher, 1879-1961

617

I serve a risen Saviour,
He's in the world today;
I know that He is living,
whatever men may say.
I see His hand of mercy,
I hear His voice of cheer,
and just the time I need Him
He's always near.

He lives, He lives,
Christ Jesus lives today!
He walks with me and talks with me
along life's narrow way.
He lives, He lives,
salvation to impart!
You ask me how I know He lives?
He lives within my heart.

2 In all the world around me
  I see His loving care,
and though my heart grows weary
  I never will despair;
I know that He is leading,
  through all the stormy blast;
the day of His appearing
  will come at last.

3 Rejoice, rejoice, O Christian,
  lift up your voice and sing
eternal hallelujahs
  to Jesus Christ the King!
The hope of all who seek Him,
  the help of all who find,
none other is so loving,
  so good and kind.

Alfred Henry Ackley, 1887-1960

618

I shall see Him in the morning,
  now the night is passing fast;
morn is breaking, comes the dawning,
  I shall see His face at last.
Born in darkness, sad and broken,
  I had wandered far from God;
then the word of life was spoken,
  pointing me to Jesu's blood.

2 I shall see Him in the morning,
  in my Father's house above;
He who bore the shame and scorning;
  O the fulness of His love!
He who was the Father's treasure
  freely left His throne on high;
such a love beyond all measure
  brought Him down to earth to die.

3 I shall see Him in the morning,
  Jesus, King of kings so fair:
crowns of joy His brow adorning,
  and His likeness I shall wear.
Sin had burnt its marks upon me,
  and my heart was dark as night;
brightest beams of grace fell on me,
  bathing me in gospel light.

4 I shall see Him in the morning;
  then my joy shall be complete,
when in wonder, all adoring,
  I kneel at His nail-scarred feet.
O the glorious revelation!
  led by grace to this sweet place,
mine the perfect consummation,
  seeing Jesus face to face.

Colin P Goldsworthy, b. 1927

619

I want the Spirit of power within,
  of love, and of a healthful mind:
of power, to conquer inbred sin;
  of love, to You and all mankind;
of health, that pain and death defies,
most vigorous when the body dies.

2 When shall I hear the inward voice
  which only faithful souls can hear?
Pardon, and peace, and heavenly joys
  attend the promised Comforter:
O come! and righteousness divine,
and Christ, and all with Christ, are
  mine.

3 O that the Comforter would come!
  nor visit as a transient guest,
but fix in me His constant home,
  and take possession of my breast,
and fix in me His loved abode,
the temple of indwelling God.

4 Come, Holy Ghost, my heart inspire!
Attest that I am born again;
come and baptize me now with fire,
nor let Your former gifts be vain:
I cannot rest in sins forgiven;
where is the earnest of my heaven?

5 Where the indubitable seal
that ascertains the kingdom mine?
The powerful stamp I long to feel,
the signature of love divine:
O shed it in my heart abroad,
fulness of love, of heaven, of God!

Charles Wesley, 1707-88

620

Jesus lives, and so shall I!
Death, your sting is gone forever:
He who came for me to die,
lives, the chains of death to sever.
He shall raise me with the just,
Jesus is my hope and trust.

2 Jesus lives, and God extends
grace to each returning sinner;
rebels He receives as friends,
and exalts to highest honour.
God is merciful and just,
Jesus is my hope and trust.

3 Jesus lives, and I am sure
nothing from His arms can take me;
Satan's threats I may ignore,
nor let pain or pleasure shake me.
None of all His saints is lost:
Jesus is my hope and trust.

4 Jesus lives, and death's dark gate
is my entrance into glory.
Courage then, my soul, and wait:
joy shall crown life's varied story.
All God's ways are right and just:
Jesus still my hope and trust.

*Christian Fürchtegott Gellert**, 1715-69

621

Jesus my Lord will love me forever,
from Him no power of evil can sever;
He gave His life to ransom my soul,
now I belong to Him.

Now I belong to Jesus,
Jesus belongs to me,
not for the years of time alone,
but for eternity.

2 Once I was lost in sin's degradation,
Jesus came down to bring me salvation,
lifted me up from sorrow and shame,
now I belong to Him.

3 Joy fills my soul for Jesus has saved me,
freed me from sin that long had enslaved me,
His precious blood He gave to redeem,
now I belong to Him.

Norman John Clayton, 1903-92

622

Jesus, I my cross have taken,
all to leave, and follow Thee;
destitute, despised, forsaken,
Thou from hence my all shalt be:
perish every fond ambition,
all I've sought, and hoped, and known;
yet how rich is my condition!
God and heaven are still mine own.

2 Let the world despise and leave me,
they have left my Saviour too;
human hearts and looks deceive me;
Thou art not, like man, untrue:

and, while Thou shalt smile upon me,
God of wisdom, love, and might,
foes may hate, and friends may shun me;
show Thy face, and all is bright.

3 Man may trouble and distress me,
'twill but drive me to Thy breast;
life with trials hard may press me,
heaven will bring me sweeter rest.
Think what Spirit dwells within thee,
what a Father's smile is thine,
what a Saviour died to win thee!
Child of heaven, shouldst thou repine?

4 Haste then on from grace to glory,
armed by faith, and winged by prayer;
heaven's eternal day's before thee;
God's own hand shall guide thee there.
Soon shall close thine earthly mission,
swift shall pass thy pilgrim days,
hope soon change to glad fruition,
faith to sight, and prayer to praise.

Henry Francis Lyte, 1793-1847

623

My faith has found a resting place,
from guilt my soul is freed;
I trust the ever-living One,
His wounds for me shall plead.

I need no other argument,
I need no other plea;
it is enough that Jesus died,
and that He died for me.

2 Enough for me that Jesus saves,
this ends my fear and doubt;
a sinful soul I come to Him,
He'll never cast me out.

3 My heart is leaning on the Word,
the written Word of God;
salvation by my Saviour's Name,
salvation through His blood.

4 My great physician heals the sick,
the lost He came to save;
for me His precious blood He shed,
for me His life He gave.

*Eliza Edmunds Hewitt**, 1851-1920

624

Now I have found the ground wherein
sure my soul's anchor may remain –
the wounds of Jesus, for my sin
before the world's foundation slain;
whose mercy shall unshaken stay,
when heaven and earth are fled away.

2 Father, Thine everlasting grace
our scanty thought surpasses far;
Thy heart still melts with tenderness,
Thine arms of love still open are
returning sinners to receive,
that mercy they may taste and live.

3 O Love, Thou bottomless abyss,
my sins are swallowed up in Thee!
Covered is my unrighteousness,
nor spot of guilt remains on me,
while Jesus' blood, through earth and skies,
'Mercy, free, boundless mercy!' cries.

4 With faith I plunge me in this sea,
here is my hope, my joy, my rest;
hither, when hell assails, I flee,
I look into my Saviour's breast:
away, sad doubt and anxious fear!
Mercy is all that's written there.

5 Though waves and storms go o'er my head,
though strength, and health, and friends be gone,
though joys be withered all and dead,
though every comfort be withdrawn,
on this my steadfast soul relies –
Father, Thy mercy never dies!

6 Fixed on this ground will I remain,
though my heart fail and flesh decay;
this anchor shall my soul sustain,
when earth's foundations melt away:
mercy's full power I then shall prove,
loved with an everlasting love.

Johann Andreas Rothe, 1688-1758;
tr. by John Wesley, 1703-91

625

O my soul, arise and bless your Maker,
for He is your master and your friend;
slow to wrath, but rich in tender mercy –
worship the Saviour, Jesus.

2 King of grace, His love is overwhelming,
bread of life, He's all I'll ever need,
for His blood has purchased me forever –
bought at the cross of Jesus.

And I will sing for all my days
of heaven's love come down;
each breath I take will speak his praise,
until He calls me home.

3 When I wake, I know that He is with me,
when I'm weak, I know that He is strong;
though I fall, His arm is there to lean on –
safe on the rock of Jesus.

4 Stir in me the songs that You are singing,
fill my gaze with things as yet unseen;
give me faith to move in works of power,
making me more like Jesus.
And I will sing…

5 Then one day I'll see Him as He sees me,
face to face, the Lover and the loved;
no more words, the longing will be over –
there with my precious Jesus.

Repeat: Then one day
(No refrain after v. 5)

Stuart Townend, b. 1963

626

Speak, I pray Thee, gentle Jesus!
O how passing sweet Thy words,
breathing o'er my troubled spirit
peace which never earth affords.
All the world's distracting voices,
all the enticing tones of ill,
at Thy accents mild, melodious,
are subdued, and all is still.

2 Tell me Thou art mine, O Saviour,
grant me an assurance clear;
banish all my dark misgivings,
still my doubting, calm my fear.
O, my soul within me yearneth
now to hear Thy voice divine;
so shall grief be gone for ever,
and despair no more be mine.

William Williams, 1717-91;
tr. Richard Morris Lewis, 1847-1918

627

When sins and fears prevailing rise,
and fainting hope almost expires,
Jesus, to You I lift my eyes,
to You I breathe my soul's desires.

2 Are You not mine, my living Lord?
And can my hope, my comfort die,
fixed on Your everlasting Word,
that Word which built the earth and sky?

3 Since my immortal Saviour lives,
then my immortal life is sure;
His Word a firm foundation gives:
here let me build, and rest secure.

4 Here let my faith unshaken dwell;
immovable Your promise stands;
not all the powers of earth or hell
can e'er dissolve the sacred bands.

5 Here, O my soul, your trust repose;
if Jesus is for ever mine,
not death itself, that last of foes,
shall break a union so divine!

Anne Steele, 1717-78

628 PSALM 23

The Lord is my shepherd; no want shall I know.
He makes me lie down where the green pastures grow;
He leads me to rest where the calm waters flow.

2 My wandering steps He brings back to His way,
in straight paths of righteousness making me stay;
and this He has done His great name to display.

3 Though I walk in death's valley, where darkness is near,
because You are with me, no evil I'll fear;
Your rod and Your staff bring me comfort and cheer.

4 In the sight of my en'mies a table You spread.
The oil of rejoicing You pour on my head;
my cup overflows and I'm graciously fed.

5 So surely Your covenant mercy and grace
will follow me closely in all of my ways;
I will dwell in the house of the Lord all my days.

SING PSALMS, 2003

629

Why should I sorrow more?
I trust a Saviour slain,
and safe beneath His sheltering cross
unmoved I shall remain.

2 Let Satan and the world
now rage or now allure;
the promises in Christ are made
immutable and sure.

3 The oath infallible
is now my spirit's trust;
I know that He who spoke the word
is faithful, true and just.

4 He'll bring me on my way
unto my journey's end;
He'll be my Father and my God,
my Saviour and my friend.

5 So all my doubts and fears
shall wholly flee away,
and every mournful night of tears
be turned to joyous day.

6 All that remains for me
is but to love and sing,
and wait until the angels come
to bear me to the King.

William Williams, 1717-91,
and Charles Haddon Spurgeon, 1834-92

630

Based on ROMANS 8

Who now shall God's elect condemn
when Christ has for their ransom died?
Rising, He intercedes for them;
and they in Him are justified.

2 Not tribulation, nakedness,
not famine, peril, or the sword,
nor persecution or distress,
shall separate from Christ the Lord.

3 Nor life nor death, nor depth nor height,
nor powers below, nor powers above,
not present things, nor things to come,
can change His purposes of love.

4 His sovereign mercy knows no bounds,
His faithfulness shall still endure;
and those who on His word rely,
shall find His truth for ever sure.

Benjamin Beddome, 1717-98

631

Through the love of God our Saviour
all will be well;
free and changeless is His favour,
all, all is well:
precious is the blood that healed us;
perfect is the grace that sealed us;
strong the hand stretched forth to shield us;
all must be well.

2 Though we pass through tribulation,
all will be well;
Christ has purchased full salvation,
all, all is well:
happy still in God confiding,
fruitful, if in Christ abiding,
holy, through the Spirit's guiding;
all must be well.

3 We expect a bright tomorrow;
all will be well;
faith can sing through days of sorrow,
all, all is well:
on our Father's love relying,
Jesus every need supplying,
then in living or in dying
all must be well.

Mary Peters, 1813-56

632

How good is the God we adore,
our faithful, unchangeable Friend!
His love is as great as His power,
and knows neither measure nor end!

2 'Tis Jesus, the first and the last,
whose Spirit shall guide us safe home;
we'll praise Him for all that is past,
and trust Him for all that's to come.

Joseph Hart, 1712-68

633

Who trusts in God, a strong abode
in heaven and earth possesses;
who looks in love to Christ above,
no fear his heart oppresses.
In You alone, dear Lord, we own
sweet hope and consolation,
our shield from foes, our balm from woes,
our great and sure salvation.

2 Though Satan's wrath beset our path,
and worldly scorn assail us,
while You are near we will not fear,
Your strength shall never fail us.
Your rod and staff shall keep us safe,
and guide our steps for ever;
nor shades of death, nor hell beneath,
our souls from You shall sever.

3 In all the strife of mortal life
our feet shall stand securely;
temptation's hour shall lose its power,
for You shall guard us surely.
O God, renew, with heavenly dew,
our body, soul and spirit,
until we stand at Your right hand,
through Jesus' saving merit.

v. 1. Joachim Magdeburg, b.c. 1525;
vv. 2 & 3 Anonymous, 1597;
tr. by Benjamin Hall Kennedy,* 1804-89

634

Why should I fear the darkest hour,
or tremble at the tempter's power?
Jesus has pledged to be my tower.

2 Though hot the fight, why quit the field?
Why must I either fly or yield,
since Jesus is my mighty shield?

3 When creature comforts fade and die,
worldlings may weep, but why should I?
Jesus still lives and still is nigh.

4 I know not what may soon betide,
or how my wants shall be supplied;
but Jesus knows, and will provide.

5 Though sin would fill me with distress,
the throne of grace I dare address,
for Jesus is my righteousness.

6 Though faint my prayers and cold my love,
my steadfast hope shall not remove,
while Jesus intercedes above.

7 Against me earth and hell combine;
but on my side is power divine;
Jesus is all, and He is mine!

John Newton, 1725-1807

Union with Christ

635

A mind at perfect peace with God;
O what a word is this!
a sinner reconciled through blood,
this, this indeed is peace!

2 By nature and by practice far –
how very far from God!
Yet now by grace brought nigh to Him,
through faith in Jesus' blood.

3 So nigh, so very nigh to God,
I cannot nearer be;
for in the person of His Son
I am as near as He.

4 So dear, so very dear to God,
more dear I cannot be;
the love wherewith He loves the Son –
such is His love to me!

5 Why should I ever anxious be,
since such a God is mine?
He watches o'er me night and day,
and tells me: 'Mine is thine'.

Catesby Paget

636

As the deer pants for the water,
so my soul longs after You,
You alone are my heart's desire
and I long to worship You.

You alone are my strength, my shield,
to You alone may my spirit yield.
You alone are my heart's desire
and I long to worship You.

2 I want You more than gold or silver,
only You can satisfy.
You alone are the real joy-giver
and the apple of my eye.

3 You're my Friend and You are my Brother,
even though You are a King.
I love You more than any other,
so much more than anything.

Martin Nystrom, b. 1956

637

Based on PHILIPPIANS 3:7-11

All I once held dear, built my life upon,
all this world reveres and wars to own,
all I once thought gain I have counted loss;
spent and worthless now, compared to this.

Knowing You, Jesus, knowing You;
there is no greater thing.
You're my all, You're the best,
You're my joy, my righteousness,
and I love you, Lord.

2 Now my heart's desire is to know You more,
to be found in You and known as Yours;
to possess by faith what I could not earn,
all-surpassing gift of righteousness.

3 O to know the power of Your risen life,
and to know You in Your sufferings;
to become like You in Your death, my Lord,
so with You to live and never die.

Graham Kendrick, b. 1950

638

Be Thou my vision, O Lord of my heart;
nought be all else to me, save that Thou art;
Thou my best thought, by day or by night,
waking or sleeping, Thy presence my light.

2 Be Thou my wisdom, Thou my true word;
I ever with Thee, Thou with me, Lord;
Thou my great Father, I Thy true son;
Thou in me dwelling, and I with Thee one.

3 Be Thou my battle-shield, sword for the fight;
be Thou my armour, be Thou my might;
Thou my soul's shelter, Thou my high tower;
raise Thou me heavenward, O power of my power.

4 Riches I heed not, nor man's empty
praise;
Thou mine inheritance, now and
always;
Thou and Thou only, first in my heart,
high King of heaven, my treasure Thou
art.

5 High King of heaven, after victory won,
may I reach heaven's joy, O bright
heaven's sun!
Heart of my own heart, whatever befall,
still be my vision, O Ruler of all.

Irish, c. 8th cent.,
from The Poem Book of the Gael;
tr. by Mary Elizabeth Byrne, 1880-1931;
versified by Eleanor Henrietta Hull,
1860-1935

639 PHILIPPIANS 3:10

Deep in my heart there is a sigh,
a longing, Lord, for Thee;
to know the depths that in Thee lie,
the grace of Calvary.
O grant that I might understand
Thy glorious mystery,
more of Thyself, and by Thy hand;
obedience stir in me.

2 Thy living power I long to prove
in resurrection might,
with overcoming grace to move
each sin that dims this light.
O grant that I may find the source
of hidden strength and stay,
which flows from Thee, and on its
course
O draw my soul each day.

3 There is a fellowship of pain
deep in Christ's heart of love,
of suffering sweet, eternal gain,
the tears of heaven above.
O grant me, Lord, to feel this joy,
these tremors of Thy grace;
engraved by Thee, none can destroy
the riches I embrace.

4 Then lead me in this wondrous way
to die to self and sin;
and take me, Lord, when Thou dost
slay,
and drive Thy grace within.
O grant me now an image sweet
impressed upon my heart;
with joy I lie beneath Thy feet,
to weep and not depart.

William Vernon Higham, b. 1926

640

Blest are the pure in heart,
for they shall see our God;
the secret of the Lord is theirs,
their soul is Christ's abode.

2 The Lord, who left the heavens
our life and peace to bring,
to dwell in lowliness with men,
their pattern and their King –

3 Still to the lowly soul
He doth Himself impart,
and for His dwelling and His throne
chooseth the pure in heart.

4 Lord, we Thy presence seek;
may ours this blessing be;
give us a pure and lowly heart,
a temple meet for Thee.

John Keble, 1792-1866, *and others*

641

Lord Jesus, are we one with Thee?
O height, O depth of love!
With Thee we died upon the tree,
in Thee we live above.

2 Such was Thy grace, that for our sake
Thou didst from heaven come down,
Thou didst of flesh and blood partake,
in all our sorrows one.

3 Our sins, our guilt, in love divine,
confessed and borne by Thee:
the gall, the curse, the wrath were Thine,
to set Thy members free.

4 Ascended now in glory bright,
still one with us Thou art;
nor life, nor death, nor depth, nor height,
Thy saints and Thee can part.

5 O teach us, Lord, to know and own
this wondrous mystery,
that Thou with us art truly one,
and we are one with Thee!

6 Soon, soon shall come that glorious day,
when, seated on Thy throne,
Thou shalt to wondering worlds display
that Thou with us art one.

James George Deck, 1802-84

642

May the mind of Christ my Saviour
live in me from day to day,
by His love and power controlling
all I do and say.

2 May the Word of God dwell richly
in my heart from hour to hour,
so that all may see I triumph
only through His power.

3 May the peace of God the Father
rule my life in everything,
that I may be calm to comfort
sick and sorrowing.

4 May the love of Jesus fill me
as the waters fill the sea;
Him exalting, self abasing,
this is victory.

5 May I run the race before me,
strong and brave to face the foe,
looking only unto Jesus
as I onward go.

6 May his beauty rest upon me
as I seek the lost to win,
and may they forget the channel,
seeing only Him.

Katie Barclay Wilkinson, 1859-1928

643

Based on PHILIPPIANS 2:5-11

Jesus! exalted far on high,
to whom a Name is given,
a Name surpassing every name
that's known in earth or heaven:

2 Before whose throne shall every knee
bow down with one accord,
before whose throne shall every tongue
confess that Thou art Lord.

3 Jesus! who in the form of God
didst equal honour claim,
yet, to redeem our guilty souls,
didst stoop to death and shame:

4 O may that mind in us be formed
which shone so bright in Thee!
May we be humble, lowly, meek,
from pride and envy free.

5 May we to others stoop, and learn
to emulate Thy love:
so shall we bear Thine image here,
and share Thy throne above.

Thomas Cotterill, 1779-1823

644

How often have they told me,
this earth is passing fair;
the hand of the Creator
is printed everywhere.
But now in vision brighter
of realms before unknown,
I see the Lord of glory,
the Man upon the throne.

2 Tell me of earth no longer,
tell me of earth no more,
the mighty love of Jesus
has made my heart run o'er;
that He should leave the brightness
of His fair home on high
and there alone in darkness
for me, yes me, to die!

3 Such love I cannot measure,
nor mind can comprehend!
The best of earth can never
such matchless love transcend.
I need no other object
on which to set my love,
enough, my fairest Jesus –
enthroned for me above.

Faith Cook, b. 1937;
based on John Macdonald, 1926

645

I lift my heart to Thee,
Saviour divine;
for Thou art all to me,
and I am Thine.
Is there on earth a closer bond than this,
that my Belovèd's mine and I am His?

2 Thine am I by all ties,
but chiefly Thine,
that through Thy sacrifice
Thou, Lord, art mine.
By Thine own cords of love, so sweetly
wound
around me, I to Thee am closely
bound.

3 To Thee, Thou dying Lamb,
I all things owe;
all that I have and am,
and all I know.
All that I have is now no longer mine,
and I am not my own; Lord, I am Thine.

4 How can I, Lord, withhold
life's brightest hour
from Thee, or gathered gold,
or any power?
Why should I keep one precious thing
from Thee,
when Thou hast given Thine own dear
self for me?

5 I pray Thee, Saviour, keep
me in Thy love,
until death's holy sleep
shall me remove
to that fair realm where, sin and sorrow
o'er,
Thou and Thine own are one for
evermore.

Charles Edward Mudie, 1818-90

646

**I'd rather have Jesus than silver or
gold,**
I'd rather be His than have riches untold;
I'd rather have Jesus than houses or
lands,
I'd rather be led by His nail-pierced
hand;

Than to be the king of a vast domain
and be held in sin's dread sway;
I'd rather have Jesus than anything
this world affords today.

2 I'd rather have Jesus than men's applause,
I'd rather be faithful to His dear cause;
I'd rather have Jesus than worldwide fame,
I'd rather be true to His holy name;

3 He's fairer than lilies of rarest bloom,
He's sweeter than honey from out the comb;
He's all that my hungering spirit needs,
I'd rather have Jesus and let Him lead;

Rhea F Miller, 1894-1966

647

In Christ alone my hope is found,
He is my light, my strength, my song;
this cornerstone, this solid ground,
firm through the fiercest drought and storm.
What heights of love, what depths of peace,
when fears are stilled, when strivings cease!
My Comforter, my all in all,
here in the love of Christ I stand.

2 In Christ alone! – who took on flesh,
fulness of God in helpless babe!
this gift of love and righteousness,
scorned by the ones He came to save:
till on that cross as Jesus dies,
the wrath of God was satisfied –
for every sin on Him was laid;
here in the death of Christ I live.

3 There in the ground His body lay,
Light of the world by darkness slain:
then bursting forth in glorious day
up from the grave He rose again!
And as He stands in victory
sin's curse has lost its grip on me,
for I am His and He is mine –
bought with the precious blood of Christ.

4 No guilt in life, no fear in death,
this is the power of Christ in me;
from life's first cry to final breath,
Jesus commands my destiny.
No power of hell, no scheme of man,
can ever pluck me from His hand;
till He returns or calls me home,
here in the power of Christ I'll stand!

Stuart Townend, b. 1963

648

I've found a Friend, O such a Friend!
He loved me ere I knew Him;
He drew me with the cords of love,
and thus He bound me to Him;
and round my heart still closely twine
those ties which nought can sever;
for I am His, and He is mine,
for ever and for ever.

2 I've found a Friend, O such a Friend!
He bled, He died to save me;
and not alone the gift of life,
but His own self He gave me.
Nought that I have mine own I'll call,
I'll hold it for the Giver;
my heart, my strength, my life, my all
are His, and His for ever.

3 I've found a Friend, O such a Friend!
all power to Him is given,
to guard me on my onward course,
and bring me safe to heaven.
The eternal glories gleam afar,
to nerve my faint endeavour;
so now to watch! to work! to war!
and then – to rest for ever.

4 I've found a Friend, O such a Friend,
so kind, and true, and tender!
so wise a counsellor and guide,
so mighty a defender!
From Him who loves me now so well
what power my soul can sever?
Shall life or death, or earth or hell?
No! I am His for ever.

James Grindlay Small, 1817-88

649

Jesus, I am resting, resting
in the joy of what Thou art;
I am finding out the greatness
of Thy loving heart.
Thou hast bid me gaze upon Thee,
and Thy beauty fills my soul,
for by Thy transforming power
Thou hast made me whole.

Jesus, I am resting, resting
in the joy of what Thou art;
I am finding out the greatness
of Thy loving heart.

2 O how great Thy loving kindness,
vaster, broader than the sea!
O how marvellous Thy goodness,
lavished all on me!
Yes, I rest in Thee, Belovèd,
know what wealth of grace is Thine,
know Thy certainty of promise,
and have made it mine.

3 Simply trusting Thee, Lord Jesus,
I behold Thee as Thou art,
and Thy love, so pure, so changeless,
satisfies my heart;
satisfies its deepest longings,
meets, supplies its every need,
compasseth me round with blessings;
Thine is love indeed!

4 Ever lift Thy face upon me,
as I work and wait for Thee;
resting 'neath Thy smile, Lord Jesus,
earth's dark shadows flee.
Brightness of my Father's glory,
sunshine of my Father's face,
keep me ever trusting, resting;
fill me with Thy grace.

Jean Sophia Pigott, 1845-82

650

Jesus, Jesus, all-sufficient,
beyond telling is Thy worth;
in Thy Name lie greater treasures
than the richest found on earth.
Such abundance
is my portion with my God.

2 In Thy gracious face there's beauty
far surpassing every thing
found in all the earth's great wonders
mortal eye hath ever seen.
Rose of Sharon,
Thou Thyself art heaven's delight.

William Williams, 1717-91; *tr. by Robert Maynard Jones (Bobi Jones)*, b. 1929

651

Jesus, Thy boundless love to me
no thought can reach, no tongue
declare;
O knit my thankful heart to Thee,
and reign without a rival there!
Thine wholly, Thine alone, I am,
be Thou alone my constant flame.

2 O grant that nothing in my soul
may dwell, but Thy pure love alone;
O may Thy love possess me whole,
my joy, my treasure, and my crown!
Strange flames far from my heart
remove;
my every act, word, thought, be love.

3 O Love, how cheering is Thy ray!
All pain before Thy presence flies,
care, anguish, sorrow, melt away,
where'er Thy healing beams arise:
O Jesus, nothing may I see,
nothing desire, or seek, but Thee!

4 Unwearied may I this pursue,
dauntless to the high prize aspire;
hourly within my soul renew
this holy flame, this heavenly fire;
and day and night be all my care
to guard the sacred treasure there.

5 In suffering, be Thy love my peace;
weakness, be Thy love my power;
and, when the storms of life shall cease,
Jesus, in that tremendous hour,
in death, as life, be Thou my guide,
and save me, who for me hast died.

Paul Gerhardt, 1607-76;
tr. by John Wesley, 1703-91

652

Nearer, still nearer, close to Thy heart,
draw me, my Saviour, so precious
Thou art;
fold me, O fold me close to Thy breast,
shelter me safe in that haven of rest.

2 Nearer, still nearer, nothing I bring,
nought as an offering to Jesus my King;
only my sinful, now contrite heart;
grant me the cleansing Thy blood doth
impart.

3 Nearer, still nearer, Lord, to be Thine,
sin, with its follies, I gladly resign,
all of its pleasures, pomp and its pride:
give me but Jesus, my Lord crucified.

4 Nearer, still nearer, while life shall last,
till all its struggles and trials are past;
then through eternity, ever I'll be
nearer, my Saviour, still nearer to Thee.

Leila Naylor Morris, 1862-1929

653

Love divine, all loves excelling,
joy of heaven, to earth come down,
fix in us Thy humble dwelling,
all Thy faithful mercies crown.
Jesus, Thou art all compassion,
pure, unbounded love Thou art;
visit us with Thy salvation,
enter every trembling heart.

2 Breathe, O breathe Thy loving Spirit
into every troubled breast;
let us all in Thee inherit,
let us find Thy promised rest.
Take away the love of sinning,
Alpha and Omega be;
end of faith, as its beginning,
set our hearts at liberty.

3 Come, almighty to deliver,
let us all Thy grace receive;
suddenly return, and never,
never more Thy temples leave:
Thee we would be always blessing,
serve Thee as Thy hosts above,
pray, and praise Thee, without ceasing,
glory in Thy perfect love.

4 Finish then Thy new creation,
pure and spotless let us be;
let us see Thy great salvation,
perfectly restored in Thee;

changed from glory into glory,
till in heaven we take our place,
till we cast our crowns before Thee,
lost in wonder, love and praise.
Charles Wesley, 1707-88

654

More about Jesus would I know,
more of His grace to others show,
more of His saving fulness see,
more of His love – who died for me.

More, more about Jesus,
more, more about Jesus;
more of His saving fulness see,
more of His love who died for me.

2 More about Jesus let me learn,
more of His holy will discern;
Spirit of God, my teacher be,
showing the things of Christ to me.

3 More about Jesus, in His Word,
holding communion with my Lord;
hearing His voice in every line,
making each faithful saying mine.

4 More about Jesus, on His throne,
riches in glory all His own;
more of His kingdom's sure increase;
more of His coming, Prince of Peace!
Eliza Edmunds Hewitt, 1851-1920

655

O how deep the love of Jesus!
and how great salvation's plan,
that our Lord, the King of Heaven
should descend to die for man.
Fierce His torment in that garden
where He prayed in agony;
O the wonder of that moment!
that my Saviour wept for me.

2 See the depth of His compassion
in love's purest form revealed,
there upon the cross of Calvary
where a broken world was healed.
There He lifted all our sorrows,
bore them high upon the tree;
prayed in love for our forgiveness,
gave Himself to set us free.

3 Now restored to Heaven's splendour,
Jesus stands before the throne,
He our Counsel and Defender
claims lost sinners as his own.
'I have paid the price of ransom:
It is finished, all is done.'
Love of God, so pure and precious,
gave us life in Christ the Son.

4 Though we walked in death's dark
shadow,
with its terrors on each side,
He in love has safely led us,
heaven's door has opened wide.
When at last our eyes shall see Him,
we will love Him ever more,
kneel before the King of Glory,
worship, praise Him and adore.
Simoney Girard, b. 1977

656

O Jesus Christ, grow Thou in me,
and all things else recede:
my heart be daily nearer Thee,
from sin be daily freed.

2 Each day let Thy supporting might
my weakness still embrace;
my darkness vanish in Thy light,
Thy life my death efface.

3 In Thy bright beams which on me fall,
fade every evil thought;
that I am nothing, Thou art all,
I would be daily taught.

4 More of Thy glory let me see,
Thou holy, wise, and true!
I would Thy living image be,
in joy and sorrow too.

5 Fill me with gladness from above,
hold me by strength divine!
Lord, let the glow of Thy great love
through my whole being shine.

6 Make this poor self grow less and less,
be Thou my life and aim;
O make me daily, through Thy grace,
more fit to bear Thy name!

Johann Caspar Lavater, 1741-1801;
tr. by Elizabeth Lee Smith, 1817-98

657

Thou hidden source of calm repose,
Thou all-sufficient love divine,
my help and refuge from my foes,
secure I am, if Thou art mine:
and lo! from sin, and grief, and shame,
I hide me, Jesus, in Thy Name.

2 Thy mighty Name salvation is,
and keeps my happy soul above;
comfort it brings, and power, and peace,
and joy, and everlasting love:
to me, with Thy dear Name, are given
pardon, and holiness, and heaven.

3 Jesus, my all in all Thou art,
my rest in toil, my ease in pain,
the medicine of my broken heart,
in war my peace, in loss my gain,
my smile beneath the tyrant's frown,
in shame my glory and my crown:

4 In want my plentiful supply,
in weakness my almighty power,
in bonds my perfect liberty,
my light in Satan's darkest hour,
my help and stay whene'er I call,
my life in death, my heaven, my all.

Charles Wesley, 1707-88

658

O Jesus, friend unfailing,
how dear art Thou to me!
Are care or fears assailing?
I find my strength in Thee.
Why should my feet grow weary
of this my pilgrim way?
Rough though the path and dreary,
it ends in perfect day.

2 What fills my soul with gladness?
'Tis Thine abounding grace:
where can I look in sadness
but, Jesus, on Thy face?
My all is Thy providing,
Thy love can ne'er grow cold:
in Thee, my refuge, hiding,
no good wilt Thou withhold.

3 Why should I droop in sorrow?
Thou'rt ever by my side:
why trembling dread the morrow?
What ill can e'er betide?
If I my cross have taken
'tis but to follow Thee;
if scorned, despised, forsaken,
nought severs Thee from me.

4 For every tribulation,
for every sore distress,
in Christ I've full salvation,
sure help and quiet rest.
No fear of foes prevailing,
I triumph, Lord, in Thee:
O Jesus, friend unfailing,
how dear art Thou to me!

Samuel Christian Gottfried Küster, 1762-1838;
tr. by Hannah Kilham Burlingham, 1842-1901

659

O Love divine, how sweet Thou art!
When shall I find my willing heart
all taken up by Thee?
I thirst, I faint, I die to prove
the greatness of redeeming love,
the love of Christ to me.

2 Stronger His love than death or hell;
its riches are unsearchable;
the first-born sons of light
desire in vain its depths to see;
they cannot reach the mystery,
the length, and breadth, and height.

3 God only knows the love of God;
O that it now were shed abroad
in this poor stony heart!
For love I sigh, for love I pine;
this only portion, Lord, be mine,
be mine this better part!

4 O that I could for ever sit
with Mary at the Master's feet!
Be this my happy choice:
my only care, delight, and bliss,
my joy, my heaven on earth, be this –
to hear the Bridegroom's voice!

Charles Wesley, 1707-88

660

Object of my first desire,
Jesus crucified for me;
all to happiness aspire,
only to be found in Thee:
Thee to praise, and Thee to know,
constitute my bliss below;
Thee to see, and Thee to love,
constitute my bliss above.

2 Lord, it is not life to live
if Thy presence Thou deny;
Lord, if Thou Thy presence give,
'tis no longer death to die:
source and giver of repose,
only from Thy smile it flows;
peace and happiness are Thine;
mine they are, if Thou art mine.

3 Whilst I feel Thy love to me,
every object teems with joy;
may I ever walk with Thee,
for 'tis bliss without alloy:
let me but Thyself possess,
total sum of happiness:
perfect peace I then shall prove,
heaven below and heaven above.

Augustus Montague Toplady, 1740-78

661

Rise with me – my soul in triumph
mounts to see the Prince of kings;
draw with me the flood which issues
from the boundless heavenly springs.
There together let us wonder,
gaze upon the Lamb that died;
bow before the victor reigning,
glory in the flowing tide.

2 O how mighty are the riches
of a grace so large and free,
full of virtue and redemption,
bought by grief and agony!
There for sinners interceding
sits the Man of sorrows now,
glory, honour, praise eternal
circle round His noble brow.

3 Stay with me, while here I glory,
raptured by His lovely face;
praise with me the King of beauty,
all the lines of favour trace.
King eternal, may Your mercy
move our souls Your grace to adore;
streams all-flowing, love abounding
satisfy for evermore.

Paul Eric Graham Cook, b. 1932

662

Show me Thy face! – one transient gleam
of loveliness divine,
and I shall never think or dream
of other love save Thine;
all lesser light will darken quite,
all lower glories wane;
the beautiful of earth will scarce
seem beautiful again.

2 Show me Thy face! – my faith and love
shall henceforth fixèd be,
and nothing here have power to move
my soul's serenity;
my life shall seem a trance, a dream,
and all I feel and see,
illusive, visionary – Thou
the one reality!

3 Show me Thy face ! – I shall forget
the weary days of yore;
the fretting ghosts of vain regret
shall haunt my soul no more;
all doubts and fears for future years
in quiet rest subside,
and nought but blest content and calm
within my breast abide.

4 Show me Thy face! – the heaviest cross
will then seem light to bear;
there will be gain in every loss,
and peace with every care;
with such light feet the years will fleet,
life seem as brief as blest,
till I have laid my burden down,
and entered into rest.

Anonymous; from STOCKWELL GEMS

663

Thou Shepherd of Israel, and mine,
the joy and desire of my heart,
for closer communion I pine,
I long to reside where Thou art:
the pasture I languish to find
where all, who their Shepherd obey,
are fed, on Thy bosom reclined,
and screened from the heat of the day.

2 Ah! show me that happiest place,
the place of Thy people's abode,
where saints in an ecstasy gaze,
and hang on a crucified God;
Thy love for a sinner declare,
Thy passion and death on the tree;
my spirit to Calvary bear,
to suffer and triumph with Thee.

3 'Tis there, with the lambs of Thy flock,
there only, I covet to rest,
to lie at the foot of the rock,
or rise to be hid in Thy breast;
'tis there I would always abide,
and never a moment depart,
concealed in the cleft of Thy side,
eternally held in Thy heart.

Charles Wesley, 1707-88

664

Thou whose name is callèd Jesus,
risen Lord of life and power,
O it is so sweet to trust Thee
every day and every hour!
Of Thy wondrous grace I sing,
Saviour, Counsellor and King.

2 Thou canst keep my feet from falling,
even my poor wayward feet –
Thou who dost present me faultless,
in Thy righteousness complete;
Jesus, Lord, in knowing Thee,
O what strength and victory!

3 All the sin in me, my Saviour,
Thou canst conquer and subdue;
with Thy sanctifying power
permeate my spirit through;
let Thy government increase,
risen, crownèd, Prince of peace.

4 Thou canst keep me upward looking,
ever upward in Thy face;
Thou canst make me stand, upholden
by the greatness of Thy grace;
every promise of Thy Word
now I claim from Thee, dear Lord.

5 O what joy to trust Thee, Jesus,
mighty victor o'er the grave,
and to learn amid earth's shadows
Thine unceasing power to save!
Only those who prove Thee know
what the grace Thou dost bestow.

6 Make my life a bright outshining
of Thy life, that all may see
Thine own resurrection power
mightily put forth in me;
ever let my heart become
yet more consciously Thy home.

Jean Sophia Pigott, 1845-82

665

Though all the world my choice deride,
yet Jesus shall my portion be;
for I am pleased with none beside;
the fairest of the fair is He.

2 Sweet is the vision of Thy face,
and kindness o'er Thy lips is shed;
lovely art Thou and full of grace,
and glory beams around Thy head.

3 E'en whilst I hated, Thou didst love,
and o'er Thy rebel creature yearn;
for me Thou pleadest still above –
and shall I not such love return?

4 Thy sufferings I embrace with Thee,
Thy poverty and shameful cross;
the pleasures of the world I flee,
and judge its treasures worthless dross.

5 Be daily dearer to my heart,
and ever let me feel Thee near;
then willingly with all I'd part,
nor count it worthy of a tear.

6 O keep my heart and love with Thee
until my mortal work is done;
and then in heaven Thy face I'll see,
to be with Thee for ever one!

Gerhard Tersteegen, 1697-1769;
tr. by Samuel Jackson, 1786-1861

666

Who can cheer the heart like Jesus,
by His presence all divine?
True and tender, pure and precious,
O how blest to call Him mine!

All that thrills my soul is Jesus;
He is more than life to me;
and the fairest of ten thousand
in my blessèd Lord I see.

2 Love of Christ so freely given,
grace of God beyond degree,
mercy higher than the heaven,
deeper than the deepest sea!

3 What a wonderful redemption!
Never can a mortal know
how my sin, though red like crimson,
can be whiter than the snow.

4 Every need His hand supplying,
every good in Him I see;
on His strength divine relying,
He is all in all to me.

5 By the crystal-flowing river
with the ransomed I will sing,
and for ever and for ever
praise and glorify the King.

Thoro Harris, 1873-1955

Fellowship with God

667 PSALM 42:1-5

As pants the hart for cooling streams,
when heated in the chase,
so longs my soul, O God, for Thee,
and Thy refreshing grace.

2 For Thee, my God, the living God,
my thirsty soul doth pine;
O when shall I behold Thy face,
Thou Majesty divine!

3 God of my strength, how long shall I,
like one forgotten, mourn,
forlorn, forsaken, and exposed
to my oppressor's scorn?

4 Why restless, why cast down, my soul?
Hope still and thou shalt sing
the praise of Him who is thy God,
thy health's eternal spring.

Nahum Tate, 1652-1715,
and Nicholas Brady, 1659-1726

668 PSALM 1

Blessèd is the man, the man who does not walk
in the counsel of the ungodly – blessèd is that man.
He who rejects the way, rejects the way of sin
and who turns away from scoffing – blessèd is that man.

But his delight, by day and night,
is the law of God Almighty.

2 He is like a tree, a tree that flourishes
being planted by the water – blessèd is that man.
He will bring forth fruit – his leaf will wither not –
for in all he does he prospers – blessèd is that man.

For his delight, by day and night
is the law of God Almighty.

3 The ungodly are not so – for they are like the chaff
which the wind blows clean away – the ungodly are not so.
The ungodly will not stand upon the judgment day
nor belong to God's own people – the ungodly will not stand.

But God knows the way of righteous men,
and ungodly ways will perish.

Blessèd is the man, the man who does not walk
in the counsel of the ungodly – blessèd is that man.

Michael Baughen, b. 1930

669 Based on MATTHEW 5:3-12

Blest are the humble souls that see
their emptiness and poverty;
treasures of grace to them are given,
and crowns of joy laid up in heaven.

2 Blest are the men of broken heart,
who mourn for sin with inward smart;
the blood of Christ divinely flows,
a healing balm for all their woes.

3 Blest are the meek, who stand afar
from rage and passion, noise and war;
God will secure their happy state,
and plead their cause against the great.

4 Blest are the souls that thirst for grace,
hunger and long for righteousness;
they shall be well supplied and fed,
with living streams and living bread.

5 Blest are the men whose hearts do move
and melt with sympathy and love;
from Christ the Lord shall they obtain
like sympathy and love again.

6 Blest are the pure, whose hearts are clean
from the defiling powers of sin;
with endless pleasures they shall see
a God of spotless purity.

7 Blest are the men of peaceful life,
who quench the coals of growing strife;
they shall be called the heirs of bliss,
the sons of God, the God of peace.

8 Blest are the sufferers who partake
of pain and shame for Jesus' sake;
their souls shall triumph in the Lord,
glory and joy are their reward.

Isaac Watts, 1674-1748

670 PSALM 1

Blest is he who loves God's precepts,
who from sin restrains his feet,
he who will not stand with sinners,
he who shuns the scorners' seat.

2 Blest is he who makes the statutes
of the Lord his chief delight,
in the law of God rejoicing,
meditating day and night.

3 He is like a tree well-planted
by the flowing river's side,
ever green of leaf and fruitful;
thus shall all his works abide.

4 Like the driven chaff the wicked
shall be swept from off the land;
with the just they shall not gather,
nor shall in the judgment stand.

5 Well the Lord will guard the righteous,
for their way to Him is known;
but the way of evildoers
shall by Him be overthrown.

From PSALTER HYMNAL, 1959

671 Based on PSALM 61:1-3

Hear my cry, O God, listen to my prayer;
from the ends of the earth will I call to You.
Hear my cry, O God!
When my heart is overwhelmed
lead me to the rock that is higher than I.
Teach me to trust in You,
to pour out my heart to You;
You are my help, my refuge and strength.
Hear my cry, O God, listen to my prayer;
from the ends of the earth will I cry to You.
Hear my cry, O God!

Andy Silver

672 — Psalm 63

O God, Thou art my God alone,
early to Thee my soul shall cry,
a pilgrim in a land unknown,
a thirsty land whose springs are dry.

2 Yet through this rough and thorny maze
I follow hard on Thee, my God;
Thine hand unseen upholds my ways;
I safely tread where Thou hast trod.

3 Thee, in the watches of the night,
when I remember on my bed,
Thy presence makes the darkness light;
Thy guardian wings are round my head.

4 Better than life itself Thy love,
dearer than all beside to me;
for whom have I in heaven above,
or what on earth, compared with Thee?

5 Praise, with my heart, my mind, my voice,
for all Thy mercy I will give;
my soul shall still in God rejoice;
my tongue shall bless Thee while I live.

James Montgomery, 1771-1854

673

Nearer, my God, to Thee,
nearer to Thee!
E'en though it be a cross
that raiseth me,
still all my song shall be,
nearer, my God, to Thee,
nearer to Thee!

2 Though, like the wanderer,
the sun gone down,
darkness be over me,
my rest a stone,
yet in my dreams I'd be
nearer, my God, to Thee,
nearer to Thee!

3 There let the way appear
steps unto heaven;
all that Thou send'st to me
in mercy given;
angels to beckon me
nearer, my God, to Thee,
nearer to Thee!

4 Then, with my waking thoughts
bright with Thy praise,
out of my stony griefs
Bethel I'll raise;
so by my woes to be
nearer, my God, to Thee,
nearer to Thee!

5 Or if on joyful wing
cleaving the sky,
sun, moon, and stars forgot,
upward I fly,
still all my song shall be,
nearer, my God, to Thee,
nearer to Thee!

6 Christ alone beareth me
where Thou dost shine;
joint-heir He maketh me
of the divine!
In Christ my soul shall be
nearest, my God, to Thee,
nearest to Thee.

Sarah Fuller Adams, 1805-48;
v. 6, Arthur Tozer Russell, 1806-74

674

O Lord, I would delight in Thee,
and on Thy care depend;
to Thee in every trouble flee,
my best, my only friend.

2 When all created streams are dried,
Thy fulness is the same;
may I with this be satisfied,
and glory in Thy Name!

3 No good in creatures can be found,
but may be found in Thee;
I must have all things, and abound,
while God is God to me.

4 O that I had a stronger faith,
to look within the veil,
to rest on what my Saviour saith,
whose word can never fail!

5 He that has made my heaven secure
will here all good provide;
while Christ is rich, can I be poor?
What can I want beside?

6 O Lord, I cast my care on Thee,
I triumph and adore;
henceforth my great concern shall be
to love and please Thee more.

John Ryland, 1753-1825

675

O Lord, Thy touch hath stirred my soul
and caused my heart to love;
my quickened mind hath been made whole
to seek those things above.

2 There is a path of thought so true
that brings me to Thy throne,
and there my heart may mercy sue
and claim Thy grace my own.

3 Eye hath not seen, nor ear hath heard
those things that Thou hast there:
for every promise of Thy Word
awaits my soul to dare.

4 O why should I let sorrow reign,
when such a God is mine,
who gives to me and gives again,
and tells me, 'Mine is thine'?

5 The riches He hath stored for me
no measurement can tell;
for in the love of Calvary
all with my God is well.

6 The Holy Spirit now hath taught
my being to adore;
the blessings Jesus Christ hath wrought
shall cause my soul to soar.

William Vernon Higham, b. 1926

676 Based on PSALM 24:3-6

O Lord, who shall ascend
that holy hill to seek Thy face?
where is the man who dares to stand
and worship in Thy holy place?

2 The man whose hands are clean,
with lowly heart, and lips kept pure,
who knows the cleansing of Christ's blood,
has access there that will endure.

3 To such the Lord shall give
the blessing of His righteousness:
He calls His saints to seek His face
and throng His courts that He may bless.

Eluned Harrison, b. 1934

677

Thou hidden love of God, whose height,
whose depth unfathomed, no man knows,
I see from far Thy beauteous light,
and inly sigh for Thy repose;
my heart is pained, nor can it be
at rest, till it finds rest in Thee.

2 Is there a thing beneath the sun
that strives with Thee my heart to share?
Ah! tear it thence, and reign alone,
the Lord of every motion there;
then shall my heart from earth be free,
when it has found repose in Thee.

3 O hide this self from me, that I
no more, but Christ in me, may live!
My vile affections crucify,
nor let one darling lust survive!
In all things nothing may I see,
nothing desire or seek, but Thee.

4 Each moment draw from earth away
my heart, that lowly waits Thy call;
speak to my inmost soul and say,
'I am thy love, thy God, thy all!'
To feel Thy power, to hear Thy voice,
to taste Thy love, be all my choice.

Gerhard Tersteegen, 1697-1769;
tr. by John Wesley, 1703-91

678

Talk with us, Lord, Thyself reveal,
while here on earth we rove;
speak to our hearts, and let us feel
the kindling of Thy love.

2 With Thee conversing, we forget
all time and toil and care;
labour is rest, and pain is sweet,
if Thou, my God, art here.

3 Here then, my God, consent to stay,
and bid my heart rejoice;
my bounding heart shall own Thy sway,
and echo to Thy voice.

4 Thou callest me to seek Thy face,
'tis all I wish to seek;
to attend the whispers of Thy grace,
and hear Thee inly speak.

5 Let this my every hour employ
till I Thy glory see,
enter into my Master's joy,
and find my heaven in Thee.

Charles Wesley, 1707-88

679

PSALM 43:3-5

O send Your light forth and Your truth;
let them be guides to me,
and bring me to Your holy hill,
e'en where Your dwellings be.
Then will I to God's altar go,
to God my chiefest joy:
yes, God, my God, Your name to praise
my harp I will employ.

2 Why are you then cast down, my soul?
Why so discouraged be?
And why with vexing thoughts are you
disquieted in me?
Still trust in God; for Him to praise
good cause I yet shall have:
He of my count'nance is the health,
my God, who will me save.

SCOTTISH PSALTER, 1650

Peace and joy

680

A sinner you may call me,
as I am, as I am,
I'm looking up to Calvary
as I am.
Where else in earth or heaven
can life to such be given
by trials and tempests driven
as I am, as I am?
I'll praise for sins forgiven
as I am.

2 The Lamb who died on Calvary
is my joy, is my joy,
the gospel of God's glory
is my joy.
The precept He has spoken,
the promise never broken,
the hearts which Christ has woken
are my joy, are my joy.
To feast with them – heaven's token –
is my joy.

Eluned Harrison, b. 1934

681

Happy the man that finds the grace,
the blessing of God's chosen race,
the wisdom coming from above,
the faith that sweetly works by love!

2 Happy beyond description he
who knows: the Saviour died for me!
the gift unspeakable obtains,
and heavenly understanding gains.

3 Wisdom divine! who tells the price
of wisdom's costly merchandise?
Wisdom to silver we prefer,
and gold is dross compared to her.

4 Her hands are filled with length of days,
true riches, and immortal praise,
riches of Christ, on all bestowed,
and honour that descends from God.

5 To purest joys she all invites,
chaste, holy, spiritual delights;
her ways are ways of pleasantness,
and all her flowery paths are peace.

6 Happy the man who wisdom gains,
thrice happy who his guest retains!
He owns, and shall for ever own:
wisdom, and Christ, and heaven are one.

Charles Wesley, 1707-88

682

Come, we that love the Lord,
and let our joys be known;
join in a song with sweet accord,
and thus surround the throne.

2 The sorrows of the mind
be banished from the place;
religion never was designed
to make our pleasures less.

3 Let those refuse to sing
that never knew our God;
but children of the heavenly King
may speak their joys abroad.

4 The men of grace have found
glory begun below;
celestial fruit on earthly ground
from faith and hope may grow.

5 The hill of Zion yields
a thousand sacred sweets,
before we reach the heavenly fields,
or walk the golden streets.

6 Then let our songs abound,
and every tear be dry;
we're marching through Immanuel's ground
to fairer worlds on high.

Isaac Watts, 1674-1748

Where the tune 'We're marching to Zion' is used, the following chorus may be sung – either after each verse, or after the first and last verses only.

We're marching to Zion,
beautiful, beautiful Zion;
we're marching upward to Zion,
the beautiful city of God.

683

How happy are they
who the Saviour obey,
and have laid up their treasure above.
Tongue cannot express
the sweet comfort and peace
of a soul in its earliest love.

2 That comfort was mine,
when the favour divine
I first found in the blood of the Lamb;
when my heart it believed,
what a joy it received,
what a heaven in Jesus' great name!

3 Jesus all the day long
was my joy and my song;
O that all His salvation may see!
He has loved me, I cried,
He has suffered, and died,
to redeem such a rebel as me.

4 O the rapturous height
of the holy delight
which I felt in the life-giving blood!
Of my Saviour possessed
I was perfectly blessed
as if filled with the fulness of God.

Charles Wesley, 1707-88

684

How vast the treasure we possess!
How rich Your bounty, King of grace!
This world is ours, and worlds to come;
earth is our lodge, and heaven our home.

2 All things are ours, the gift of God,
the purchase of a Saviour's blood;
while the good Spirit shows us how
to use, and to improve them too.

3 If peace and plenty crown my days,
they help me, Lord, to speak Your praise;
if bread of sorrows be my food,
those sorrows work my lasting good.

4 I would not change my blest estate
for all the world calls good or great;
and while my faith can keep her hold,
I envy not the sinner's gold.

5 Father, I wait Your daily will;
You shall divide my portion still:
grant me on earth what You deem best,
till death and heaven reveal the rest.

Isaac Watts, 1674-1748

685

I hear the words of love,
I gaze upon the blood,
I see the mighty sacrifice,
and I have peace with God.

2 'Tis everlasting peace,
sure as Jehovah's Name;
'tis stable as His steadfast throne,
for evermore the same.

3 The clouds may come and go,
and storms may sweep my sky –
this blood-sealed friendship changes not:
the cross is ever nigh.

4 My love is oft-times low,
my joy still ebbs and flows;
but peace with Him remains the same –
no change Jehovah knows.

5 I change, He changes not,
the Christ can never die;
His love, not mine, the resting-place,
His truth, not mine, the tie.

Horatius Bonar, 1808-89

686

Jesus, priceless treasure,
source of purest pleasure,
truest friend to me.
Ah! how long I've panted,
and my heart hath fainted,
thirsting, Lord, for Thee!
Thine I am, O spotless Lamb,
I will suffer nought to hide Thee,
nought I ask beside Thee.

2 In Thine arm I rest me;
foes who would molest me
cannot reach me here;
though the earth be shaking,
every heart be quaking,
Jesus calms my fear;
sin and hell in conflict fell
with their bitter storms assail me:
Jesus will not fail me.

3 Hence, all fears and sadness!
for the Lord of gladness,
Jesus, enters in.
Those who love the Father,
though the storms may gather,
still have peace within;
yea, whate'er I here must bear,
still in Thee lies purest pleasure,
Jesus, priceless treasure!

Johann Franck, 1618-77;
tr. by Catherine Winkworth, 1827-78

687

Like a river glorious
is God's perfect peace,
over all victorious
in its bright increase;
perfect, yet it floweth
fuller every day;
perfect, yet it groweth
deeper all the way.

Stayed upon Jehovah
hearts are fully blest,
finding, as He promised,
perfect peace and rest.

2 Hidden in the hollow
of His blessèd hand,
never foe can follow,
never traitor stand;
we may trust Him fully
all for us to do;
they who trust Him wholly
find Him wholly true.

Frances Ridley Havergal, 1836-79

688 Based on Psalm 4

Lord of my life, my hope, my joy,
my never failing friend,
my helper all my life till now,
O help me to the end!

2 While worldly minds impatient grow
more prosperous yet to be,
O let the glories of Your face
shine brighter, Lord, on me.

3 So shall my days be filled with joys
more lasting and more true,
than all the transient happiness
they eagerly pursue.

4 Then down in peace I'll lay my head
my needful rest to take;
no other guard I ask or need –
whether I sleep or wake.

*Henry Francis Lyte**, 1793-1847

689

Loved with everlasting love,
led by grace that love to know,
Spirit, breathing from above,
You have taught me it is so.
O this full and perfect peace!
O this rapture all divine!
In a love which cannot cease,
I am His and He is mine.

2 Heaven above is softer blue,
earth around is sweeter green;
something lives in every hue
Christless eyes have never seen:
birds with gladder songs o'erflow,
flowers with deeper beauties shine,
since I know, as now I know,
I am His and He is mine.

3 His for ever, only His;
who the Lord and me shall part?
Ah, with what a rest of bliss
Christ can fill the loving heart!
Heaven and earth may fade and flee,
first-born light in gloom decline,
but while God and I shall be,
I am His and He is mine.

George Wade Robinson, 1838-77

690

My God, I am Thine;
what a comfort divine,
what a blessing to know that my Jesus
is mine!
In the heavenly Lamb
thrice happy I am,
and my heart it doth dance at the
sound of His name.

2 True pleasures abound
in the rapturous sound;
and whoever hath found it hath
paradise found.
My Jesus to know,
and feel His blood flow,
'tis life everlasting, 'tis heaven below.

3 Yet onward I haste
to the heavenly feast:
that, that is the fulness; but this is the
taste!
And this I shall prove,
till with joy I remove,
to the heaven of heavens in Jesus'
great love.

Charles Wesley, 1707-88

691

**Not what I am, O Lord, but what
Thou art!**
that, that alone, can be my soul's
true rest;
Thy love, not mine, bids fear and doubt
depart,
and stills the tempest of my tossing
breast.

2 Thy name is Love! I hear it from yon
cross;
Thy name is Love! I read it in yon
tomb;
all meaner love is perishable dross,
but this shall light me through time's
thickest gloom.

3 Girt with the love of God on every side,
breathing that love as heaven's own
healing air,
I work or wait, still following my guide,
braving each foe, escaping every
snare.

4 'Tis what I know of Thee, my Lord and God,
that fills my soul with peace, my lips with song;
Thou art my health, my joy, my staff and rod;
leaning on Thee, in weakness I am strong.

5 More of Thyself, O show me hour by hour,
more of Thy glory, O my God and Lord;
more of Thyself, in all Thy grace and power;
more of Thy love and truth, incarnate Word!

Horatius Bonar, 1808-89

692

Peace, perfect peace, in this dark world of sin?
The blood of Jesus whispers peace within.

2 Peace, perfect peace, by thronging duties pressed?
To do the will of Jesus, this is rest.

3 Peace, perfect peace, with sorrows surging round?
On Jesus' bosom nought but calm is found.

4 Peace, perfect peace, with loved ones far away?
In Jesus' keeping we are safe, and they.

5 Peace, perfect peace, our future all unknown?
Jesus we know, and He is on the throne.

6 Peace, perfect peace, death shadowing us and ours?
Jesus has vanquished death and all its powers.

7 It is enough: earth's struggles soon shall cease,
and Jesus call us to heaven's perfect peace.

Edward Henry Bickersteth, 1825-1906

693

PSALM 23

The King of love my Shepherd is,
whose goodness faileth never;
I nothing lack, if I am His,
and He is mine for ever.

2 Where streams of living waters flow,
my ransomed soul He leadeth,
and, where the verdant pastures grow,
with food celestial feedeth.

3 Perverse and foolish oft I strayed,
but yet in love He sought me,
and on His shoulder gently laid,
and home, rejoicing, brought me.

4 In death's dark vale I fear no ill,
with Thee, dear Lord, beside me;
Thy rod and staff my comfort still,
Thy cross before to guide me.

5 And so through all the length of days,
Thy goodness faileth never:
good Shepherd, may I sing Thy praise
within Thy house for ever!

Henry Williams Baker, 1821-77

694

We bless Thee for Thy peace, O God,
deep as the unfathomed sea,
which falls like sunshine on the road
of those who trust in Thee.

2 We ask not, Father, for repose
which comes from outward rest,
if we may have through all life's woes
Thy peace within our breast –

3 That peace which suffers and is strong,
trusts where it cannot see,
thinks not the trial-way too long,
but leaves the end with Thee;

4 That peace which flows serene and deep,
a river in the soul,
whose banks a living verdure keep –
God's sunshine o'er the whole.

5 O Father, give our hearts this peace,
whate'er the outward be,
till all life's discipline shall cease,
and we go home to Thee.

From CHRISTIAN MELODIES, 1858

Thankfulness and love

695

Awake, and sing the song
of Moses and the Lamb;
wake every heart and every tongue
to praise the Saviour's name.

2 Sing of His dying love;
sing of His rising power;
sing how He intercedes above
for those whose sins He bore.

3 You pilgrims, on the road
to Zion's city, sing;
rejoice now in the Lamb of God,
in Christ, the eternal King.

4 Soon shall we hear Him say,
'Come blessèd children, come!'
Soon will He call us hence away,
and take His wanderers home.

5 There shall each raptured tongue
His endless praise proclaim,
and sing in sweeter notes the song
of Moses and the Lamb.

William Hammond, 1718-83

696

Awake, my soul, in joyful lays,
and sing thy great Redeemer's praise;
He justly claims a song from thee:
His lovingkindness, O how free!

2 He saw me ruined in the Fall,
yet loved me, notwithstanding all;
He saved me from my lost estate:
His lovingkindness, O how great!

3 Though numerous hosts of mighty foes,
though earth and hell my way oppose,
He safely leads my soul along:
His lovingkindness, O how strong!

4 When trouble like a gloomy cloud,
has gathered thick and thundered loud,
He near my soul has always stood:
His lovingkindness, O how good!

5 Often I feel my sinful heart
prone from my Saviour to depart;
but though I have Him oft forgot,
His lovingkindness changes not.

6 Soon shall I pass the gloomy vale,
soon all my mortal powers must fail;
O may my last expiring breath
His lovingkindness sing in death!

7 Then let me mount and soar away
to the bright world of endless day,
and sing with rapture and surprise
His lovingkindness in the skies.

Samuel Medley, 1738-99

697

Belovèd, let us love:
love is of God;
in God alone hath love
its true abode.

2 Belovèd, let us love:
for they who love,
they only, are His sons,
born from above.

3 Belovèd, let us love:
for love is rest,
and he who loveth not
abides unblest.

4 Belovèd, let us love:
in love is light,
and he who loveth not,
dwelleth in night.

5 Belovèd, let us love:
for only thus
shall we behold that God
who loveth us.

Horatius Bonar, 1808-89

698

Hark, my soul! it is the Lord;
'tis thy Saviour, hear His word;
Jesus speaks, and speaks to thee:
'Say, poor sinner, lov'st thou Me?

2 'I delivered thee when bound,
and, when bleeding, healed thy wound;
sought thee wandering, set thee right,
turned thy darkness into light.

3 'Can a woman's tender care
cease towards the child she bare?
Yes, she may forgetful be,
yet will I remember thee.

4 'Mine is an unchanging love,
higher than the heights above,
deeper than the depths beneath,
free and faithful, strong as death.

5 'Thou shalt see My glory soon,
when the work of grace is done;
partner of My throne shalt be:
say, poor sinner, lov'st thou Me?'

6 Lord, it is my chief complaint
that my love is weak and faint;
yet I love Thee, and adore;
O for grace to love Thee more!

William Cowper, 1731-1800

699

Beyond all things created
in earth or heaven above,
how vast the breadth and fulness
of Jesus' timeless love.
It brought Him from the glory
to die on Calvary's tree.
The mighty love of Jesus,
it could no greater be!

2 Away with every rival
however dear or fair;
for none but Christ in glory
my heart, my love, shall share.
He loved, and still will love me
right to the very end;
the mighty love of Jesus,
no thought can comprehend.

3 Surpassing love of Jesus,
my life-long song shall be;
and it will be my anthem
to all eternity.
Unbounded, uncreated,
unmeasured, full and free;
the mighty love of Jesus,
it could no greater be!

Faith Cook, b. 1937;
based on John Macdonald, 1926

700

Christ Jesus lay in death's strong bands
for our offences given;
but now at God's right hand He stands,
and brings us life from heaven:
let us give thanks and joyful be,
and to our God sing faithfully
loud songs of hallelujah!

2 It was a strange and dreadful strife,
when life and death contended;
the victory was gained for life,
the reign of death was ended:
stripped of its power, no more it reigns:
an empty form alone remains;
its sting is lost forever.

3 Let us obey His heavenly call
by which the Lord invites us;
Christ is Himself the joy of all,
the sun who warms and lights us;
in love and mercy He imparts
eternal sunshine to our hearts;
the night of sin is ended.

4 Let us His people feast this day
upon the bread of heaven.
The Word of grace has purged away
the old corrupting leaven.
Now Christ alone our souls will feed,
He is our meat and drink indeed,
faith lives upon no other.

Martin Luther, 1483-1546;
tr. by Richard Massie, 1800-87

701

Come, every thankful heart
that loves the Saviour's name,
your noblest powers exert
to celebrate His fame!
Tell all above and all below
the debt of love to Him you owe.

2 He left His starry crown,
He laid His robes aside,
on wings of love came down,
and wept, and bled, and died.
What He endured no tongue can tell,
to save our souls from death and hell.

3 From the dark grave He rose,
the mansion of the dead,
and thence His mighty foes
in glorious triumph led:
up through the sky the conqueror rode,
and reigns on high the Saviour God.

4 From thence He'll quickly come,
His chariot will not stay,
and bear our spirits home
to realms of endless day:
then shall we see His lovely face,
and ever dwell in His embrace.

5 Jesus, we ne'er can pay
the debt we owe Your love;
yet tell us how we may
our gratitude approve:
our hearts, our all, to You we give,
the gift, though small, O Lord receive.

Samuel Stennett, c. 1727-95

702

I have not seen Thy face, O Lord,
yet with my heart I love Thee;
for Thou hast plucked each tender cord
with pleasing touch of mercy.
O Saviour, Lord, my King and friend,
I worship Thee with gladness;
and by Thy grace I will defend
the Name that brought me kindness.

2 I have not known Thee here on earth,
yet with my soul I trust Thee;
for Thou hast stirred my thought to birth
of God and heaven and glory.
O precious Saviour, hear my praise
with songs of joy and wonder;
for Thou hast taught my lips to raise
a theme of words so tender.

3 Now I have seen Thy glorious face,
with eyes of faith unveiling
the splendour of the theme of grace,
all to my mind revealing.
Such bliss and happiness is mine
to know the God of glory;
for who could call the Lord divine
but for Thy grace and mercy?

William Vernon Higham, b. 1926

703

Give thanks with a grateful heart,
give thanks to the Holy One,
give thanks because He's given
Jesus Christ, His Son.
Give thanks with a grateful heart,
give thanks to the Holy One,
give thanks because He's given
Jesus Christ, His Son.

2 And now let the weak say, 'I am strong',
let the poor say, 'I am rich',
because of what the Lord
has done for us.
And now let the weak say, 'I am strong',
let the poor say, 'I am rich',
because of what the Lord
has done for us.

Give thanks. *(Last time only)*

Henry Smith

704

Come, Thou Fount of every blessing,
tune my heart to sing Thy grace;
streams of mercy, never ceasing,
call for songs of loudest praise.
Teach me some melodious measure,
sung by flaming tongues above;
O the vast, the boundless treasure
of my Lord's unchanging love!

2 Here I raise my Ebenezer,
hither by Thy help I'm come,
and I hope by Thy good pleasure
safely to arrive at home.
Jesus sought me when a stranger,
wandering from the fold of God;
He, to rescue me from danger,
interposed His precious blood.

3 O to grace how great a debtor
daily I'm constrained to be!
Let that grace, Lord, like a fetter,
bind my wandering heart to Thee.
Prone to wander, Lord, I feel it,
prone to leave the God I love –
Take my heart, O take and seal it,
seal it from Thy courts above!

Robert Robinson, 1735-90

705 PSALM 116

I love the Lord who heard my cry
and granted my request;
in Him who hears and answers prayer
my trust through life shall rest.

2 When deadly sorrows compassed round,
my heart was full of grief;
then to the Lord I made my prayer,
that He would send relief.

3 The Lord is just and merciful,
and gracious to the meek;
He saved me when I cried to Him,
though I was poor and weak.

4 Return now to your rest, my soul,
no longer troubled be.
The Lord's sustaining love has dealt
most graciously with me.

5 Before my Saviour I will live;
from death He saved my soul,
my eyes from tears, my feet from falls,
and He has made me whole.

6 In my affliction this I found,
that human help deceived;
but ever faithful was the Lord
in whom my soul believed.

THE PSALTER, 1912

706 PSALM 40:1-5,11

I waited for the Lord my God,
and patiently did bear;
at length to me He did incline,
my voice and cry to hear.

2 He took me from a fearful pit
and from the miry clay,
and on a rock He set my feet,
establishing my way.

3 He put a new song in my mouth,
our God to magnify;
many shall see it, and shall fear,
and on the Lord rely.

4 O blessèd is the man whose trust
upon the Lord relies,
respecting not the proud, nor such
as turn aside to lies.

5 O Lord my God, full many are
the wonders You have done;
Your gracious thoughts to us-ward far
above all thoughts are gone.

6 Your tender mercies, Lord, from me
O Lord do not restrain;
Your lovingkindness and Your truth,
let them me still maintain.

SCOTTISH PSALTER, 1650

707

I will sing the wondrous story
of the Christ who died for me;
how He left His home in glory
for the cross on Calvary.
I was lost: but Jesus found me,
found the sheep that went astray;
threw His loving arms around me,
drew me back into His way.

2 I was bruised; but Jesus healed me –
faint was I from many a fall;
sight was gone, and fears possessed me:
but He freed me from them all.
Days of darkness still come o'er me;
sorrow's paths I often tread;
but the Saviour still is with me,
by His hand I'm safely led.

3 He will keep me till the river
rolls its waters at my feet:
then He'll bear me safely over,
where the loved ones I shall meet.
Yes, I'll sing the wondrous story
of the Christ who died for me;
sing it with the saints in glory,
gathered by the crystal sea.

Francis Harold Rowley, 1854-1952

708

Jesus, my Lord, my God, my all,
hear me, blest Saviour, when I call;
hear me, and from Thy dwelling-place
pour down the riches of Thy grace:

Jesus, my Lord, I Thee adore;
O make me love Thee more and more.

2 Jesus, too late I Thee have sought;
how can I love Thee as I ought?
And how extol Thy matchless fame,
the glorious beauty of Thy Name?

3 Jesus, what didst Thou find in me,
that Thou hast dealt so lovingly?
How great the joy that Thou hast brought,
so far exceeding hope or thought!

4 Jesus, of Thee shall be my song;
to Thee my heart and soul belong;
all that I have or am is Thine,
and Thou, blest Saviour, Thou art mine.

Henry Collins, 1827-1919

709

In tenderness He sought me,
weary and sick with sin,
and on His shoulders brought me
back to His fold again;
while angels in His presence sang,
until the courts of heaven rang.

O the love that sought me!
O the blood that bought me!
O the grace that brought me to the fold,
wondrous grace that brought me to the fold!

2 He washed the bleeding sin-wounds,
and poured in oil and wine;
He whispered to assure me
'I've found thee, thou art Mine';
I never heard a sweeter voice,
it made my aching heart rejoice.

3 He pointed to the nail-prints –
for me His blood was shed;
a mocking crown so thorny
was placed upon His head:
I wondered what He saw in me
to suffer such deep agony.

4 I'm sitting in His presence,
the sunshine of His face,
while with adoring wonder
His blessings I retrace.
It seems as if eternal days
are far too short to sound His praise.

5 So, while the hours are passing,
all now is perfect rest;
I'm waiting for the morning,
the brightest and the best,
when He will call us to His side
to be with Him, His spotless bride.

W Spencer Walton, 1850-1906

710

Majestic sweetness sits enthroned
upon the Saviour's brow;
His head with radiant glories crowned,
His lips with grace o'erflow.

2 He saw me plunged in deep distress,
He flew to my relief;
for me He bore the shameful cross,
and carried all my grief.

3 To Him I owe my life and breath,
and all the joys I have;
He makes me triumph over death,
He saves me from the grave.

4 To heaven, the place of His abode,
He brings my weary feet;
shows me the glories of my God,
and makes my joys complete.

5 Since from His bounty I receive
such proofs of love divine,
had I a thousand hearts to give
Lord, they should all be Thine!

Samuel Stennett, c. 1727-95

711

Let us love, and sing, and wonder,
let us praise the Saviour's Name!
He has hushed the law's loud thunder,
He has quenched Mount Sinai's flame;
He has washed us with His blood,
He has brought us nigh to God.

2 Let us love the Lord who bought us,
pitied us when enemies,
called us by His grace, and taught us,
gave us ears, and gave us eyes:
He has washed us with His blood,
He presents our souls to God.

3 Let us sing, though fierce temptations
threaten hard to bear us down!
For the Lord, our strong salvation,
holds in view the conqueror's crown:
He who washed us with His blood
soon will bring us home to God.

4 Let us wonder; grace and justice
join, and point to mercy's store;
when through grace in Christ our trust is,
justice smiles, and asks no more.
He who washed us with His blood
has secured our way to God.

5 Let us praise, and join the chorus
of the saints enthroned on high;
here they trusted Him before us,
now their praises fill the sky:
'You have washed us with Your blood;
You are worthy, Lamb of God.'

John Newton, 1725-1807

712

Lord of the cross of shame,
set my cold heart aflame
with love for You, my Saviour and my Master;
who on that lonely day
bore all my sins away,
and saved me from the judgment and disaster.

2 Lord of the empty tomb,
born of a virgin's womb,
triumphant over death, its power defeated;
how gladly now I sing
Your praise, my risen King,
and worship You, in heaven's splendour seated.

3 Lord of my life today,
teach me to live and pray
as one who knows the joys of sins forgiven,
so may I ever be,
now and eternally,
one with my fellow-citizens in heaven.

Michael Saward, b. 1932

713

My God how shall I tell the grace,
or how the tender mercy trace,
that looked upon an erring race
and then laid hold on me?

2 The mighty angels stood amazed,
the seraphim in wonder gazed,
then loud their gladdest anthems raised
when Christ laid hold on me.

3 Who, who can plumb such mystery?
no tongue can tell – then let me be
surprised to all eternity
that Christ laid hold on me.

4 And how may I such love return?
O let my soul with passion burn,
while prostrate at His feet I learn
why Christ laid hold on me.

5 To know Him more I would aspire,
to love Him with a heart of fire,
wrapped up in Him, my one desire,
who first laid hold on me.

6 Then onward to that mark I press,
till I the heavenly prize possess,
and with the ransomed throng confess
my Christ laid hold on me.

Faith Cook, b. 1937

714

O Lord my God, I stand and gaze in wonder
on the vast heavens Thy wisdom hath ordained;
sun, moon and stars continue at Thy pleasure,
from nothing called and by Thy power sustained.

O mighty God, my heart cries out to Thee:
How great Thou art! how great Thou art!
Thy praise shall sound throughout eternity:
How great Thou art! how great Thou art!

2 Sometimes I hear the heavens rent by thunder,
or see dread lightning leap across the sky,
then in the cloud I see the promised rainbow
stilling my fears with mercy from on high.

3 This earth once heard the sound of angels singing –
this earth that wept the day that Adam fell –
for Jesus came from purest heights of glory,
an infant weak, to break the powers of hell.

4 Nailed to a tree, the great Creator suffered
when that dread weight of foulest sin He bare.
Lo! Satan flees! the Lord of glory triumphs!
Nothing can with this mighty love compare.

Eluned Harrison, b. 1934;
based on Carl Gustaf Boberg, 1856-1940

715

My Jesus, I love Thee, I know Thou art mine;
for Thee all the pleasures of sin I resign;
my gracious Redeemer, my Saviour art Thou,
if ever I loved Thee, my Jesus, 'tis now.

2 I love Thee because Thou hast first lovèd me,
and purchased my pardon on Calvary's tree;
I love Thee for wearing the thorns on Thy brow,
if ever I loved Thee, my Jesus, 'tis now.

3 I will love Thee in life, I will love Thee in death,
and praise Thee as long as Thou lendest me breath;
and say, when the death-dew lies cold on my brow,
if ever I loved Thee, my Jesus, 'tis now.

4 In mansions of glory and endless delight,
I'll ever adore Thee in heaven so bright;
I'll sing with the glittering crown on my brow,
if ever I loved Thee, my Jesus, 'tis now.

William Ralph Featherston, 1842-70

716

Not the grandeur of the mountains,
nor the splendour of the sea,
can excel the ceaseless wonder
of my Saviour's love to me:

For His love to me is faithful
and His mercy is divine;
and His truth is everlasting,
and His perfect peace is mine.

2 Not the streams that fill the valleys,
nor the clouds that drift along,
can delight me more than Jesus
or replace my grateful song:

3 Yet these all convey His beauty
and proclaim His power and grace –
for they are among the tokens
of the love upon His face:

Michael Perry, 1942-96

717

O what a wonderful, wonderful day,
day I will never forget!
After I'd wandered in darkness away,
Jesus my Saviour I met!
O what a tender, compassionate friend,
He met the need of my heart,
shadows dispelling, with joy I am telling,
He made all the darkness depart.

Heaven came down and glory filled my soul,
when at the cross the Saviour made me whole;
my sins were washed away,
and my night was turned to day,
heaven came down and glory filled my soul.

2 Born of the Spirit with life from above
into God's family divine,
justified fully through Calvary's love,
O what a standing is mine!
And the transaction so quickly was made
when as a sinner I came,
took of the offer of grace He did proffer,
He saved me, O praise His dear name!

3 Now I've a hope that will surely endure
after the passing of time,
I have a future in heaven for sure,
there in those mansions sublime.
And it's because of that wonderful day,
when at the cross I believed;
riches eternal and blessings supernal
from His precious hand I received.

John W Peterson, b. 1921

718

Such love, pure as the whitest snow;
such love weeps for the shame I know;
such love, paying the debt I owe;
O Jesus, such love!

2 Such love, stilling my restlessness;
such love, filling my emptiness;
such love, showing me holiness;
O Jesus, such love!

3 Such love springs from eternity;
such love, streaming through history;
such love, fountain of life to me;
O Jesus, such love!

Graham Kendrick, b. 1950

719

Thee will I love, my strength, my tower,
Thee will I love, my joy, my crown,
Thee will I love with all my power,
in all Thy works, and Thee alone;
Thee will I love, till the pure fire
fill my whole soul with chaste desire.

2 In darkness willingly I strayed,
I sought Thee, yet from Thee I roved,
far wide my wandering thoughts were spread,
Thy creatures more than Thee I loved;
and now if more at length I see,
'tis through Thy light, and comes from Thee.

3 I thank Thee, uncreated Sun,
that Thy bright beams on me have shined;
I thank Thee, who hast overthrown
my foes and healed my wounded mind;
I thank Thee, whose enlivening voice
bids my freed heart in Thee rejoice.

4 Uphold me in the doubtful race,
nor suffer me again to stray;
strengthen my feet with steady pace
still to press forward in Thy way;
my soul and flesh, O Lord of might,
transfigure with Thy heavenly light.

5 Thee will I love, my joy, my crown,
Thee will I love, my Lord, my God;
Thee will I love, beneath Thy frown
or smile, Thy sceptre or Thy rod;
what though my flesh and heart decay?
Thee shall I love in endless day!

Johann Scheffler, 1624-77;
tr. by John Wesley, 1703-91

720

There is a Redeemer,
Jesus, God's own Son,
precious Lamb of God, Messiah,
Holy One.

Thank you, O my Father,
for giving us Your Son,
and leaving Your Spirit
till the work on earth is done.

2 Jesus my Redeemer,
Name above all names,
precious Lamb of God, Messiah,
once for sinners slain.

3 When I stand in glory
I will see His face,
and there I'll serve my King for ever
in that holy place.

Melody Green, b. 1946

Growth in grace

721

And dost Thou say, 'Ask what thou wilt'?
Lord, I would seize the golden hour;
I pray to be released from guilt,
and freed from sin and Satan's power.

2 More of Thy presence, Lord, impart,
more of Thine image let me bear;
erect Thy throne within my heart,
and reign without a rival there.

3 Give me to read my pardon sealed,
and from Thy joy to draw my strength,
to have Thy boundless love revealed,
its height, and depth, its breadth, and length.

4 Grant these requests, I ask no more,
but to Thy care the rest resign;
living or dying, rich or poor,
all shall be well if Thou art mine.

John Newton, 1725-1807

722

Believe not those who say
the upward path is smooth,
lest you should stumble in the way
and faint before the truth.

2 It is the only road
up to the realms of joy;
but he who seeks that blest abode
must all his powers employ.

3 Arm, arm you for the fight!
cast useless loads away;
watch through the darkest hours of night;
toil through the hottest day.

4 To labour and to love,
to pardon and endure,
to lift your heart to God above,
and keep your conscience pure –

5 Be this your constant aim,
your hope, your chief delight;
what matter who should whisper blame
or who should scorn or slight,

6 If but your God approve,
and if, within your breast,
you feel the comfort of His love,
the earnest of His rest.

Anne Brontë, 1820-49

723

Burn in me, Fire of God,
burn till my heart is pure;
burn till Your life shines out in me,
steadfast and strong and sure.

2 Burn in me, Fire of God,
spare not for price or pain;
burn till all dross of earth consume,
only Your gold remain.

3 Burn in me, Fire of God,
burn till Your eyes can see
Jesus' own image, strong and sure,
formed by Your grace in me!

Margaret Clarkson, b. 1915

724

Christ, of all my hopes the ground,
Christ, the spring of all my joy,
still in You may I be found,
still for You my powers employ.

2 Let Your love my heart inflame,
keep Your fear before my sight,
be Your praise my highest aim,
be Your smile my chief delight.

3 Fountain of o'erflowing grace,
freely from Your fulness give;
till I close my earthly race,
may I prove it 'Christ to live'.

4 Firmly trusting in Your blood,
nothing shall my heart confound;
safely I shall pass the flood,
safely reach Immanuel's ground.

5 Thus, O thus, an entrance give
to the land of cloudless sky;
having known it 'Christ to live',
let me know it 'gain to die'.

Ralph Wardlaw, 1779-1853

725 PSALM 1

Blessed is the one who turns away
from where the wicked walk,
who does not stand in sinners' paths
or sit with those who mock.

2 Instead he finds God's holy law
his joy and great delight;
he makes the precepts of the LORD
his study day and night.

3 He prospers ever like a tree
that's planted by a stream,
and in due season yields its fruit;
its leaves are always green.

4 Not so the wicked! They are like
the chaff that's blown away.
They will not stand when judgement comes
or with the righteous stay.

5 It is the LORD who sees and knows
the way the righteous go,
but those who live an evil life
the LORD will overthrow.

SING PSALMS, 2003

726

Come, Holy Ghost, all-quickening fire,
come, and my hallowed heart inspire,
sprinkled with the atoning blood;
now to my soul Thyself reveal,
Thy mighty working let me feel,
and know that I am born of God.

2 Humble, and teachable, and mild,
O may I, as a little child,
my lowly Master's steps pursue!
Be anger to my soul unknown,
hate, envy, jealousy, be gone;
in love create Thou all things new.

3 Let earth no more my heart divide,
with Christ may I be crucified,
to Thee with my whole soul aspire;
dead to the world and all its toys,
its idle pomp, and fading joys,
be Thou alone my one desire!

4 My will be swallowed up in Thee;
light in Thy light still may I see,
beholding Thee with open face;
called the full power of faith to prove,
let all my hallowed heart be love,
and all my ransomed life be praise.

Charles Wesley, 1707-88

727

Compared with Christ, in all beside
no comeliness I see;
the one thing needful, dearest Lord,
is to be one with Thee.

2 The sense of Thy expiring love
into my soul convey;
Thyself bestow; for Thee alone,
my all in all, I pray.

3 Less than Thyself will not suffice
my comfort to restore;
more than Thyself I cannot crave;
and Thou canst give no more.

4 Loved of my God, for Him again
with love intense I burn;
chosen of Thee ere time began,
I choose Thee in return.

5 Whate'er consists not with Thy love,
O teach me to resign;
I'm rich to all the intents of bliss,
if Thou, O God, art mine!

Augustus Montague Toplady, 1740-78

728

Father of peace, and God of love,
we own Your power to save,
that power by which our Shepherd rose
victorious o'er the grave.

2 We triumph in that Shepherd's name,
still watchful for our good;
who brought the eternal covenant down,
and sealed it with His blood.

3 So may Your Spirit seal our souls,
and mould them to Your will,
that our weak hearts no more may
stray,
but keep Your covenant still;

4 Still may we gain superior strength,
and press with vigour on;
till full perfection crown our hopes,
and fix us near Your throne.

Philip Doddridge, 1702-51

729

Jesus, all-atoning Lamb,
Thine, and only Thine, I am:
take my body, spirit, soul;
only Thou possess the whole.

2 Thou my one thing needful be;
let me ever cleave to Thee;
let me choose the better part;
let me give Thee all my heart.

3 Fairer than the sons of men,
do not let me turn again,
leave the fountain-head of bliss,
stoop to creature-happiness.

4 Whom have I on earth below?
Thee, and only Thee, I know;
whom have I in heaven but Thee?
Thou art all in all to me.

5 All my treasure is above,
all my riches is Thy love:
who the worth of love can tell?
Infinite, unsearchable!

Charles Wesley, 1707-88

730

He is the way,
the end of all my searching;
He is the truth –
I'll trust His every word;
He is the life
abundant, everlasting:
this is the Christ,
the Saviour of the world!

2 More of the way,
dear Lord, be this my choosing;
more of the truth,
Lord, teach me day by day;
more of the life
for ever satisfying:
more of Yourself –
the Life, the Truth, the Way.

Gordon Brattle, 1917-91

731

PSALM 119:1-8

How blest are those whose way is pure,
and free from guilt or blame,
who honour all the laws of God,
and glorify His Name!

2 How blest are those who keep His word,
and ever are inclined
to seek the one eternal God
with all their heart and mind.

3 They shun the paths that lead to sin,
and only walk the way
of God's commands, which He has called
His people to obey.

4 O that my ways were firmly fixed
according to His will,
that all His precepts I might keep,
and all His laws fulfil.

5 Then shall I not be put to shame
but shall respond with praise,
in gratitude for what I've learned
of all God's righteous ways.

6 The statutes of the Lord I'll keep,
and His decrees obey.
Do not abandon me, O God;
forsake me not, I pray.

Graham D S Deans, b. 1953

732

Jesus, keep me near the cross:
there a precious fountain,
free to all, a healing stream,
flows from Calvary's mountain.

In the cross, in the cross,
be my glory ever,
till my raptured soul shall find
rest beyond the river.

2 Near the cross, a trembling soul,
love and mercy found me;
there the bright and morning Star
shed its beams around me.

3 Near the cross! O Lamb of God,
bring its scenes before me;
help me walk from day to day
with its shadow o'er me.

4 Near the cross I'll watch and wait,
hoping, trusting ever,
till I reach the golden strand,
just beyond the river.

Frances Jane Van Alstyne, 1820-1915

733

Based on Psalm 61

Listen to my prayer, Lord,
hear my humble cry;
when my heart is fainting,
to Your throne I fly.

2 In earth's farthest corner
You will hear my voice:
set me on Your rock, Lord,
then I shall rejoice.

3 You have been my shelter
when the foe was near,
as a tower of refuge
shielding me from fear.

4 I will rest for ever
in Your care and love,
guarded and protected
as by wings above.

5 All that I have promised,
help me to fulfil;
and in all who love You
work Your perfect will.

6 May Your truth and mercy
keep me all my days;
let my words and actions
be my songs of praise.

James Edward Seddon, 1915-83

734

Jesus, my strength, my hope,
on Thee I cast my care,
with humble confidence look up,
and know Thou hear'st my prayer.
Give me on Thee to wait,
till I can all things do,
on Thee, almighty to create,
almighty to renew.

2 I want a godly fear,
a quick-discerning eye
that looks to Thee when sin is near,
and sees the tempter fly;
a spirit still prepared,
and armed with jealous care,
for ever standing on its guard
and watching unto prayer.

3 I want a true regard,
a single, steady aim,
unmoved by threatening or reward,
to Thee and Thy great Name;
a jealous, just concern
for Thine immortal praise;
a pure desire that all may learn
and glorify Thy grace.

4 I rest upon Thy Word;
the promise is for me;
my succour and salvation, Lord,
shall surely come from Thee:
but let me still abide,
nor from my hope remove,
till Thou my patient spirit guide
into Thy perfect love.

Charles Wesley, 1707-88

735

Jesus, Your all-victorious love
shed in my soul abroad;
then shall my feet no longer rove,
rooted and fixed in God.

2 O that in me the sacred fire
might now begin to glow,
burn up the dross of base desire
and make the mountains flow!

3 O that it now from heaven might fall,
and all my sins consume!
Come, Holy Ghost, for You I call;
Spirit of burning, come!

4 Refining fire, go through my heart,
illuminate my soul;
scatter Your life through every part,
and sanctify the whole.

5 My steadfast soul, from falling free,
shall then no longer move,
while Christ is all the world to me,
and all my heart is love.

Charles Wesley, 1707-88

736

O Jesus Christ, most holy,
Head of the church, Your bride,
each day in us more fully
Your Name be magnified!

2 O may in each believer
Your love its power display,
and none among us ever
from You, our Shepherd, stray.

Nicolaus Ludwig von Zinzendorf, 1700-60;
tr. by Christian Gottfried Clemens, 1743-1815

737

From Psalm 119

O that the Lord would guide my ways
to keep His statutes still!
O that my God would grant me grace
to know and do His will!

2 O send Your Spirit down to write
Your law upon my heart;
nor let my tongue indulge deceit,
nor act the liar's part.

3 From vanity, Lord, turn my eyes;
let no corrupt design,
nor covetous desires arise
within this soul of mine.

4 Order my footsteps by Your Word,
and make my heart sincere;
let sin have no dominion, Lord,
but keep my conscience clear.

5 Make me to walk in Your commands;
'tis a delightful road;
nor let my head, or heart, or hands,
offend against my God.

Isaac Watts, 1674-1748

738

**More love to Thee, O Christ,
more love to Thee!**
Hear Thou the prayer I make on bended knee;
this is my earnest plea:
more love, O Christ, to Thee,
more love to Thee,
more love to Thee.

2 Once earthly joy I craved – sought peace and rest;
now Thee alone I seek; give what is best:
this all my prayer shall be:
more love, O Christ, to Thee,
more love to Thee,
more love to Thee.

3 Let sorrow do its work: send grief or pain;
sweet are Thy messengers, sweet their refrain,
when they can sing with me,
more love, O Christ, to Thee,
more love to Thee,
more love to Thee.

4 Then shall my latest breath whisper Thy praise;
this be the parting cry my heart shall raise,
this still my prayer shall be;
more love, O Christ, to Thee,
more love to Thee,
more love to Thee.

Elizabeth Payson Prentiss, 1818-78

739

O for a heart to praise my God,
a heart from sin set free;
a heart that always feels Thy blood
so freely shed for me;

2 A heart resigned, submissive, meek,
my great Redeemer's throne,
where only Christ is heard to speak,
where Jesus reigns alone;

3 A humble, lowly, contrite heart,
believing, true, and clean,
which neither life nor death can part
from Him that dwells within;

4 A heart in every thought renewed
and full of love divine,
perfect and right and pure and good:
a copy, Lord, of Thine.

5 Thy nature, gracious Lord, impart;
come quickly from above;
write Thy new name upon my heart,
Thy new best name of love.

Charles Wesley, 1707-88

740

Seek this first, not earthly pleasure,
fading joy and failing treasure;
but the love that knows no measure –
Seek this first.

2 Seek this first: God's peace and blessing –
you have all if this possessing;
come, your need and sin confessing:
Seek Him first.

3 Seek Him first; then, when forgiven,
pardoned, made an heir of heaven,
let your life to Him be given:
Seek this first.

4 Seek this first: be pure and holy,
like the Master, meek and lowly,
yielded to His service wholly:
Seek this first.

5 Seek this first, His promise trying –
it is sure, all need supplying;
heavenly things – on Him relying –
Seek this first.

Georgianna Mary Taylor, 1848-1915

741

So let our lips and lives express
the holy gospel we profess;
so let our works and virtues shine,
to prove the doctrine all divine.

2 Thus shall we best proclaim abroad
the honours of our Saviour God,
when His salvation reigns within,
and grace subdues the power of sin.

3 Our flesh and sense must be denied,
passion and envy, lust and pride,
while justice, temperance, truth and love,
our inward godliness approve.

4 Religion bears our spirits up,
while we expect that blessèd hope,
the bright appearing of the Lord:
and faith stands leaning on His Word.

Isaac Watts, 1674-1748

742

Take time to be holy, speak oft with your Lord;
abide in Him always, and feed on His Word.
Make friends of God's children, help those who are weak;
forgetting in nothing His blessing to seek.

2 Take time to be holy, the world rushes on;
spend much time in secret with Jesus alone.
By looking to Jesus like Him you shall be;
your friends, in your conduct, His likeness shall see.

3 Take time to be holy, let Him be your guide:
and run not before Him whatever betide:
in joy or in sorrow still follow your Lord,
and, looking to Jesus, still trust in His Word.

4 Take time to be holy, be calm in your soul;
each thought and each temper beneath His control.
Thus led by His Spirit and filled with His love,
you soon shall be fitted for service above.

William Dunn Longstaff, 1822-94

743

Walk in the light, and you shall own
your darkness passed away,
because that light has on you shone
in which is perfect day.

2 Walk in the light, and you shall find
your heart made truly His
who dwells in cloudless light enshrined,
in whom no darkness is.

3 Walk in the light and sin, abhorred,
shall ne'er defile again;
the blood of Jesus Christ your Lord
shall cleanse from every stain.

4 Walk in the light, and you shall know
that fellowship of love
His Spirit only can bestow,
who reigns in light above.

5 Walk in the light, and e'en the tomb
no fearful shade shall wear;
glory shall chase away its gloom,
for Christ has conquered there.

6 Walk in the light; pursue your way
till faith be turned to sight;
for in the land of endless day
God is Himself the light.

*Bernard Barton**, 1784-1849

Spiritual conflict

744

Begone, unbelief;
my Saviour is near,
and for my relief
will surely appear:
by prayer let me wrestle,
and He will perform;
with Christ in the vessel,
I smile at the storm.

2 Though dark be my way,
since He is my guide,
'tis mine to obey,
'tis His to provide;
though plans all be broken,
and creatures all fail,
the word He has spoken
shall surely prevail.

3 His love in time past
forbids me to think
He'll leave me at last
in trouble to sink;
each sweet Ebenezer
I have in review
confirms His good pleasure
to help me quite through.

4 Determined to save,
He watched o'er my path,
when, Satan's blind slave,
I sported with death;
and can He have taught me
to trust in His Name,
and thus far have brought me
to put me to shame?

5 Why should I complain
of want or distress,
temptation or pain?
He told me no less;
the heirs of salvation,
I know from His Word,
through much tribulation
must follow their Lord.

6 Since all that I meet
shall work for my good,
the bitter is sweet,
the medicine is food;
though painful at present,
'twill cease before long;
and then, O how pleasant
the conqueror's song!

John Newton, 1725-1807

745

Christian, seek not yet repose;
cast your dreams of ease away;
you are in the midst of foes:
Watch and pray.

2 Principalities and powers,
mustering their unseen array,
wait for your unguarded hours:
Watch and pray.

3 Gird your heavenly armour on;
wear it ever, night and day;
ambushed lies the evil one:
Watch and pray.

4 Hear the victors who o'ercame;
still they mark each warrior's way;
all with one sweet voice exclaim:
Watch and pray.

5 Hear, above all, hear your Lord,
whom you love and would obey;
hide within your heart His word:
Watch and pray.

6 Watch, as if on that alone
hung the issue of the day;
pray, that help may be sent down:
Watch and pray.

Charlotte Elliott, 1789-1871

746

Christian, do you see them
on the holy ground,
how the powers of darkness
compass you around?
Christian, up and smite them,
counting gain but loss;
for your mighty Saviour
triumphed on the cross.

2 Christian, do you feel them,
how they work within,
striving, tempting, luring,
goading into sin?
Christian, never tremble,
never be downcast;
arm you for the conflict,
watch and pray and fast.

3 Christian, do you hear them,
how they speak so fair? –
'Always fast and vigil?
always watch and prayer?'
Christian, answer boldly,
'While I breathe I pray';
peace shall follow battle,
night shall end in day.

4 'Well I know your trouble,
O My servant true;
you are very weary –
I was weary too:
but that toil shall make you
some day all My own,
and the end of sorrow
shall be near My throne.'

John Mason Neale, 1818-66

747

Fight the good fight with all thy might;
Christ is thy strength, and Christ thy right;
lay hold on life, and it shall be
thy joy and crown eternally.

2 Run the straight race through God's good grace,
lift up thine eyes and seek His face;
life with its path before thee lies,
Christ is the way, and Christ the prize.

3 Cast care aside, lean on thy guide;
His boundless mercy will provide;
trust, and thy trusting soul shall prove
Christ is its life and Christ its love.

4 Faint not nor fear, His arms are near;
He changeth not and thou art dear;
only believe and thou shalt see
that Christ is all in all to thee.

John Samuel Bewley Monsell, 1811-75

748

I asked the Lord that I might grow
in faith, and love, and every grace,
might more of His salvation know,
and seek more earnestly His face.

2 'Twas He who taught me thus to pray,
and He, I trust, has answered prayer;
but it has been in such a way
as almost drove me to despair.

3 I hoped that in some favoured hour
at once He'd answer my request;
and, by His love's constraining power,
subdue my sins, and give me rest.

4 Instead of this, He made me feel
the hidden evils of my heart,
and let the angry powers of hell
assault my soul in every part.

5 Yes, more, with His own hand He seemed
intent to aggravate my woe,
crossed all the fair designs I schemed,
blasted my gourds, and laid me low.

6 'Lord, why is this?' I trembling cried,
'will You pursue Your worm to death?'
''Tis in this way', the Lord replied,
'I answer prayer for grace and faith.

7 'These inward trials I employ,
from self and pride to set you free,
and break your schemes of earthly joy,
that you may seek your all in Me.'

John Newton, 1725-1807

749

Soldiers of Christ, arise,
and put your armour on;
strong in the strength which God supplies,
through His eternal Son;
strong in the Lord of hosts,
and in His mighty power;
who in the strength of Jesus trusts
is more than conqueror.

2 Stand, then, in His great might,
with all His strength endued;
and take, to arm you for the fight,
the panoply of God.
To keep your armour bright
attend with constant care,
still serving in your Captain's sight,
and watching unto prayer.

3 From strength to strength go on;
wrestle and fight and pray;
tread all the powers of darkness down,
and win the well-fought day;
that, having all things done,
and all your conflicts past,
you may o'ercome through Christ alone,
and stand entire at last.

Charles Wesley, 1707-88

750 Based on Psalm 27

God is my strong salvation;
what foe have I to fear?
In darkness and temptation
my light, my help is near.

2 Though hosts encamp around me,
firm to the fight I stand;
what terror can confound me,
with God at my right hand?

3 Then on the Lord relying,
my soul, with courage wait;
His truth your strength supplying,
when faint and desolate.

4 His might your heart shall strengthen,
His love your joy increase;
mercy your days shall lengthen;
the Lord will give you peace.

*James Montgomery**, 1771-1854

751

In the hour of trial,
Jesus, pray for me,
lest by base denial
I depart from Thee;
when Thou seest me waver,
with a look recall,
nor, for fear or favour,
suffer me to fall.

2 With its witching pleasures
would this vain world charm,
or its sordid treasures
spread to work me harm –
bring to my remembrance
sad Gethsemane,
or, in darker semblance,
cross-crowned Calvary.

3 If with sore affliction
Thou in love chastise,
pour Thy benediction
on the sacrifice;
then, upon Thine altar
freely offered up,
though the flesh may falter,
faith shall drink the cup.

4 When in dust and ashes
to the grave I sink,
while heaven's glory flashes
o'er the shelving brink,
on Thy truth relying
through that mortal strife,
Lord, receive me, dying,
to eternal life.

James Montgomery, 1771-1854

752

Lord Jesus, think on me,
and purge away my sin;
from earthborn passions set me free,
and make me pure within.

2 Lord Jesus, think on me,
with care and woe opprest;
let me Thy loving servant be,
and taste Thy promised rest.

3 Lord Jesus, think on me,
amid the battle's strife;
in all my pain and misery
be Thou my health and life.

4 Lord Jesus, think on me,
nor let me go astray;
through darkness and perplexity
point Thou the heavenly way.

5 Lord Jesus, think on me,
when flows the tempest high;
when on doth rush the enemy,
O Saviour, be Thou nigh.

6 Lord Jesus, think on me,
that, when the flood is past,
I may the eternal brightness see,
and share Thy joy at last.

Synesius of Cyrene, 375-430;
tr. by Allen William Chatfield, 1808-96

753

Oppressed with sin and woe,
a burdened heart I bear;
opposed by many a mighty foe,
yet will I not despair.

2 With this polluted heart,
I dare to come to Thee –
holy and mighty as Thou art –
for Thou wilt pardon me.

3 I feel that I am weak,
and prone to every sin;
but Thou who giv'st to those who seek,
wilt give me strength within.

4 I need not fear my foes;
I need not yield to care;
I need not sink beneath my woes,
for Thou wilt answer prayer.

5 In my Redeemer's name
I give myself to Thee;
and, all unworthy as I am,
my God will welcome me.

Anne Brontë, 1820-49

754

Search me, O God! my actions try,
and let my life appear
as seen by Thine all-searching eye –
to mine my ways make clear.

2 Search all my sense, and know my heart,
who only canst make known;
and let the deep, the hidden part
to me be fully shown.

3 Throw light into the darkened cells,
where passion reigns within;
quicken my conscience till it feels
the loathsomeness of sin.

4 Search all my thoughts, the secret springs,
the motives that control;
the rebel heart where evil things
hold empire o'er the soul.

5 Search, till Thy fiery glance has cast
its holy light through all,
and I by grace am brought at last
before Thy face to fall.

6 Thus prostrate I shall learn of Thee,
what now I feebly prove,
that God alone in Christ can be
unutterable love!

Francis Bottome, 1823-94

755

My God shall be my strength
throughout my pilgrim way,
my sure defence, my guard, my guide,
my shield and stay:
secure in Him my heart is strong
and lifts aloft faith's triumph song.

2 My God shall be my strength,
though fierce may be the foe;
no hosts of hell my trusting soul
shall overthrow.
Through Christ I conquer: by His power
I triumph in the evil hour.

3 My God shall be my strength,
though flesh and heart may fail;
in want or weakness, by His strength
I shall prevail.
In Christ I triumph over pain
and rise to face the foe again.

4 My God shall be my strength
in sorrow's bitter hour;
in anguish, grief or loss I plead
His sovereign power.
No harm can pass His perfect will,
and in His love my heart is still.

5 My God shall be my strength
when death shall press his claim,
when powers shall fail and weakness spoil
this mortal frame:
through Christ triumphant I shall rise
to sing His praise in paradise.

Margaret Clarkson, b. 1915

756

O safe to the Rock that is higher than I
my soul in its conflicts and sorrows would fly;
so sinful, so weary, Thine, Thine would I be;
Thou blest Rock of Ages, I'm hiding in Thee!

Hiding in Thee! hiding in Thee!
Thou blest Rock of Ages,
I'm hiding in Thee!

2 In the calm of the noontide, in sorrow's lone hour,
in times when temptation casts o'er me its power,
in the tempests of life, on its wide heaving sea,
Thou blest Rock of Ages, I'm hiding in Thee!

3 How oft in the conflict, when pressed by the foe,
I have fled to my refuge and breathed out my woe!
How often, when trials like sea-billows roll,
have I hidden in Thee, O Thou Rock of my soul!

William Orcutt Cushing, 1823-1903

757

O Jesus, I have promised
to serve Thee to the end;
be Thou for ever near me,
my master and my friend:
I shall not fear the battle
if Thou art by my side,
nor wander from the pathway
if Thou wilt be my guide.

2 O let me feel Thee near me:
the world is ever near;
I see the sights that dazzle,
the tempting sounds I hear;
my foes are ever near me,
around me and within;
but, Jesus, draw Thou nearer,
and shield my soul from sin.

3 O let me hear Thee speaking
in accents clear and still,
above the storms of passion
the murmurs of self-will;
O speak to reassure me,
to hasten or control;
O speak, and make me listen,
Thou guardian of my soul.

4 O Jesus Thou hast promised
to all who follow Thee,
that where Thou art in glory
there shall Thy servant be;
and, Jesus, I have promised
to serve Thee to the end:
O give me grace to follow,
my master and my friend.

5 O let me see Thy footmarks,
and in them plant mine own:
my hope to follow duly
is in Thy strength alone.
O guide me, call me, draw me,
uphold me to the end;
and then in heaven receive me,
my Saviour and my friend.

John Ernest Bode, 1816-74

758

O Lamb of God, still keep me
close to Thy piercèd side:
'tis only there in safety
and peace I can abide.

2 What foes and snares surround me,
what lusts and fears within!
The grace that sought and found me
alone can keep me clean.

3 'Tis only in Thee hiding
I feel myself secure;
only in Thee abiding,
the conflict can endure.

4 Thine arm the victory gaineth
o'er every hateful foe;
Thy love my heart sustaineth
in all its cares and woe.

5 Soon shall my eyes behold Thee
with rapture face to face;
one half hath not been told me
of all Thy power and grace.

6 Thy beauty, Lord, and glory,
the wonders of Thy love,
shall be the endless story
of all Thy saints above.

James George Deck, 1802-84

759

O Thou, the contrite sinner's Friend,
who, loving, lovest to the end,
on this alone my hopes depend,
that Thou wilt plead for me.

2 When, weary in the Christian race,
far off appears my resting-place,
and, fainting, I mistrust Thy grace,
then, Saviour, plead for me.

3 When I have erred, and gone astray
afar from Thine and wisdom's way,
and see no glimmering, guiding ray,
still, Saviour, plead for me.

4 When Satan, by my sins made bold,
strives from Thy cross to loose my hold,
then with Thy pitying arms enfold,
and plead, O plead for me!

5 And when my dying hour draws near,
darkened with anguish, guilt, and fear,
then to my fainting sight appear,
pleading in heaven for me.

6 When the full light of heavenly day
reveals my sins in dread array,
say, 'I have washed them all away,
I plead, yea, plead for thee.'

Charlotte Elliot, 1789-1871

760

Oft in danger, oft in woe,
onward, Christians, onward go;
fight the fight, maintain the strife,
strengthened with the Bread of Life.

2 Onward, Christians, onward go!
join the war, and face the foe.
Will you flee in danger's hour?
Know you not your Captain's power?

3 Let your drooping hearts be glad;
march, in heavenly armour clad;
fight, nor think the battle long:
soon shall victory tune your song.

4 Let not sorrow dim your eye,
soon shall every tear be dry;
let not fears your course impede,
great your strength, if great your need.

5 Onward then to battle move;
more than conquerors you shall prove;
though opposed by many a foe,
Christian soldiers, onward go.

Henry Kirke White, 1785-1806
and Frances Sara Colquhoun, 1809-77

761

Onward! Christian soldiers,
marching as to war,
looking unto Jesus,
who is gone before:
Christ, the royal Master,
leads against the foe;
forward into battle,
see, His banners go!

Onward! Christian soldiers,
marching as to war,
looking unto Jesus,
who is gone before.

2 At the name of Jesus,
Satan's host doth flee;
on then, Christian soldiers,
on to victory!
Hell's foundations quiver
at the shout of praise:
brothers, lift your voices;
loud your anthems raise.

3 Like a mighty army
moves the church of God;
brothers, we are treading
where the saints have trod:
we are not divided,
all one body we,
one in hope and doctrine,
one in charity.

4 Crowns and thrones may perish,
kingdoms rise and wane;
but the church of Jesus
constant will remain:
gates of hell can never
'gainst that church prevail;
we have Christ's own promise,
and that cannot fail.

5 Onward, then, you people!
join our happy throng;
blend with ours your voices
in the triumph-song:
'Glory, praise, and honour,
unto Christ the King!'
This through countless ages
men and angels sing.

Sabine Baring-Gould, 1834-1924

762

Stand up, stand up for Jesus,
you soldiers of the cross!
Lift high His royal banner,
it must not suffer loss.
From victory unto victory
His army shall He lead,
till every foe is vanquished,
and Christ is Lord indeed.

2 Stand up, stand up for Jesus!
the trumpet-call obey;
forth to the mighty conflict
in this His glorious day!
You that are men, now serve Him
against unnumbered foes;
let courage rise with danger,
and strength to strength oppose.

3 Stand up, stand up for Jesus!
stand in His strength alone:
the arm of flesh will fail you;
you dare not trust your own.
Put on the gospel armour,
each piece put on with prayer;
where duty calls, or danger,
be never wanting there.

4 Stand up, stand up for Jesus!
the strife will not be long;
this day the noise of battle,
the next the victor's song.
To him that overcometh
a crown of life shall be;
he with the King of glory
shall reign eternally.

George Duffield, 1818-88

763

'We rest on Thee', our Shield and our Defender!
We go not forth alone against the foe;
strong in Thy strength, safe in Thy keeping tender,
'We rest on Thee, and in Thy name we go.'

(Repeat last two lines)

2 Yes, 'in Thy name', O Captain of salvation!
In Thy dear name, all other names above;
Jesus our righteousness, our sure foundation,
our Prince of glory and our King of love.

3 'We go' in faith, our own great weakness feeling,
and needing more each day Thy grace to know;
yet from our hearts a song of triumph pealing:
'We rest on Thee, and in Thy name we go.'

4 'We rest on Thee', our Shield and our Defender!
Thine is the battle; Thine shall be the praise!
When passing through the gates of pearly splendour,
victors, we rest with Thee through endless days.

Edith Adeline Gilling Cherry, 1872-97

764

Yield not to temptation, for yielding is sin;
each victory will help you some other to win;
fight manfully onward; dark passions subdue;
look ever to Jesus, He will carry you through.

Ask the Saviour to help you,
comfort, strengthen, and keep you;
He is willing to aid you,
He will carry you through.

2 Shun evil companions; bad language disdain;
God's name hold in reverence, nor take it in vain;
be thoughtful and earnest, kind-hearted and true;
look ever to Jesus, He will carry you through.

3 To him that o'ercometh God giveth a crown;
through faith we shall conquer, though often cast down;
He who is our Saviour our strength will renew;
look ever to Jesus, He will carry you through.

Horatio Richmond Palmer, 1834-1907

765

Who is on the Lord's side?
Who will serve the King?
Who will be His helpers
other lives to bring?
Who will leave the world's side?
Who will face the foe?
Who is on the Lord's side?
Who for Him will go?

By Thy call of mercy,
by Thy grace divine,
we are on the Lord's side;
Saviour, we are Thine.

2 Jesus, Thou hast bought us,
not with gold or gem,
but with Thine own life-blood,
for Thy diadem.
With Thy blessing filling
each who comes to Thee,
Thou hast made us willing,
Thou hast made us free.
By Thy great redemption,
by Thy grace divine,
we are on the Lord's side;
Saviour, we are Thine.

3 Fierce may be the conflict,
strong may be the foe;
but the King's own army
none can overthrow.
Round His standard ranging,
victory is secure;
for His truth unchanging
makes the triumph sure.
Joyfully enlisting,
by Thy grace divine,
we are on the Lord's side;
Saviour, we are Thine.

4 Chosen to be soldiers
in an alien land,
chosen, called, and faithful,
for our Captain's band,
in the service royal
let us not grow cold;
let us be right loyal,
noble, true, and bold.
Master Thou wilt keep us,
by Thy grace divine,
always on the Lord's side,
Saviour, always Thine.

Frances Ridley Havergal, 1836-79

766 PSALM 27

Whom shall I fear on earth below
with such a God on high?
My light to guide, my strength to save –
Thou, Lord, art ever nigh.
Let wicked men, my enemies,
rise in malicious pride,
in this will I be confident:
safe in my Lord I hide.

2 One thing desired I of the Lord,
one thing alone I've sought:
that long as life shall last on earth
I may to Thee be brought.
Within Thy house my days I'd spend,
Thy beauty to behold,
enquire of Thee, and sing that praise
whose end can ne'er be told.

3 He'll hide me in His secret place
when trouble rages sore;
upon the rock of steadfast love
my feet are set secure.
He lifts my head in triumph high
mine enemies above;
and so with joy my praise shall rise
to God, the King of love.

4 Hear, gracious Lord, this voice that cries;
have mercy, is my plea:
let not Thine anger hide Thy face
far, far away from me.
Thou only hast my helper been;
forsake me not, I sigh;
lift up Thy lovely face, and shine
its beauty from on high.

5 Unless I had believed to see
His goodness while below,
what else in this sad land of sin
but faintness would I know?
Wait on the Lord, with courage wait,
and thy weak heart shall find
the mighty strength of God within
thy heart and soul and mind.

Graham Stuart Harrison, b. 1935

Pilgrimage and guidance

767

A pilgrim in a desert land,
I wander far and wide,
expecting I may some time come
close to my Father's side.

2 Ahead of me I think I hear
sounds of a heavenly choir,
a conquering host already gone
through tempest, flood and fire.

3 Come, Holy Spirit, fire by night,
pillar of cloud by day;
lead, for I dare not take a step
unless You show the way.

4 So prone am I when on my own
to stray from side to side,
I need, each step to paradise,
my God to be my guide.

5 I have a yearning for that land,
where the unnumbered throng
extol the death on Calvary
in heaven's unending song.

William Williams, 1717-91;
tr. by Robert Maynard Jones
(Bobi Jones), b.1929

768

Thy way, not mine, O Lord,
however dark it be!
Lead me by Thine own hand,
choose out the path for me.

2 Smooth let it be, or rough,
it will be still the best;
winding, or straight, it leads
right onward to Thy rest.

3 I dare not choose my lot;
I would not if I might;
choose Thou for me, my God,
so shall I walk aright.

4 The kingdom that I seek
is Thine, so let the way
that leads to it be Thine,
else I must surely stray.

5 Take Thou my cup, and it
with joy or sorrow fill,
as best to Thee may seem;
choose Thou my good and ill.

6 Choose Thou for me my friends,
my sickness or my health;
choose Thou my cares for me,
my poverty or wealth.

7 Not mine, not mine the choice,
in things or great or small;
be Thou my guide, my strength,
my wisdom, and my all.

Horatius Bonar, 1808-89

769

A pilgrim through this lonely world,
the blessèd Saviour passed;
a mourner all His life was He,
a dying Lamb at last.

2 That tender heart, that felt for all,
for us its life-blood gave;
it found on earth no resting-place,
save only in the grave.

3 Such was our Lord – and shall we fear
the cross, with all its scorn?
Or love a faithless, evil world,
that wreathed His brow with thorn?

4 No! facing all its frowns or smiles,
like Him, obedient still,
we homeward press, through storm or calm,
to Zion's blessèd hill.

5 In tents we dwell amid the waste,
nor turn aside to roam
in folly's path, nor seek our rest
where Jesus had no home.

6 Dead to the world with Him who died
to win our hearts, our love,
we, risen with our risen Head,
in spirit dwell above.

Edward Denny, 1796-1889

770

All the way my Saviour leads me:
what have I to ask beside?
Can I doubt His tender mercy,
who through life has been my guide?
Heavenly peace, divinest comfort,
here by faith in Him to dwell!
For I know whate'er befall me,
Jesus doeth all things well.

2 All the way my Saviour leads me:
cheers each winding path I tread,
gives me grace for every trial,
feeds me with the living bread.
Though my weary steps may falter,
and my soul athirst may be,
gushing from the rock before me,
lo! a spring of joy I see.

3 All the way my Saviour leads me;
O the fulness of His love!
Perfect rest to me is promised
in my Father's house above.
When my spirit, clothed, immortal,
wings its flight to realms of day,
this my song through endless ages –
Jesus led me all the way.

Frances Jane Van Alstyne, 1820-1915

771

Called together by the Father,
strengthened by the Spirit's power,
following a living Saviour,
rise to meet this hour.

My presence shall go with you,
My presence shall go with you.
Hear the voice of God your Father,
'I will give you rest,
I will give you rest.'

2 Facing paths you have not taken,
walking on an untracked way,
never will you be forsaken,
hear your Father say:

3 Enemies are there before you
holding ground that you must win,
faithful is the One who calls you,
fix your eyes on Him.

4 Trust the promise He has spoken,
plant your footsteps on His Word,
faith will need no other token,
act on what you've heard:

Colin P Goldsworthy, b. 1927

772

Captain of Israel's host, and guide
of all who seek the land above,
beneath Your shadow we abide,
the cloud of Your protecting love;
our strength, Your grace; our rule, Your Word;
our end, the glory of the Lord.

2 By Your unerring Spirit led,
we shall not in the desert stray;
we shall not full direction need,
nor miss our providential way;
as far from danger as from fear,
while love, almighty love, is near.

Charles Wesley, 1707-88

773

Children of the heavenly King,
as ye journey, sweetly sing;
sing your Saviour's worthy praise,
glorious in His works and ways.

2 We are travelling home to God
in the way the fathers trod;
they are happy now, and we
soon their happiness shall see.

3 Shout, ye little flock and blest!
You on Jesus' throne shall rest;
there your seat is now prepared,
there your kingdom and reward.

4 Lift your eyes, ye sons of light;
Zion's city is in sight;
there our endless home shall be,
there our Lord we soon shall see.

5 Fear not, brethren; joyful stand
on the borders of your land;
Jesus Christ, your Father's Son,
bids you undismayed go on.

6 Lord, obediently we go,
gladly leaving all below:
only Thou our leader be,
and we still will follow Thee.

John Cennick, 1718-55

774

Father, although I cannot see
the future You have planned,
and though the path is sometimes dark
and hard to understand,
yet give me faith, through joy and pain,
to trace Your loving hand.

2 When I recall that in the past
Your promises have stood
through each perplexing circumstance
and every changing mood,
I rest content that all things work
together for my good.

3 Whatever, then, the future brings
of good or seeming ill,
I ask for strength to follow You
and grace to trust You still;
and I would look for no reward,
except to do Your will.

John Eddison, b. 1916

775

Guide me, O Thou great Jehovah,
pilgrim through this barren land;
I am weak, but Thou art mighty,
hold me with Thy powerful hand;
bread of heaven,
feed me till I want no more.

2 Open Thou the crystal fountain
whence the healing stream doth flow;
let the fiery, cloudy pillar
lead me all my journey through;
strong deliverer,
be Thou still my strength and shield.

3 When I tread the verge of Jordan,
bid my anxious fears subside;
death of death, and hell's destruction,
land me safe on Canaan's side;
songs of praises
I will ever give to Thee.

William Williams, 1717-91;
tr. by Peter Williams, 1722-96

776

I know not where tomorrow's road
may turn my pilgrim way,
I may not taste its joy or care
nor see beyond today;
but this I know – my Father plans
the path I cannot see;
He knows each turn, each hill, each
dale,
and He will walk with me.

2 I know not if my way be bright
or dark with storm and rain,
I know not what it holds for me
of pleasure, grief, or pain;
but this I know – my Saviour's love
prepares my path each day,
and held within His mighty hand
I need not fear the way.

3 I know not what the future holds,
nor what life's evening brings,
but with the glad salute of faith
I hail its opening wings.
For this I know – in God the Lord
shall all my needs be met;
I'll trust tomorrow to His love
who has not failed me yet.

Margaret Clarkson, b. 1915

777

Jesus, still lead on,
till our rest be won;
and, although the way be cheerless,
we will follow, calm and fearless;
guide us by Your hand
to our fatherland.

2 If the way be drear,
if the foe be near,
let not faithless fears o'ertake us,
let not faith and hope forsake us;
for, through many a foe,
to our home we go.

3 When we seek relief
from a long-felt grief,
when oppressed by new temptations,
Lord, increase and perfect patience;
show us that bright shore
where we weep no more.

4 When sweet earth and skies
fade before our eyes;
when through death we look to
heaven,
and our sins are all forgiven,
from Your bright abode,
call us home to God.

5 Jesus, still lead on,
till our rest be won;
heavenly leader, still direct us,
still support, console, protect us,
till we safely stand
in our fatherland.

Nicolaus Ludwig von Zinzendorf, 1700-60;
tr. by Jane Laurie Borthwick, 1813-97

778

In heavenly love abiding,
no change my heart shall fear;
and safe is such confiding,
for nothing changes here:
the storm may roar without me,
my heart may low be laid;
but God is round about me,
and can I be dismayed?

2 Wherever He may guide me,
no want shall turn me back;
my Shepherd is beside me,
and nothing can I lack:
His wisdom ever waketh,
His sight is never dim;
He knows the way He taketh,
and I will walk with Him.

3 Green pastures are before me,
which yet I have not seen;
bright skies will soon be o'er me,
where the dark clouds have been:
my hope I cannot measure,
my path to life is free;
my Saviour has my treasure,
and He will walk with me.

Anna Laetitia Waring, 1823-1910

779

Leader of faithful souls, and guide
of all who travel to the sky,
come and with us, even us, abide,
who would on You alone rely,
on You alone our spirits stay,
while held in life's uneven way.

2 Strangers and pilgrims here below,
this earth, we know, is not our place;
but hasten through the vale of woe,
and, restless to behold Your face,
swift to our heavenly country move,
our everlasting home above.

3 We've no abiding city here,
but seek a city out of sight;
thither our steady course we steer,
aspiring to the plains of light,
Jerusalem, the saints' abode,
whose founder is the living God.

4 Through You, who all our sins have
borne,
freely and graciously forgiven,
with songs to Zion we return,
contending for our native heaven;
that palace of our glorious King,
we find it nearer while we sing.

5 Raised by the breath of love divine,
we urge our way with strength
renewed;
the church of the first-born to join,
we travel to the mount of God,
with joy upon our heads arise,
and meet our Captain in the skies.

Charles Wesley, 1707-88

780

Lead us, heavenly Father, lead us
o'er the world's tempestuous sea;
guard us, guide us, keep us, feed us,
for we have no help but Thee;
yet possessing every blessing
if our God our Father be.

2 Saviour, breathe forgiveness o'er us;
all our weakness Thou dost know;
Thou didst tread this earth before us,
Thou didst feel its keenest woe;
faint and weary, journey dreary,
through the desert Thou didst go.

3 Spirit of our God, descending,
fill our hearts with heavenly joy,
love with every passion blending,
pleasure that has no alloy;
thus provided, pardoned, guided,
nothing can our peace destroy.

James Edmeston, 1791-1867

781

O God of Bethel! by whose hand
Your people still are fed;
who through this weary pilgrimage
have all our fathers led:

2 Our vows, our prayers, we now present
before Your throne of grace:
God of our fathers, be the God
of their succeeding race.

3 Through each perplexing path of life
our wandering footsteps guide;
give us each day our daily bread,
and raiment fit provide.

4 O spread Your covering wings around,
till all our wanderings cease,
and at our Father's loved abode
our souls arrive in peace.

5 Such blessings from Your gracious hand
our humble prayers implore;
and You shall be our chosen God,
and portion evermore.

Philip Doddridge, 1702-51,
as in SCOTTISH PARAPHRASES, 1781

782

When, O my Jesus, when shall I
look on Your face serene,
rejoice in heaven's perpetual day,
without a veil between?

2 Assist me while I wander here
amidst a world of cares;
incline my heart to pray with love,
and then accept my prayers.

3 Spare me, O God, O spare the soul
that longs Your own to be!
Take all that I possess below,
but give Yourself to me.

4 Your Spirit, O my Saviour, give,
to be my guide and friend,
to light my path to ceaseless joys,
where Sabbaths have no end.

James Montgomery, 1771-1854

783

PSALM 84

Pleasant are Thy courts above,
in the land of light and love;
pleasant are Thy courts below,
in this land of sin and woe.
O! my spirit longs and faints
for the converse of Thy saints,
for the brightness of Thy face,
for Thy fulness, God of grace!

2 Happy birds that sing and fly
round Thine altars, O most High!
Happier souls that find a rest
in a heavenly Father's breast!
Like the wandering dove that found
no repose on earth around,
they can to their ark repair,
and enjoy it ever there.

3 Happy souls! their praises flow
even in this vale of woe;
waters in the desert rise,
manna feeds them from the skies.
On they go from strength to strength,
till they reach Thy throne at length,
at Thy feet adoring fall,
who hast led them safe through all.

4 Lord, be mine this prize to win;
guide me through a world of sin;
keep me by Thy saving grace;
give me at Thy side a place.
Sun and shield alike Thou art;
guide and guard my erring heart:
grace and glory flow from Thee;
shower, O shower them, Lord, on me!

Henry Francis Lyte, 1793-1847

784

PSALM 121

Unto the hills around do I lift up
my longing eyes;
O whence for me shall my salvation
come,
from whence arise?
From God the Lord doth come my
certain aid,
from God the Lord, who heaven and
earth hath made.

2 He will not suffer that thy foot be moved:
safe shalt thou be.
No careless slumber shall His eyelids
close,
who keepeth thee.
Behold our God, the Lord, He
slumbereth ne'er,
who keepeth Israel in His holy care.

3 Jehovah is Himself thy keeper true,
thy changeless shade;
Jehovah thy defence on thy right hand
Himself hath made.
And thee no sun by day shall ever
smite,
no moon shall harm thee in the silent
night.

4 From every evil shall He keep thy soul,
from every sin;
Jehovah shall preserve thy going out,
thy coming in.
Above thee watching, He, whom we
adore,
shall keep thee henceforth, yea, for
evermore.

John Douglas Sutherland Campbell,
1845-1914

785

**Stupendous height of heavenly
love,**
of pitying tenderness divine!
It brought the Saviour from above,
it caused the springing day to shine;
the Sun of righteousness to appear,
and gild our gloomy hemisphere.

2 God did in Christ Himself reveal,
to chase our darkness by His light,
our sin and ignorance dispel,
direct our wandering feet aright,
and bring our souls, with pardon blest,
to realms of everlasting rest.

3 Come then, O Lord, Your light impart,
the faith that bids our terrors cease;
into Your love direct our heart,
into Your way of perfect peace;
and cheer the souls of death afraid,
and guide them through the dreadful
shade.

4 Answer Your mercy's whole design,
my God incarnated for me;
my spirit make Your radiant shrine,
my light and full salvation be;
and through the shades of death
unknown
conduct me to Your dazzling throne.

Charles Wesley, 1707-88

786

The Lord has helped me hitherto;
here will I stand.
Before time's dawn His tender love
my pathway planned,
nor will He leave me till I reach
heaven's brighter land.

2 Though rough and long the pilgrim way
my steps have trod,
my guide still leads me safely on
by staff and rod,
all undismayed while I still cling
close to my God.

3 And should my path lead into night,
or fears appal,
stayed on that mighty unseen arm
I need not fall;
while Christ is mine and I am His
I still have all.

4 Should Jordan's flood before me spread
both deep and wide,
His power can cleave those gloomy depths,
a path provide,
to bring my conquering soul at last
to Jesu's side.

5 So shall I own my Father's care
with gladdest praise!
A monument of grateful love
I'll ever raise,
until I dwell at His right hand
through timeless days.

Faith Cook, b. 1937

787 PSALM 23

The Lord's my Shepherd, I'll not want:
He makes me down to lie
in pastures green; He leadeth me
the quiet waters by.

2 My soul He doth restore again,
and me to walk doth make
within the paths of righteousness,
e'en for His own name's sake.

3 Yea, though I walk in death's dark vale,
yet will I fear none ill;
for Thou art with me, and Thy rod
and staff me comfort still.

4 My table Thou hast furnishèd
in presence of my foes;
my head Thou dost with oil anoint,
and my cup overflows.

5 Goodness and mercy all my life
shall surely follow me;
and in God's house for evermore
my dwelling-place shall be.

SCOTTISH PSALTER, 1650

788

Who would true valour see,
let him come hither;
one here will constant be,
come wind, come weather;
there's no discouragement
shall make him once relent
his first avowed intent
to be a pilgrim.

2 Whoso beset him round
with dismal stories,
do but themselves confound;
his strength the more is.
No lion can him fright;
he'll with a giant fight,
but he will have a right
to be a pilgrim.

3 Hobgoblin nor foul fiend
can daunt his spirit;
he knows he at the end
shall life inherit.
Then fancies fly away,
he'll fear not what men say;
he'll labour night and day
to be a pilgrim.

John Bunyan, 1628-88

789

Through the night of doubt and sorrow,
onward goes the pilgrim band,
singing songs of expectation,
marching to the promised land.

2 Clear before us through the darkness
gleams and burns the guiding light;
brother clasps the hand of brother,
stepping fearless through the night.

3 One the light of God's own presence,
o'er His ransomed people shed,
chasing far the gloom and terror,
brightening all the path we tread;

4 One the object of our journey,
one the faith which never tires,
one the earnest looking forward,
one the hope our God inspires;

5 One the strain that lips of thousands
lift as from the heart of one;
one the conflict, one the peril,
one the march in God begun;

6 One the gladness of rejoicing
on the far eternal shore,
where the one almighty Father
reigns in love for evermore.

7 Onward therefore, pilgrim brothers,
onward with the cross our aid!
Bear its shame, and fight its battle,
till we rest beneath its shade.

8 Soon shall come the great awaking,
soon the rending of the tomb;
then the scattering of all shadows,
and the end of toil and gloom.

Bernhardt Severin Ingemann, 1789-1862;
tr. by Sabine Baring-Gould, 1834-1924

Patience, submission and trust

790

Be still, my soul: the Lord is on your side;
bear patiently the cross of grief or pain;
leave to your God to order and provide;
in every change He faithful will remain.
Be still, my soul: your best, your heavenly Friend
through thorny ways leads to a joyful end.

2 Be still, my soul: your God will undertake
to guide the future as He has the past.
Your hope, your confidence, let nothing shake;
all now mysterious shall be bright at last.
Be still, my soul: the waves and winds still know
His voice who ruled them while He dwelt below.

3 Be still, my soul: the hour is hastening on
when we shall be for ever with the Lord,
when disappointment, grief and fear are gone,
sorrow forgot, love's purest joys restored.
Be still, my soul: when change and tears are past,
all safe and blessèd we shall meet at last.

Katharina von Schlegel, b. 1697;
tr. by Jane Laurie Borthwick, 1813-97

791

God holds the key of all unknown,
and I am glad:
if other hands should hold the key,
or if He trusted it to me,
I might be sad.

2 What if tomorrow's cares were here
without its rest?
I'd rather He unlocked the day,
and, as the hours swing open, say
'My will is best.'

3 The very dimness of my sight
makes me secure;
for groping in my misty way,
I feel His hand; I hear Him say,
'My help is sure.'

4 I cannot read His future plans;
but this I know:
I have the smiling of His face,
and all the refuge of His grace,
while here below.

5 Enough: this covers all my wants;
and so I rest!
For what I cannot, He can see,
and in His care I saved shall be,
for ever blest.

Joseph Parker, 1830-1902

792

Give to the winds thy fears;
hope, and be undismayed:
God hears thy sighs, and counts thy tears;
God shall lift up thy head.

2 Through waves, and clouds, and storms
He gently clears thy way;
wait thou His time, so shall this night
soon end in joyous day.

3 Leave to His sovereign sway
to choose and to command;
so shalt thou wondering own His way,
how wise, how strong His hand.

4 Far, far above thy thought
His counsel shall appear,
when fully He the work hath wrought
that caused thy needless fear.

5 Thou seest our weakness, Lord;
our hearts are known to Thee:
O lift Thou up the sinking hand,
confirm the feeble knee!

6 Let us in life, in death,
Thy steadfast truth declare,
and publish with our latest breath
Thy love and guardian care.

Paul Gerhardt, 1607-76;
tr. by John Wesley, 1703-91

793

Have faith in God, my heart,
trust and be unafraid;
God will fulfil in every part
each promise He has made.

2 Have faith in God, my mind,
although your light burns low;
God's mercy holds a wiser plan
than you can fully know.

3 Have faith in God, my soul,
His cross for ever stands;
and neither life nor death can tear
His children from His hands.

4 Lord Jesus, make me whole;
grant me no resting place
until I rest mind, heart and soul,
the captive of Your grace.

Bryn Austin Rees, 1911-83

794

When we walk with the Lord,
in the light of His Word,
what a glory He sheds on our way!
While we do His good will,
He abides with us still,
and with all who will trust and obey!

Trust and obey!
For there's no other way
to be happy in Jesus
but to trust and obey.

2 Not a burden we bear,
not a sorrow we share,
but our toil He will richly repay:
not a grief nor a loss,
not a frown nor a cross,
but is blest if we trust and obey.

3 But we never can prove
the delights of His love
until all on the altar we lay;
for the favour He shows,
and the joy He bestows,
are for those who will trust and obey.

4 Then in fellowship sweet
we will sit at His feet,
or we'll walk by His side in the way;
what He says we will do,
where He sends we will go –
never fear, only trust and obey!

John Henry Sammis, 1846-1919

795

Have Thine own way, Lord,
have Thine own way;
Thou art the potter,
I am the clay.
Mould me and make me
after Thy will,
while I am waiting
yielded and still.

2 Have Thine own way, Lord,
have Thine own way;
search me and try me,
Master, today.
Whiter than snow, Lord,
wash me just now,
as in Thy presence
humbly I bow.

3 Have Thine own way, Lord,
have Thine own way;
wounded and weary,
help me, I pray.
Power, all power,
surely is Thine;
touch me and heal me,
Saviour divine.

4 Have Thine own way, Lord,
have Thine own way;
hold o'er my being
absolute sway.
Fill with Thy Spirit
till all shall see
Christ only, always,
living in me.

Adelaide Addison Pollard, 1862-1934

796

I am not skilled to understand
what God has willed, what God has planned;
I only know at His right hand
stands One who is my Saviour.

2 I take Him at His word and deed:
'Christ died for sinners', this I read;
and in my heart I find a need
of Him to be my Saviour.

3 That He should leave His place on high,
and come for sinful man to die,
you count it strange? – so once did I,
before I knew my Saviour.

4 And O that He fulfilled may see
the travail of His soul in me,
and with His work contented be,
as I with my dear Saviour!

5 Yes, living, dying, let me bring
my strength, my solace, from this spring,
that He who lives to be my King
once died to be my Saviour.

Dorothy Greenwell, 1821-82

797

PSALM 123

I lift my eyes to You,
to heaven Your royal throne;
as servants watch their master's hand,
we look to You alone.

2 Have mercy, Lord, we pray,
and hear Your people's cries;
until Your mercy reaches us,
on You we fix our eyes.

3 The proud have mocked us long;
their scorn we have endured:
our days are filled with their contempt –
we look to You, O Lord.

Christopher Idle, b. 1938

798

Lord, it belongs not to my care
whether I die or live;
to love and serve You is my share,
and this Your grace must give.

2 If life be long, I will be glad
that I may long obey;
if short, yet why should I be sad
to soar to endless day?

3 Christ leads me through no darker rooms
than He went through before;
and he that to God's kingdom comes
must enter by this door.

4 Come, Lord, when grace has made me meet
Your blessèd face to see;
for if Your work on earth be sweet,
what will Your glory be?

5 Then I shall end my sad complaints
and weary, sinful days;
and join with the triumphant saints
who sing Jehovah's praise.

6 My knowledge of that life is small,
the eye of faith is dim:
but 'tis enough that Christ knows all,
and I shall be with Him.

Richard Baxter, 1615-91

799

Jesus, our best-belovèd friend,
draw out our souls in pure desire;
Jesus, in love to us descend,
baptize us with Thy Spirit's fire.

2 On Thy redeeming Name we call,
poor and unworthy though we be;
pardon and sanctify us all;
let each Thy full salvation see.

3 Our souls and bodies we resign
to fear and follow Thy commands;
O take our hearts, our hearts are Thine,
accept the service of our hands.

4 Firm, faithful, watching unto prayer,
may we Thy blessèd will obey,
toil in Thy vineyard here, and bear
the heat and burden of the day.

5 Yet, Lord, for us a resting-place
in heaven at Thy right hand prepare;
and till we see Thee face to face
may our best joys and hopes be there.

*James Montgomery**, 1771-1854

800

Leave God to order all thy ways,
and hope in Him whate'er betide;
thou'lt find Him in the evil days
thy all-sufficient strength and guide:
who trusts in God's unchanging love
builds on the rock that nought can move.

2 Only thy restless heart keep still,
and wait in cheerful hope, content
to take whate'er His gracious will,
His all-discerning love, hath sent;
nor doubt our inmost wants are known
to Him who chose us for His own.

3 Sing, pray, and swerve not from His ways,
but do thine own part faithfully;
trust His rich promises of grace,
so shall they be fulfilled in thee:
God never yet forsook at need
the soul that trusted Him indeed.

Georg Christian Neumark, 1621-81;
tr. by Catherine Winkworth, 1827-78

801

My times are in Thy hand:
my God, I wish them there;
my life, my friends, my soul I leave
entirely to Thy care.

2 My times are in Thy hand,
whatever they may be,
pleasing or painful, dark or bright,
as best may seem to Thee.

3 My times are in Thy hand:
why should I doubt or fear?
A Father's hand will never cause
His child a needless tear.

4 My times are in Thy hand,
Jesus, the crucified;
those hands my cruel sins had pierced
are now my guard and guide.

5 My times are in Thy hand:
I'll always trust in Thee;
and, after death, at Thy right hand
I shall for ever be.

William Freeman Lloyd, 1791-1853

802

My heart is resting, O my God,
I will give thanks and sing;
my heart is at the secret source
of every precious thing:
now the frail vessel You have made
no hand but Yours shall fill;
the waters of the earth have failed,
and I am thirsty still.

2 I thirst for springs of heavenly life,
and here all day they rise;
I seek the treasure of Your love,
and close at hand it lies;
and a new song is in my mouth
to long-loved music set:
glory to You for all the grace
I have not tasted yet!

3 Glory to You for strength withheld,
for want and weakness known,
the fear that sends me to Your breast
for what is most my own.
I have a heritage of joy
that yet I must not see;
the hand that bled to make it mine
is keeping it for me.

4 My heart is resting, O my God,
my heart is in Your care;
I hear the voice of joy and health
resounding everywhere.
'You are my portion, says my soul,'
ten thousand voices say;
the music of their glad Amen
will never die away.

Anna Laetitia Waring, 1823-1910

803

O Love, that wilt not let me go,
I rest my weary soul in Thee;
I give Thee back the life I owe,
that in Thine ocean depths its flow
may richer, fuller be.

2 O Light, that followest all my way,
I yield my flickering torch to Thee;
my heart restores its borrowed ray,
that in Thy sunshine's blaze its day
may brighter, fairer be.

3 O Joy, that seekest me through pain,
I cannot close my heart to Thee;
I trace the rainbow through the rain,
and feel the promise is not vain
that morn shall tearless be.

4 O cross, that liftest up my head,
I dare not ask to fly from thee;
I lay in dust life's glory dead,
and from the ground there blossoms red
life that shall endless be.

George Matheson, 1842-1906

804

O Lord, how happy should we be
if we could cast our care on Thee,
if we from self could rest;
and feel at heart that One above,
in perfect wisdom, perfect love,
is working for the best!

2 How far from this our daily life,
how oft disturbed by anxious strife,
by sudden wild alarms!
O, could we but relinquish all
our earthly props, and simply fall
on Thine almighty arms!

3 Could we but kneel and cast our load,
e'en while we pray, upon our God,
then rise with lightened cheer,
sure that the Father, who is nigh
to still the famished raven's cry,
will hear, in that we fear.

4 We cannot trust Him as we should:
so chafes weak nature's restless mood
to cast its peace away;
but birds and flowers around us preach,
and all the present evil teach
sufficient for the day.

5 Lord, make these faithless hearts of ours
such lessons learn from birds and flowers;
make them from self to cease,
leave all things to a Father's will,
and taste, on Him relying still,
e'en in affliction, peace.

Joseph Anstice, 1808-36

805

Based on PSALM 91

Safe in the shadow of the Lord,
beneath His hand and power,
I trust in Him,
I trust in Him,
my fortress and my tower.

2 My hope is set on God alone
though Satan spreads his snare;
I trust in Him,
I trust in Him,
to keep me in His care.

3 From fears and phantoms of the night
from foes about my way,
I trust in Him,
I trust in Him,
by darkness as by day.

4 His holy angels keep my feet
secure from every stone;
I trust in Him,
I trust in Him,
and unafraid go on.

5 Strong in the everlasting Name,
and in my Father's care,
I trust in Him,
I trust in Him,
who hears and answers prayer.

6 Safe in the shadow of the Lord,
possessed by love divine,
I trust in Him,
I trust in Him,
and meet His love with mine.

Timothy Dudley-Smith, b. 1926

806

When I survey life's varied scene
amid the darkest hours,
sweet rays of comfort shine between,
and thorns are mixed with flowers.

2 Lord, teach me to adore the hand
whence all my comforts flow,
and let me in this desert land
a glimpse of Canaan know.

3 And O, whate'er of earthly bliss
Thy sovereign will denies,
accepted at Thy throne of grace
let this petition rise:

4 Give me a calm, a thankful heart,
from every murmur free;
the blessings of Thy grace impart,
and let me live to Thee.

5 Let the sweet hope that Thou art mine
my path of life attend,
Thy presence through my journey shine,
and crown my journey's end.

Anne Steele, 1717-78

807

Teach me Your way, O Lord,
teach me Your way;
Your gracious aid afford,
teach me Your way;
help me to walk aright,
more by faith, less by sight;
lead me with heavenly light:
teach me Your way.

2 When doubts and fears arise,
teach me Your way;
when storms o'erspread the skies,
teach me Your way;
shine through the cloud and rain,
through sorrow, toil, and pain;
make then my pathway plain:
teach me Your way.

3 Long as my life shall last,
teach me Your way;
where'er my lot be cast,
teach me Your way;
until the race is run,
until the journey's done,
until the crown is won,
teach me Your way.

Benjamin Mansell Ramsey, 1849-1923

808

PSALM 23

The Lord's my Shepherd, I'll not want,
He makes me lie in pastures green.
He leads me by the still, still waters,
His goodness restores my soul.

And I will trust in You alone,
And I will trust in You alone.
For Your endless mercy follows me,
Your goodness will lead me home.

2 He guides my ways in righteousness,
and He anoints my head with oil,
and my cup it overflows with joy,
I feast on His pure delights.

3 And though I walk the darkest path,
I will not fear the evil one,
for You are with me and Your rod and staff
are the comfort I need to know.

Stuart Townend, b. 1963

809

When peace, like a river, attendeth my way,
when sorrows, like sea-billows, roll,
whatever my lot, Thou hast taught me to say,
'It is well, it is well with my soul.'

2 Though Satan should buffet, though trials should come,
let this blest assurance control,
that Christ has regarded my helpless estate,
and has shed His own blood for my soul.

3 My sin – O the bliss of this glorious thought! –
my sin, not in part, but the whole,
is nailed to His cross, and I bear it no more:
praise the Lord, praise the Lord, O my soul!

4 For me be it Christ, be it Christ hence to live!
If Jordan above me shall roll,
no pang shall be mine, for in death as in life
Thou wilt whisper Thy peace to my soul.

5 But, Lord, 'tis for Thee, for Thy coming, we wait;
the sky, not the grave, is our goal;
O trump of the angel! O voice of the Lord!
Blessèd hope! blessèd rest of my soul!

Horatio Gates Spafford, 1828-88

810

Why should cross and trial grieve me?
Christ is near
with His cheer;
never will He leave me.
Who can rob me of the heaven
that God's Son
for my own
to my faith hath given?

2 God oft gives me days of gladness;
shall I grieve
if He give
seasons, too, of sadness?
God is good and tempers ever
all my ill,
and He will
wholly leave me never.

3 Death can not destroy for ever;
from our fears,
cares and tears,
it will us deliver.
It will close life's mournful story,
make a way
that we may
enter heavenly glory.

4 Lord, my Shepherd, take me to Thee;
Thou art mine,
I was Thine,
even ere I knew Thee.
I am Thine, for Thou hast bought me;
lost I stood,
but Thy blood
free salvation brought me.

5 Thou art mine; I love and own Thee;
Light of joy,
ne'er shall I
from my heart dethrone Thee!
Saviour, let me soon behold Thee
face to face;
may Thy grace
evermore enfold me!

Paul Gerhardt, 1607-76;
based on translation by John Kelly, 1834-90

811

PSALM 3

Your promise, Lord, is perfect peace,
and yet my trials still increase;
till fears at times my soul beset
that Satan will defeat me yet.

2 Then, Saviour, let me to You fly,
find in Your strength a refuge nigh;
O hear me from Your holy hill,
and calm, and keep, and help me still.

3 Beneath Your care secure I sleep,
for what can harm the souls You keep?
I'll wake and know You at my side,
my omnipresent guard and guide!

4 For how can earth or hell distress,
with God so strong, so near to bless?
From You alone salvation flows,
my only refuge and repose.

Henry Francis Lyte, 1793-1847

Zeal and service

812

Facing a task unfinished,
that drives us to our knees,
a need that, undiminished,
rebukes our slothful ease,
we, who rejoice to know You,
renew before Your throne
the solemn pledge we owe You
to go and make You known.

2 Where other lords beside You
hold their unhindered sway,
where forces that defied You
defy You still today,
with none to heed their crying
for life, and love, and light,
unnumbered souls are dying,
and pass into the night.

3 We bear the torch that flaming
fell from the hands of those
who gave their lives proclaiming
that Jesus died and rose.
Ours is the same commission,
the same glad message ours,
fired by the same ambition,
to You we yield our powers.

4 O Father who sustained them,
O Spirit who inspired,
Saviour, whose love constrained them
to toil with zeal untired,
from cowardice defend us,
from lethargy awake!
Forth on Your errands send us
to labour for Your sake.

Frank Houghton, 1894-1972

813

A charge to keep I have,
a God to glorify,
a never-dying soul to save,
and fit it for the sky:

2 To serve the present age,
my calling to fulfil:
O may it all my powers engage
to do my Master's will!

3 Arm me with jealous care,
as in Your sight to live;
and O Your servant, Lord, prepare
a strict account to give!

4 Help me to watch and pray,
and on Yourself rely,
and let me ne'er my trust betray,
but press to realms on high.

*Charles Wesley**, 1707-88

814

All for Jesus, all for Jesus!
this our song shall ever be;
He our only hope and Saviour,
His the love that sets us free!

2 All for Jesus: He will give us
strength to serve Him hour by hour;
none can move us from His presence
while we trust His grace and power.

3 All for Jesus – He has loved us,
all for Jesus – He has died,
all for Jesus – He is with us,
all for Jesus crucified.

4 All for Jesus, all for Jesus!
this the church's song shall be,
till at last His people gather,
one in Him eternally.

William John Sparrow-Simpson, 1859-1952

815

Awake, my soul, stretch every nerve,
and press with vigour on;
a heavenly race demands your zeal,
and an immortal crown.

2 A cloud of witnesses around
hold you in full survey:
forget the steps already trod,
and onward urge your way.

3 'Tis God's all-animating voice
that calls you from on high;
'tis His own hand presents the prize
to your aspiring eye.

4 Blest Saviour, introduced by You,
have I my race begun;
and, crowned with victory, at Your feet
I'll lay my honours down.

Philip Doddridge, 1702-51

816

Fill Thou my life, O Lord my God,
in every part with praise,
that my whole being may proclaim,
Thy being and Thy ways.

2 Not for the words of praise alone,
nor e'en the praising heart,
I ask, but for a life made up
of praise in every part:

3 Praise in the common things of life,
its goings out and in;
praise in each duty and each deed,
however small and mean.

4 Fill every part of me with praise;
let all my being speak
of Thee and of Thy love, O Lord,
poor though I be and weak.

5 So shalt Thou, Lord, from me, e'en me,
receive the glory due;
and so shall I begin on earth
the song for ever new.

6 So shall no part of day or night
from sacredness be free;
but all my life, in every step,
be fellowship with Thee.

Horatius Bonar, 1808-89

817

I'm not ashamed to own my Lord,
or to defend His cause;
maintain the honour of His Word,
the glory of His cross.

2 Jesus, my God! I know His Name,
His Name is all my trust;
nor will He put my soul to shame,
nor let my hope be lost.

3 Firm as His throne His promise stands,
and He can well secure
what I've committed to His hands
till the decisive hour.

4 Then will He own my worthless name
before His Father's face;
and, in the new Jerusalem,
appoint my soul a place.

Isaac Watts, 1674-1748

818

Forth in Thy Name, O Lord, I go,
my daily labour to pursue,
Thee, only Thee, resolved to know
in all I think, or speak, or do.

2 The task Thy wisdom hath assigned
O let me cheerfully fulfil,
in all my works Thy presence find,
and prove Thy good and perfect will.

3 Thee may I set at my right hand,
whose eyes my inmost substance see,
and labour on at Thy command,
and offer all my works to Thee.

4 Give me to bear Thy easy yoke,
and every moment watch and pray,
and still to things eternal look,
and hasten to Thy glorious day;

5 For Thee delightfully employ
whate'er Thy bounteous grace hath given,
and run my course with even joy,
and closely walk with Thee to heaven.

Charles Wesley, 1707-88

819

Go, labour on; spend, and be spent,
your joy to do the Father's will;
it is the way the Master went;
should not the servant tread it still?

2 Go, labour on; 'tis not for nought;
your earthly loss is heavenly gain;
men heed you, love you, praise you not;
the Master praises: what are men?

3 Go, labour on; your hands are weak,
your knees are faint, your soul cast down;
yet falter not; the prize you seek
is near – a kingdom and a crown!

4 Go, labour on, while it is day;
the world's dark night is hastening on;
speed, speed your work, cast sloth away;
it is not thus that souls are won.

5 Toil on, faint not, keep watch, and pray;
be wise the erring soul to win;
go forth into the world's highway,
compel the wanderer to come in.

6 Toil on, and in your toil rejoice;
for toil comes rest, for exile home;
soon shall you hear the Bridegroom's voice,
the midnight cry, 'Behold, I come!'

Horatius Bonar, 1808-89

820

Jesus, I long to find
Your zeal for God in me,
Your yearning pity for mankind,
Your burning charity.

2 In me Your Spirit dwell;
in me Your mercies move:
so shall the fervour of my zeal
be the pure flame of love.

Charles Wesley, 1707-88

821

From heaven You came, helpless babe,
entered our world, Your glory veiled;
not to be served but to serve,
and give Your life that we might live.

This is our God, the Servant King
He calls us now to follow Him,
to bring our lives as a daily offering,
of worship to the Servant King.

2 There in the garden of tears,
my heavy load He chose to bear;
His heart with sorrow was torn,
'Yet not my will but Yours,' He said.

3 Come, see His hands and His feet,
the scars that speak of sacrifice,
hands that flung stars into space
to cruel nails surrendered.

4 So let us learn how to serve,
and in our lives enthrone Him;
each other's needs to prefer,
for it is Christ we're serving.

Graham Kendrick, b. 1950

822

Jesus calls us o'er the tumult
of our life's wild restless sea,
day by day His sweet voice sounding,
saying, 'Christian, follow Me!'

2 As of old apostles heard it
by the Galilean lake,
turned from home and toil and kindred,
leaving all for His dear sake.

3 Jesus calls us from the worship
of the vain world's golden store,
from each idol that would keep us,
saying, 'Christian, love Me more!'

4 In our joys and in our sorrows,
days of toil and hours of ease,
still He calls, in cares and pleasures,
that we love Him more than these.

5 Jesus calls us! By Your mercies,
Saviour, make us hear Your call,
give our hearts to Your obedience,
serve and love You best of all.

Cecil Frances Alexander, 1818-95

823

Lord, speak to me, that I may speak
in living echoes of Thy tone;
as Thou hast sought, so let me seek
Thy erring children lost and lone.

2 O lead me, Lord, that I may lead
the wandering and the wavering feet;
O feed me, Lord, that I may feed
Thy hungering ones with manna sweet.

3 O strengthen me, that, while I stand
firm on the rock, and strong in Thee
I may stretch out a loving hand
to wrestlers with the troubled sea.

4 O teach me, Lord, that I may teach
the precious things Thou dost impart;
and wing my words, that they may reach
the hidden depths of many a heart.

5 O give Thine own sweet rest to me,
that I may speak with soothing power
a word in season, as from Thee,
to weary ones in needful hour.

6 O fill me with Thy fulness, Lord,
until my very heart o'erflow
in kindling thought and glowing word,
Thy love to tell, Thy praise to show.

7 O use me, Lord, use even me,
just as Thou wilt, and when, and where,
until Thy blessèd face I see,
Thy rest, Thy joy, Thy glory share.

Frances Ridley Havergal, 1836-79

824

Jesus, and shall it ever be
a mortal man ashamed of Thee,
ashamed of Thee, whom angels praise,
whose glories shine through endless
days?

2 Ashamed of Jesus, of my God,
who purchased me with His own blood!
of Him who, to retrieve my loss,
despised the shame, endured the cross?

3 Ashamed of Jesus, that dear friend,
on whom my hopes of heaven depend!
No, when I blush, be this my shame,
that I no more revere His name.

4 Ashamed of Jesus! yes, I may
when I've no guilt to wash away,
no tear to wipe, no good to crave,
no fears to quell, no soul to save.

5 Ashamed of Jesus, of my Lord,
by all heaven's glorious hosts adored!
No, I will make my boast of Thee,
in time and in eternity!

6 Till then, nor is my boasting vain,
till then I boast a Saviour slain!
And O may this my glory be,
that Christ is not ashamed of me!

Joseph Grigg, c. 1720-68,
and Benjamin Francis, 1734-99

825

**Master, speak! Thy servant
heareth,**
waiting for Thy gracious word,
longing for Thy voice that cheereth,
Master, let it now be heard.
I am listening, Lord, for Thee;
what hast Thou to say to me?

2 Speak to me by name, O Master,
let me know it is to me;
speak, that I may follow faster,
with a step more firm and free,
where the Shepherd leads the flock
in the shadow of the Rock.

3 Master, speak! though least and lowest,
let me not unheard depart;
Master, speak! for O Thou knowest
all the yearning of my heart;
knowest all its truest need;
speak, and make me blest indeed.

4 Master, speak! and make me ready,
when Thy voice is truly heard,
with obedience glad and steady
still to follow every word.
I am listening, Lord, for Thee;
Master, speak! O speak to me!

Frances Ridley Havergal, 1836-79

826

My gracious Lord, I own Thy right
to every service I can pay;
and call it my supreme delight
to hear Thy dictates and obey.

2 What is my being but for Thee,
its sure support, its noblest end;
Thy ever-smiling face to see,
and serve the cause of such a friend?

3 I would not breathe for worldly joy,
or to increase my worldly good;
nor future days or powers employ
to spread a sounding name abroad.

4 'Tis to my Saviour I would live,
to Him who for my ransom died:
nor could untainted Eden give
such bliss as blossoms at His side.

5 His work my hoary age shall bless,
when youthful vigour is no more;
and my last hour of life confess:
His love hath animating power.

Philip Doddridge, 1702-51

827

O Thou who camest from above
the pure celestial fire to impart,
kindle a flame of sacred love
on the mean altar of my heart!

2 There let it for Thy glory burn
with inextinguishable blaze,
and trembling to its source return
in humble prayer and fervent praise.

3 Jesus, confirm my heart's desire
to work and speak and think for
Thee;
still let me guard the holy fire,
and still stir up Thy gift in me.

4 Ready for all Thy perfect will,
my acts of faith and love repeat,
till death Thine endless mercies seal,
and make the sacrifice complete.

Charles Wesley, 1707-88

828

Saviour, Thy dying love
Thou gavest me;
nor should I aught withhold,
my Lord, from Thee;
in love my soul would bow,
my heart fulfil its vow,
some offering bring Thee now,
something for Thee.

2 At the blest mercy-seat
pleading for me,
my feeble faith looks up,
Jesus, to Thee;
help me the cross to bear,
Thy wondrous love declare,
some song to raise, or prayer –
something for Thee.

3 Give me a faithful heart,
likeness to Thee,
that each departing day
henceforth may see
some work of love begun,
some deed of kindness done,
some wanderer sought and won –
something for Thee.

4 All that I am and have,
Thy gifts so free,
in joy, in grief, through life,
O Lord, for Thee!
And when Thy face I see,
my ransomed soul shall be,
through all eternity,
something for Thee.

Sylvanus Dryden Phelps, 1816-95

829

Tell all the world of Jesus,
our Saviour, Lord and King;
and let the whole creation
of His salvation sing:
proclaim His glorious greatness
in nature and in grace;
Creator and Redeemer,
the Lord of time and space.

2 Tell all the world of Jesus,
that everyone may find
the joy of His forgiveness –
true peace of heart and mind:

proclaim His perfect goodness,
His deep, unfailing care;
His love so rich in mercy,
a love beyond compare.

3 Tell all the world of Jesus,
that everyone may know
of His almighty triumph
defeating every foe:
proclaim His coming glory,
when sin is overthrown,
and He shall reign in splendour –
the King upon His throne!

James Edward Seddon, 1915-83;

830

Take my life, and let it be
consecrated, Lord, to Thee;
take my moments and my days,
let them flow in ceaseless praise.

2 Take my hands, and let them move
at the impulse of Thy love;
take my feet, and let them be
swift and beautiful for Thee.

3 Take my voice, and let me sing
always, only for my King;
take my lips, and let them be
filled with messages from Thee.

4 Take my silver and my gold,
not a mite would I withhold;
take my intellect, and use
every power as Thou shalt choose.

5 Take my will, and make it Thine;
it shall be no longer mine:
take my heart, it is Thine own;
it shall be Thy royal throne.

6 Take my love; my Lord, I pour
at Thy feet its treasure-store:
take myself, and I will be
ever, only, all for Thee!

Frances Ridley Havergal, 1836-79

831

The battle is the Lord's!
The harvest fields are white:
how few the reaping hands appear,
their strength, how slight!
Yet victory is sure –
we face a vanquished foe;
then forward with the risen Christ
to battle go!

2 The battle is the Lord's!
Not ours is strength and skill,
but His alone in sovereign grace,
to work His will.
Ours, counting not the cost,
unflinching to obey;
and in His time His holy arm
shall win the day!

3 The battle is the Lord's!
The Victor crucified
must with the travail of His soul
be satisfied.
The powers of hell shall fail,
and all God's will be done
till every soul whom He has given
to Christ be won.

4 The battle is the Lord's!
Stand still, my soul, and view
the great salvation God has wrought
revealed for you.
Then resting in His might,
lift high His triumph song,
for power, dominion, kingdom, strength
to Christ belong.

Margaret Clarkson, b. 1915

832

To Him we come,
Jesus Christ our Lord,
God's own living Word,
his dear Son.
In Him there is no east and west,
in Him all nations shall be blessed;
to all He offers peace and rest,
loving Lord!

2 In Him we live,
Christ our strength and stay,
life and truth and way,
friend divine:
His power can break the chains of sin,
still all life's storms without, within,
help us the daily fight to win,
living Lord!

3 For Him we go,
soldiers of the cross,
counting all things loss
Him to know;
going to every land and race,
preaching to all redeeming grace,
building His church in every place,
conquering Lord!

4 With Him we serve,
His the work we share
with saints everywhere,
near and far;
one in the task which faith requires,
one in the zeal which never tires,
one in the hope his love inspires,
coming Lord!

5 Onward we go,
faithful, bold and true,
called His will to do
day by day,
till, at the last, with joy we'll see
Jesus, in glorious majesty;
live with Him through eternity,
reigning Lord!

James Edward Seddon, 1915-83,

833

Thy life was given for me,
Thy blood, O Lord, was shed,
that I might ransomed be,
and quickened from the dead:
Thy life was given for me;
what have I given for Thee?

2 Long years were spent for me
in weariness and woe,
that through eternity
Thy glory I might know:
long years were spent for me;
have I spent one for Thee?

3 Thou, Lord, hast borne for me
more than my tongue can tell
of bitterest agony,
to rescue me from hell:
Thou suffer'dst all for me;
what have I borne for Thee?

4 And Thou hast brought to me
down from Thy home above
salvation full and free,
Thy pardon and Thy love:
great gifts Thou broughtest me;
what have I brought to Thee?

5 O let my life be given,
my years for Thee be spent,
world-fetters all be riven,
and joy with suffering blent:
Thou gav'st Thyself for me;
I give myself to Thee.

Frances Ridley Havergal, 1836-79

Restoration and perseverance

834

Awake, our souls! away, our fears!
let every trembling thought be gone!
Awake, and run the heavenly race,
and put a cheerful courage on.

2 True, narrow is the thorny road
and mortal spirits tire and faint;
but they forget the mighty God
who feeds the strength of every saint,

3 Our mighty God, whose matchless power
is ever new, and ever young,
and firm endures, while endless years
their everlasting circles run.

4 From You, the overflowing spring,
our souls shall drink a fresh supply;
while such as trust their native strength
shall melt away, and droop, and die.

5 Swift as the eagle cuts the air,
we'll mount aloft to Your abode;
on wings of love our souls shall fly,
nor tire along the heavenly road.

Isaac Watts, 1674-1748

835

Based on Genesis 32:24-32
(Shorter version)

Come, O Thou Traveller unknown,
whom still I hold, but cannot see!
My company before is gone,
and I am left alone with Thee;
with Thee all night I mean to stay,
and wrestle till the break of day.

2 I need not tell Thee who I am,
my misery and sin declare;
Thyself hast called me by my name;
look on Thy hands, and read it there:
but who, I ask Thee, who art Thou?
Tell me Thy Name, and tell me now.

3 In vain Thou strugglest to get free;
I never will unloose my hold!
Art Thou the Man that died for me?
The secret of Thy love unfold:
wrestling, I will not let Thee go,
till I Thy Name, Thy nature know.

4 Yield to me now; for I am weak,
but confident in self-despair;
speak to my heart, in blessings speak,
be conquered by my instant prayer;
speak, or Thou never hence shalt move,
and tell me if Thy Name is Love.

5 'Tis Love! 'tis Love! Thou diedst for me!
I hear Thy whisper in my heart;
the morning breaks, the shadows flee,
pure, universal Love Thou art;
to me, to all, Thy mercies move:
Thy nature and Thy Name is Love.

6 I know Thee, Saviour, who Thou art,
Jesus, the feeble sinner's Friend;
nor wilt Thou with the night depart,
but stay and love me to the end;
Thy mercies never shall remove:
Thy nature and Thy Name is Love.

Charles Wesley, 1707-88

(Full version)

Come, O Thou Traveller unknown,
whom still I hold, but cannot see!
My company before is gone,
and I am left alone with Thee;
with Thee all night I mean to stay,
and wrestle till the break of day.

2 I need not tell Thee who I am,
my misery and sin declare;
Thyself hast called me by my name;
look on Thy hands, and read it there:
but who, I ask Thee, who art Thou?
Tell me Thy Name, and tell me now.

3 In vain Thou strugglest to get free;
I never will unloose my hold!
Art Thou the Man that died for me?
The secret of Thy love unfold:
wrestling, I will not let Thee go,
till I Thy Name, Thy nature know.

4 Wilt Thou not yet to me reveal
Thy new, unutterable Name?
Tell me, I still beseech Thee, tell;
to know it now resolved I am:
wrestling, I will not let Thee go,
till I Thy Name, Thy nature know.

5 What though my shrinking flesh complain,
and murmur to contend so long?
I rise superior to my pain,
when I am weak, then I am strong;
and when my all of strength shall fail,
I shall with the God-Man prevail.

6 Yield to me now; for I am weak,
but confident in self-despair;
speak to my heart, in blessings speak,
be conquered by my instant prayer;
speak, or Thou never hence shalt move,
and tell me if Thy Name is Love.

7 'Tis Love! 'tis Love! Thou diedst for me!
I hear Thy whisper in my heart;
the morning breaks, the shadows flee,
pure, universal Love Thou art;
to me, to all, Thy mercies move:
Thy nature and Thy Name is love,

8 My prayer hath power with God; the grace
unspeakable I now receive;
through faith I see Thee face to face,
I see Thee face to face, and live!
In vain I have not wept and strove:
Thy nature and Thy Name is Love.

9 I know Thee, Saviour, who Thou art,
Jesus, the feeble sinner's Friend;
nor wilt Thou with the night depart,
but stay and love me to the end;
Thy mercies never shall remove:
Thy nature and Thy Name is Love.

10 The Sun of righteousness on me
hath risen with healing in His wings;
withered my nature's strength, from Thee
my soul its life and succour brings;
my help is all laid up above:
Thy nature and Thy Name is Love.

11 Contented now upon my thigh
I halt, till life's short journey end;
all helplessness, all weakness, I
on Thee alone for strength depend;
nor have I power from Thee to move:
Thy nature and Thy Name is Love.

12 Lame as I am, I take the prey,
hell, earth, and sin with ease o'ercome;
I leap for joy, pursue my way
and as a bounding hart fly home,
through all eternity to prove
Thy nature and Thy Name is Love.

Charles Wesley, 1707-88

836

Cast your burden on the Lord;
only lean upon His Word;
you will soon have cause to bless
His eternal faithfulness.

2 He sustains you by His hand;
He enables you to stand;
those whom Jesus once has loved
from His grace are never moved

3 Human counsels come to nought;
that shall stand which God has wrought;
His compassion, love and power
are the same for evermore.

4 Heaven and earth may pass away,
God's free grace shall not decay;
He has promised to fulfil
all the pleasure of His will.

5 Jesus, guardian of Your flock,
be for us our constant rock;
make us, by Your powerful hand,
strong as Zion's mountain stand.
From Rowland Hill's PSALMS AND HYMNS, 1783

837

PSALM 6

Gently, gently, lay Your rod
on my sinful head, O God,
stay Your wrath, in mercy stay,
lest I sink before its sway.

2 Heal me, for my flesh is weak;
heal me, for Your grace I seek;
this my only plea I make,
heal me for Your mercy's sake.

3 Who within the silent grave
shall proclaim Your power to save?
Lord, my trembling soul reprieve,
speak, and I shall rise and live.

4 Lo! He comes! He heeds my plea!
Lo! He comes! the shadows flee!
Glory round me dawns once more;
rise my spirit, and adore!
Henry Francis Lyte, 1793-1847

838

How can we sing with joy to God,
how can we pray to Him,
when we are far away from God
in selfishness and sin?

2 How can we claim to do God's will
when we have turned away
from things of God to things of earth,
and willed to disobey?

3 How can we praise the love of God
which all His works make known,
when all our works turn from His love
to choices of our own?

4 God knows how often we have sinned
and joined with godless men,
yet in His love he calls to us
to win us back again.

5 So we will turn to God again –
His ways will be our ways,
His will our will, His love our love,
and He Himself our praise!
Brian Foley, b. 1919

839

Depth of mercy! can there be
mercy still reserved for me?
Can my God His wrath forbear?
Me, the chief of sinners, spare?

2 I have long withstood His grace,
long provoked Him to His face,
would not hearken to His calls,
grieved Him by a thousand falls.

3 Whence to me this waste of love?
Ask my Advocate above!
See the cause in Jesu's face,
now before the throne of grace.

4 There for me the Saviour stands;
shows His wounds and spreads His hands.
God is love; I know, I feel;
Jesus lives, and loves me still.

5 Jesus, answer from above:
Is not all Thy nature love?
Wilt Thou not the wrong forget?
Suffer me to kiss Thy feet?

6 If I rightly read Thy heart,
if Thou all compassion art,
bow Thine ear, in mercy bow;
pardon and accept me now.

Charles Wesley, 1707-88

840

Far off I see the goal;
O Saviour, guide me;
I feel my strength is small;
be Thou beside me:
with vision ever clear,
with love that conquers fear,
and grace to persevere,
O Lord, provide me.

2 Whene'er Thy way seems strange,
go Thou before me;
and, lest my heart should change,
O Lord, watch o'er me;
but should my faith prove frail,
and I through blindness fail,
O let Thy grace prevail,
and still restore me.

3 Should earthly pleasures wane,
and joy forsake me,
if lonely hours of pain
at length o'ertake me,
my hand in Thine hold fast
till sorrow be o'erpast,
and gentle death at last
for heaven awake me.

4 There with the ransomed throng
who praise for ever
the love that made them strong
to serve for ever,
I too would see Thy face,
Thy finished work retrace,
and magnify Thy grace,
redeemed for ever.

Robert Rowland Roberts, 1865-1945

841

From a life of weariness,
from my guilt and my distress,
Saviour, to Your side I flee –
bring me back to Calvary.

2 I am sinful, prone to fall,
unresponsive to Your call;
yet I long Your own to be –
bring me back to Calvary.

3 When the wonders of Your love
fail my bitter heart to move,
draw me, Lord, Your wounds to see –
bring me back to Calvary.

4 Though distractions crowd my day,
though I'm weak and slow to pray,
let Your Spirit strengthen me –
bring me back to Calvary.

5 Bring me back to where Your blood
washed me clean, O Son of God,
where its power has set me free,
at the cross of Calvary.

6 Bring me back to follow You,
serve the way You want me to,
tell Your praise eternally,
Jesus, Lamb of Calvary!

Emma Turl, b. 1946

842 PSALM 130

From deep distress I cry to Thee,
Lord, hear me, I implore Thee;
bend down Thy gracious ear to me,
regard my prayer before Thee;
if Thou should'st look on all my sin,
and mark down every wrong within,
who, Lord, could stand before Thee?

2 Our pardon is Thy gift; Thy love
and grace alone avail us;
our works could ne'er our guilt remove,
the strictest life would fail us;
before Thy presence none can boast,
but Thou art all forgiving grace;
that each may learn to fear Thee.

3 And thus my hope is in the Lord
and not in mine own merit;
I rest upon His faithful word
to them of contrite spirit;
that He is merciful and just –
here is my comfort and my trust;
His help I wait with patience.

4 Though great our sins and sore our woes,
His grace much more aboundeth;
His helping love no limit knows,
our utmost need it soundeth;
our kind and faithful Shepherd He,
who shall at last set Israel free
from all their sin and sorrow.

Martin Luther, 1483-1546;
tr. by Catherine Winkworth, 1827-78;
altd by John D Manton, b. 1930

843

He giveth more grace when the burdens grow greater,
He sendeth more strength when the labours increase;
to added affliction He addeth His mercy,
to multiplied trials, His multiplied peace.

His love has no limit, His grace has no measure,
His power has no boundary known unto men;
for out of His infinite riches in Jesus
He giveth, and giveth, and giveth again!

2 When we have exhausted our store of endurance,
when our strength has failed ere the day is half done,
when we reach the end of our hoarded resources,
our Father's full giving is only begun.

Annie Johnson Flint, 1866-1932

844

Based on Psalm 30

I worship You, O Lord,
for You have raised me up;
I cried to You for help,
and You restored my life.
You brought me back from death
and saved me from the grave.

2 Sing praises to the Lord
all those who know His name;
for while His wrath is brief
His favour knows no end.
Though tears may flow at night,
the morning brings new joy.

3 I said, 'I am so strong,
I never shall be moved';
but You, Lord, shook my life –
my heart was in distress.
I cried for You to help,
and pleaded for Your grace.

4 My mourning You have turned
to dancing and to joy;
my sadness You dispelled
as gladness filled my soul.
And so I'll sing Your praise,
my God, through all my days.

James Edward Seddon, 1915-83

845

Jesus, to Thee our hearts we lift –
may all our hearts with love
o'erflow –
with thanks for Thy continued gift,
that still Thy precious name we know,
retain our sense of sin forgiven,
and wait for all our inward heaven.

2 What mighty troubles hast Thou shown
Thy feeble, tempted followers here!
We have through fire and water gone,
but saw Thee on the floods appear,
but felt Thee present in the flame,
and shouted our Deliverer's name.

3 All are not lost or wandered back;
all have not left Thy church and
Thee;
there are who suffer for Thy sake,
enjoy Thy glorious infamy,
esteem the scandal of the cross,
and only seek divine applause.

4 Thou who hast kept us to this hour,
O keep us faithful to the end!
when, robed with majesty and power,
our Jesus shall from heaven descend,
His friends and witnesses to own,
and seat us on His glorious throne.

Charles Wesley, 1707-88

846

O for a closer walk with God,
a calm and heavenly frame,
a light to shine upon the road
that leads me to the Lamb!

2 Where is the blessedness I knew
when first I saw the Lord?
Where is the soul-refreshing view
of Jesus and His Word?

3 What peaceful hours I once enjoyed!
How sweet their memory still!
But they have left an aching void
the world can never fill.

4 Return, O holy Dove! return,
sweet messenger of rest!
I hate the sins that made Thee mourn,
and drove Thee from my breast.

5 The dearest idol I have known,
whate'er that idol be,
help me to tear it from Thy throne,
and worship only Thee.

6 So shall my walk be close with God,
calm and serene my frame;
so purer light shall mark the road
that leads me to the Lamb.

William Cowper, 1731-1800

847

O Jesus, full of truth and grace,
more full of grace than I of sin,
yet once again I seek Your face;
open Your arms, and take me in,
and freely my backslidings heal,
and love the faithless sinner still.

2 You know the way to bring me back,
my fallen spirit to restore:
O for Your truth and mercy's sake,
forgive, and bid me sin no more;
the ruins of my soul repair,
and make my heart a house of prayer.

3 The stone to flesh again convert,
the veil of sin again remove;
sprinkle Your blood upon my heart,
and melt it by Your dying love;
this rebel heart by love subdue,
and make it soft, and make it new.

4 Ah! give me, Lord, the tender heart
that trembles at the approach of sin;
a godly fear of sin impart,
implant, and root it deep within,
that I may dread Your gracious power,
and never dare to offend You more.

Charles Wesley, 1707-88

848

The heroes of Scripture
with hearts full of faith,
their eyes on the city,
engaged in the race.
With hope in the promise,
encouraged to see
invisible glories
and joys yet to be.

Consider your mighty Saviour King,
enduring the cross,
and run with a holy joyful strength
the race to the last.

2 Each hindrance discarded
and sin laid aside,
with patient endurance
see Christ as your prize.
The hardships you suffer,
your sorrows and care,
though painful at present
will righteousness bear.

3 The Jesus who called you
the race to begin,
is waiting to crown you
when glory you win.
Let hands be uplifted,
let strength flow from grace,
with Christ as your champion
you'll finish the race.

John Tindall, b. 1942

When sung to 'St. Denio',
the chorus is omitted

849

Rejoice, believer, in the Lord,
who makes your cause His own!
The hope that's built upon His Word
can ne'er be overthrown.

2 Though many foes beset your road,
and feeble is your arm,
your life is hid with Christ in God,
beyond the reach of harm.

3 Weak as you are, you shall not faint,
or fainting, shall not die;
Jesus, the strength of every saint,
will aid you from on high.

4 Though unperceived by mortal sense,
faith sees Him always near,
a guide, a glory, a defence;
then what have you to fear?

5 As surely as He overcame
and triumphed once for you,
so surely you that love His name
shall triumph in Him too.

John Newton, 1725-1807

850

Return, O wanderer, return,
and seek an injured Father's face;
those warm desires that in you burn
were kindled by reclaiming grace.

2 Return, O wanderer, return,
and seek a Father's melting heart;
whose pitying eyes your grief discern,
whose hand can heal your inward smart.

3 Return, O wanderer, return;
He heard your deep repentant sigh;
He saw your softened spirit mourn
when no intruding ear was nigh.

4 Return, O wanderer, return;
your Saviour bids your spirit live;
go to His bleeding feet, and learn
how freely Jesus can forgive.

William Bengo Collyer, 1782-1854

851

See! the storms of life are breaking,
faithless fears our hearts are shaking;
swiftly for our aid awaking,
Lord and Saviour, help us.

2 See! the world, from You rebelling,
round Your church in pride is swelling;
with Your word their madness quelling,
Lord and Saviour, help us.

3 We on Your command relying,
we our onward task applying,
while to You for safety sighing,
Lord and Saviour, help us.

4 Steadfast we, in faith abiding,
in Your secret presence hiding,
in Your love and grace confiding;
Lord and Saviour, help us.

5 By Your birth, Your cross, Your passion,
by Your tears of deep compassion,
by Your mighty intercession,
Lord and Saviour, help us.

*Henry Alford**, 1810-71

The hope of glory

852

Abide with me: fast falls the eventide;
the darkness deepens; Lord, with me abide!
When other helpers fail, and comforts flee,
help of the helpless, O abide with me.

2 Swift to its close ebbs out life's little day;
earth's joys grow dim, its glories pass away;
change and decay in all around I see:
O Thou who changest not, abide with me.

3 I need Thy presence every passing hour;
what but Thy grace can foil the tempter's power?
Who like Thyself my guide and stay can be?
Through cloud and sunshine, Lord, abide with me.

4 I fear no foe, with Thee at hand to bless;
ills have no weight, and tears no bitterness:
where is death's sting? where, grave, thy victory?
I triumph still, if Thou abide with me.

5 Hold Thou Thy cross before my closing eyes;
shine through the gloom, and point me to the skies;
heaven's morning breaks, and earth's vain shadows flee:
in life, in death, O Lord, abide with me.

Henry Francis Lyte, 1793-1847

853

By the sea of crystal,
saints in glory stand,
myriads in number,
drawn from every land.
Robed in white apparel,
washed in Jesus' blood,
they now reign in heaven
with the Lamb of God.

2 Out of tribulation,
death and Satan's hand,
they have been translated
at the Lord's command.
In their hands they're holding
palms of victory;
hark! the jub'lant chorus
shouts triumphantly:

3 'Unto God Almighty,
sitting on the throne,
and the Lamb, victorious,
be the praise alone.'
God has wrought salvation,
He did wondrous things.
Who shall not extol Him,
holy King of kings?

William Kuipers, 1884-1933

854

'For ever with the Lord!'
Amen, so let it be!
Life from the dead is in that word,
'tis immortality.
Here in the body pent,
absent from Him I roam,
yet nightly pitch my moving tent
a day's march nearer home.

2 My Father's house on high,
home of my soul, how near
at times to faith's foreseeing eye
thy golden gates appear!
Ah! then my spirit faints
to reach the land I love,
the bright inheritance of saints,
Jerusalem above.

3 'For ever with the Lord!'
Father, if 'tis Thy will,
the promise of that faithful word
e'en here to me fulfil.
Be Thou at my right hand,
then can I never fail;
uphold Thou me, and I shall stand;
fight, and I must prevail.

4 So when my latest breath
shall rend the veil in twain,
by death I shall escape from death,
and life eternal gain.
That resurrection word,
that shout of victory:
once more, 'For ever with the Lord!'
Amen, so let it be!

James Montgomery, 1771-1854

855

Jerusalem the golden,
with milk and honey blest,
beneath thy contemplation
sink heart and voice oppressed:
I know not, O I know not
what joys await us there,
what radiancy of glory,
what bliss beyond compare.

2 They stand, those halls of Zion,
all jubilant with song,
and bright with many an angel,
and all the martyr throng;
the Prince is ever in them;
the daylight is serene;
the pastures of the blessèd
are decked in glorious sheen.

3 There is the throne of David;
and there, from care released,
the shout of them that triumph,
the song of them that feast;
and they, who with their Leader
have conquered in the fight,
for ever and for ever
are clad in robes of white.

4 O sweet and blessèd country,
the home of God's elect!
O sweet and blessèd country
that eager hearts expect!
Jesus, in mercy bring us
to that dear land of rest,
who art, with God the Father
and Spirit, ever blest!

Bernard of Cluny, 12th cent.;
tr. by John Mason Neale, 1818-66

856

Give me the wings of faith to rise
within the veil, and see
the saints above, how great their joys,
how bright their glories be.

2 Once they were mourning here below,
with sighing and with tears;
they wrestled hard, as we do now,
with sins and doubts and fears.

3 I ask them whence their victory came;
they, with united breath,
ascribe their conquest to the Lamb,
their triumph to His death.

4 They marked the footsteps that He trod,
His zeal inspired their breast,
and, following their incarnate God,
possess the promised rest.

5 Our glorious Leader claims our praise
for His own pattern given;
while the long cloud of witnesses
show the same path to heaven.

Isaac Watts, 1674-1748

857

Based on REVELATION 7:13-17

How bright these glorious spirits shine!
Whence all their white array?
How came they to the blissful seats
of everlasting day?

2 Lo! these are they from sufferings great
who came to realms of light;
and in the blood of Christ have washed
those robes that shine so bright.

3 Now with triumphal palms they stand
before the throne on high,
and serve the God they love amidst
the glories of the sky.

4 His presence fills each heart with joy,
tunes every voice to sing;
by day, by night, the sacred courts
with glad hosannas ring.

5 Hunger and thirst are felt no more,
nor sun with scorching ray;
God is their sun, whose cheering beams
diffuse eternal day.

6 The Lamb, who dwells amidst the throne,
shall o'er them still preside,
feed them with nourishment divine,
and all their footsteps guide.

7 In pastures green He'll lead His flock,
where living streams appear;
and God the Lord from every eye
shall wipe off every tear.

8 To Him who sits upon the throne,
the God whom we adore,
and to the Lamb that once was slain,
be glory evermore!

Isaac Watts, 1674-1748;
as in SCOTTISH PARAPHRASES, 1781

858

From heavenly Jerusalem's towers,
the path through the desert they trace;
and every affliction they suffered
redounds to the glory of grace;
their look they cast back on the tempests,
on fears, on grim death and the grave,
rejoicing that now they're in safety,
through Him that is mighty to save.

2 And we, from the wilds of the desert,
shall flee to the land of the blest;
life's tears shall be changed to rejoicing,
its labours and toil into rest.
There we shall find refuge eternal,
from sin, from affliction, from pain,
and in the sweet love of the Saviour,
a joy without end shall attain.

David Charles, 1762-1834;
tr. by Lewis Edwards, 1809-87

859

I saw a new vision of Jesus,
a view I'd not seen here before,
beholding in glory so wondrous
with beauty I had to adore.
I stood on the shores of my weakness,
and gazed at the brink of such fear;
'twas then that I saw Him in newness,
regarding Him fair and so dear.

2 My Saviour will never forsake me,
unveiling His merciful face,
His presence and promise almighty,
redeeming His loved ones by grace.
In shades of the valley's dark terror,
where hell and its horror hold sway,
my Jesus will reach out in power,
and save me by His only way.

3 For yonder a light shines eternal,
which spreads through the valley of
gloom;
Lord Jesus, resplendent and regal,
drives fear far away from the tomb.
Our God is the end of the journey,
His pleasant and glorious domain;
for there are the children of mercy,
who praise Him for Calvary's pain.

William Vernon Higham, b. 1926
© *Author*

860

Lo! round the throne, a glorious band,
the saints in countless myriads stand,
of every tongue, redeemed to God,
arrayed in garments washed in blood.

2 Through tribulation great they came;
they bore the cross, despised the
shame;
from all their labours now they rest,
in God's eternal glory blest.

3 They see their Saviour face to face,
and sing the triumphs of His grace;
Him day and night they ceaseless
praise,
to Him the loud thanksgiving raise:

4 'Worthy the Lamb, for sinners slain,
through endless years to live and reign;
You have redeemed us by Your blood,
and made us kings and priests to God.'

5 So may we tread the sacred road
that saints and holy martyrs trod;
wage to the end the glorious strife,
and win, like them, a crown of life.

From COTTERILL'S SELECTION, 1810;
based on Rowland Hill, 1744-1833

861

The sands of time are sinking;
the dawn of heaven breaks;
the summer morn I've sighed for,
the fair, sweet morn, awakes:
dark, dark hath been the midnight,
but day-spring is at hand,
and glory, glory dwelleth
in Immanuel's land.

2 The King there, in His beauty,
without a veil is seen;
it were a well-spent journey,
though seven deaths lay between;
the Lamb with His fair army
doth on Mount Zion stand,
and glory, glory dwelleth
in Immanuel's land.

3 O Christ, He is the fountain,
the deep, sweet well of love;
the streams on earth I've tasted,
more deep I'll drink above;
there, to an ocean fulness,
His mercy doth expand,
and glory, glory dwelleth
in Immanuel's land.

4 With mercy and with judgment
my web of time He wove,
and aye the dews of sorrow
were lustred with His love:
I'll bless the hand that guided,
I'll bless the heart that planned,
when throned where glory dwelleth
in Immanuel's land.

5 The bride eyes not her garment,
but her dear bridegroom's face;
I will not gaze at glory,
but on my King of grace;
not at the crown He giveth,
but on His piercèd hand:
The Lamb is all the glory
of Immanuel's land.

6 I've wrestled on towards heaven,
'gainst storm and wind and tide;
now, like a weary traveller
that leans upon his guide,
amid the shades of evening,
while sinks life's lingering sand,
I hail the glory dawning
from Immanuel's land.

Anne Ross Cousin, 1824-1906

862

When this passing world is done,
when has sunk yon radiant sun,
when I stand with Christ on high,
looking o'er life's history,
then, Lord, shall I fully know,
not till then, how much I owe.

2 When I stand before the throne,
dressed in beauty not my own,
when I see Thee as Thou art,
love Thee with unsinning heart,
then, Lord, shall I fully know,
not till then, how much I owe.

3 When the praise of heaven I hear,
loud as thunders to the ear,
loud as many waters' noise,
sweet as harp's melodious voice,
then, Lord, shall I fully know,
not till then, how much I owe.

4 Chosen, not for good in me,
wakened up from wrath to flee,
hidden in the Saviour's side,
by the Spirit sanctified,
teach me, Lord, on earth to show
by my love how much I owe.

Robert Murray M'Cheyne, 1813-43

863

There is a land of pure delight,
where saints immortal reign;
infinite day excludes the night,
and pleasures banish pain.

2 There everlasting spring abides,
and never-withering flowers;
death, like a narrow sea, divides
this heavenly land from ours.

3 Sweet fields, beyond the swelling flood,
stand dressed in living green;
so to the Jews old Canaan stood,
while Jordan rolled between.

4 But timorous mortals start and shrink
to cross this narrow sea,
and linger shivering on the brink,
and fear to launch away.

5 O could we make our doubts remove,
those gloomy doubts that rise,
and see the Canaan that we love
with unbeclouded eyes;

6 Could we but climb where Moses stood,
and view the landscape o'er,
not Jordan's stream, nor death's cold flood,
should fright us from the shore.

Isaac Watts, 1674-1748

864

There is an hour when I must part
with all I hold most dear;
and life with its best hopes will then
as nothingness appear.

2 There is an hour when I must sink
beneath the stroke of death,
and yield to Him, who gave it first,
my struggling, vital breath.

3 There is an hour when I must stand
before the judgment-seat,
and all my sins, and all my foes,
in awful vision meet.

4 There is an hour when I must look
on one eternity;
and nameless woe, or blissful life,
my endless portion be.

5 O Saviour, then, in all my need,
be near, be near to me;
and let my soul by steadfast faith
find life and heaven in Thee.

Andrew Reed, 1787-1862

865

When the trumpet of the Lord shall sound,
and time shall be no more,
and the morning breaks eternal, bright and fair;
when the saved of earth shall gather
over on the other shore,
and the roll is called up yonder,
I'll be there.

When the roll is called up yonder,
when the roll is called up yonder,
when the roll is called up yonder,
when the roll is called up yonder,
I'll be there.

2 On that bright and cloudless morning,
when the dead in Christ shall rise,
and the glory of His resurrection share;
when His chosen ones shall gather to
their home beyond the skies,
and the roll is called up yonder,
I'll be there.

3 Let us labour for the Master from the dawn till setting sun,
let us talk of all his wond'rous love and care;
then when all of life is over, and our
work on earth is done,
and the roll is called up yonder,
I'll be there.

James Milton Black, 1856-1938

866 Based on Revelation 7:13-17

Who are these in bright array,
this innumerable throng,
round the altar night and day
hymning one triumphant song:
'Worthy is the Lamb once slain,
blessing, honour, glory, power,
wisdom, riches to obtain,
new dominion every hour'?

2 These through fiery trials trod,
these from great afflictions came;
now before the throne of God,
sealed with His almighty Name;
clothed in garments pure and white,
victor palms in every hand,
through their dear Redeemer's might,
more than conquerors they stand.

3 Hunger, thirst, disease unknown,
on immortal fruits they feed;
there the Lamb amidst the throne,
shall to living fountains lead:
joy and gladness banish sighs,
perfect love dispels all fears,
and for ever from their eyes
God shall wipe away the tears.

James Montgomery, 1771-1854

SPECIAL OCCASIONS
Beginning and ending of year

867

Another year has now begun
with silent pace its course to run;
our hearts and voices let us raise
to God in prayer and songs of praise.

2 Father, Thy bounteous love we bless,
for gifts and mercies numberless;
for life and health, for grace and peace,
for hope of joys that never cease.

3 O Son of God, in faith and fear
teach us to walk as strangers here,
with hearts in heaven, that we may come
to where Thou art, our Father's home.

4 Grant us, O Comforter, Thy grace,
and speed us on our earthly race,
in body, spirit, and in soul,
right onward to the heavenly goal.

5 Thou, Lord, who makest all things new,
O give us hearts both pure and true;
that we, as jewels, ever Thine,
in new Jerusalem may shine.

6 Blest Three in One, to Thee we pray;
defend and guide us on our way;
that we at last with joy may see
the new year of eternity!

Christopher Wordsworth, 1807-85

868

Come, let us anew
our journey pursue,
roll round with the year,
and never stand still till the Master appear.

2 His adorable will
let us gladly fulfil,
and our talents improve,
by the patience of hope and the labour of love.

3 Our life is a dream;
our time as a stream
glides swiftly away,
and the fugitive moment refuses to stay.

4 O that each in the day
of His coming may say:
'I have fought my way through,
I have finished the work that You gave me to do!'

5 O that each from his Lord
may receive the glad word:
'Well and faithfully done;
enter into My joy, and sit down on My throne!'

Charles Wesley, 1707-88

869

Great God, we sing that guiding hand
by which supported still we stand;
the opening year Your mercy shows,
let mercy crown it till it close.

2 By day, by night, at home, abroad,
still are we guarded by our God,
by His incessant bounty fed,
by His unerring counsel led.

3 With grateful hearts the past we own;
the future, all to us unknown,
we to Your guardian care commit,
and peaceful leave before Your feet.

4 In scenes exalted or depressed,
You are our joy, You are our rest;
Your goodness all our hopes shall raise,
adored through all our changing days.

5 When death shall interrupt these songs,
and seal in silence mortal tongues,
our helper, God, in whom we trust,
in better worlds our souls shall boast.

*Philip Doddridge**, 1702-51

870

My helper, God! I bless His Name,
whose love for ever is the same;
the tokens of whose gracious care
open, and crown, and close the year.

2 I midst ten thousand dangers stand,
supported by His guardian hand,
and see, when I review my ways,
ten thousand monuments of praise.

3 Thus far His arm has led me on,
thus far I make His mercy known;
and while I tread this desert land,
new mercies shall new songs demand.

4 My grateful soul, on Jordan's shore,
shall raise one sacred pillar more;
then bear in His bright courts above
inscriptions of immortal love.

Philip Doddridge, 1702-51

871

Father, let us dedicate
all this year to You,
for the service small or great
You would have us do;
not from any painful thing
freedom can we claim;
but in all that we may bring
glory to Your Name.

2 Can a child presume to choose
where or how to live?
Can a father's love refuse
all the best to give?
More You give us every day
than we dare to claim,
and our grateful voices say,
'Glory to Your Name.'

3 If You call us to a cross
and its shadows come
turning all our gain to loss,
shrouding heart and home,
let us think how Your dear Son
to His triumph came,
then through pain and tears pray on,
'Glory to Your Name.'

4 If in mercy You prepare
joyful years ahead,
if through days serene and fair
peaceful paths we tread;
then, whatever life may bring,
let our lips proclaim
and our glad hearts ever sing,
'Glory to Your Name.'

Lawrence Tuttiett, 1825-97

872

Sing to the great Jehovah's praise;
all praise to Him belongs;
who kindly lengthens out our days
demands our choicest songs.

2 His providence has brought us through
another various year;
we all with vows and anthems new
before our God appear.

3 Father, Thy mercies past we own;
Thy still continued care;
to Thee presenting, through Thy Son,
whate'er we have or are.

4 Our lips and lives shall gladly show
the wonders of Thy love,
while on in Jesu's steps we go
to see Thy face above.

5 Our residue of days or hours
Thine, wholly Thine, shall be;
and all our consecrated powers
a sacrifice to Thee:

6 Till Jesus in the clouds appear
to saints on earth forgiven,
and bring the grand sabbatic year,
the jubilee of heaven.

Charles Wesley, 1707-88

National and harvest

873

Almighty God, before Your throne
Your mourning people bend;
'tis on Your pardoning grace alone
our prostrate hopes depend.

2 Dire judgments from Your heavy hand
Your dreadful power display;
yet mercy spares our guilty land,
and still we live to pray.

3 O turn us, turn us, mighty Lord,
by Your subduing grace;
so shall our hearts obey Your Word,
and we shall see Your face.

4 When evil smites, when foes invade,
we shall not sink or fear,
secure of all-sufficient aid
when God, our God, is near!

Anne Steele, 1717-78

874

O God of love, O King of peace,
make wars throughout the world to
cease;
the wrath of sinful man restrain;
give peace, O God, give peace again.

2 Remember, Lord, Your works of old,
the wonders that our fathers told;
remember not our sin's dark stain;
give peace, O God, give peace again.

3 Whom shall we trust but You, O Lord,
where rest but on Your faithful Word?
None ever called on You in vain;
give peace, O God, give peace again.

4 Where saints and angels dwell above,
all hearts are knit in holy love;
O bind us in that heavenly chain;
give peace, O God, give peace again.

Henry Williams Baker, 1821-77

875

Eternal Father, strong to save
whose arm hath bound the restless wave,
who bidd'st the mighty ocean deep
its own appointed limits keep:
O hear us when we cry to Thee
for those in peril on the sea!

2 O Christ, whose voice the waters heard,
and hushed their raging at Thy word,
who walkedst on the foaming deep,
and calm amid the storm didst sleep;
O hear us when we cry to Thee
for those in peril on the sea!

3 O Holy Spirit, who didst brood
upon the waters dark and rude,
and bid their angry tumult cease,
and give, for wild confusion, peace:
O hear us when we cry to Thee
for those in peril on the sea!

4 O Trinity of love and power,
our brethren shield in danger's hour;
from rock and tempest, fire and foe,
protect them wheresoe'er they go:
thus evermore shall rise to Thee
glad hymns of praise from land and sea.

William Whiting, 1825-78

876

O God, whose all-sustaining hand
is over this and every land,
whose laws from age to age have stood,
sure guardians of our common good,
may love of justice rule our days
and ordered freedom guide our ways.

2 Be near to those who strive to see
our homes from harm and terror free,
who live their lives at duty's call
and spend themselves in serving all:
receive for them Your people's prayer,
uphold them by Your constant care.

3 Teach us to serve our neighbour's need,
the homeless help, the hungry feed,
the poor protect, the weak defend,
and to the friendless prove a friend;
the wayward and the lost reclaim
for love of Christ and in His Name.

4 So may our hearts remember yet
that cross where love and justice met,
and find in Christ our fetters freed,
whose mercy answers all our need:
who lives and reigns, our risen Lord,
where justice sheathes her righteous sword.

Timothy Dudley-Smith, b. 1926

877

Great King of nations, hear our prayer,
while at Your feet we fall,
and humbly, with united cry,
to You for mercy call.

2 The guilt is ours, but grace is Yours;
O turn us not away,
but hear us from Your lofty throne,
and help us when we pray.

3 Our fathers' sins were manifold,
and ours no less we own;
yet wondrously from age to age
Your goodness has been shown.

4 When dangers like a stormy sea
beset our country round,
to You we looked, to You we cried,
and help in You we found.

5 With one consent, we meekly bow
beneath Your chastening hand,
and pouring our confessions forth
mourn with our grieving land.

6 With pitying eyes behold our need:
to You we lift our prayer;
correct us with Your judgements, Lord,
then let Your mercy spare.

John Hampden Gurney, 1802-62

878

O Lord of heaven, and earth, and sea,
to Thee all praise and glory be;
how shall we show our love to Thee,
who givest all?

2 The golden sunshine, vernal air,
sweet flowers and fruits, Thy love declare;
where harvests ripen, Thou art there,
who givest all.

3 For peaceful homes and healthful days,
for all the blessings earth displays,
we owe Thee thankfulness and praise,
who givest all.

4 Thou didst not spare Thine only Son,
but gav'st Him for a world undone,
and freely with that blessèd One
Thou givest all.

5 Thou giv'st the Spirit's blessèd dower,
Spirit of life, and love, and power,
and dost His sevenfold graces shower
upon us all.

6 For souls redeemed, for sins forgiven,
for means of grace and hopes of heaven,
Father, what can to Thee be given,
who givest all?

7 To Thee, from whom we all derive
our life, our gifts, our power to give!
O may we ever with Thee live,
who givest all!

Christopher Wordsworth, 1807-85

879

Praise O praise the Lord of harvest,
providence and love!
Praise Him in His earthly temples,
and above!

2 Praise Him, every living creature,
by His goodness fed,
whose rich mercy daily giveth
daily bread.

3 Sing Him thanks for all the bounties
of His gracious hand;
smiling peace and welcome plenty
o'er our land.

4 Praise His Name that war's loud thunder
breaks not on our shore!
Fields of harvest, not of plunder,
yield their store.

5 Quickened unto life eternal,
bear we heavenly fruit;
lest, if barren, He reject us
branch and root.

6 Speed, O speed that glorious harvest
of the souls of men,
when Christ's members, here long scattered,
meet again.

7 Glory to the Lord of harvest,
holy Three in One!
To the Father, Son, and Spirit,
praise be done!

James Hamilton, 1819-96

880

We plough the fields, and scatter
the good seed on the land,
but it is fed and watered
by God's almighty hand;
He sends the snow in winter,
the warmth to swell the grain,
the breezes and the sunshine,
and soft refreshing rain.

All good gifts around us
are sent from heaven above,
then thank the Lord, O thank the Lord,
for all His love.

2 He only is the Maker
of all things near and far;
He paints the wayside flower;
He lights the evening star;
the winds and waves obey Him;
by Him the birds are fed;
much more to us, His children,
He gives our daily bread.

3 We thank You, then, O Father,
for all things bright and good,
the seed-time and the harvest,
our life, our health, our food:
no gifts have we to offer
for all Your love imparts,
but that which You desire,
our humble, thankful hearts.

Matthias Claudius, 1740-1815;
tr. by Jane Montgomery Campbell, 1817-78

881

Come, ye thankful people, come,
raise the song of harvest-home:
all is safely gathered in
ere the winter storms begin;
God our maker doth provide
for our wants to be supplied:
come to God's own temple, come,
raise the song of harvest-home.

2 All the world is God's own field,
fruit unto His praise to yield;
wheat and tares together sown,
unto joy or sorrow grown;
first the blade, and then the ear,
then the full corn shall appear:
Lord of harvest, grant that we
wholesome grain and pure may be.

3 For the Lord our God shall come,
and shall take His harvest home;
from His field shall in that day
all offences purge away;
give His angels charge at last
in the fire the tares to cast,
but the fruitful ears to store
in His garner evermore.

4 Even so, Lord, quickly come
to Thy final harvest-home:
gather Thou Thy people in,
free from sorrow, free from sin;
there, for ever purified,
in Thy presence to abide:
come, with all Thine angels come,
raise the glorious harvest-home.

Henry Alford, 1810-71

Marriage, home and family

882

For the beauty of the earth,
for the beauty of the skies,
for the love which from our birth
over and around us lies:

Gracious God, to Thee we raise
this our sacrifice of praise.

2 For the beauty of each hour
of the day and of the night,
hill and vale, and tree and flower,
sun and moon and stars of light:

3 For the joy of human love,
brother, sister, parent, child,
friends on earth and friends above,
for all gentle thoughts and mild:

4 For each perfect gift of Thine
to our race so freely given,
graces human and divine,
flowers of earth and buds of heaven:

Folliott Stanford Pierpoint, 1835-1917

883

Except the Lord the house should build
the builder toils in vain.
Except the Lord the city keep
it cannot safe remain.
This couple, Lord, look up to Thee –
their builder and their guardian be.

2 At Cana's wedding feast a guest
turned water into wine,
and natural human things transformed
by that which is divine.
Of Him alone we make request –
be Thou an ever-present guest.

3 As Jesus on Emmaus road
the scriptures opened up,
then sat with them around their board
and shared their bread and cup,
this couple, Lord, we bring to Thee –
their wisdom and companion be.

4 Upon this couple blessing pour,
our Saviour and true vine;
increase them, Lord, in every way,
and make their increase Thine.
Bless them, O Lord, to endless days
in harmony to sing Thy praise.

Eluned Harrison, b. 1934

884

Jesus, the Lord of love and life,
draw near to bless this man and wife;
as they are now in love made one,
let Your good will for them be done.

2 Give them each day Your peace and joy,
let no dark clouds these gifts destroy;
in growing trust may love endure,
to keep their marriage-bond secure.

3 As they have vowed to have and hold,
each by the other be consoled;
in wealth or want, in health or pain,
till death shall part, let love remain.

4 Deepen, O Lord, their love for You,
and in that love their own renew;
each in the other find delight,
as lives and interests now unite.

5 Be to them both a guide and friend,
through all the years their home
defend;
Jesus, the Lord of love and life,
stay near and bless this man and wife.

James Edward Seddon, 1915-83

885

O perfect Love, all human thought transcending,
lowly we kneel in prayer before Thy throne,
that theirs may be the love which knows no ending
whom Thou for evermore dost join in one.

2 O perfect Life, be Thou their full assurance
of tender charity and steadfast faith,
of patient hope, and quiet brave endurance,
with childlike trust that fears nor pain nor death.

3 Grant them the joy which brightens earthly sorrow;
grant them the peace which calms all earthly strife;
and to life's day the glorious unknown morrow
that dawns upon eternal love and life.

Dorothy Frances Gurney, 1858-1932

886

We worship Thee, the King of grace,
with heart and soul and voice;
O grant that mercy's smiling face
may cause us to rejoice!

2 Along life's path we have been led
by Thee, our Lord and friend;
and we have tasted of the Bread
of Life, which Thou dost send.

3 We come to Thee for blessing now
upon this wedding-day;
we ask Thee, Lord, Thy grace bestow
and may Thy presence stay.

4 We come our promises to make,
present our vows to Thee;
our humble prayer O gently take,
that we may faithful be.

5 Upon our hearts O grant Thy peace,
Thy guidance in our lives;
that we may walk the way of grace,
and be in all things wise.

6 Upon our home Thy blessing give,
a haven from the storm,
a place of comfort, where we live
in harmony and calm.

7 We look to Thee, our sovereign God,
for unction and for grace;
and when our journey we have trod,
we'll see Thy blessèd face.

William Vernon Higham, b. 1926

887

God of mercy, hear our prayer
for the children Thou hast given;
let them all Thy blessings share,
grace on earth, and bliss in heaven!

2 In the morning of their days
may their hearts be drawn to Thee;
let them learn to lisp Thy praise
in their earliest infancy.

3 Cleanse their souls from every stain,
through the Saviour's precious blood;
let them all be born again,
and be reconciled to God.

4 For this mercy, Lord, we cry;
bend Thine ever-gracious ear;
while on Thee our souls rely,
hear our prayer, in mercy hear!

Thomas Hastings, 1784-1872

888

Happy the home when God is there,
and love fills every breast;
when one their wish, and one their prayer,
and one their heavenly rest.

2 Happy the home where Jesus' name
is sweet to every ear;
where children early lisp His fame,
and parents hold Him dear.

3 Happy the home where prayer is heard,
and praise is wont to rise;
where parents love the sacred Word
that makes us truly wise.

4 Lord, let us in our homes agree,
this blessèd peace to gain;
unite our hearts in love to Thee,
and love to all will reign.

Henry Ware, 1794-1843

889

O Lord, behold us at Thy feet,
a needy, sinful band;
as suppliants round Thy mercy-seat
we come at Thy command.

2 'Tis for our children we would plead,
the offspring Thou hast given;
where shall we go in time of need
but to the God of heaven?

3 We ask not for them wealth or fame,
amid the worldly strife;
but in the all-prevailing Name,
we ask eternal life.

4 We crave the Spirit's quickening grace,
to make them pure in heart,
that they may stand before Thy face,
and see Thee as Thou art.

Thomas Hastings, 1784-1872

890

Our children, Lord, in faith and prayer
we now present to Thee;
let them Thy covenant mercies share,
and Thy salvation see.

2 Such helpless babes Thou didst embrace,
while dwelling here below;
to us and ours, O God of grace,
the same compassion show.

3 In early days their hearts secure
from worldly snares, we pray;
and may they to the end endure
in every righteous way.

4 Before them let their parents live
in godly faith and fear,
then, Lord, to heaven their souls receive,
and bring their children there.

*Thomas Haweis**, 1733-1820

HYMNS FOR CHILDREN†

891

All things bright and beautiful,
all creatures great and small,
all things wise and wonderful,
the Lord God made them all.

Each little flower that opens,
each little bird that sings,
He made their glowing colours,
He made their tiny wings:

2 The purple-headed mountain,
the river running by,
the sunset, and the morning
that brightens up the sky:

3 The cold wind in the winter,
the pleasant summer sun,
the ripe fruits in the garden,
He made them every one:

4 He gave us eyes to see them,
and lips that we might tell
how great is God almighty,
who has made all things well:

Cecil Frances Alexander, 1818-95

892

Gentle Jesus, meek and mild,
look upon a little child;
pity my simplicity,
suffer me to come to Thee.

2 Fain I would be as Thou art;
give me Thy obedient heart;
Thou art pitiful and kind;
let me have Thy loving mind.

3 Above all, let me fulfil
God my heavenly Father's will,
never His good Spirit grieve,
only to His glory live.

4 Thou didst live to God alone;
Thou didst never seek Thine own;
Thou Thyself didst never please;
God was all Thy happiness.

5 Loving Jesus, gentle Lamb,
in Thy gracious hands I am;
make me, Saviour, what Thou art;
live Thyself within my heart.

6 I shall then show forth Thy praise,
serve Thee all my happy days;
then the world shall always see
Christ, the holy child, in me.

Charles Wesley, 1707-88

893

God, who made the earth,
the air, the sky, the sea,
who gave the light its birth –
He cares for me.

2 God, who made the grass,
the flower, the fruit, the tree,
the day and night to pass –
He cares for me.

3 God, who made the sun,
the moon, the stars, is He
who, when life's troubles come,
will care for me.

†While songs used for children have changed considerably in recent times, we have sought to retain some of the best and most frequently used hymns from the previous edition of the book.

4 God, who sent His Son
to die on Calvary,
He, if I trust in Him,
will care for me.
Sarah Betts Rhodes, 1829-1904

894

I love to think, though I am young,
my Saviour was a child;
that Jesus walked this earth along,
with feet all undefiled.

2 He kept His Father's word of truth,
as I am taught to do;
and while He walked the paths of
youth,
He walked in wisdom too.

3 I love to think that He who spake
and made the blind to see,
and called the sleeping dead to wake,
was once a child like me:

4 That He who wore the thorny crown,
and tasted death's despair,
had a kind mother like my own,
and knew her love and care.

5 I know 'twas all for love of me
that He became a child,
and left the heavens, so fair to see,
and trod earth's pathway wild.

6 Then, Saviour, who wast once a child,
a child may come to Thee;
and O in all Thy mercy mild,
dear Saviour, come to me!
Edwin Paxton Hood, 1820-85

895

Around the throne of God in heaven
thousands of children stand,
children whose sins are all forgiven,
a holy, happy band:

Singing, 'Glory, glory, glory!'
Singing, 'Glory, glory, glory!'

2 In flowing robes of spotless white
see every one arrayed,
dwelling in everlasting light
and joys that never fade:

3 What brought them to that world above,
that heaven so bright and fair,
where all is peace, and joy, and love?
How came those children there?

4 Because the Saviour shed His blood
to wash away their sin;
bathed in that pure and precious flood,
behold them white and clean!

5 On earth they sought the Saviour's
grace,
on earth they loved His name;
so now they see His blessèd face,
and stand before the Lamb:
Anne Shepherd, 1809-57

896

Hushed was the evening hymn,
the temple courts were dark,
the lamp was burning dim
before the sacred ark,
when suddenly a voice divine
rang through the silence of the shrine.

2 The priest of Israel slept,
the old man meek and mild;
watch in the temple kept
the little Levite child;
and what from Eli's sense was sealed
the Lord to Hannah's son revealed.

3 O give me Samuel's ear,
the open ear, O Lord!
alive and quick to hear
each whisper of Thy word:
like him to answer at Thy call,
and to obey Thee first of all.

4 O give me Samuel's heart!
a lowly heart that waits
where in Thy house Thou art,
or watches at Thy gates;
by day and night a heart that still
moves at the breathing of Thy will.

5 O give me Samuel's mind!
a sweet unmurmuring faith,
obedient and resigned
to Thee in life and death;
that I may read with childlike eyes
truths that are hidden from the wise.

James Drummond Burns, 1823-64

897

It is a thing most wonderful,
almost too wonderful to be,
that God's own Son should come from heaven,
and die to save a child like me.

2 And yet I know that it is true;
He came to this poor world below,
and wept and toiled and mourned and died,
only because He loved us so.

3 I cannot tell how He could love
a child so weak and full of sin;
His love must be most wonderful,
if He could die my love to win.

4 I sometimes think about the cross,
and shut my eyes, and try to see
the cruel nails, and crown of thorns,
and Jesus crucified for me.

5 But even could I see Him die,
I could but see a little part
of that great love which like a fire,
is always burning in His heart.

6 It is most wonderful to know
His love for me so free and sure;
how shameful then it is to see
my love for Him so faint and poor.

7 And yet I want to love Thee, Lord;
O light the flame within my heart,
and I will love Thee more and more,
until I see Thee as Thou art.

William Walsham How, 1823-97

898

Jesus loves me, this I know,
for the Bible tells me so;
little ones to Him belong,
they are weak, but He is strong.

Yes, Jesus loves me,
yes, Jesus loves me,
yes, Jesus loves me,
the Bible tells me so.

2 Jesus loves me! He who died
heaven's gate to open wide;
He will wash away my sin,
let His little child come in.

3 Jesus loves me! loves me still,
when I'm very weak and ill;
from His shining throne on high
watches with me where I lie.

4 Jesus loves me! He will stay
close beside me all the way;
if I trust Him, when I die
He will take me home on high.
Anna Bartlett Warner, 1827-1915

899

I often say my prayers,
but do I ever pray?
And do the wishes of my heart
go with the words I say?

2 I may as well kneel down
and worship gods of stone,
as offer to the living God
a prayer of words alone.

3 For words without the heart
the Lord will never hear;
nor will He to those lips attend
whose prayers are not sincere.

4 Lord, teach me what I need,
and teach me how to pray;
but do not let me seek Your grace,
not meaning what I say.
John Burton, 1803-77

900

Praise Him, praise Him, all you little children;
God is love, God is love.

2 Thank Him, thank Him, all you little children,
God is love, God is love.

3 Love Him, love Him, all you little children,
God is love, God is love.

4 Crown Him, crown Him, all you little children,
God is love, God is love.
Anonymous, c. 1890

901

There is a city bright;
closed are its gates to sin;
nought that defileth,
nought that defileth
can ever enter in.

2 Saviour, I come to Thee!
O Lamb of God, I pray,
cleanse me and save me,
cleanse me and save me,
wash all my sins away.

3 Lord, make me, from this hour,
Thy loving child to be;
kept by Thy power,
kept by Thy power
from all that grieveth Thee:

4 Till in the snowy dress
of Thy redeemed I stand,
faultless and stainless,
faultless and stainless,
safe in that happy land!
Mary Ann Sanderson Deck, 1813-1903

902

Jesus, high in glory,
lend a listening ear;
when we bow before You,
children's praises hear.

2 Though You are so holy,
heaven's almighty King,
You will stoop to listen
when Your praise we sing.

3 Save us, Lord, from sinning;
watch us day by day;
help us now to love You;
take our sins away.

4 Then, when You will call us
to our heavenly home,
we will gladly answer,
'Saviour, Lord, we come'.

Harriot Burn McKeever, 1807-87

903

Jesus, who lived above the sky,
came down to be a man and die;
and in the Bible we may see
how very good He used to be.

2 He went about, He was so kind,
to cure poor people who were blind;
and many who were sick and lame,
He pitied them and did the same.

3 And more than that, He told them too
the things that God would have them do;
and was so gentle and so mild,
He would have listened to a child.

4 But such a cruel death He died:
He was hung up and crucified!
and those kind hands that did such
good,
they nailed them to a cross of wood!

5 And so He died! and this is why
He came to be a man and die:
the Bible says He came from heaven,
that we might have our sins forgiven.

6 He knew how wicked man had been,
and knew that God must punish sin;
so, out of pity, Jesus said
He'd bear the punishment instead.

Ann Gilbert, 1782-1866

904

Saviour, like a shepherd lead us,
much we need Thy tender care;
in Thy pleasant pastures feed us;
for our use Thy folds prepare:
blessèd Jesus!
Thou hast bought us, Thine we are.

2 We are Thine; do Thou befriend us;
be the guardian of our way;
keep from ill; from sin defend us;
seek us when we go astray:
blessèd Jesus!
hear, O hear us, when we pray.

3 Thou hast promised to receive us,
poor and sinful though we be;
Thou hast mercy to relieve us,
grace to cleanse, and power to free:
blessèd Jesus!
early let us turn to Thee.

4 Early let us seek Thy favour,
early let us do Thy will;
blessèd Lord and only Saviour,
with Thy love our bosoms fill:
blessèd Jesus!
Thou hast loved us, love us still.

Anonymous; HYMNS FOR THE YOUNG, 1836

905

There's a Friend for little children
above the bright blue sky,
a Friend who never changes,
whose love will never die.
Unlike our friends by nature,
who change with changing years,
this Friend is always worthy
the precious name He bears.

2 There's a rest for little children
above the bright blue sky,
who love the blessèd Saviour,
and 'Abba Father' cry –
a rest from every trouble,
from sin and danger free,
where every little pilgrim
shall rest eternally.

3 There's a home for little children
above the bright blue sky,
where Jesus reigns in glory,
a home of peace and joy;
no home on earth is like it,
or can with it compare;
for every one is happy,
nor could be happier, there.

4 There's a crown for little children
above the bright blue sky,
and all who look to Jesus
shall wear it by and by –
a crown of brightest glory,
which He will then bestow
on all who love the Saviour,
and walk with Him below.

5 There's a song for little children
above the bright blue sky,
a song that will not weary
though sung continually,
a song which even angels
can never, never sing;
they know not Christ as Saviour,
but worship Him as King.

Albert Midlane, 1825-1909

SONGS AND CHORUSES

906

Abba, Father, let me be
Yours and Yours alone.
May my will for ever be
evermore Your own.
Never let my heart grow cold,
never let me go;
Abba, Father, let me be
Yours and Yours alone.

Dave Bilbrough, b. 1955

907

All hail, King Jesus!
All hail, Emmanuel!
King of kings,
Lord of lords, bright morning star;
every day You give me breath,
I'll sing Your praises,
and I'll reign with You throughout
eternity.

Dave Moody, b. 1948

908

As we are gathered, Jesus is here,
one with each other, Jesus is here;
joined by the Spirit, washed in His
blood,
part of the body, the Church of God.
As we are gathered, Jesus is here,
one with each other, Jesus is here.

John Daniels

909 Based on Deuteronomy 32:3-4

Ascribe greatness to our God, the Rock,
His work is perfect and all His ways are
just.
Ascribe greatness to our God, the Rock,
His work is perfect and all His ways are
just.
A God of faithfulness and without
injustice,
good and upright is He;
a God of faithfulness and without
injustice,
good and upright is He.

Mary Kirkbride-Barthow
& Mary-Lou King

910 Based on Psalm 46:10-11

Be still and know that I am God,
be still and know that I am God,
be still and know that I am God.

2 I am the Lord that keepeth thee…

3 In Thee, O Lord, I put my trust…

911

Come among us, Lord,
gathered round Your Word;
to mind and heart Your truth impart,
O living Word.
In this morning (*evening*) hour,
Lord, reveal Your power!
May souls be fed with living bread –
Come among us, Lord.

Gordon Brattle, 1917-91

912 PSALM 51:7,10

Create in me a clean heart, O God,
and renew a right spirit in me.
Create in me a clean heart, O God,
and renew a right spirit in me.
Wash me, cleanse me, purify me,
make my heart as white as snow.
Create in me a clean heart, O God,
and renew a right spirit in me.

David Fellingham, b. 1945

913

Father, we love You, we worship and adore You,

Glorify Your name in all the earth,
glorify Your name, glorify Your name,
glorify Your name in all the earth.

2 Jesus we love You, we worship and adore You,

3 Spirit, we love You, we worship and adore You,

Donna Adkins, b. 1940

914 ISAIAH 9:6

For unto us a child is born,
unto us a Son is given;
and the government
shall be upon His shoulders.
And His name shall be called
Wonderful, Counsellor, the Mighty God,
the Everlasting Father,
and the Prince of Peace is He.

915

Give me oil in my lamp, keep me burning,
give me oil in my lamp, I pray;
give me oil in my lamp, keep me burning,
keep me burning till the break of day.

Sing hosanna, sing hosanna,
sing hosanna to the King of kings!
Sing hosanna, sing hosanna,
sing hosanna to the King.

2 Give me joy in my heart, keep me singing,
give me joy in my heart, I pray;
give me joy in my heart, keep me singing,
keep me singing till the break of day.

3 Give me love in my heart, keep me serving,
give me love in my heart, I pray;
give me love in my heart, keep me serving,
keep me serving till the break of day.

Anonymous

916

Hallelujah! for the Lord our God
the almighty reigns.
Hallelujah! for the Lord our God
the almighty reigns.
Let us rejoice and be glad and give
the glory unto Him.
Hallelujah! for the Lord our God
the almighty reigns.

Dale Garratt

917

Hallelujah, my Father,
for giving us Your Son;
sending Him into the world
to be given up for men,
knowing we would bruise Him
and smite Him from the earth.
Hallelujah, my Father,
in His death is my birth.
Hallelujah, my Father,
in His life is my life.

Tim Cullen

918 Based on PHILIPPIANS 2:10-11

He is Lord, He is Lord!
He is risen from the dead
and He is Lord!
Every knee shall bow,
every tongue confess
that Jesus Christ is Lord.

Marvin Frey, 1918-92

919

He rose triumphantly
in power and majesty;
the Saviour rose no more to die.
O let us now proclaim
the glory of His name
and tell to all, He lives today!

Oswald J Smith, 1889-1986
and Bentley D Ackley, 1872-1958

920

Higher than the hills,
deeper than the sea,
broader than the skies above
is my Redeemer's love for me.
To His cross of shame,
Jesus freely came,
bearing all my sin and sorrow –
wondrous love!

Norman John Clayton, 1903-92

921

His name is higher than any other,
His name is Jesus, His name is Lord.
His name is Wonderful,
His name is Counsellor,
His name is Prince of peace,
the mighty God.
His name is higher than any other,
His name is Jesus, His name is Lord.

Anonymous

922

His name is wonderful, His name is wonderful,
His name is wonderful, Jesus my Lord.
He is the mighty King, master of everything,
His name is wonderful, Jesus my Lord.
He's the great shepherd, the rock of all ages,
almighty God is He;
bow down before Him, love and adore Him,
His name is wonderful, Jesus my Lord.

Audrey Mieir, b. 1916

923 Based on Psalm 36:7-9

How precious, O Lord,
is Your unfailing love;
we find refuge
in the shadow of Your wings.
We feast, Lord Jesus,
on the abundance of Your house
and drink from Your river of delights.

With You is the fountain of life,
in Your light we see light,
with You is the fountain of life,
in Your light we see light.

Phil Rogers, b. 1949

924

I know a fount where sins are washed away,
I know a place where night is turned to day,
burdens are lifted, blind eyes made to see.
There's a wonder-working power
in the blood of Calvary.

Oliver Cooke, 1873-1945

925 Based on Psalm 118:19,20,24

I will enter His gates with thanksgiving in my heart,
I will enter His courts with praise,
I will say, 'This is the day that the Lord has made',
I will rejoice for He has made me glad.
He has made me glad,
He has made me glad,
I will rejoice for He has made me glad.

He has made me glad,
He has made me glad,
I will rejoice for He has made me glad.

Leona von Brethorst, b. 1923

926 Psalm 57:9-11

I will give thanks to You,
O Lord, among the people.
I will sing praises to You
among the nations.
For Your steadfast love is great,
is great to the heavens,
and Your faithfulness,
Your faithfulness, to the clouds.

Be exalted, O God,
above the heavens.
Let Your glory be over all the earth!
Be exalted, O God,
above the heavens.
Let Your glory be over all the earth!

(last time only)
Let Your glory, let Your glory,
let Your glory be over all the earth!

Brent Chambers, b. 1948

927

In my need Jesus found me,
put His strong arm around me,
brought me safe home
into the shelter of the fold.
Gracious Shepherd that sought me,
precious life-blood that bought me
out of the night,
into the light and near to God.

Gordon Brattle, 1917-91

928

Jesus, Name above all names,
beautiful Saviour, glorious Lord;
Emmanuel, God is with us,
blessèd Redeemer, living word.

Naida Hearn, b. 1944

929

Jesus shall take the highest honour,
Jesus shall take the highest praise,
let all earth join heaven exalting
the Name which is above all other names.
Let's bow the knee in humble adoration,
for at His Name every knee must bow;
let every tongue confess He is Christ,
God's only Son.

Sovereign Lord, we give You glory now,
for all honour and blessing and power
belong to You, belong to You.
All honour and blessing and power
belong to You, belong to You,
Lord Jesus Christ, Son of the living God.

Chris Bowater, b. 1947

930

Let the beauty of Jesus be seen in me,
all His wondrous compassion and purity.
O, Thou, Spirit divine,
all my nature refine,
till the beauty of Jesus be seen in me.

Albert Orsborn, 1886-1967

931 Based on Psalm 139:23-24

Search me, O God,
and know my heart today;
try me, O Lord,
and know my thought, I pray.
See if there be some wicked way in me;
cleanse me from every sin and set me free.

J Edwin Orr, 1912-87

932 Based on Matthew 6:33; 4:4; 7:7,8

Seek ye first the kingdom of God
and His righteousness,
and all these things shall be added unto you.
Allelu, alleluia.
Seek ye first…

2 Man shall not live by bread alone,
but by every word
that proceeds from the mouth of God.
Allelu, alleluia.
Man shall not…

3 Ask and it shall be given unto you,
seek and ye shall find;
knock and the door shall be opened up to you.
Allelu, alleluia.
Ask and it shall…

Karen Lafferty, b. 1948

933

Spirit of the living God,
fall afresh on me;
Spirit of the living God,
fall afresh on me:
break me, melt me,
mould me, fill me.
Spirit of the living God,
fall afresh on me.

Daniel Iverson, 1890-1977

934 Based on LAMENTATIONS 3:22-23

The steadfast love of the Lord never ceases,
His mercies never come to an end;
they are new every morning, new every morning:
great is Your faithfulness, O Lord,
great is Your faithfulness.

Edith McNeill, b. 1923

935

There's a way back to God
from the dark paths of sin;
there's a door that is open
and you may go in:
at Calvary's cross is where you begin,
when you come as a sinner to Jesus.

Eric Swinstead, 1882-1950

936

There's no greater name than Jesus,
name of Him who came to save us;
in that saving name so gracious
every knee shall bow.

2 Let everything that's beneath the ground,
let everything in the world around,
let everything exalted on high
bow at Jesus' name.

3 In our minds, by faith professing,
in our hearts, by inward blessing,
on our tongues by words confessing,
Jesus Christ is Lord!

Michael Baughen, b. 1930

937 Based on PSALM 118:24

This is the day,
this is the day that the Lord has made,
that the Lord has made.
We will rejoice,
we will rejoice and be glad in it,
and be glad in it.
This is the day that the Lord has made,
we will rejoice and be glad in it.
This is the day,
this is the day that the Lord has made.

2 This is the day … when He rose again.
We will rejoice and be glad in it.

3 This is the day … when the Spirit came.
We will rejoice and be glad in it.

Les Garratt, b. 1944

938

Within the veil I now would come,
into the holy place to look upon Your face.
I see such beauty there, no other can compare,
I worship You my Lord, within the veil.

Ruth Dryden

939 Based on REVELATION 5:12-13

Worthy is the Lamb, seated on the throne,
worthy is the Lamb, who was slain,
to receive power and riches, and wisdom and strength,
honour and glory,
glory and praise,
for ever and evermore.

Arranged by David J Hadden

940

Wounded for me, wounded for me,
there on the cross He was wounded for me.
Gone my transgressions and now I am free;
all because Jesus was wounded for me.

Gladys W Roberts b. 1888

941

Yesterday, today, for ever,
Jesus is the same;
all may change but Jesus never,
glory to His name;
glory to His name,
glory to His name;
all may change, but Jesus never,
glory to His name.

Author unknown

942

You are the King of glory,
You are the Prince of peace,
You are the Lord of heaven and earth,
You're the Son of righteousness.
Angels bow down before You,
worship and adore,
for You have the words of eternal life,
You are Jesus Christ the Lord.

Hosanna to the Son of David!
Hosanna to the King of kings!
Glory in the highest heaven,
for Jesus the Messiah reigns!

Mavis Ford

INDEX OF FIRST LINES

INDEX OF FIRST LINES

Index of first lines

INDEX OF FIRST LINES

Index of first lines

INDEX OF FIRST LINES

Index of first lines

INDEX OF FIRST LINES

Index of first lines

INDEX OF FIRST LINES

Index of first lines

INDEX OF FIRST LINES

Index of first lines

INDEX OF FIRST LINES

Index of first lines

INDEX OF FIRST LINES

INDEX OF FIRST LINES

Index of first lines

INDEX OF FIRST LINES

Index of first lines

INDEX OF FIRST LINES